Devadasis in South India – A Journey from Sacred to Profane Spaces

Devadasis in South India – A Journey from Sacred to Profane Spaces

S. Jeevanandam and Rekha Pande

KALPAZ

ISBN: 978-93-5128-210-5

Price: ₹ 1225

First Published, 2016

Published by

Kalpaz Publications
C-30, Satyawati Nagar,
Delhi – 110052
E-mail: kalpaz@hotmail.com
Ph.: 9212142040

Printed at: G. Print Process, Delhi

Cataloging in Publication Data—DK
Courtesy: D.K. Agencies (P) Ltd. <docinfo@dkagencies.com>

Jeevanandam, S., author.
Devadasis in South India : a journey from sacred to profane spaces / S. Jeevanandam and Rekha Pande.
pages cm
Includes bibliographical references.
ISBN 9789351282105

1. Devadāsīs—India, South—History. I. Pande, Rekha, 1955- author. II. Title.

BL1237.58.D48J44 2016 DDC 294.538 23

Contents

Preface 7
Acknowledgements 9
Abbreviations 11

1. Introduction 13
2. Pre-Colonial South India: - The Historical Context 51
3. Emergence and Growth of the Devadasi System: - Pre-Colonial Period 77
4. The Devadasi System: - The Colonial Period 109
5. The Twentieth century Debate on Devadasi System 153
6. The Life Stories of Some Selected Devadasis of South India 209
7. Conclusion 249

Bibliography 263
Appendixes 303
Index 317

Preface

The present book, **Devadasis in South India – A Journey from Sacred to Profane Spaces,** looks at a very important area in history and women's studies i.e. The Devadasis. The patriarchal understanding of the history writings have marginalised women and their historical experience. Writing women's history is not just meant for the glorification of historical personalities but it is an important intellectual engagement in the reconstruction of a gender sensitised historical past. In general, women's history traces the historical experiences of women. In India, women in history are placed within the "private" domain, but recorded history generally focuses the "public" domain. Further, the centrality of the Indian culture lay in its religious roots. The patriarchal values are established and monitored through religious ideas. Religious values have restricted women's access to the public sphere. Devadasi, a temple women who could share the public domain, which was not possible for other women in the society becomes a very interesting exercise in the creation of women's history.

Devadasi is a dedicated women to any particular deity or symbol. In the past, the custom was widely spread in South Asia, especially in India. They were an integral part of the temple organisation. The strong historical lineage of devadasi institution has gone through many changes due to various historical reasons. This book attempts to focus on the historical development and transition of the devadasi system from the early medieval to modern period with a special focus on Tamilakam.The region Tamilakam, includes the modern states of Tamil Nadu, Kerala, and some parts of Telangana, Andhra Pradesh and Karnataka.

The entire arguments of devadasi discourse is able to establish the fact that the gradual transition of the devadasi system from the early medieval to the modern society, went through various ups and downs. The political economy determined the condition of devadasis. The imperial Cholas understood the importance of the religion to sustain their power. They made liberal endowment to the temples. The sustained temple economy patronage the devadasis and thus they were economically resourceful. But later, the failure of the Empire collapsed the temple economy, which made the devadasis face economic hardships. Meanwhile, the Vijayanagar kingdom revived the 'Hindu' religion and patron the temple institutions under the control of Kumara Kampana. However, devadasis could not regain their earlier status. The later medieval sources highlighted the problems in the devadasi system. The intervention of the colonial power introduced new economic patterns such as *zamindari* and *ryotwari* and it influenced new kinds of social structure. The nation building process of the nineteenth century was largely constructed on female sexuality that brought concepts such as 'social purity', 'good women', and 'motherhood'. This further weakened the social acceptance of the Devadasi women. In the early twentieth century devadasi lost both their social and economic bases and became 'common' prostitutes and eventually the Devadasi institution faded away.

This study uses qualitative methods, especially the methodologies of history and gender studies. It has used a lot of archival sources such as inscriptions, official government records, newspapers, collected speeches and writings, reports and minutes, memories and autobiographies, oral histories, personal letters, diaries, and songs as well as monographs. This book also uses unstructured interviews with an expert and the last surviving devadasi to understand their experiences and perspectives on devadasi institution. We hope that this will be of use to both students and researchers of history, women's history, women's studies and religion.

Acknowledgements

We owe our thanks to a large number of people who have helped us at each and every step. Dr M.N. Rajesh (University of Hyderabad) for his support and help. We are very much obliged to the non-teaching staff of the Centre for Women's studies especially, Mr Prasad, G for his patience and timely assistance at various stages, of this project.

We also acknowledge the support received from Professor Kalpana Kannabiran (Council for Social Development, Hyderabad) for her kind guidance. We are also thankful to Professor S. Anandhi (MIDS, Chennai), Ms B. Jeevasundari (Writer, Chennai), Ms A. Arulmozhi (Lawyer, Chennai), Professor Angayarkanni (Tamil University, Thanjavur), Professor K. Sadasivan (MS University, Tirunelveli), Mr B.M. Sundaram (Musicologist), 'Padma Shri' P.R. Tilakam (music teacher) for their suggestions and advises in collecting material. We like to specifically mention Professor Su.Ba. Veerapandian (Social Activist, Chennai), Professor Geraldine Forbes (State University of New York Oswego), Dr V. Krishna Ananth, Dr Vijay Kumar Thangellapali, Dr S. Manivannan of Sikkim University, and Dr S.S. Sundaram (University of Madras, Chennai) for their inspiration and support.

We are also grateful to Mr Kovindan (Librarian, Periyar Rationalist Research Library Research Centre, Chennai) for his help to access the valuable collections of the library sources. We are also thankful to the Librarians and other staff of various libraries such as Indira Gandhi Memorial Library (University of Hyderabad), Connemara Public Library, Anna Centenary Library, Roja Muthiah Research Library, The Adyar Library and Research Centre, Perasiriyar Research Library (Anna Arivalayam), Mahamahopadyaya Dr U.V. Swaminathaiyer Library, University of Madras, Tamil Nadu State Archives, Government Oriental Manuscripts Library and Research Centre, Archaeological Survey of India, Chennai circle and state museum and Ananda Vikatan (all are in Chennai), French Institute of Pondicherry (Puducherry), University of Kerala and Kerala Council for Historic Research (Thiruvananthapuram), Jawaharlal Nehru University and Delhi University (New Delhi), Department of Archaeology and Museum, Government of Andhra Pradesh and Council for Social Development (Hyderabad) for their kind co-operation in providing all the necessary research materials.

Our friends, who have been a great support include, Mr K. Karthick and Dr M. Viji. Thanks also to Dr N. Prakash Prabhu (University of Hyderabad), Mr Chandra Sekar, Dr Dinesan, Dr Murugananth Kumar, Mr Anthony Raj (Arul Anandar College, Madurai), Mr Justin Selvaraj (Madurai Kamaraj University), Mr Prem Ram, Mr Vellaisamy, Mr Kishore Kumar, Dr Raj Kumar, Dr Raja Kumar, Mr Kabalishwaran, Mr Bharath, Ms Suchitra, Mr Venky, Mr Sabur Ali, Mr Dickens, Mr Nelson, Mr Dheepanjan, Dr Prabu, Dr Ramakrishna and Dr Harish Srinivasa (University of Allahabad) for their encouragement.

We both acknowledge the patience and support of our respected families, Jeevanandam to his wife, Archana. S, for her assistance, cooperation and moral support, his grandparents Ms Nainammal and Mr Gopal, parents Mr S. Sankar and Ms S. Kasthuri for their blessings, love and dedication, sister Ms S. Vinothapriya, Mr S. Suresh, Ms S. Lakshya and Mr S. 'Kula Keerthi' Kirthik, Mr J.A. Siddhardhan and his family members Ms Rajam and Mr Sivaprakashan for their affection and care. Rekha to her husband Dr Suresh and sons Mr Sankalp, Dr Tarun and Mr Varun for their continuous support.

S. Jeevanandam, Rekha Pande

Abbreviations

AR	: Annual Report
A.R.I.E.	: Annual Report of Indian Epigraphy
A.R.S.I.E.	: Annual Report of South Indian Epigraphy
ASI	: Archaeological Survey of India
Ch.	: Chapter
Comp.	: Compilation, Compiled
EC	: Epigraphia Carnatica
Ed.	: Edited, Edition
EI	: Epigraphia Indica
FNSI	: Foreign Notices of South India
Fn	: Foot Note
GO	: Government Order
HAS	: Hyderabad Archaeological Series
HISI	: Historical Inscriptions of South India
IA	: Indian Antiquary
Ibid.	: in the same place
IEASHR	: Indian Economic and Social History Review
JAHRS	: Journal of the Andhra Historical Research Society
JAU	: Journal of Annamalai University
JIH	: Journal of Indian History
JIAS	: Journal of the Institute of Asian Studies
JMU	: Journal of Madras University
K.K.	: Kanyakumari Kalvettukal (Kanyakumari Inscriptions)
l.	: Line
ll.	: Lines
lit.	: Literature
MAMP	: Manual of Administration of Madras Presidency
M.E.R.	: Madras Epigraphy Report

Ml.	: Malayalam
MLC	: Madras Legislative Council
Ms.	: Manuscript
Mss.	: Manuscripts
n.d.	: no date
No.	: Number
Nos.	: Numbers
Op.cit	: in the work cited
PMLC	: Proceedings of the Madras Legislative Council
P.S.I.	: Pudukkottai State Inscriptions
pt.	: Part
SATLS	: Studies in Ancient Tamil Law and Society
S.I.I.	: South Indian Inscriptions
S.I.T.I.	: South Indian Temple Inscriptions
Skt.	: Sanskrit
sl.	: Sloka
sls.	: Slokas
S.N.D.P.	: Sree Narayana Dharma Paripalana
st.	: Stanza
Ta.	: Tamil
T.A.S.	: Travancore Archaeological Series
Tl.	: Tamil
T.M.S.S.M.	: Thanjavur Maharajah Serfoji's Sarasvati Mahal Library
Tr.	: Translation, Translated
T.T.D.E.S.	: Tirumalai Tirupati Devasthanam Epigraphical Series
Up.	: Unpublished
v.	: verse
Vol.	: Volume
vs.	: verses.

Chapter - 1

Introduction

History writing is very biased in its nature, because it has given a very male centric view of the past. The conventional history marginalised everyday lives of women into irrelevance and virtual non-existence.[1] In general, the voices of women are not represented in the historical reconstruction. It is essential that these voices are heard in order to get an understanding of gender sensitised past. Gerda Lerner, a historian, mentioned that the experience of women in history has been obscured and neglected by patriarchal understanding, a fact that has significantly affected by the psychology of men and women.[2] She further stated that women have been systematically excluded from the enterprise of creating symbol systems, philosophies, science, and law.[3]

Writing women's history is not a process of creating or constructing the history of few great women of the past. It is just a process of recording the experience of women in history. In the words of Carroll Smith-Rosenberg, women's history have to explore the complexity of the female experience and not to create a pantheon of ideologically correct heroines, but to analyse the evolution of women's roles, in the context of the effect of economic changes upon a society's allocation of economic resources and power, institutional developments, and ideological conceptualisations.[4] With regards experience, Gerda Lerner cited that women have a significantly different historical experience from men.[5] In general, the patriarchal attitudes deny the historical agency of women. In Indian society, women are placed within the "private" domain but recorded history focuses the "public" domain. Hence, in order to reconstruct history and to get a balanced view of the past, we need to look for sources, which will give us some information about women of Indian society. One of the principal goal of women's history is to redefine the canons of traditional history and that events and processes central to women's experience assume historical centrality and recognise women as an active agent of social change.[6]

Ratna Sharma specified that to construct the general status of a culture, one have to assess the position of women in its society.[7] Historically, there are very few details available from inscriptions about the condition of the women. This phenomenon is common in almost all the parts of Indian Subcontinent, especially in South India. Swaminathan, an art historian, mentioned that there is no evidence available on women education, social status, marriages and so on.[8] In general, women of medieval India were positioned as subordinate to men. They appeared to have participated in the household activities and religious ceremonies. The feature of the slavery prevailed with women. Subramanian, a South Indian historian, compared the relationship between a husband and wife with the relationship of *guru-sisya*.[9] The wives were insisted to look after their husbands as their gods. The male dominated society treated homemakers as bearer and nurse to bring up their children and men were free from all these responsibilities. The patriarchal institution restricted women to claim property.

According to the Indian tradition, women were treated as a perpetual minor. The medieval religious texts, stressed monogamy for women and polygamy for men. Usually, marriage was constructed as sacred and condition of the wedlock could not be ended with divorce even after her husband's death. They became widow of the dead, otherwise, they performd *sati*. The word *sati* literally meant chaste wives and inalienable duty of chaste wives was to be united with her husband even after his death. However, the *sati* practice was not widely common in Tamilakam.[10] *Sati* was considered as an act of heroism and the custom paralleled with the hero stone worship of South India.[11] One who did not commit *sati* had to lead the life of an ascetic and they shaved their head, shed their ornaments, forgo edible food and sufficient sleep. They were cursed as inauspicious.[12]

Interestingly, a section of women were free from these clutches, accessed considerable liberation which other women could not even imagine, formed a community and later became a unique feature of Indian history. The name of the community is popularly called as devadasi, temple women. The history of South India is incomplete without the inclusion of the institution of devadasi. Saskia Kersenboom-Story, an Indologist, stated that devadasi were an object of romantic reminiscence of the past.[13] In South India, devadasis were very important functionary in the 'Hindu' society and were closely associated with the cult of fertility.[14] Their ritual dancing was part of religious service in a long history of temple. A.K. Singh, a historian, said that in India, the practices originated and developed during the early medieval period onwards.[15] There are a large number of inscriptions, which provided a lot of information regarding devadasi. The institution of devadasi had taken such deep roots in the temple organisation in South Indian society.[16] Several South Indian inscriptions proved the association of temple girls with temple service since ninth century.[17] The study of this institution helps us to reconstruct the history of South India and also analyse the position and general status of the women of that particular society.

A study of this institution is important in understanding not only the temple activities but also their contributions to the South Indian society. It helps us to understand the role of women in perpetuating a particular ideology and understanding the complexity of women's situation in terms of oppression within a patriarchal structure. Devadasis were prominent women in public domain, who often played a prominent role in political and social events. Saskia Kersenboom-Story pointed out that devadasi were a very expressive semiotic unit signifying the mythical-ascetic-cum-ritual object residing in the collective consciousness of 'Hindu' tradition.[18] Latha Iyer and Kanakalatha Mukund also stressed that the historical significance of devadasihood and their various roles in local society.[19] Historically, devadasi employed in temples as dancers, singers, musicians and for offering certain services to the deities.

Devadasi

Devadasi or *devaradiyar* (a female slave) is a woman who was dedicated and attached to any specific temple.[20] It was a pan-Indian phenomenon.[21] Devadasi means a woman who was enslaved for the service of some deity or sacred object. They were unmarried temple servants who had been dedicated to temple deities when young through the rites, which resembled 'Hindu' marriage ceremonies.[22] The married temple girls were eternally free from the 'inauspicious' widowhood. In this context, Saskia Kersenboom-Story referred devadasi as *nityasumangali*.[23]

The word devadasi is to be a Sanskritized form of Tamil word *devaradiyar*, which meant a woman who is enslaved for the service of some specific deity or sacred object.[24] In general, the word is the feminine form of *deva-dasa*, a man who enslaved for the service of a deity.[25] However, the term has its origin in Sanskrit, the prevailing custom and practices are in no way related to the gods or deities mentioned in Sanskrit literature, especially the Trinity.[26] Leslie Orr, a historian, stated that the devadasi or temple women was women, one who may or may not be a prostitute or dancer and one who is associated with temple, either by having some kind of regular service function in a temple or because her primary social identity is defined with reference to a temple.[27]

Edgar Thurston, a colonial ethnographer, described devadasis as *dasis* or *deva-dasis* are dancing girls attached to the Tamil temples, who subsist by dancing and music, and the practice of 'the oldest profession in the world'.[28] Further, he stated that the rise of the caste and its euphemistic name seem to date from the ninth and tenth century, during which many activities prevailed in Southern India in the matter of building temples, and elaborating the services held in them. The dancing girls' duties, then as now, were to fan the idol with *charmaras* (Tibetan ox tails), to carry the sacred light called *kumbarti*, and to sing and dance before the god when he was carried in procession.[29]

In a book *Religious Thought and Life in India*, Monier-Williams described devadasis in a way that they were held to be married to the god, and had no other duty but to dance before the shrine and belonged to the god's, hence they were called the god's slaves (*deva-dasi*), and were generally considered to follow patterns of piety and propriety.[30] He further pointed out that, in the present day, they are still called by the same name, but are rather slaves to the licentious passions of the profligate Brahmins of the temples to which they belonged. He was surprised to see the number and weightage of the ornaments of devadasi, especially in Southern India. He referred that a profitable trade was done by devadasi under the sanction of religion.[31] The arguments of Joep Bor was also similar with Monier-William. He detailed that devadasis as pretty temple servants who dressed conspicuously and were privileged in that they were taught reading, writing, singing and dancing. Their main duty was to worship the gods with songs and dances, but according to travellers, their gestures were lascivious and their songs obscene. Travellers noted that the dancers were public prostitutes.[32]

Frederique Apffel Marglin, an anthropologist, considered devadasis as a very specialised, unusual group of women and one who acted as the harbingers of auspiciousness to a state and society.[33] They do not marry any mortal men and their dedication to temple service was regarded as constituting a marriage with the main deity.[34] Venkatramaiah, a Tamil scholar, said that some women were employed in temples as workers and those well versed in dance and music (*See Appendix*: - 1) and would dance and sing in the temples on certain specific occasions. They were not harlots or prostitutes. They were spinsters who might leave the service in the temples and enter into married life if they should so desire.[35]

A Concise Dictionary on Hindu Religion mentioned that the devadasis were the celestial dancing women otherwise a women one who do service in temples.[36] Ramanathan in his dictionary mentioned that the devadasi meant *devadiyal.*[37] *Kazhakap Puzhavar Kuzhuvinar* mentioned that *devadi* meant palace[38] and *patiyilar* meant *kanikaiyar*, women.[39] The first European encounter of the term devadasi appeared in the *Lettres ediffiantes et curieuses* (1713) in which a Jesuit missionary mentioned them as a 'divine slave'.[40] Dutch pastor Francois Valentyn (1726) used the term *deva-dasikal.*[41] Sonnerat was probably the first author to change the commonly used Portuguese term *bailadeira* into the French word *bayadere.*[42] *Webster's Unabridged Dictionary* (1999) mentioned that the word *bayadere* meant a professional female dancer of India.[43]

Devadasis were a common feature in almost all the major brahmanical temples.[44] Ibn Battuta, a Moroccan explorer, referred the dance of five hundred dancing girls before God of Dineswara in 1342-1343.[45] Abbe Dubois, a French Catholic missionary activist, recorded the devadasi practices in his book *A Description of the Character, Manner and Customs of the People of India*. In every temple, based on its size, entertains a band of these, to the number of eight, twelve, or more.[46] *Kudi Arasu*, the radical newspaper of the Self-Respect Movement, mentioned that every temples had nearly ten to thirty devadasi and even in major temples carried more than hundred of them.[47] The service they performed consists of dancing and singing. In smaller temples, the Brahmins themselves did the services, attended by the music, the dancing girls and other assistants.[48] Abbe Dubois referred that devadasi were the important persons next to the sacrificers.[49] The *Travancore State Manual* recorded that in the Southern districts of Travancore there was entertainment provided by dancing girls and musicians with their instruments at the *pagoda* (temple), and they attended five times a day, early in the morning, at forenoon, at noon, in the evening and at night. In all those occasions, one or two singers also attended the temple, who were paid twenty five and thirty *panams* per mensem.[50]

In general, devadasi was not allowed marrying any mortal. Her unmarried status was equalled to being ritually celibate. Selvy Thiruchandran, a feminist critic, explained that a mother or grandmother of devadasi advertised the availability of young devadasi to the public. Soon after that, her patron was decided. According to the devadasi custom, the married men should be the patron. She was not expected to serve the patron as a wife. Her non-domestic role was emphasised.[51] Ramachandram described about devadasi that they had a plaited hair, wore *kashayam* (tunics), and lived upon the small ration, which were given to them out of the cooked rice offered to God, so as to keep body and soul together and they lived like ascetics.[52]

The illustration of devadasi occurred even outside the temple institution. They became an integral feature of the social life and no important social occasions would be complete without the presence of devadasi.[53] They had certain de facto rights in the temple and society. They were permitted to hold land and to transfer the land. Politically, they were permitted to use their umbrella, flag, palanquin, etc. They were allowed to have children and could adopt female children. Abbe Dubois mentioned that devadasi were the only females in India who may learn to read, to sing, and to dance.[54] Biswanath Joardar pointed out that the Bengali girls were careful never to sing or to dance. Because it considered as a sign of immodesty, which would scandalise the neighbours and disgrace the family.[55] There were no restriction imposed on their sexual activities. However, the sexual relation to the lower caste men was considered as social stigma. During the funeral, flowers, sandal wood paste and garland of the deity were offered to devadasi to honour her lifelong servitude. According to the tradition, the funeral procession was halted for some time in front of the temple, the deity observed a daylong pollution and no *puja* was conducted on the day. Usually, the fire to lit the funeral pyre was carried from the temple kitchen.[56]

The evolution of the devadasi system

There are many speculations and theories[57] regarding the origin of the devadasi system. The system of dedicating women for the ritual service was an ancient and universal practice. The customs were differed from each country based on the period and their culture. Mesopotamia, Egypt, Greece, Babylonia and Cyprus were the few countries, where the system of dedicating women to the religious service flourished from several thousand years ago.[58] In the temples of Osiris and Isis, Aphrodite[59], Anu, and Ishtar, women were used for sacred services.

Generally, the practice of dedicating women in the name of religion is termed as theogamy. James Frazer viewed that theogamy was the result of Mother Goddess worship.[60] The custom was found in ancient India. The religious women occupied a divine status, their roles personified in the forms of Mother Goddess, and numerous material gifts were offered to her.[61] In the meantime, the Mother Goddess tradition came under the influence of Sanskritic tradition through two processes. One was that, the new myths were created and propagated, and another one was they were subjected by powerful male deities. The powers and capacities of the male deity were glorified. The concept of ritual purity and pollution were introduced. The shift from matriarchy to patriarchy reduced their status as mere ritual functionaries. [62]

J.N. Farquhar stated that every well established 'Hindu' temple aimed at being an earthly reproduction of the paradise of the god in whose honour it was built…The *gandharvas* (celestial men) were represented by the temple band, the *apsarasas* (celestial women) by the courtesans who sing and dance in the service. These were dedicated to the service of the god; but they gave their favours to their worshippers. They usually called as devadasis, hand maidens of the god…They did their dancing and singing performance in temple and procession. Hence, the common name for them everywhere was *nautch* girls, dancing girls…[63]

Yande in his *Naik-Maratha Mandal* mentioned that Krishna married more than sixteen thousand women and numerous allusions in the *puranam* to the king who patronised prostitute for the purpose of dancing and singing in the court. Moreover, the imitation of these legendary monarchical kings and a young unmarried damsels were about the best things to charm the gods of the savage tribes whom they practiced the ghost worship and fetish worship. Some of the Indian aboriginal races must have gone through this phase of religious worship.[64] *Kudi Arasu* revealed that Vashistar, the *puranic* saint, was born as a son of devadasi called Urvasi.[65] Jamanadas mentioned that the effect of fall of Buddhism in ancient India was the momentum for the establishment of devadasi system.[66] Yande noted that the Buddhist institution of *Bhikshunees* was responsible for the origin of this custom of dedication.[67] He further added that this most immoral custom had been completely converted to the Aryan cult and all their actions were regulated by the religious duties prescribed by that cult.[68]

Parasher-Sen, an ancient historian, considered the service of women in the temples in India was an innovation of the *puranic* religion.[69] A.K. Singh mentioned that the devadasi institution in India did not go back to third century B.C.E.[70] because the practice of worship in public temples was taking shape in the early centuries of the Common era.[71] However, the system existed in early centuries, but the custom was much practiced and prevailed from the early medieval period onwards. Altekar pointed out that, after the magnificent construction of the temples of 'Hindu' gods, people began to feel in course of time, that there should be singing girls attached to shrines to play music on the occasions of the different services and worships of the day.[72] Leslie Orr opined that the system prevailed from early medieval period onwards.[73] M.G.S. Narayanan, a South Indian historian, believed that the expansion of the temple system and growth of the *bhakti* movement brought into existence the class of temple dancing girls.[74]

The development of the devadasi institution was not uniform in its nature.[75] Historically, the origin of the devadasi custom was not clear. For some scholars, the system had emerged out of the fertility cult.[76] The earliest literary source mentioned that the association of women with temple was in the hymns of Tamil *bhakti* saints in seventh century.[77] Campantar, a prominent Saivite saint, mentioned that the temple woman as *kuravankamazh narumenkuzhal arivai* which meant a woman who had fragrance on tress hair.[78] The earliest inscriptional evidence, which discussed about the devadasi in South India was found in eighth century.[79] The devadasi custom had become an institution towards the end of fifth and sixth century, under the patronage of the Pallavas and the Pandiya.[80] In general, the system widely prevailed in the South Asia especially in modern South India and some parts of Sri Lanka.

The medieval temple organisation did not strike roots before the fourth century. However, the practice of worshipping images in public temples was taking shape in the early centuries of the Common era, but the institutional character of the temple and its importance in the socio-economic life of the people did not become noticeable until the fourth and fifth century.[81] The study of inscriptions showed that the inscription of devadasi started taking roots in the seventh and eighth century.[82] The central part of the feudal age in

India, from the ninth to twelfth century marked the origin, development and maturity of the devadasi institution in South India.[83]

In India, the whole process of social formation (from fifth to sixth century onwards) appear to be inseparably connected with developments in the field of religion. The conflict between Saivism and Vaishnavism and other religious values propagated the new religious ideology. This marked the new era in the religious temple preface. The religious sanctification of the political authority was an important characteristic of feudal polity.[84] The temple was the hub of the social and economic life in a locality.[85] The temples with devadasi drew liberal patronage from both the rulers and the private individuals.[86] Even outside the temple, devadasi was an integral part of the social life.[87] They emerged as sub-caste, with their own traditions, rules of behaviour and etiquette.[88] The inscriptions also revealed that the eleventh and twelfth century, marked the period of maximum growth.[89] The devadasi institution was established in regions that were economically and politically well developed such as the riverine of the Cauveri delta of Tamilakam.[90]

The custom gained support from religious, political, economic and social situations that prevailed in the society during the period and region. All the royal courts in India were associated with the devadasi who were good dancers and singers.[91] However, the devadasi system was prevalent throughout India; it did not flourish to a great extent in Northern India due to various reasons. In North India, it neither emerged as an institution having strong base in the society nor a common feature of majority of the temples.[92] The political instability of the Northern India and the strong non-Hindu rulers[93] such as Persian and Moghuls did not patronage the temples and confused to understand the alien custom. Khafi Khan, a historian, noted the condition of devadasi of North India especially in the reign of Aurangzeb. He pointed out that the proclamation of Aurangzeb on the prohibition against women to dance and sing. He further referred the king's order that all the dancing girls in the country should marry, otherwise they were instructed to expel from the kingdom.[94] During the same period, there were very little sources available on devadasis of Central India.[95] Even in South India, the development of the devadasi institution was not uniform.[96] Though the system was very much in existence, it did not affect the non-Hindu invasions or the external influence. So the details of the rituals were completely deep rooted in the minds of the people comparatively rest of South India.[97] As a part of 'Hindu' ritual structure, devadasi custom had its own status, roles, rules and functions.

In South India, the earliest inscription that mentioned about devadasi was as late as the eighth century.[98] The earliest literary sources to mention the association of devadasi with temple was in the hymns of Tamil Nayanmar Campantar in the seventh century.[99] The devadasi custom had become an institution towards the end of the fifth and sixth century under the patronage of Pallavas and Pandiyas.[100] The Chokkur inscription of Goda Ravi dated Kollam era 107 (932) obtained from Malabar (northern districts of modern Kerala) contained the first recorded information of the devadasi system in Kerala.[101] Sreedhara Menon mentioned that devadasi were mentioned in several inscriptions from the tenth century onwards. The institution made much head away in the eleventh century.[102]

The sources for the origin of the custom largely based on the literary records of ancient Tamils, particularly in *Tolkappiyam* and *Chilappathikaram*. The practice of ritual dancing practiced by ancient Tamil tribe such as the Maravar hunters, and the gradual transformation of it under the influence of the Brahmanical religion, seems to point towards the probable inspiration for the system of temple dancing.[103] In Sangam literature[104], the dancing women and prostitutes were frequently mentioned. However, there was no evidence of temple women. From the early medieval period, the devotional literature of Alvars and Nayanmars extensively used the concepts such as women as celestial, offerings to worship, and singing and dancing in the temples. The Tamil *bhakti* ideologies of self-surrender and devotion to service had a huge impact on the society[105] and it resulted in the construction of temples.

The temples had a huge bureaucracy and it had command over the temple girls, who were employed in the service of God. Devadasi became significant officiating dignitaries. They were the most important ritual performers, and no celebration was completed in the temple without the performance of the temple girls. Hence, the employment of these dancing girls became customary on the part of the *devasthanam* (temple institution), which was gradually institutionalised into a professional organisation. The institution of devadasi became an integral part of medieval temple organisation.[106] Rajarajan I, the Chola emperor, was responsible for the introduction of the devadasi system in Ilankai (modern Sri Lanka). He constructed 'Hindu' temples and introduced the devadasi system in Ilankai.[107] The devadasis of Tamil Nadu used to visit Ilankai in the month of February and danced in the 'Hindu' temple of Yalpanam (Jaffna, Sri Lanka).[108]

After the decline of the Cholas and the Pandiyas, the political instability overshadowed the Tamil society. The devadasi system faced the struggle for existence. The interlude of non-Hindu rulers further weakened the temple institutions and the devadasi system.[109] The invaders perceived the temples to be a great source of wealth. They invaded the new regions, targeted temples and looted the wealth [110] Amir Khusru (1253-1325), a medieval scholar, mentioned that the large quantities of wealth and jewels which were carried away to Northern India.[111] Due to the loss of patronage, many professional communities remained unemployed, and the workers suffered from want and misery.[112] The emergence of the Vijayanagar rule in South India marked a significant move in the reformulation of the system. Kumara Kampana, the army chief of Vijayanagar, captured Tondaimandalam from Sambuvarayar in 1352. Following the event, Kumara Kampana initiated the process of devadasi restoration in Tamilakam.[113]

The fall of the Vijayanagar kingdom witnessed the collapse of the devadasi system. During the Nayaka period (1565 and 1800), the symptoms of the decline of the system made their explicit appearance.[114] The political instability of the state, irrelevance of the temple institution, political intervention and repeated transfers of devadasis from temple to temple, the graded hierarchical structure and poverty distracted the 'sacred' services of devadasi and victimise them as prostitutes. During the colonial period, they were criminalised as prostitutes.[115]

Devadasi and the question of caste

The caste system was deep rooted in every sections of the Indian subcontinent. The question of caste was associated with the devadasi system. However, devadasi system did not identify as a separate caste. E.V. Ramasami, the founder of the Self-Respect Movement, spoke about the different caste affiliation with the devadasi women. In Kodumudi (town in Erode district, modern Tamil Nadu) meeting, E.V. Ramasami mentioned that the devadasis were identified as *Goundar* caste in Kongu region, *Pillai* in Thanjavur and Tirunelveli and they were categorised as *Mudaliyar* in Chennai.[116] Ramachandreir mentioned that a relation of any caste-men with devadasi did not strike the caste and their social status.[117] According to the Hindu notion, that any persons or things appertaining to a deity or temple was sacred, pure and incapable of polluting others.[118] In general, any relationship and intimacy between the caste-man and non-caste woman was treated as social crime and the person was tabooed, placed out of caste and completely denied all his caste privileges. But an open intimacy and association of caste-man with temple woman as a concubine or prostitute did not strike the caste-man as an act of inconsistent to the caste system and rules, and he was not deprived from his caste status.[119] Ironically, his position was strengthened in the society.

Aloysius, a sociologist, mentioned that a caste is an occupational endogamous community as well as rank ordered and ritually legitimated *Varna*.[120] Ketkar defined caste as a social group, which should carry two characteristics such as membership is confined to those who are born of members and includes all persons so born, and an inexorable social law forbids the members to marry outside the group.[121] In this sense, devadasi should be a woman from any caste order. The customs of devadasi could accumulate girls from various castes, customs and regions.[122] They were dedicated to different Hindu deities.[123] Abbe Dubois mentioned in his note that the profession of dancing girls was opened to embraces all persons with irrespective of their caste affiliation.[124] The Hindu Law recognised the legitimacy of the adopted child. So naturally, devadasi would not be classified as separate caste but it was a homogenous community, which carried similar characteristics with one another.

The Hindu Law recognised the dancing girls as a separate class and acknowledged the civil rights and status.[125] The High Court of colonial Madras acknowledged that the dancing girls were a separate community and had no caste, or belonged to any caste, and that consequently they could adopt a girl from any caste or no caste.[126] Yande reported that all the other castes, either high or low, look down upon the castes in which this custom of dedicating girls to gods prevails, and even the 'lowest caste' would never be induced to dedicate their girls to gods and allowed them to carry on the most infamous trade of prostitution.[127] It was known fact that the devadasis were recruited from various castes from the Hindu community and having different names in different districts.[128] The strength of the community was laid by the adoption from other communities because when the old devadasis become sterile, which was often the nature of their profession, they bought girls from other caste-Hindu and reduce the misery of such a life.[129] Usually, the succession to the profession was matrilineal. Devadasi was identified with their mothers, and the property was transferred through the female lineage.[130]

The role of caste

Sadasivan, a historian, mentioned that the girl meant for the dedication must have been of the devadasi caste.[131] Saskia Kersenboom-Story stressed that the nature of devadasihood was *murai* (professional ethics) or *vrtti* (way of life) which meant functions or task not as *jati* (caste).[132] Sadasivan also mentioned that the gradation of devadasi was called *murai* and those who came under *muraikkaris*.[133] Amrit Srinivasan pointed out that the temple dancing girls were not a *jati*.[134] Even further that a highly systematized knowledge about caste was developed over the latter half of the nineteenth century.[135]

However, caste played a significant role within the system. Based on their caste affiliation, the hierarchy was formed and nature of work was determined. Sadasivan mentioned the graded hierarchy of devadasi system.[136] In Suchindram temple of modern Kanyakumari district, Tamil Nadu, there were special customs called *muththa kudi* (traditional family) and *sirappu kudi* (family with special respect).[137] An Epigraph of 1343-1344 from Tiruvorriyur categorised them into *patiyilar* (not of a specific temple or husbandless), *devaradiyar* (servants of god) and *ishabattaliyilar* (those of the Siva temple).[138] The dedicated girls from the upper caste were allowed to perform ritual services and the rest had to do the secular works like cleaning the temple premises and utensils.[139]

In general, the girls from upper caste did the ritualistic performances and the others had to do the non-ritualistic performances.[140] At the same time, the upper castes girls became the concubines of the upper caste men, and the rest to be commercial prostitutes.[141] Sadasivan mentioned that the low-grade devadasi was paid so cheap.[142] John Shortt, the Superintendent of Vaccination in the Madras Presidency, referred that devadasi were permitted to do prostitution with any individual of an equal or superior caste or to live in a professional concubinage.[143] *Naik-Maratha Mandal* mentioned that the devadasis were the castes of hereditary prostitutes.[144] However, the early twentieth century developments of the Self-Respect Movement encouraged the inter-caste marriages of devadasi women to men of other caste. In 1929, the self-respecters, S. Guruswami of *Mudaliyar* caste and Kunjitham of *Isai Vellalar* got into a self-respect marriage.[145]

The dedication of devadasi

According to the devadasi tradition, the dedication was an important occasion and it was considered as meritorious in the life of devadasi. The dedication occurred both on voluntary and non-voluntary basis. Vidyadhar Agnihotri referred that the people dedicated their daughters to different deities while the others purchased girls for dedication to ensure their posthumous reward of a heavenly abode.[146] The voluntary dedication happened due to various reasons such as superstition, carrying tradition, etc. John Shortt referred that the dedication was made because of vow of the parents whom they were sick or other affliction, or when surrounded by troubles and trials, to give one of their daughters to some particular temple.[147] Yande pointed out that the poor, ignorant and superstitious families generally became the victims of the custom which were depended almost entirely on the profit they gained.[148]

Abbe Dubois mentioned that usually the perilous pregnant women were making vow to dedicate their daughter to the temple service for their safe delivery.[149] Alice Van Doren highlighted the event that the parents made pledge to dedicate their youngest daughter because of the critical condition of their first-born son who was near to death. After the recovery of the son, the parents fulfilled the oath of their dedication of eight years old daughter to the temple.[150] Ramachendrier, an assistant collector of Tiruchirappalli, stated that the custom was permitted the dedication of the elder daughter to the goddess Basavi.[151] Further, he stated that the girls were holding a stick and Margosa leaves in their hand and danced during the procession especially on the prevalence of epidemics.[152]

The non-voluntary dedication otherwise forced servitude was also common among the dedication. The adoption was a common feature in the devadasi system. Vidyadhar Agnihotri mentioned that devadasis used to purchase girls from outside the family to dedicate to temple to ensure their posthumous reward of a heavenly abode.[153] In general, they purchased girls from the poor caste-Hindus.[154] Based on the tradition, no women could dedicate themselves to the temple, and the immoral life of the dedicated daughters would not bring any disgrace to the family.[155] They were instructed to get the approval from the respective authorities of the temple administration. Ramachendrier remarked that prostitutes, women from non-devadasi community, married women, who deserted or discarded by their husbands, and widows, leading adulterous lives, could not claim the status of dancing girls. However, the daughters of such women could join the community of dancing girls and become devadasis.[156] The introduction of a virgin girl into the family of a dancing girl was sufficient to entitle her to be treated as daughter and no matter how she was obtained and to what caste she belonged.[157] Usually, the selection of girls for adoption was based on their physical charm. John Shortt referred in his note that the good looking and well-made girls were chosen for the dedication.[158]

The dedicated girls were trained in music, dancing and all other fine accomplishments to make them attractive to vice. Muthulakshmi Reddi, the first women legislator of Madras Presidency, mentioned that these accomplished girls were well tutored in the art of evil trade.[159] She mentioned that they were trained, as a practice of their caste-duty or *dharma*.[160] Here, she highlighted the word 'trained' but the custom of caste was based on their birth alone. Abbe Dubois mentioned that they were bred to this profligate life from their infancy. They were taken from any caste, and were frequently of respectable birth.[161] Their profession requires of them to be open to the embraces of persons of all castes.[162] Yande mentioned that all the other castes, either high or low, look down upon the castes in which this custom of dedicating girls to gods prevailed, and even the so called lowest caste will never be induced to dedicate their girls to gods and allow them to carry on the most infamous trade of prostitution.[163]

The selected girls should undergo the ritual ceremonies to become a devadasi. Even a daughter of devadasi had to go through a number of rites to attain the status of her inherent rights and duties.[164] The girls pass through a certain ceremony in the temples and the temple priest conducting *puja* as a representative of the particular deity. As per the custom of the devadasi order, the selected girls underwent certain ceremonies like *pottu kattuthal* (tying *pottu*), *gejja puja* (anklet ceremony) and puberty.

The dedication ceremony

Devadasis were existed in the most of the temples in South India. The dedication happened in both Saiva and Vaishnava temples. B.M. Sundaram, a musicologist, referred the Vaishnava temple *dasis* such as Thanjavur Mohanambal of Venkatesa Perumal *koyil*[165] and Thanjavur Kokilambal of

Rajagopalaswami *koyil.*[166] Usually, the dedication varied from temples to temples.[167] Natural and as well as adopted daughters of dancing girls were made, when young, to dedicate themselves to the idol of the temple to which their mother belonged. Traditionally, the girls between six and nine years of age were dedicated while before they attained puberty. The name of the girl was recommended by a head devadasi to the temple authorities. The ritual was done on the auspicious day either in the temple quarters or in the house of devadasi. The expenses of the ceremony was partly borne by senior devadasi and rest would be part of the patron and temple authorities.

The dedication ceremony was called as *pottu kattuthal.* The ceremony resembled the brahmanical marriage. The bridegroom was the presiding deity of the temple. In general, the priest and Brahmin were conducting *puja*, as a representative of the god. The priest tied golden *pottu* (symbol) on the neck of the girls. The ceremony stamped the girl as devadasi, after that they were exclusively associated for the temple services.[168] The ceremony of *pottu kattuthal* signified the person, one who pledge to sacrifice their life for the service of the god.[169]

The girl one who undertook the ceremony should marry either an object or dagger.[170] Sarma mentioned that the ceremony of *pottu* was the symbol of the religion, which denoted the pledge of the women as an ascetic for the rest of their life.[171] It resembled that the women would lead an ascetic life, if it would not happen, she would sacrifice her life to the sword.[172] He mentioned the ritual that resembled the girl should not violate the rituals and sacredness. If it happed, the sword would take away their life.[173] As per the Hindu custom, Lord Siva considered the dedicated girls as his women, so they were denoted as *rudrakanikai* and their service to the deity identify them as devadasi.[174] Based on their sect (Saivism and Vaishnavism), the dedicated girls used to wear rosaries or sacred beads and *vibhuthy* or *srechurnam* (ash).[175]

The *Census of India, 1901: - Travancore* detailed the ritual ceremony of the *pottu kattuthal* in Suchindram temple. Usually, the girl to be wedded took bath and moved to the temple with two pieces of cloth, a *tali* (wedlock), betel, areca nut, and coconut. The ceremonial artefacts were placed before the priest and later the priest kept those artefacts under the feet of idol. The young girl seated to face towards the deity. The priest kindled the sacred fire and went through the rituals of the *Tirukkalyanam* (sacred marriage). The priest used *Panchakshara mantra* in Saiva temple and *Ashakshara mantra* in Vaishnava temple. The priest tied *tali* around her neck and did all the rituals of the bridegroom on behalf of the deity. The grand ceremony was celebrated for four days.[176] Samy Chidambaranar, an ideologue of the Self-Respect Movement, stated that the naming ritual itself branded the young girls as wife of god.[177] Interestingly, *Kamikamam*, the brahmanical text, referred devadasi as the wife of the priest.[178] Following the rituals, the dedicated girl was allotted with grants and confirmed some special privileges, and they received certain sums as wages, the amount was dependent on the worth, sanctity, and popularity of the temple to which they were dedicated.[179]

Gejja puja and puberty

In general, training was an important part in the life of young devadasi. They were expected to undergo a rigorous training in dance and music under the apprenticeship of *nattuvanar* (teacher). Later, they became accomplished performers and their services being required in temples for various rituals.[180] Tamil lexicon mentioned that devadasi as dancing girl, dedicated to the service of a god or celestial dancing girl.[181] In addition to the artistic performances, devadasi had to do a series of other services in the temple. Ramachandram mentioned that the engagement of devadasi in cleaning, decoration, flooring, burnishing its vessels and lamps, collecting flowers, making garlands, and offering them to God in the temple.[182] William Taylor in his note mentioned that the service of devadasi such as lighting lamp, powdering sandal and garland making on the temple service for both in the morning and evening rituals.[183] He further stated that the customary offerings and performances were glad and struck his eyes with great piety.[184] In Tiruvarur, devadasi practiced two *murai* (traditions) which were *periya murai* (big tradition) and *china murai* (small tradition). Also, devadasi performed their daily rituals in every evening in the sanatorium and showed sixteen types of hand signals which was known as *kaikattum murai*.[185] In *periya murai*, devadasi stood in the sanatorium and did rituals which carried *arati* (sacred light) to the gods. Usually, the ritual was done by the senior devadasi who reached menopause. According to *chinna murai*, devadasi was not allowed to use the sacred light but they carried out the rituals out of the sanctorium in the temple premises.[186]

The ceremony of *gejja puja* was considered an important ceremony next to *pottu kattuthal*. The *gejja puja* was a ceremony, which honoured the young devadasi with anklet on her leg. The ceremony signalled that the dedicated girl would start to learn dance. Following the ceremony, the elders in the family taught the artistic forms to the children and then, they were sent to teachers outside the family whose style was compatible.[187] John Shortt mentioned that the young devadasi were taught to dance at the early age of five.[188] There was an equal distribution of hours devoted to singing and dancing practices.[189] In general, the lessons in dancing and music were given daily, two hours in the morning and the evening. In three years, the child was supposed to master the arts of singing and dancing, and then they continued their performance until the age of thirty and forty.[190] The tradition insisted devadasi to dance six times a day, at the temple, before the deity, while the priests were officiating the rituals. The duties of the devadasi was synchronised by their turns.[191]

After *gejja puja*, the festival for puberty of the dedicated girl became grand. Traditionally, devadasi considered puberty as a meritorious one. *Muvaraiyan Virali Vitu Tutu*, the seventeenth century Tamil literature, mentioned the puberty celebration of the devadasi. According to the text, devadasi celebrated the day of her puberty as *thiranda nal*, which meant 'matured day'.[192] During the day, she conducted a grand festival with the traditional songs of *villupattu*, *kooththu* and *kaniyan kooththu*.[193] On the day, she worshipped the demi-god called Madan and sacrificed animals.[194]

In general, devadasis had to master all the fields. The performances of devadasis were categorised into ritualistic and non-ritualistic.[195] The ritualistic performance was primarily considered as dancing and singing. Devadasis did the various dance performances (*aryak-kooththu*, *santik-kooththu*, etc.) in the temples and other festivals with meticulous care, devotion and dedication. Usually, devadasis were the good dancers and singers and their performances were held in the specific halls like *natakasalai* and *nrttamandapam*.[196] The songs and dances of devadasi became a source of attraction to the lay worshippers and pilgrims.[197] The artistic qualities became an iconic identity of devadasis. Altekar pointed out that the people visited temples not to pay their respects to deities, but as to carry their love intrigues with the singing girls who was employed in the temples.[198] The kings, nobles, temples, and *sabhas* (village assembly) remunerated devadasi with *manya* (gift) and *jivita* (allowances), as a recognition of their performance and other multifarious activities.[199] The non-ritualistic performances included activities such as washing, sweeping, collecting flowers, sounding bells, fanning the deity.[200] The South Indian inscription mentioned that the women who served in temple *madaippali* (kitchen) were called as *adukkalaip-pendugal*.[201]

Categories of devadasis

The prolonged continuity of the tradition created different categories among the devadasi institution. *Abithana Chintamani*, an encyclopedia on Tamil literature, classified devadasis into seven kinds, based on their method of dedication.[202] According to the encyclopedia, *thathai* was a woman, one who dedicated herself to the god; *vikkirathai* was one who sold for the temple worship; *piruhuthya* was one dedicated herself for the welfare of the clan; *pakthai* was a person dedicated herself to the god for the devotion; *haritha* was a person who was mesmerised by the god; *alankarai* was one who sent by the king due to her excellence in her field; and *rudrakanikai* was one who served the temple for the remuneration.[203] All the women were subdivided into *vazhankai* and *idankai dasis*. Usually, *vazhankai dasis* served *idankai dasis*.

Edgar Thurston pointed out the seven classes of *dasis* from the old 'Hindu' texts. His monumental work, *Castes and Tribes of Southern India* referred *datta* was a girl, one who gave herself as a gift to a temple, *vikrita* was one who sold herself for the same purpose of dedication, *bhritya* was a girl, who offered herself as a temple servant for the prosperity of her family, *bhakta* was one who joined a temple out of devotion, *hrita* was one who enticed away, and presented to a temple, *alankara* was one who being well trained in her profession and profusely decked and was presented to a temple by kings and noblemen and *rudrakanika* or *gopika* was one who received regular wages from a temple, and were employed for singing and dancing.[204]

Other names for devadasis

The devadasi tradition was ancient and widespread in the culture of India. Therefore, the name of the institution also varied from regions to regions. The earliest elements of devadasi system were found in Sangam literature. In general, Sangam literature was considered as the most secular literary contribution of Tamil to the Indian culture. Sangam literature portrayed the images of dancing women and prostitutes. *Tolkappiyam*, *Ettuttogai*, *Pattupattu* and *Pathinenkilkanakku*[205] gave the earliest reference of the 'captive women' (*kondi mahalir*), one who engaged in divine service.[206] All the other Sangam classics referred *viraliyar* (minstrels), *kuttiyar* (dancing girls), and *parattaiyar* (prostitutes). Later, all these customs merged to evolve the devadasi system in Tamilakam.[207]

The materials related to the evolution of the devadasi system were evident from the Tamil epics of *Chilappathikaram*, *Manimekalai* and *Civakachintamani*.[208] The Sangam literature and post-Sangam sources such as *Chilappathikaram* and *Manimekalai* did not mention anything directly about devadasi system or religious sexuality. However, it portrayed prostitutes in their work. The Sangam text referred the women who acted as *velan veriyadal*, *kuri solluthal* and *virali*, but there was no reference for the dedication of women to any particular deity. Even, the term *paraththai* (prostitutes) were denoted as *ayilai mahalir*[209], *nerilai mahalir*[210], *vilaik kanikai*[211], *vilai nalap pendir*[212], *kurumahal*[213], *manilai mahalir*[214], *valilai mahalir*[215], *kurunthodi mahalir*[216], *kanankulaiyavar*[217], *ezhil unkan nallar*[218], *kodiyannar*[219], *ezhilnallar*[220], *thunaimalark kothaiyar*[221], *kadikkondar*[222], *ethilar*[223], *kondi mahalir*,[224] *padini*[225], *kama kilaththiyar*, *paraththaiyar*, *kamakkilaththi* (concubine), *katharpparaththai*, *irparaththai* and *cheripparaththai*.[226] The characteristics of prostitute were categorised on the basis of dance, beauty and youthfulness. In general, family women were differentiated and identify them as *kula mahalir* (family women).

The historians could not trace the visible elements of devadasi system during the Kalabhra interim.[227] The contemporary literature is the importance evidence of the period. The core of Kalabhras literature was morality. In general, women were mute. *Pathinenkilkanakku* mentioned prostitute in different terms such as *ainthodiyar*[228], *panpin mahalir*[229], *porut pendir*[230], *maya mahalir*[231], *manilaiyar*[232], *irumanap pendir*[233], *vesaiyar*[234], *vanna mahalir*[235], *pudaippendir*[236], *punguzhaiyar*[237], *ayilaiyal*[238], *thalirannar*[239], *onnuthlar*[240], *kanikai*[241], *varaivin mahalir, vilai mahalir*. The other post-Sangam works also detailed about the prostitute in different terms such as *adal kooththiyar*[242], *arankak kooththi*[243], *arankiyan mahalir*[244], *kadai kazhi mahalir*[245], *kanikai*[246], *kothiyar*[247], *thoriya madanthaiyar*[248], *nadaka madanthaiyar*[249], *puvilai madanthaiyar*[250], *vampap paraththai*[251], *koththiyanmadanthaiyar*[252], *kondi mahalir*[253], *pothuvar*[254], *porul vilaiyatti*[255], *dasi*[256], *kalaiyunar mahalir*[257], *arivaiyar*[258], *adan mahalir*[259], *poga mahalir*[260], *kalaiyindra sollal*[261], *adan mankaiyar*[262] and *paraththai.*[263]

The devotional literature of Tamil, *puranas* and *stalapuranas* (temple myths) of the medieval period detailed the devadasi custom. The devotional literature of Alvars and Nayanmars (composed between sixth and ninth century) referred the women as a celestial human being. *Periyapuranam*, the twelfth century Saivite hagiology, detailed the devadasi system. During the reigns of Vijayanagar, Nayaka, Maratha and Poligars, there were innumerable minor literary works were composed in Tamilakam. Those literatures such as the *parani*, *ula*, *tutu* and *kovai* detailed the general conditions of devadasis. The medieval *Manipravala* literature, threw the valuable lights on the growing influence of the devadasi system.[264]

The cultural and geographical indicators played a significant role in the variations of the devadasi institution. According to the *Census of India, 1901: - Travancore*, Tamil devadasis were known as *padham* and Malayalam known as *padhamangalam* in South Travancore. The Malayalam speaking devadasis used to wear white cloths in Suchindram and Padmanabapuram temple.[265] In addition, they did not engage in the private performance such as Tamil *dasis* did.[266] Devadasis were called by several names in the Indian subcontinent. In Tamil Nadu, devadasis were identified as *devadasi, devaradiyar, patiyilar*[267], *talichcheri pendukal, devanar makal, koottikal, adikalmar, manikkam* or *manikkattar, kanikaiyar*[268], *devadiyal, emperumanadiyar, koyil pillaimar*[269], *rudrakanikai, koyil pinakkal*[270] and so on. The devadasis of Kerala noted as *kuttiyar* (officially known as *atumpatrams*)[271], *kudikari, marampavaiyar, devidicchi, nangaimar*[272], *muraikkari, kootachi, koothichi*, and *attakkari*[273]. In Andhra Pradesh, they were called as *bhogam-vandhi, sanis, bhogam* and *jogin*,[274] Devadasi in the Karnataka region were known as *suleyar*[275], *sule, poti, basavi* (young devadasi) and *jogtis* (old devadasi) (The term '*basavi*' refers to feminine form of '*basava*', a bull which roams the village at will without any restriction. Hence, '*basavi*' alludes to the foot loose position of the woman.).[276] In Assam, devadasis were called as *Natis*[277], *kurmapus kudipus*, and *darikas*[278]. The devadasi system in Odisha was identified with the terms *patras* and *maharis*. In Konkani belt, devadasi were denoted by *bhavanis*, *bhavin*, *kudikar* and *kalavant*. Further, in Marathi speaking region, devadasi system was referred in terms such as *murali*, *jogateen* and *aradhini*[279]. Sadasivan mentioned that the devadasis' in the Bombay presidency were identified in different terms, based on their temple affiliation.[280] Often, the devadasi system was confused with prostitution. However, the Tamil word clearly differentiates the devadasi and prostitution, the word *vesi* referred prostitutes and *dasi* meant slave women who attached to the temple.[281]

Proverbs on devadasi

There were many proverbs, which were closely associated with devadasi. The proverbs reflected the public consensus on the general status of the devadasi system. A proverb, *thevaradiyal irunthu aththal seththal kottu melam, thevadiyal seththal onrumillai* meant that if the dancing girl is alive, and her mother dies, there will be beating of drums; but if the dancing girl dies there will be no such display. Which meant that to get the favour of the dancing girl, many men would attend her mother's funeral; but if the dancing girl dies, there will be nothing gained by attending her funeral. It also meant that a devadasi's property remained with her family only as long as she lived and her death usually left the house without a single penny.[282]

Another proverb, *kozhukkattaikku thalaiyumillai, kooththadichchikku muraiyumillai* meant that the cake has no point like dancing girl does not have any ethics in their life.[283] In the same way, *siraichchalaikku azhakillai thevadiyalukku muraiyillai* referred a prison has no ethics and a dancing girl does not regard the ties of relationship.[284] *Thelukku kodukkile visam, thevadiyalukku udampile visam, unakko sarvankam visam*, which meant scorpions have poison in their tail, harlots in their body, but to you, your whole body, is poison.[285]

Some proverbs detailed the poverty of devadasi girls. *Kovil sorrukku kumattina thevadiyal, kadich chorrukku karanampodukiral* meant the dancing girl who was formerly more than filled with good food in the temple, now turns a somersault to get a poor man's rice.[286] *Orukku oru thevadiyal yarukkendru aduval* referred the village has only one dancing girl; for whom is she to dance? (As all want her services, she is not only in doubt where to go, but also suffers from being overworked.).[287] *Adamattatha thevadiyal pothathu enralam* pointed the dancing girl, who could not dance, said that the hall was not big enough.[288] *Than pathiniyanal, thevadiyal thervilum kudiyirukkalam* stated if a matron is chaste, she may live in the dancing- girls' street.[289]

Sources for the study of the devadasis

This study used both primary and secondary sources. According to the historical context, the natures of sources are differed. The study extensively used the historical narratives such as epigraphy, travelogues, literary sources, official records, newspapers, collected speeches and writings, reports and minutes, memories and autobiographies, oral narratives, personal letters, and diaries as well as monographs and folk songs.

The study of inscriptions provided the information about the devadasi. It helped us to situate devadasi within the particular historical context of the medieval South India. From eleventh century onwards, the inscriptions that dealt with devadasi was available in every part of Indian subcontinent. In general, the inscriptions were engraved on rocks, boulders, walls of temples, pillars and loose slabs. Some of the inscriptions are unfortunately buried under earth as hundreds of inscriptions engraved on copper and silver plates.[290] The epigraphical evidences detailed the social status of devadasi women. The recorded gifts explained the charitable activities of devadasis. Usually, devadasis were made different endowments such as lands, lamps, sheep, cow, gold, jewels, and other ornaments to the temple and other the public charities.[291] The sources highlighted the role of the temple and the dancing girls in early medieval, medieval and even later period. The earliest epigraphical reference to devadasi occurred in the reign of the Pallava king, Nandivarma Pallavamalla (731-796).[292] The inscriptions were published in the series of *South Indian Inscriptions* (*S.I.I.*), *the Inscriptions of Pudukkottai State* (*P.S.I.*), *South Indian Temple Inscriptions* (*S.I.T.I.*), *Annual Report on Indian Epigraphy* (*A.R.I.E.*), *Travancore Archaeological Series* (*T.A.S.*), *Epigraphica Indica*, etc.

The historical remains such as sculptures and paintings reflected the respective society and elegant of devadasi women. In general, the sculptures of the dancing girls were depicted in the walls and towers of the temples. For example, the paintings of the dancing girls were depicted in the temples of Kailasanatha (Kanchipuram), Vaigunthaperumal (Kanchipuram), Vettuvarkoil (Kalugumalai), Rajarajesvaram (Thanjavur), Chittannavasal cave (Pudukkottai), Tiruvarur temple and Thiyagarajar temple.[293]

In addition to inscriptions, we have other sources from time to time. Thanjavur Marathas of the eighteenth century, used *Modi* scripts, which were popularly known as the *Modi* records. However, the documentation of *Modi* records has not been done systematically. So referring *Modi* source was a little difficult (*See Appendix*: - 2).[294] The translated works of K.M. Venkatramaiah and Vivekanandagopal were helpful while using those sources. Further, the government orders (GO), legislative council debates, different volumes of census reports of India and contemporary newspapers and magazines from the colonial period gave valuable information about the devadasis in colonial India.

Usually, literature furnishes primary data for the study of devadasi. It throws light on contemporary events and substantiates the information, which was found in the inscriptions. The present book used mostly Sangam and post-Sangam literature, *bhakti* literature and other minor literature, especially the literary genres of *tutu* and *Kalambagam*, the songs of Arunakirinathar and Kalamekam.

The records of Arab, Chinese and European travellers provided the references of the temple women of India. Huan Tsang (c. seventh century), Abu Zaid al Hasan (930), Al-Beruni (1030), Chau-ju-Kua (twelfth century), Marco Polo (1290), Wasaf (fourteenth century), Ibn Batuta (fourteenth century), Durate Barbosa (1504-1514) and Abbe Dubois (1799) were few notable travellers, who recorded the institution of devadasis. Al-Beruni stated that the institution of devadasi was started to degenerate as early as the tenth to eleventh century.[295] Abdul Razaak, a Turkish ambassador from Persia, described that the prostitution of dancing girls was a great source of revenue to the kingdom, and out of the income of the dancing girls, the entire upkeep of the police force was paid.[296] Nicolo Conti (fifteenth century), Paes and Nuniz (sixteenth century) were detailed the devadasi institution of the Vijayanagar period. Abbe Dubois (1799) said that devadasi granted their favours to anyone demanding them, in return for ready money. He further added that the people perceived devadasis or the handmaids of god as a prostitute.[297] The sixteenth century missionary letters of Fr. Immanuel de Veiga and Fr. Vico detailed the devadasi system.[298]

The study largely depended on the personal writings such as 'personal documents' or 'documents of life' which include diaries, letters, autobiographies, biographies, memoranda and other materials.[299] The writings of E.V. Ramasami and other self-respecters, Muthulakshmi Reddi and her personal communication with Gandhi were useful. With regards to biography, the life of Ramamirtham was referred from the writings of Ramamirtham in her novel *Dasikal Mosavalai alladhu Mathipetra Mminar* (Dasis web of deceit or enlightened Playboy) and newspapers of the Self-Respect Movement and the biography of Jeevasunadari. The life of Nagarathnam was reconstructed from the work of Sriram (*The Devadasi and the Saint: The Life and Times of Bangalore Nagarathnamma*) and Balasaraswati's life from Douglas M. Knight Jr's *Balasaraswathi: Her Art and Life*. And T.J.S. George's *MS: A Life in Music* is helpful to refer the life of M.S. Subbulakshmi.

Review of literature

There are two kinds of secondary sources, used for this research. One that exclusively discussed about the devadasi and its institution. The next one is the works, which detailed the issues, which were related to women, society and ideologies such as the works of M.S.S. Pandian, K.N. Panikkar, V. Geetha, K.A.N. Sastri, etc.

There are good numbers of secondary sources available on studying devadasi system. The sources partly or completely analysed devadasi and the institution. Frederique Apffel Marglin, Saskia Kersenboom-Story, Leslie C. Orr, Sadasivan, A.K. Singh, Tarachand, Priyadarshini Vijaisri, Kunal M. Parker, Shashi Panjrath and O.P. Ralhan, Jogan Shankar, Kay K. Jordan, Nagendra Kr. Singh,[300] Indira Viswanathan Peterson, Davesh Soneji, Amrit Srinivasan,[301] Rekha Pande, Lakshmi Subramanian, Kalpana Kannabiran and Lakshmi Viswanathan are the few prominent scholars who did extensive research on devadasi institution.

A.K. Singh's *Devadasi System in Ancient India* discussed the evolution of devadasi system in a historical perspective. Inscriptions were the primary sources for his study. The book discussed about the origin of the system and further detailed the functions and activities of the organisation, their regional distribution and their paramours. Shashi Panjrath and O.P. Ralhan detailed the institution in a historical perspective.[302] They pointed about the temple institution and its performance and influence in the respective society. It further detailed the role of devadasi, their royal patronage, rituals and practices, duties and rewards in South India. Rekha Pande in her article *Devadasis* detailed devadasi of a medieval South India. She discussed about the relationship between temple organisation and devadasi, their land grant which popularly known as *devadana* and the functions of devadasis in temple institution.[303]

Saskia Kersenboom-Story's *Nityasumangali* is one of the pioneering works in the study of devadasi system. The work considered the institution as semiotic unit. She did not analyse the institution based historical perspective. She understood the system and its functions within the fold Hindu tradition.[304] She traced the concept of the devadasi from the Sangam Age beginning in 100 B.C.E. and lasting until the collapse of the Thanjavur court in 1947. She provided a detailed analysis of the role of the devadasi in both the daily and festival temple rituals based on Sanskrit manuals, inscriptions, and informants' accounts. Leslie C. Orr's *Donors, Devotees, and Daughters of God* marked an important addition to the study of this system.[305] This book is based on an exhaustive study of temple inscriptions and claimed to reveal the actuality of temple women's lives, from those inscriptional records from the Chola Empire (850-1300) in Tamil Nadu. The body of the book is loaded with statistics and tables. She challenged the image of women dancers as prostitutes and produced valuable information on them. She portrayed devadasis in three categories as donors, devotees and at the same time as daughters of god. *Devadasi System in Medieval Tamil Nadu* of Sadasivan detailed the devadasi institution of medieval Tamil Nadu. It was one of the extensive researches on the devadasi institution of Tamil society. His research was based on inscription and epigraphical records.

The work brought out the general condition on devadasis during periods of Chola, later Pandiya and Nayaka.

Frederique Apffel Marglin studied the devadasi institution of eastern India, especially devadasis associated with the temple of Jagannath in Puri, Orissa. It provided an ethnographic data. It combined with description of the involvements of devadasis in palace and temple rituals, their sexual initiations, caste and geographical structures on their sexual availability, and their culturally askew kinship systems. It centred on all such discussion on auspiciousness/ inauspiciousness as an axial pair of Hindu values. Marglin highlighted that the secularised nature of kingly role in India.[306] Tarachand's anthropological work, *Devadasi Custom* theoretically contributes to understand the concept of religious tradition, marriage union, lineage inheritance, family leadership, status, authority and so on. The work theorized the various concepts of the origin of the system. It basically set on the post-colonial village of Wada in Maharashtra.[307] *Devadasi Cult* of Jogan Shankar analysed the devadasi system of Yellamma tradition. It based on the sociological perspective. It detailed on the post-colonial period.[308] Priyadarshini Vijaisri's *Recasting the Devadasi* focused on the sacred prostitution of South India, during colonial period with special focused on Karnataka and Telugu speaking area (Mysore state and Maratha country). It locates various manifestations of this custom in a culturally pluralistic context.[309] Kalpana Kannabiran's article *Judiciary, Social Reform and Debate on 'Religious Prostitution' in Colonial India* discussed devadasis system in the colonial India. It detailed the struggle between the reformist and the revivalist and the role of devadasi.[310] Moreover, her another work, *Muvalur Ramamirthammal's Web of Deceit* was a translated work of the notable devadasi of colonial Tamil Nadu, Muvalur Ramamirthammal.[311]

Kunal M. Parker's *A Corporation of Superior Prostitutes' Anglo-Indian Legal Conceptions of Temple Dancing Girls, 1800- 1914* was a detailed work on the various judicial issues on the abolition devadasi system in colonial period. It analysed the problems between the indigenous custom, Hindu and colonial law. It further discussed about the labialisation of devadasi as prostitutes.[312] Jordan's *From Sacred Servants to Profane Prostitutes* was one of the prominent works that related to the different judicial policies that were enacted during the colonial period for the abolition of devadasi system. It detailed the colonial transformation of the Indian legal system towards the issues of devadasis.[313] Amrit Srinivasan's *Judiciary, Social Reform and Debate on 'Religious Prostitution' in Colonial India* examined the official debate in the colonial judiciary on the devadasi institution of the Madras Presidency. The study of the devadasi institution undertook with a two-fold purposes. The first was an attempt to understand the relationship between women, religion and the state in pre-colonial and colonial South India, and the second was to try and disentangle this complex process, specifically looked, how far the projects of colonialism, reforms and revivals were based on an understanding of the material reality of the practice between 1860-1935.[314]

Indira Viswanathan Peterson and Davesh Soneji's *Performing Pasts: Reinventing the Arts in Modern South India* was a book, which contained the important collection of articles on performing arts and modernity in South India.[315] It illuminated the tension between modernity and tradition. It critically interrogated colonialism and nationalism in the context of the "invention" of South India's performing arts in the nineteenth and twentieth century. The articles in the volume, discussed the various issues on devadasi custom during colonial period. Lakshmi Subramanian's *From the Tanjore Court to the Madras Music Academy* was a critical study, which discussed the transformation of devadasi arts from its nature to modern. The work was set the on colonial background. Her book focused on the modernisation the devadasi's art form.[316] Lakshmi Viswanathan a explored the world of the devadasi in the historical context in her book *Women of Pride*. It gave a general information on devadasi institution and provided the interviews of devadasis and *nautch* women of colonial India.[317]

The work of A.K. Singh and Shashi Panjrath and O.P. Ralhan, Rekha Pande provided general details of devadasi and their situation. Saskia Kersenboom-Story, Leslie Orr and Sadasivan focused the temple women of Tamilakam. Saskia Kersenboom-Story analysed the system within the Hindu custom. Leslie C. Orr detailed on devadasi on medieval Tamil Chola Empire. Sadasivan historically detailed the medieval temple institution. Frederique Apffel Marglin, Tarachand and Priyadarshini Vijaisri focused the devadasi institution in Orissa, Karnataka and Mysore region respectively. Kunal M. Parker and Kay K. Jordan preceded the legal things of devadasi in colonial context. Indira Viswanathan Peterson and Davesh Soneji, Amrit Srinivasan, Lakshmi Subramanian, and Kalpana Kannabiran set their research in colonial context and analysed the transformation from its traditional way of performance to modernity. All the above-mentioned research works focused on different issues related to devadasis. However, they did not concentrate on the historical connectivity of the evolution of the institution and its reformulated structure in the Tamil country which we plan to do.

Methodology

This study uses qualitative methods, especially the methodologies of History and Gender Studies. The researcher carried out unstructured interviews with the last surviving devadasi to understand their experiences and opinions on devadasi institution.

This research used a large amount of translation. With regard the transliteration, the thesis followed its own pattern – for instance, the word mother was transliterated as *amma* instead of *ammaa* or *ammâ*; and the meaning was given either in brackets or in the endnotes. The historical discourse engaged with many historical personalities. Those eminent Person were usually identified with their surnames like E.V. Ramasami as *Thanthai Periyar* and M.K. Gandhi as *Mahatma*. The present book tries to avoid their popular names or pseudonyms and has attempted to use their proper names alone.

Objectives

This book has five objectives to comprehend the evolution and reformulation the devadasi system:

- To understand the concept and nature of devadasi institution.
- To know the historical background of the devadasi system in Tamilakam. The study also focuses on social, religious, political and economic condition of the Tamilakam.
- To study the life of devadasi in the historical context.
- The study concentrates on the historical transformation of the devadasi institution from sacred place to profane.
- To find the role of reformist and revivalist in the process of abolition of the system.

To achieve its object, this study has to face few challenges. The first one is in the form of sources. Sources are the backbone for every historical study. Regarding this study we have to utilise various kinds of primary sources. Each kind has its own nature and problem. Few of the medieval Tamilakam inscriptions were scripted in Prakrit language. The next issue is in the form of *stalapuranas*. These give details regarding temples, its origin, deity, worshipping pattern and auspicious days etc. However, *stalapuranas* were infused with the mythological elements. Therefore, we have to focus on those evidences in a rational and historical way. In the same way, the devotional songs of Alvars and Nayanars carried the devotional elements. Raghavan had characterised the saints as "mystics who spoke the language of experience and poetry and not of argument and logic."[318] The other challenge was in the identification of the exact sacred centres of the medieval period. The names of the places mentioned in the primary sources have changed in course of time.

Chapterisation

The present book is divided into seven chapters:

The first chapter is titled *Introduction*. It details the concept of devadasi, meaning and features of the devadasi institution. It analysis the sources and historiography of the study. Then it discusses about the methodologies that have been used and followed in collecting and analysing the data and concludes with the details of the chapterisation of this research.

The second chapter is *Pre-Colonial South India: - The Historical Context*. It discusses the historical development which led to the formation of devadasi institution of South India with special focus on Tamilakam. This chapter focuses on the social condition of the age that influenced in the emergence of devadasi system in South India. It looks at the political background. It also explores the economic, social and religious situation in South India.

The third chapter, *Emergence and Growth of the Devadasi System: - Pre-Colonial Period* analyses the position of devadasi in pre-colonial South India and further, it details the effective participation of temple women in the South Indian society.

The fourth chapter, *The Devadasi System: - The Colonial Period* vividly lists the transformation of the devadasi system from one mode of political condition to another one. It analyses various causes for the degradation of the system. The conclusion of this chapter is highlights the general condition of devadasis of colonial South India.

The fifth chapter, *The Twentieth Century Debate on Devadasi System* discusses the role of reformist and revivalist in the move of the abolition and restoration of the devadasi custom in the society.

The sixth chapter, *The Life Stories of Some Selected Devadasis of South India* gives different perspective on devadasis and their institution in their contemporary society. It details the portrayal of devadasis in their contemporary media and its influence over the system.

The last and concluding chapter, *Conclusion* gives a valedictory note of this work and summarises the facts from the chapters.

References

1. Iyer, Latha and Kanakalatha Mukund. "Herstory: Women in South India in the Seventeenth and Eighteenth Centuries." *Indica* 32, no. 1. (1995): p. 29.
2. Lerner, Gerda. *The Creation of Patriarchy*. Oxford University Press: New York, 1986: p. 6.
3. *Ibid*. p. 5.
4. Carroll Smith-Rosenberg in Morgan, Sue. Ed. *The Feminist History Reader*. London: Routledge, 2006: p. 100.
5. Lerner, Gerda. 1986. *Op.cit.,* p. 5.
6. Carroll Smith-Rosenberg in Morgan, Sue. Ed. 2006. *Op.cit.,* p. 99.
7. Sharma, Ratna. "Devadasi: The Sacred Veil on Priestly Prostitution." *Adhyayan* VI, no. 1 and 2. (1996): p. 20.
8. Swaminathan, S. *The Early Cholas History, Art and Culture*. Delhi: Sharada Publicating House, 1998: p. 124.

9. Subramanian, N. *History of Tamilnad.* Madurai: Koodal Publishers, 1978: p. 344.
10. The geographical boundary is not a permanent phenomenon and it could change with time. Hence, defining the exact geographical boundary of Tamilakam is tough. According to *Chilappathikaram*, the limits of Tamilakam were from Venkata Hills (Tirupathi) in the North to Cape Comorin in the South and from the Bay of Bengal in the East, to the Arabian Sea in the West. (Kanakasabhai, V. *The Tamils Eighteen Hundred Years Ago*. New Delhi: Asian Educational Services, 1904 (Rpt. 1979): 10.) Subramanian stated that the Tamil country called Tamil Nadu or Tamilakam lies to the South of the Mysore plateau in the North and North West and the Tirupathi hills in the North East, and is bounded on the West by the Arabian Sea, on the South by the Indian Ocean and on the east by the Bay of Bengal. (Subramanian, N. 1978. *Op.cit.*, p. 1.)
11. Hero Stones are the small establishment made on the buried person whose act was considered as valiant. In general, people used to offer or worship the establishment.
12. Subramanian, N. 1978. *Op.cit.*, p. 344.
13. Kersenboom, Saskia C. *Nityasumangali*. Delhi: Motilal Banarsidas, 1987: p. IX.
14. Sharma, Ratna. 1996. *Op.cit.*, p. 20.
15. Singh, A.K. *Devadasis System in Ancient India*. Delhi: H.K. Publishers and Distributors, 1990: p. 7.
16. Tarachand, K.C. *Devadasi Custom: Rural and Social Structure and Flesh Markets*. New Delhi: Reliance Publishing House, 1991: p. 12.
17. Sharma, Ratna. 1996. *Op.cit.*, p. 23.
18. Kersenboom, Saskia C. 1987. *Op.cit.*, p. XVI.
19. Iyer, Latha and Kanakalatha Mukund. 1995. *Op.cit.*, p. 38.
20. Wilson, H.H. *A Glossary of the Judicial and Revenue Terms: And of the Useful Words Occurring in Official Documents Relating to the Administration of the Government of British India*. London: W.H. Allen and Co, 1855: p. 133.
21. Basham, A.L. *The Wonder That Was India*. New Delhi: Rupa. Co, 1954 (Rpt. 2002): p. 185.
22. Parker, Kunal M. "A Corporation of Superior Prostitutes' Anglo-Indian Legal Conceptions of Temple Dancing Girls, 1800-1914." *Modern Asian Studies* 32, no. 3. (July, 1998): p. 559.
23. Kersenboom, Saskia C. 1987. *Op.cit.*
24. *Ibid.*, p. XV.
25. Tarachand, K.C. 1991. *Op.cit.*, p. 1.
26. *Ibid.*
27. Orr, Leslie. C. *Donors, Devotees and Daughters of God: Temple Women in Medieval Tamilnadu*. Oxford: Oxford University Press, 2000: p. 5.
28. Thurston, Edgar and K, Rangachari. *Castes and Tribes of Southern India*. Vol. II- C to J. New Delhi: Asian Educational Services, 1987 (Rpt. 1909): pp. 125-126.
29. *Ibid.*

30. Williams, Monier M. *Religious Thought and Life in India: An Account of the Religious of the Indian Peoples, Based on a Life's Study of their Literature and on Personal Investigations in their Own Country*. Part. I. London: John Murray, 1885: p. 451.
31. *Ibid.*
32. Bor, Joep. "Mamia, Ammani and Other Bayaderes: Europe's Portrayal of India's Temple Dancers." In Davesh Soneji. Ed. *Bharathanatyam: A Reader*. New Delhi: Oxford University Press, 2010: p. 48.
33. Marglin, Frederique Apffel. *Wives of the God- King: The Rituals of the Devadasis of Puri*. Delhi: Oxford University Press, 1985: p. 18-19.
34. *Ibid.*, p. 18.
35. Venkatramaiah, K.M. *Administration and Social Life under the Maratha Rulers of Thanjavur* (in Tamil). Thanjavur: Tamil University, 1984: p. 490.
36. *Hindu Samayach Chollakarathi* (A Concise Dictionary on Hindu Religion) (in Tamil). Kokkalai Jerajan. Comp. Chennai: Maharani, 1992 (2001): p. 410.
37. *Irupatham Norrandu Tamil Peyaragarathi* (Twentieth Century Tamil Dictionary) (in Tamil). P. Ramanathan. Comp. Chennai: Institute of South Indian Studies, 1909 (1991): p. 770.
38. *Kazhakath Tamil Agarathi* (Tamil Dictionary of an Association) (in Tamil). Kazhakap Puzhavar Kuzhuvinar. Comp. Tirunelveli: The South India Saiva Siddhanta Works Publishing Society, 1964 (2000): p. 576.
39. *Ibid.*
40. Bor, Joep. 2007. *Op.cit.*, pp. 45.
41. Valentyn, Francois. *Oud en Nieuw Oost-Indien*. Vol. 5. Dordrecht and Amsterdam: Joannes van Braam and Gerard Onder den Linden, 1726: p. 54.
42. Bor, Joep. 2007. *Op.cit.*, p. 46.
43. *Webster's Unabridged Dictionary*. Random House. New York: Random House, 1999: p. 179.
44. Singh, A.K. 1990. *Op.cit.*, p. 13.
45. Krishnaswami Aiyengar, S. *South India and Her Muhammadan Invaders*. London: Oxford University Press, 1921: p. 233.
46. Dubois, Abbe J.A. *A Description of the Character, Manner and Customs of the People of India*. Madras: J. Higginbotham, 1862: p. 295.
47. *Swamikalum Devadiyalkalum* (Gods and Prostitutes) (in Tamil). 04/09/1927. *Kudi Arasu*.
48. Dubois, Abbe J.A. 1862. *Op.cit.*, p. 294.
49. *Ibid.*
50. *The Travancore State Manual*. Vol. III. V. Nagam Aiya. Trivandrum: The Travancore Government Press, 1906: p. 523.
51. Thiruchandran, Selvy. *The Spectrum of Femininity: A Process of Deconstruction*. New Delhi: Vikas Publishing House Pvt Ltd, 1998: p. 26.
52. Ramachandram, M. *The Devadasi*. Conjeeveram: S.K.B. Press, June, 1900: p. 2.
53. Singh, A.K. 1990. *Op.cit.*, p. 12.

54. Dubois, Abbe J.A. 1862. *Op.cit.*, p. 295.
55. Joardar, Biswanath. *Prostitution in Nineteenth and Early Twentieth Century Calcutta*. New Delhi: Inter-India Publications, 1985: p. 13.
56. Srinivasan, Amrit. "Reform and Revival: The Devadasi and Her Dance." *Economic and Political Weekly* 20, no. 44. (November 2, 1985): pp. 1869-1876.
57. Tarachand detailed the different theories, which were associated with the origin of the devadasi system. According to him, the theories are occupation and mother goddess theory, religious tradition theory, Sanskritisation theory, racial theory, political or selfless citizen theory, matriarchy to patriarchy theory, lineage continuation theory and traditional theory. (Tarachand, K.C. 1991. *Op.cit.*, pp. 19-23).
58. Singh, A.K. 1990. *Op.cit.*, p. 7.
59. Lewinsohn, Richard. *A History of Sexual Customs*. New York: Harper & Brothers, 1958: p. 28.
60. Frazer, James George. *The Golden Bough: A Study of Magic and Religion*. London and Basingstoke: Macmillan Press, 1922 (Rpt. 1983).
61. Tarachand, K.C. 1991. *Op.cit.*, pp. XI-XII.
62. *Ibid.*, p. XIII.
63. Farquhar, J.N. *Modern Religious Movements in India*. New Delhi: Munshiram Manoharlal, 1914 (Rpt. 1967): pp. 408-409.
64. Yande, D.S. *Dedication of Girls to Gods: Plea for Prohibition by Law by Naik-Maratha Mandal*. Bombay: V.P. Vengurlekar, (n.d.): pp. 9-10.
65. *Adhuvakumo Ithu?* (Is it became that?) (in Tamil). 25/08/1929. *Kudi Arasu*.
66. Jamanadas, K. "Devadasis Were Degraded Buddhist Nuns". (March 28, 2000.): *http://www.ambedkar.org/buddhism/Devadasis_Were_Degraded_Buddhist_Nuns.htm* accessed on December 30, 2012.
67. Yande, D.S. (n.d.) *Op.cit.*, p. 11.
68. *Ibid.*, p. 12.
69. Parasher, Aloka and Usha Naik. "Temple Girls of Medieval Karnataka." *Indian Economic and Social History Review* 23, no. 1. (1986): p. 77.
70. Singh, A.K. 1990. *Op.cit.*, p. 24.
71. *Ibid.*
72. Altekar, A.S. *The Position of Women in Hindu Civilisation*. Delhi: Motilal Banarsidass, 1959 (Rpt. 1983): pp. 182-183.
73. Orr, Leslie. C. 2000. *Op.cit.*, p. 5.
74. Narayanan, M.G.S. "Handmaids of God." in *Aspects of Aryanisation in Kerala*. Trivandrum: Kerala Historical Society, 1973.
75. Singh, A.K. 1990. *Op.cit.*, p. 13.
76. Parasher, Aloka and Usha Naik. 1986. *Op.cit.*, pp. 63- 91.
77. Singh, A.K. 1990. *Op.cit.*, p. 23.
78. *kuravangkamazh narumenkuzhal arivaiyaval veruvap*. *Tevaram Tirumurai*. I. Song no. 130. l. 1.
79. Singh, A.K. 1990. *Op.cit.*, p. 23.
80. Sadasivan, K. *Devadasi System in Medieval Tamilakam*. Trivandrum: CBH Publications, 1993: p. 5.

81. Singh, A.K. 1990. *Op.cit.,* p. 24.
82. *Ibid.*
83. *Ibid.*, pp. 14-15.
84. *Ibid.*, p. 11.
85. *Ibid.*, p. 12.
86. *Ibid.*
87. *Ibid.*
88. *Ibid.*, p. 13.
89. *Ibid.*, p. 24.
90. *Ibid.*, pp. 13, 24.
91. Tarachand, K.C. 1991. *Op.cit.,* p. 13.
92. Singh, A.K. 1990. *Op.cit.,* p. 12.
93. Tarachand, K.C. 1991. *Op.cit.,* p. 11.
94. Penzer, N.M. *The Ocean of Story*. Vol. I. tr. C.H. Tawney. London: Chas. J. Sawyer Ltd., 1924: p. 238.
95. Tarachand, K.C. 1991. *Op.cit.,* p. 11.
96. Singh, A.K. 1990. *Op.cit.,* p. 13.
97. Tarachand, K.C. 1991. *Op.cit.,* p. 12.
98. *Ibid.*, p. 23.
99. *Ibid.*
100. Sadasivan, K. 1993. *Op.cit.,* p. 5.
101. Sreedhara Menon, A. *Cultural heritage of Kerala*. Kottayam: D.C. Books, 1978 (Rpt. 2008): p. 243.
102. *Ibid.*
103. Singh, A.K. 1990. *Op.cit.,* p. 24.
104. Sangam literature is the earliest collection of poems of ancient Tamils. The unique anthology is divided into *akam* (inner world) and *puram* (outer world) based on the content, which it discussed.
105. Orr, Leslie. C. 2000. *Op.cit.,* p. 22.
106. Singh, A.K. 1990. *Op.cit.,* p. 24.
107. Raghavan, M.D. *India in Ceylonese History, Society and Culture*. Bombay: Asia Publishing House, 1964: p. 68.
108. De Zoete, Beryl. *Dance and Magic Drama in Ceylon*. London: Faber and Faber Limited, 1957: p. 64.
109. Sadasivan, K. 1993. *Op.cit.,* p. 112.
110. Elliot, H.M. and John Dowson. *The History of India as told by its own Historians: The Muhammadan Period*. Vol. III. London: Trubner and Co, 1871: p. 74.
111. *Ibid.*, pp. 91-92.
112. Sadasivan, K. 1993. *Op.cit.,* p. 112.
113. *Annual Reports of Indian Epigraphy* (*A.R.I.E.*) of 1916. No. 64.
114. Sadasivan, K. 1993. *Op.cit.,* p. 112
115. Parker, Kunal M. July, 1998. *Op.cit.,* p. 560.

116. *Devadasi Olippu Murai* (The Abolition of Devadasi Custom) (in Tamil). 31/08/1959. *Viduthalai.*
117. Ramachendrier, C. *Collection of the Decisions of the High Courts and the Privy Council on the Law of Succession, Maintenance and C (Applicable to Dancing Girls and their issues, Prostitutes not belonging o Dancing Girls' Community, Illegitimate Sons and Bastards and Illatom Affiliation up to December 1891.).* Madras: Scottish Press, 1892: p. v.
118. *Ibid.*, p. v.
119. *Ibid.*, p. iii.
120. Aloysius, G. "Caste in and Above History". in S.L. Sharma and T.K. Oomen. Ed. *Nation and National Identity in South Asia.* Hyderabad: Oriental Longman, 2000: p. 151.
121. Ketkar, S.V. *History of Caste in India.* Delhi: Low Price Publications, 1909 (Rpt. 2010): p. 15.
122. Muthulakshmi Reddi, S. *Why Should the Devadasi Institution in the Hindu Temples be Abolished?* Madras: Central Co-operative Printing Works, Ltd, 1927: p. 1.
123. Tarachand, K.C. 1991. *Op.cit.,* p. 2.
124. Dubois, Abbe J.A. 1862. *Op.cit.,* p. 295.
125. Ramachendrier, C. 1892. *Op.cit.,* p. ii.
126. *Ibid.*, p. 9.
127. Yande, D.S. (n.d.) *Op.cit.,* p. 2.
128. *The Proceedings of the Madras Legislative Council: Second Session of the Third Legislative Council.* Vol. XXXVIII. October 31-November 5, 1927: p. 416.
129. *Ibid.*
130. Shortt, John. "The Bayaderes: or, Dancing Girls of Southern India." *Council of the Anthropological Society of London* III. (1870): p. 185.
131. Sadasivan, K. 1993. *Op.cit.,* p. 123.
132. Kersenboom, Saskia C. "Devadasi Murai." *Sangeet Natak*, no. 96. (April-June, 1990): p. 48.
133. Sadasivan, K. 1993. *Op.cit.,* p. 136.
134. Srinivasan, Amrit. November 2, 1985. *Op.cit.,* p. 1869.
135. Parker, Kunal M. (July, 1998). *Op.cit.,* p. 589.
136. Sadasivan, K. 1993. *Op.cit.,* p. 140,
137. *K.K.* No. 1968/203. and K.K. No. 1968/230.
138. *South Indian Temple Inscriptions* (*S.I.T.I.*). Vol. I. No. 525.
139. Tarachand, K.C. 1991. *Op.cit.,* p. 2.
140. *Ibid.*
141. *Ibid.*
142. Sadasivan, K. 1993. *Op.cit.,* p. 73.
143. Shortt, John. 1870. *Op.cit.,* p. 182.
144. Yande, D.S. (n.d.) *Op.cit.,* p. 1.

145. The self-respect marriage is a form of marriage, which is held without any rituals and Brahmin proceedings. (Rasagopalan, Sarala. *Thiru.Vi.Ka. Pennurimaich Chinthanaigal* (The feminist thoughts of Thiru.Vi.Ka) (in Tamil). Chennai: Olip Pathippakam, 2007: p. 147.)
146. Agnihotri, Vidyadhar. *Fallen Women: A Study with Special Reference to Kanpur.* Kanpur: Maharaja Printers, 1954: p. 3.
147. Shortt, John. 1870. *Op.cit.,* p. 183.
148. Yande, D.S. (n.d.) *Op.cit.,* p. 2.
149. Dubois, Abbe J.A. 1862. *Op.cit.,* p. 295.
150. Van Doren B. Alice. *Lighted to Lighten: The Hope of India.* Massachusetts. The Central Committee on the United Study of Foreign Missions, 1922: pp. 25-26.
151. Ramachendrier, C. 1892. *Op.cit.,* p. vi.
152. *Ibid.*
153. Agnihotri, Vidyadhar. 1954. *Op.cit.,* p. 3.
154. Muthulakshmi Reddi, S. 1927. *Op.cit.,* p. 1.
155. Dubois, Abbe J.A. 1862. *Op.cit.,* p. 295.
156. Ramachendrier, C. 1892. p. i.
157. *Ibid.*
158. Shortt, John. 1870. *Op.cit.,* p. 183.
159. Muthulakshmi Reddi, S. 1927. *Op.cit.,* p. 2.
160. *Ibid.*
161. Dubois, Abbe J.A. 1862. *Op.cit.,* p. 295.
162. *Ibid.*
163. Yande, D.S. (n.d.) *Op.cit.,* p. 2.
164. Kersenboom, Saskia C. April-June, 1990. *Op.cit.,* p. 48.
165. Sundaram, B.M. *Marbu Thantha Manikkankal* (The Gifts of the Tradition) (in Tamil). Chennai: Dr. V. Raghavan Centre for Performing Arts, 2003: p. 79.
166. *Ibid.*, p. 83.
167. Knight Jr, Douglas M. *Balasaraswathi: Her Art and Life.* Chennai: Tranquebar Press, 2010: p. 27.
168. Ramachendrier, C. 1892. *Op.cit.*, p. i.
169. Sarma, R.B. *Pottukkattum Vazhakkam Ikkalaththirkup Poruthuma?* (Is it Relevant the pottu ceremony for this Age?) (in Tamil). Madras: C. Munisawmy Mudaliar and Sons, (n.d.): p. 4.
170. Muthulakshmi Reddi, S. 1927. *Op.cit.,* p. 2.
171. Sarma, R.B. (n.d.). *Op.cit.,* p. 4.
172. *Ibid.*, p. 2.
173. *Ibid.*, p. 4.
174. *Ibid.*
175. Ramachandram, M. June, 1900. *Op.cit.,* p. 2.
176. *Census of India, 1901, Travancore.* N. Subramhanya Aiyar. Vol. XXVI. Part. 1. Trivandrum: Malabar Mail Press, 1903: pp. 275-277.

177. Chidambaranar, Samy. *Sivanesarkalin Seikai* (The Activities of Saiva Saints) (in Tamil). 02/11/1930. *Kudi Arasu*.
178. Rasagopalan, Sarala. 2007. *Op.cit.*, p. 135.
179. Shortt, John. 1870. *Op.cit.*, p. 183.
180. Natarajan, Srividya. "Another Stage in the Life of the Nation: Sadir, Bharathanatyam, Feminist Theory". PhD diss., University of Hyderabad, 1997: p. VIII.
181. *Tamil Lexicon*. Vol. IV. Part. I. Madras: University of Madras, 1982: p. 2064.
182. Ramachandram, M. June, 1900. *Op.cit.*, p. 2.
183. Taylor, William. *Oriental Historical Manuscripts*. Vol. I. Madras: Charles Josian Taylor, 1835: p. 35.
184. *Ibid.*
185. Sundaram, B.M. 2003. *Op.cit.*, p. 170.
186. *Ibid.*
187. Knight Jr, Douglas M. *Balasaraswathi: Her Art and Life*. Chennai: Tranquebar Press, 2010: p. 49.
188. Shortt, John. 1870. *Op.cit.*, p. 183.
189. *Ibid.*
190. *Ibid.*
191. *Ibid.*, p. 184.
192. *centa□irk kai nallal thiranda naal-vanthu thotta; madan enra thevathaikku vaichchu vanankuvalam*. Nagasamy, R. "Introduction." In *Muvaraiyan Virali Vitu Tutu*. Mithilaippattich Chitrampala Kavirayar. Chennai: Mahamahopaththiyaya Dr. U.Ve. Saminathaiyer Library, 1982: pp. XXXVI-XXXVI.
193. *villupattu*, *kottu* and *kaniyan koothu* are the traditional art forms of Tamil.
194. *adu panri kozhi ivai allamal-padukindra; villam murasam kaikottum kaniyanum; ella vakaikkum elzhupathu pon*. (Nagasamy, R. "Introduction." In *Muvaraiyan Virali Vitu Tutu*. Mithilaippattich Chitrampala Kavirayar. Chennai: Mahamahopaththiyaya Dr. U.Ve. Saminathaiyer Library, 1982: p. XXXVII.)
195. Pande, Rekha. "Devadasis." In J.S. Grewal. Ed. *Religious Movements and Institution in Medieval India*. in the series of D.P. Chattopadhyaya. Ed. *History of Science, Philosophy and Culture in Indian Civilisation*. Vol. VII. Part 2. New Delhi: Oxford University Press, 2006: p. 498.
196. Sadasivan, K. 1993. *Op.cit.*, p. 8.
197. Singh, A.K. 1990. *Op.cit.*, p. 12.
198. Altekar, A.S. 1959. *Op.cit.*, pp. 182-183.
199. Sadasivan, K. 1993. *Op.cit.*, p. 8.
200. Tarachand, K.C. 1991. *Op.cit.*, p. 8.
201. *South Indian Inscriptions: Miscellaneous Inscriptions in Tamil, Telugu and Kannada*. Ed. H. Krishna Sastri. Vol. IV. New Delhi: Archaeological Survey of India, 1986: No. 34.
202. Singaravelu Mudaliyar, A and A Sivaprakasa Mudaliyar. *Abithana Chintamani: Tamil Kalaikazhanjiyam* (Abithana Chintamani: A Tamil Dictionary). Chennai: Seethai Pathippakam, 1899 (Rpt. 2004): p. 1083.

203. *Ibid.*
204. Thurston, Edgar and K, Rangachari. 1987 (Rpt. 1909). *Op.cit.*,
205. *Pathinenkilkanakku* is an anthology of eighteen-post Sangam literature. Those are *Nalatiyar, Nanmanikkatikai, Inna Narpathu, Iniyavai Narpathu, Kar Narpathu, Kalavazhi Narpathu, Ainthinai Aimpathu, Thinaimozhi Aimpathu, Ainthinai Ezhupathu, Thinaimalai Nurru Aimpathu, Tirukkural, Thirikatukam, Acharakkovai, Pazhamozhi Nanuru, Siruppanchamulam, Muthumozhikkanchi, Elathi* and *Kainnilai*. The songs were written by various authors. The style and content of the works are different from earlier Sangam literature.
206. *Manimekalai*. Song no. 18. l. 109.
207. Sadasivan, K. 1993. *Op.cit.,* p. 10.
208. *Ibid.*, p. 11.
209. *Akananuru*. Song no. 206. l. 8.
210. *Ibid.*, Song no. 336. l. 11.
211. *Paripadal*. Song no. 20. l. 49.
212. *Purananuru*. Song no. 365. l. 8.
213. *Narrinai*. Song no. 1. l. 20.
214. *Ibid.*, Song no. 30. l. 5.
215. *Ibid.*, Song no. 380. l. 5. and *Kuruntogai*. Song no. 45. l. 2.
216. *Kuruntogai*. Song no. 384. l. 2.
217. *Kalittogai*. Section. 3. Song no. 66. l.13.
218. *Ibid.*, Section. 3. Song no. 67. l. 6.
219. *Ibid.*, Section. 3. Song no. 67. l. 10.
220. *Ibid.*, Section. 3. Song no. 67. l. 14.
221. *Ibid.*, Section. 3. Song no. 70. l. 9.
222. *Ibid.*, Section. 3. Song no. 72. l. 9.
223. *Ibid.*, Section. 3. Song no. 78. l. 13. and Section. 3. Song no. 84. l. 20.
224. *vanava mahalir manaka kandor; nenju nadunkuruvuk kondi mahalir. Maduraikanji*. l. 583.
225. *puram porra vaya vendhan; maram padiya padini yumme. Purananuru*. Song no. 11. ll. 10-11.
226. The representation of women in Sangam and Post-Sangam literature is referred from the work of Narmadha. *Thamizhagathil Thevaradiyar Marabu-Panmuga Nokku* (A Multi-Dimensional Approach towards Devadasis of Tamilnadu) (in Tamil). Chennai: Bodhi Vanam, 2006: p. 24-25.
227. The period between the post Sangam and emergence of Pallavas and Pandiyas (third to fifth century) is marked as Kalabhra period in the South Indian history. The period is also marked as dark ages due to unavailability of historical evidences.
228. *Tirukkural*. Section. 2. *Varaivin mahalir*. Song no. 911.
229. *Ibid.*, Section. 2. *Varaivin mahalir*. Song no. 912.
230. *Ibid.*, Section. 2. *Varaivin mahalir*. Song no. 913.
231. *Ibid.*, Section. 2. *Varaivin mahalir*. Song no. 918.
232. *Ibid.*, Section. 2. *Varaivin mahalir*. Song no. 919.

233. *Ibid.*, Section. 2. *Varaivin mahalir*. Song no. 920.
234. *Acharakkovai*. Song no. 51. l. 1.
235. *Ibid.*, Song no. 82. l. 1.
236. *Nalatiyar*. Song no. 368. l. 2.
237. *Ibid.*, Song no. 370. l. 1.
238. *Ibid.*, Song no. 372. l. 1.
239. *Ibid.*, Song no. 373. l. 3.
240. *Ibid.*, Song no. 379. l. 1. and Song no. 380. l. 1.
241. *Thirikatukam*. Song no. 24. l. 1; Song no. 76. l. 2 and Song no. 81. l. 1.
242. *Chilappathikaram*. Part. 1. Section. 5. l. 50.
243. *Manimekalai*. Song no. 18. l. 35. and Song no. 24. l. 22.
244. *Ibid.*, Song no. 7. l. 44.
245. *Chilappathikaram*. Part. 2. Section. 14. l. 71.
246. *Chilappathikaram*. Part. 1. Section. 5. l. 50. and *Manimekalai*. Song no. 11. l. 13.
247. *Chilappathikaram*. Part. 2. Section. 14. l. 156; *Manimekalai*. Song no. 12. l. 51. and *Civakachintamani*. Section no. 7. l. 1651.
248. *Chilappathikaram*. Part. 2. Section. 14. l. 155.
249. *Ibid.*, Part. 2. Section. 22. l. 142.
250. *Ibid.*, Part. 1. Section. 5. l. 51.
251. *Ibid.*, Part. 1. Section. 10. l. 219.
252. *Manimekalai*. Song no. 18. l. 6.
253. *Ibid.*, Song no. 18. l. 109.
254. *Ibid.*, Song no. 28. l. 51.
255. *Ibid.*, Song no. 5. l. 87.
256. *Civakachintamani*. Section no. 7. l. 1675.
257. *Ibid.*, Section no. 7. l. 1625.
258. *Ibid.*, Section no. 9. l. 2079.
259. *Ibid.*, Section no. 10. l. 2118.
260. *Ibid.*, Section no. 10. l. 2173.
261. *Ibid.*, Section no. 11. l. 2351.
262. *Ibid.*, Section no. 12. l. 2399.
263. *Ibid.*, Section no. 13. l. 2722.
264. Sadasivan, K. 1993. *Op.cit.*, p. 25.
265. Perumal, A.K. *Thenkumariyin Kadhai* (History of Kanyakumari) (in Tamil). Chennai: United Writers, 2003: pp. 234-235.
266. *Ibid.*, p. 235.
267. *Tamil Lexicon*. Vol. IV. Part. I. 1982: p. 2474.
268. Sathyabama, K, "Mechanize Tamil Chuvadikal Chuttum Makkal Valviyal" (Life Stories of People on the basis of Mackenzie Tamil Documents) (in Tamil)" PhD diss., Tamil University, 1998: p. 204.

269. *Koyil Pillaimar* lived in Thazhakkudi, Krishnan Koyil, Tirupathicharam, Sucindrum, Budhappandi and Nagercoil in modern Tamil Nadu. This *koyil pillaimar* had a marriage alliance with Vellalar of Nanchil Nadu and later the community was faded away. These details are pointed out by Nanjil Nadan in his book. (Nadan, Nanjil. Naanjil Naattu Vellalar Vaazhkai (Ethnography of Vellalars of Nanjilnadu, Kanyakumari District) (in Tamil). Chennai: Kalachuvadu Pathippagam, 2003 (Rpt. 2008): p. 29).
270. Swaminathan, A. *Tamilaka Varalarum Panpadum* (History and Culture of Tamil) (in Tamil). Chennai: Deepa Pathppakam, 1992: p. 150.
271. *Census of India, 1901, Travancore*. N, Subramhanya Aiyar. Vol. XXVI. Part. 1. Trivandrum: Malabar Mail Press, 1903: p. 276.
272. Orr, Leslie. C. 2000. *Op.cit.*, p. 49.
273. Philip, George. "A Historical Anatomy of the Evolution of Social Revolution in Travancore" PhD diss., Mahatma Gandhi University, March, 2005: p. 66.
274. Orr, Leslie. C. 2000. *Op.cit.*, p. 49.
275. *Ibid.*
276. Jogan Shankar. *Devadasi Cult: A Sociological Analysis*. New Delhi: Ashish Publishing House, 1990. (Rpt. 1994): p. 157.
277. Jamanadas, K. March 28, 2000. *Op.cit.,*
278. Orr, Leslie. C. 2000. *Op.cit.*, p. 49.
279. *Encyclopedia of Religion*. Ed. Denise Cush; Catherine Robinson and Michael York. London: Routledge, 2008: p. 180.
280. Sadasivan, K. 1993. *Op.cit.*, pp. 1-2.
281. Shortt, John. 1870. *Op.cit.*, p. 182.
282. *Thevaradiyal irunthu aththal seththal kottu melam, thevadiyal seththal onrumillai*. (Jensen, Herman. Rev. *A Classified Collection of Tamil Proverbs*. New Delhi: Asian Educational Services, 1897 (Rpt. 1986): p. 40).
283. *Kozhukkattaikku thalaiyumillai, kooththadichchikku muraiyumillai*. (*Ibid*., p. 43.)
284. *Siraichchalaikku azhakillai thevadiyalukku muraiyillai*. (*Ibid*.)
285. *Thelukku kodukkile visam, thevadiyalukku udampile visam, unakko sarvankam visam*. (*Ibid*., p. 49.)
286. *Koyil sorrukkuk kumattina thevadiyal, kadich chorrukkuk karanampodukiral*. (*Ibid*., p. 60.)
287. *Orukku oru thevadiyal yarukkendru aduval*. (*Ibid*., p. 153.)
288. *Adamattatha thevadiyal pothathu enralam*. (*Ibid*., p. 201.)
289. *Than pathiniyanal, thevadiyal thervilum kudiyirukkalam*. (*Ibid*., p. 335.)
290. Mahalingam, T.V. "Inscription in Tamilnadu." In J.P. De Souza and C.M. Kulkarni. Ed. *Historiography in Indian Languages*. Delhi: Oriental Publishers, 1972: p. 81.
291. *Annual Reports* for 1913. part. II. paragraph no. 4.
292. Mahalingam, T.V. *Kancipuram in Early South Indian History*. Bombay: Asia Publishing House, 1969: p. 137.

293. Sadasivan, K. 1993. *Op.cit.*, p. 9.
294. *Thanjai Marattiya Mannar Modi Avanath Tamizhakkamum Kurippuraiyum* (Tamil Translation and notes of Modi Documents of Thanjavur Maratha King) (in Tamil). Vol. I-III. K.M. Venkatramaiah and R. Vivekanandagopal. Ed. Thanjavur: Tamil University, 1989: p. VI.
295. Sadasivan, K. 1993. *Op.cit.*, p. 14.
296. Tarachand, K.C. 1991. *Op.cit.*, p. 12.
297. Dubois, Abbe J.A. *Hindu Customs and Ceremonies*. New Delhi: Asian Educational Services, 1996 (Rpt. 1906).
298. Sadasivan, K. 1993. *Op.cit.*, p. 15.
299. Roberts, Brian. *Biographical Research*. Buckingham: Open University Press, 2002: p. 1.
300. Singh, Nagendra Kr. *Divine Prostitution*. New Delhi: A.P.H Publishing Corporation, 1997.
301. Srinivasan, Amrit. "Reform or Continuity?: Temple 'Prostitution' and the Community in the Madras Presidency." In Bina Agarwal. Ed. *Structures of Patriarchy: State, Community and Household in Modernizing Asia*. New Delhi: Kali for Women, 1988. (Rpt. 1991): pp. 175-198; Srinivasan, Amrit. "Women and Reform of Indian Tradition: Gandhian Alternative to Liberalism." *Economic and Political Weekly* 22, no. 51. (December 19, 1987): pp. 2225-2228.
302. Panjrath, Shashi and O.P. Ralhan. *Devadasi System in India*. Faridabad: Om Publications, 2000.
303. Pande, Rekha. 2006. *Op.cit.*, pp. 493-504.
304. Kersenboom, Saskia C. 1987. *Op.cit.*, p. IX.
305. Ali, Daud. "Reviewed work: Donors, Devotees, and Daughters of God: Temple Women in Medieval Tamilnadu by Leslie C. Orr". *The English Historical Review* 116, no. 467. (June, 2001.): pp. 708-709.
306. Marglin, Frederique Apffel. 1985. *Op.cit.,*
307. Tarachand, K.C. 1991. *Op.cit.,*
308. Shankar, Jogan. 1990. (Rpt. 1994). *Op.cit.,*
309. Vijaisri, Priyadarshini. *Recasting the Devadasi: Patterns of Sacred Prostitution in Colonial South India*. New Delhi: Kanishka Publishers, Distributors, 2004.
310. Kannabiran, Kalpana. "Judiciary, Social Reform and Debate on 'Religious Prostitution' in Colonial India." *Economic and Political Weekly* 30, no. 43. (October 28, 1995): pp. WS59-WS69.
311. Kannabiran, Kalphana and Vasanth Kannabiran. *Muvalur Ramamirthammal's Web of Deceit: Devadasi Reform in Colonial India*. Delhi: Kali for Women.
312. Parker, Kunal M. July, 1998. *Op.cit.*, pp. 559-633.
313. Jordan, Kay. K. *From Sacred Servants to Profane Prostitute: A History of the Changing Legal Status of the Devadasis in India, 1857-1947*. New Delhi: Manohar, 2003.
314. Srinivasan, Amrit November 2, 1985. *Op.cit.*, pp. 1869-1876.
315. Peterson, Indira Viswanathan and Davesh Soneji. and Davesh Soneji. *Performing Pasts: Reinventing the Arts in Modern South India*. New Delhi: Oxford University Press, 2008.

316. Subramanian, Lakshmi. *From the Tanjore Court to the Madras Music Academy: A Social History of Music in South India*. New Delhi: Oxford University Press, 2006.

317. Viswanathan, Lakshmi. *Women of Pride: The Devadasi Heritage*. New Delhi: Roli Books, 2008.

318. Raghavan, V. "The Great Integrators: - The Saint Singers of South India." Delhi: *Ministry of Information and Broadcasting*, 1966: p. 37.

Chapter - 2

Pre-colonial South India: The Historical Context

The devadasi system was not an independent one. It was an integral element of the society. It was associated with the power structure of the medieval society. It flourished under certain political conditioning of South India. Kay. K. Jordan pointed out that the medieval temple represented as an intersection with the sacred realm that gives meaning to both kingship and the service of the devadasi.[1] The process was manifested tenable changes in kinship organisation and economic relations in the establishment of religious and state bureaucracies, and in the shift in cosmogonies expressing the ascendancy of male god figures.[2] This particular chapter discusses about the historical development of the devadasi system, and how the different social conditions had led to the establishment of the devadasi institution in South India.

The South Indian society

The South Indian polity, especially the ancient Tamil was divided into number of tribal units and the main difference between them was largely due to its geographical environment.[3] There was an unequal society, which existed in South India from the early times of Chola period onwards.[4] The primitive Tamil society was tribal, horizontal and communalised in nature. They distributed themselves over five different geographical regions such as hilly, pastoral, agricultural, littoral and desert. The stratification of society was hierarchically arranged. In the beginning, it was based on profession, and later it became a rigid birth based castes. The earlier communities like Paraiar (drummers), Minavar (fishermen), Umanar (salt traders), Vellalar (peasants), weavers and Kollar (artisans) were all classified and referred as communities not as caste. Whenever the new art and craft was developed, a new community came to exist.[5] From sixth or fifth century B.C.E. onwards, the wave of Brahmin migration might have taken place in the Tamil country, and in later centuries they became an integral part of Tamil society.[6] The Sangam corpus *Purananuru* mentioned the four fold community divisions, calling each community as *kudi*.[7] "There are no *kudis* other than these four" but later all these classification were considered as untouchables. However, Tevaram, the Saivite canon of medieval South India, highlighted many castes in the South Indian society. The *Varna* system of Aryan was super-imposed on the indigenous tribal system of the South.[8] The *gotras* of Aryans and the totems of tribal intermingled to create a new social order, which was peculiar to Indian caste system. The horizontal division of the pre-Aryan Tamil society moved towards the vertical and exclusive *Varna* system.[9] The regional version of the theoretical *Varna* system was developed, and it became much more rigid.[10] The interaction of Brahmins and peasant folk constituted the primary cultural nexus of medieval South India.[11] Subramanian, a historian, said that these processes created a new social stratification, which was peculiar to South India.[12] Later, it made society much more complex.[13] Champakalakshmi, witnessed the presence of the brahmanical tradition in an amalgamated form in the early Sangam age.[14] The late Sangam and post-Sangam works of the fourth century to sixth century, *Paripadal* and *Tirumurukarruppadai* marked a new era in Tamil culture, and a new milieu in the South Indian religion and worship.[15] An idea of absolute or universal godhead entered into the South Indian ethos.[16] The vernacular rendering of the Puranic religion was established. The elements of the folk cult incorporated the brahmanical traditions of Vedic religion.

The culture of caste is an element in the character of Indian societies. Burton Stein, a medieval historian, detailed the vital distinction between the Aryan *Varna* system and South Indian caste system. According to him, the former consisted the four fold classifications of Brahmin, Kshatriya, Vaishya and Sudra and the later consisted only the two-fold of Brahmin and non-Brahmin.[17] The caste principles were pertaining to kingship, marriage and occupation as well, as to matters directly involving Brahmins. In ancient South Indian society, even the kings and the merchants were not different from the ordinary peasants.[18] The kings could freely marry within the non-brahmanical community. In South India, the relative isolation on autonomy of peasant localities was reinforced by kinship and marriage practices.[19] The impact of the *Varna* system divided the society in different basis. The Aryan framework set a sort of example and later it became prestigious. Otherwise, the horizontal communities would have developed hierarchical attitudes. The tendency to imitate the brahmanical order was popular among the indigenous groups and it generated the comparative prestige within the groups. However, the early sacrificing Brahmin priest had no legitimate rights in the temple, but in the course of time, they became the temple priest and also brought the entire area of religion under their control. The Brahmins continued to hold their position of supremacy in Pallava and Chola period, but they slowly became a distinct group in the community and confined themselves to a particular sub-urban areas and generally disdaining manual labours.[20]

The political ideologies of the South Indian kingdoms under the Pandiyas and the more powerful Pallavas differed from those of the South Indian kings during the Sangam period. In ancient times, the kings and the numerous petty chiefs had legitimatised their power through personal acts of magnanimity and heroism, which attracted the loyalty of personal for relatively small-scale military adventures. The Pallavas developed a variant of north Indian political order based on a duality between the ruler, as wielder of physical force, and ritual specialists as possessors of spiritual expertise.[21]

The domination of the Brahmin in society logically implies the dominance of the patriarchal structure. The Vedic Brahmanical structure determines the ascriptive and prescriptive roles of women and the lower castes.[22] The brahmanical interpretation which became important under the Pallavas, the Brahmins were the crucial actors in the political system, exemplifying the highest levels of ritual purity, and passing down the lore of the Vedas which maintained dharma. The Pallava rulers supported Brahmins and their Sanskrit institutions, bestowing on Brahmin communities control over numerous agrarian villages and giving lavishly in return for services at large scale royal rituals.[23] The Vellalar and Brahmin officials constituted the ruling elites in the Chola state, and the ideology, which provided a strong basis for the Chola ruling system, was communal as well as Brahmanical.[24] Frederique Apffel Marglin, an ethno-historian, explained the process of ritual sanction by the Brahmin to the tribal chiefs to get the religious status thorough conducting brahmanical rituals and the settlement of Brahmins.[25] The Velvikkudi Grant of Parantakan Nedunjadaiyan (769 - 770) mentioned that the village Velvikkudi was gifted to one Narkorran also known as Korkai Kilan by the Pandiya ruler, Palyagasalai Mudukudumipperuvazhudi when he completed *velvi* (yagna).[26] The Pandiya ruler Kadungon (590 - 620) gifted a village of Srimangalam as a *brahmadeyam* (Brahmin settlement) to twelve Brahmins.[27]

Champakalakshmi pointed out that in the early medieval period (from the sixth century onwards), the brahmanical tradition with the Vedic *yagna* along with the Puranic worldview became the norms for political legitimacy.[28] The patronage was not entirely without its return. The patronage helped the patrons to use the symbols of the religion for their benefit. The exercise of the power in a particular socio-political formation was achieved primarily with the symbols of the agamic Hindu religion, which was propagated through the aggressive *bhakti* movement and its institutional expressions. The symbols associated with the temples were used for purposes of political mobilisation as a metaphor of power.[29] The religious institutions started to function as the state itself in a surrogate way.[30] The kings were created by the performance of *srata* sacrifice under Vedic Brahmins.

The temple

The power structure of South India co-existed with religion, religious institution and symbols. The religious institutions such as temples played a crucial role. The constructed temples made a huge impact in the South Indian society. The South Indian temples were not only noted for its religiosity, but they performed multi-dimensional functions. The medieval temples were constructed for different reasons. Parabrahma Sastry, a historian, pointed out that the temples of the medieval period were a symbolic representation of the various social activities.[31] The earlier temples functioned as fortresses, treasuries, knowledge centre, warehouses, parks, exhibition sheds, auditorium, amusement, and so on. Champakalakshmi stressed that the religious institutions were a primary causative factor for the medieval pre-industrial and traditional agrarian South Indian society.[32] Rajeev H. Dehejia and Vivek H. Dehejia mentioned that religious thoughts and economic activities were closely intertwined with the history of India.[33] *Kudi Arasu*, the Tamil rational weekly detailed that the constructions of the temples by the ancient rulers was mainly due to widespread cooperation, unity, discipline and devotion among the people.[34] The institution of devadasi had taken a deep root in the temple organisation of South India and they were an essential part of the temple complex.

The Chola, Pandiya and Chera occupied the fertile riverine agrarian basins of Cauveri, Vaikai and Periyaru respectively. The polity of the strong agrarian base was able to dominate the other small chieftains like Velir, Aye, Ori, Pari, etc. After the fall of Sangam order, the Kalabhras started to govern the Tamil country. There were many misconceptions about this period due to the lack of historical evidences. During the Sangam period, there was paucity of the historical evidence for the existence of the structural temples. Initially, the sacred abodes were constructed by clay with the wooden roof. The temples, which were constructed by sand, were known as *manthali* (sand temple). The wood structure of the temple construction was still somewhat prevalent in Chidambaram and parts of modern Kerala.[35]

In the beginning of the early medieval period, the reign of Kalabhra power was overshadowed by Pallavas and Pandiyas.[36] It marked a new beginning in the social and cultural space of South India. The period of Pallavas had been identified as transitional in a number of important ways, which is related to the development of South Indian society and culture. During this period, the concept of land grants was introduced.[37] The transition period witnessed a great wave of immigration and settlement of the Brahmins.[38] The medieval rulers settled down Brahmins in the conquered tribal areas and they tamed and taught the tribal people to obey the king and his suzerainty.[39] In the proceeding period, the Brahmins started to control over the court and countryside.[40] The period witnessed the process of temple building, foundation of the *bhakti* cult, introduction of the women into the sacred shrines and efflorescence of essentially rural brahmanical institutions as loci Sanskrit learning and the establishment of kingship based upon *chakravarty* model of kingship.[41]

During the early medieval period, Pallavas and Cholas (fourth century to ninth century) reined extreme South India. The Pallava period witnessed the promotion of Sanskrit as a court language and placing the brahmanical culture to an exalted position in the social polity. The Pallavas had established their kingdom at Kanchipuram under Simhavarman I in 275. Simhavishnu extended Pallava domain beyond Kanchipuram. Later Pallava successors Mahendravarman I (571-630) and Narasimhavarman I (630-668) brought glory to the kingdom. Narasimhavarman II (695-722) established the town Mamallapuram and initiated the art of single rock cut temples and constructed the Kailasanatha temple in Kanchipuram and seashore temple in Mamallapuram.[42] The reign of Dandivarman (796-846) marked the beginning point for the glorious Pallava kingdom. During his reign, Rastrakutas and Cholas emerged in North and South respectively. The supremacy of Pallavas ended with Nirpatungavarman and the battle of Tirumpurambiyam sounded the death knell to end of the rule of Aparajitavarman and the great Pallavas.

The rise of the Cholas had occurred in the days of Vijayalaya in the mid-ninth century. He ruled Palaiyarai and later he was able to seize Thanjavur from Muttaraiyar, a feudatory chief. After his victory over Pudukkottai and Thanjavur, Vijayalaya constructed the temple Nisumpasodini for his victory.[43] The long reign of Parantakan I, the grandson of Vijayalaya had extended the territories of Cholas from Kalahasti to river Cauveri. The Kerala chiefs, Paluvettaraiyar and Velir had accepted the suzerainty of Cholas. The death of Parantakan I (955) created a political instability in the Chola court. After the thirty years of interval, Rajarajan I (985) succeed the throne. The accession of Rajarajan I led the Cholas to their ultimate place in Southern India and it became the first Tamil dynasty that tried to bring the entire South India under their common rule and extended its territory as much as possible. The king Rajarajan I constructed the Rajarajesvara temple in Thanjavur as a mark of his great kingdom. The king brought four hundred women from the different parts of his kingdom and dedicated them to the temple.[44] Rajendran I extended the glory of Cholas. He was capable to invade northern India and hold his power over Ilankai (modern Sri Lanka). The agamic variety of brahmanical religion, rooted in South India by the seventh century or eighth century. In monarchial state, patronage of the temple meant patronage of the powerful

Brahmin groups. The northern invasion of Rajendran I brought further large number of Brahmins into the South.[45] The stable rule of the Cholas was considered as the heyday of Brahmanic religion, temple and other temple establishments. There was a constant flow of endowment that was made to temples not only for economic concern, but also to consolidate their political power. In general, these temple constructions and religious endowments were considered as an act of legalisation. James Heitzman, a historian, explained the driving force behind the donations was the concept of the legitimation of their authority, whereby gifts to the gods or their representatives on earth resulted in a transfer of divine sanctity and merit to the givers.[46] The temples received major grants from royal houses especially the ones who adopted the *bhakti* ideology to promote the temple's role.[47]

The imperial Cholas started to govern the vast geographical territory compared to the other kingdoms of Pallava and later Pandiya. The success of these medieval South Indian kings was mainly based on their relationship with the people and their alliance and control over the small chiefdoms. The relations between the kings and his subordinates decided the longevity of the kingdom. The Adigamans of Tagadur changed their loyalty from the Chera to imperial Cholas that could be attributed to the considerable decline in the Chera power after the Sangam age in South India. When the reign of Nolambas from the Mysore border made incursions into the Pallava Nirpatungavarman territory, but they were promptly checked by Banas, the subordinate of Pallavas. Subramanian pointed out that pre-Vijayanagar Tamil kingdom was multiple monarchies supported or hammered as the case may be by lesser chieftains. Banas, Gangas, Kadavas, Sambavarayars, Adigamans, Muttaraiyars and Kodumbalur Chieftains were the prominent petty rulers of the medieval South India.[48] To consolidate so many local chieftainships of the macro regions and prove their supremacy over others, the medieval South Indian kings practiced the theory of divine rights. The concept of divine rights justified the absolute power of the king over his chieftains and subject. The theory had helped to convert the tribal pattern of Sangam kingship into the absolute *Kshatriya* mode of kingship. In this sense, Pallavas had become the first South Indian kingdom, which incorporated the use of ritual authority as the basis of their authority.[49]

The period between 850 and 1200 is considered as a golden period of temple expansion and endowments.[50] During this period, temples acquired a great position of centrality as a symbol of political power. The temples acted as a means of consolidating local communities and integrating them into the government and state. Therefore, the construction of temples and endowment towards it became a regular act. The temples had received major grants from ruling families who adopted the *bhakti* ideology[51] to promote the temple's role. The processes of institutionalising the temple as an ideological apparatus was still in their initial stages under the Pallavas. The reign of Rajasimman noted the construction of structural temples.[52] During the early medieval period, many new temples were established. They were much concerned towards architecture and it helped to spread the style of stone architecture in and around Tamilakam. The temples of Pallavas were classified into cave temples[53], single rock temples and structural temples. Mahendravarman and Narasimhavarman II constructed cave temples and single rock cut temples. Pandiyas constructed temples at Tirumeiyam, Kundrakkudi, Malaiyadipatti, Kunnandar *koyil*, Kudumiyanmalai, Kazhukumalai, Tirupparankunram, Anaimalai and Tirumalpuram.[54] Pandiyas constructed more cave temples than Pallavas.[55] Vettuvan *Koyil* in Kazhukumalai is a single rock cut temple. Soman alias Adhiyendhiran[56] constructed two cave temples in Namakkal (modern district in Tamil Nadu). The two temples belonged to lord Vishnu.[57] Paluvettaraiyar, the petty chieftains constructed temples in their capital Pazhuvur.[58] In general, temples in Tamilakam were denoted by different names such as *koyil, niyamam, nagaram, kottam, palli, thali* and *thaṇam*.[59] The temples that were constructed for lord Siva is known as *echchuram* (*Isvarakiraham*) and lord Vishnu is known as *vinnakaram* (*Vishnukiraham*).

The institutions of temple were actively involved in both direct and indirect economic activities of the medieval society. The temples acquired the rights in land and accumulated the agrarian wealth. The temples promoted agriculture and they became the production centres. They also obscured all the other forms of productions.[60] Subramanian compared the activities of the temples with a bank.[61] The temple functioned as a big employer.[62] Therefore, the medieval rulers increasingly made endowments to the temples in the form of lands, livestock, gold and money. The land largely became the main item of gift and it made the temple as a major landowner. The new temple-centred-economy positioned on the fertile tracts of land, which often maintained a good number of girls who received substantial endowments.[63] So the medieval rulers consciously used temple as a means of extending their agricultural activities and thereby, expanding their resource bases.[64] The socio-religious activity of dedicating girls to temples as part of the overall ideology of *bhakti* cannot be viewed in an isolation from the general economic and historical developments of the time.[65] The largest number of medieval temples had come from the fertile regions of Cauveri basin. The north and south bank of the river Cauveri carried 63 and 190 Saivite temples respectively and 40 Vaishnavite shrines were established in this particular geographical region alone.[66]

The temples and kingship

Noboru Karashima, a medieval historian, noted that the medieval temples functioned as the nexus of local as well as state.[67] Champakalakshmi further strengthened the argument. She mentioned that the medieval temples not only functioned for the development of the *bhakti* cult, it equated with the *koyil* (palace). It was also of crucial institutional significance in assisting the process of the simultaneous expansion of divine and royal authority by establishing the symbolism of the cosmos and temple territory.[68] The Sangam notion of king and kingship were transferred to the sacred power of the deity in the temple as *iraivan*, *peruman* (lord) in the *koyil*, temple or palace.[69] Arjun Appadurai, a cultural anthropologist, discussed the relationship of human kings to the temple deities in South India. He also stated that it was an elegant and symbiotic division of the sovereignty, and the sovereign deity was the paradigm of royal authority.[70] The copper plate of the larger Leiden grant stated the phrase that the King became a God.[71] The divine origin of monarchs was equated with the divine rights of their rule. The deity was related with the king.

The medieval rulers used temple construction as an act of legitimising their power to govern the larger portions of the South India. According to Kesavan Veluthat, the medieval society reflected its existing social order and recreated a parallel world of authority in the realm of religion.[72] The god in his temple was treated as earthly king. Basham, a historian, pointed that the God had wives, ministers, attendants and all other paraphernalia of a court, which included his prostitutes, often the children of mothers of the same profession.[73] The administrative divisions of the kingdom resembled the order of the Hindu mythology. The medieval kings were compared with the omnipresent and his ministers and chieftains were equated with petty Gods. The subjects were unconsciously bounded within it. In the patriarchal medieval society, the administrative units such as *valanadu* and *mandalam* were generally placed under the control of some senior members of the royal household. The seniormost of the ruling family reined from the capital and others were controlling the ancillary ones.

The kings were equated with *devas* and the temple and palace were noted as *koyil*. The deity was conceived to be paradigmatic sovereign.[74] The Tamil word *koyil* referred both temple and royal palace. The charters of early Pallavas did not refer the divine origin of their kingship, but from the period of Nandivarman II, the ideas of the divine origin of kingship were elaborately related in their copper plates.[75] The Chola and Chera rulers were identified with *Surya vamsam*, Pandiyas with *Chandra vamsam* and Pallavas with *Brahmaksatra*. Pallavas claimed their descent from sages and Vedic gods; they were *dharma maharajas*.[76] The Pallava rulers traced their lineage from Lord Brahma and Pandiyas from the lotus of Vishnu navel.[77] Based on the myths, the divine origin of their dynasty was created. Systematically, the divinity of the personality over kings was fused. The success of the rulers and prominent incident of the royal court was equated with the divine or *puranic* figures.[78] In *Tiruvaimozhi*, Kulacekara Varman was equated with Vishnu and Kanyakumari inscription described Parantakan I as *Srinilaya* or abode of Lakshmi.[79]

The paraphernalia attached to temple deities was indistinguishable from the paraphernalia of human kings: conches, palanquins, umbrella, elephants, fly whisks and so on.[80] The kings who had ruled the South India were custodial despotic, though, perhaps benevolent and got invariably the loyalty of the people.[81] However, there was no known rights or *dharma* by which that loyalty could be demanded, that right was precisely what the brahmanical social theory provided; considering the advantages the kings derived in return, provision of an honourable place for the Brahmin in that society. It was a cheap reciprocal consideration for the kings to offer. The chieftains wanted their position to be legitimised by the prerogative of antiquity.[82]

The Throne, the Crown, the Royal umbrella and other paraphernalia like a horse, an elephant, the whisk, the conch, and sword constituted the royal emblems of royalty. The crown had ritual significance for the royalty. There was a dynastic crest or emblem like the tiger for Cholas, the fish for Pandiyas, the bow for Cheras and the bull for Vijayanagar or occasionally lion for Pallavas. These were not only used for the official purpose but as the symbols of divinity, as many Vedic gods carried these emblems. However, the reason for the choice of a particular emblem was not clear, but these resembled the principles, ideology and religion of the particular dynasty. Pandiyas adopted fish as their emblem because of the proto-historic fisher folk relation, Cholas' tiger emblem resembled their magnanimity and the fertile landscape of Cauveri, and Cheras used bow and arrow to signify the hunting tradition. Pallavas used bull as their religious identity.

The imperial titles and *abisekanamas* were equated with the divine connotations.[83] *Prasasti* or *meykkirti* showed clearly the effort by those subsequent kings to make the people of their kingdom aware of their glorious achievements and even felt their presence in the locality.[84] Pallava kings had assumed several *birudas* (surnames) and additionally, kings had adopted many titles of *bhattaraka*. Mahendravarman I started the practice of inscribing these *birudas* on monuments, which he had dedicated to his favourite Gods.[85] Tiruchirappalli Cave Temple and Pallavaram Cave Temple have their titles engraved. Mahendravarman I had adorned the titles like *Purusottama*, *Vidhi*, *Sthanu*, *Kalahapriya* (Narada), *Manprava* (Siva, the Supreme Being), *Mahamegha*, *Vicittracittan*, *Chendakari* (Builder of Temples), *Mandavilacan* (Seeker of Pleasures) and *Cittirakarapuli* (Tiger of Painters).[86] Narasimhavarman II was attributed with more than 250 titles like *Rajasimha*, *Sankarapuktu* and *Aahama Priyan*.[87] The Pandiya king Arikesari Maravarman was portrayed in *Pandikovai* as *Nedumaran*, *Puliyan*, *Minavan*, *Neriyan*,

Vanavanmaran, *Arikesari, Parangusan*, *Vikari*, *Adicayan*, *Ranodayan*, and *Ranandagan*.[88]

The King-God concept was developed and derived substantially from the *arrupadai* tradition of Tamil literary genre. Later, it was further developed by the *bhakti* saints. Nayanmars, the bhakti poets of the Saiva sects, transposed the metaphor, *vallal* (philanthropist).[89] They referred lord Siva as *vallal*. The deity was equated with Lord and the devotee was compared with the vassals.[90] The words *udaiyar* or *tambiran* (lord), *adiyar* (serf) were frequently used in the medieval *bhakti* literature. The Alvars noted that the presence of the king made them to think about Lord Tirumal.[91] The pyramid structure was formed. The deity or the king was kept in supreme and the Brahmins were placed next to that order. Cundarar, the Saiva saint, mentioned that Brahmin in the society could not be a slave of others.[92] Further, he claimed himself to be the slave of the slaves of the Brahmins of *Thillai* (Chidambaram).[93] There were direct and indirect evidences that the Saivite saints in particular put themselves in the minstrel place vis-à-vis Lord Siva as the patron.[94] The mature development and ramifications of the king-God concept became evident during the glorious period of the Chola Empire that arranged endowments for every artistic activity.[95] In many occasions, the worship conducted in the Rajarajesvara temple that was centred on the king Rajarajan I.[96] Hultzsch in his introduction of the South Indian Inscription volume mentioned that the Rajarajesvara temple at Thanjavur has evidently served as a model for a large number of other temples in Southern India.[97]

From the ninth and tenth century onwards, the royal titles were superimposed on the deities of the South Indian temples such as Varadharaja of Kanchipuram, Rangaraja of Srirangam, Nataraja and Govindharaja of Chidambaram and Thiyagarajar of Tiruvarur emerged as the royal deities with increasingly elaborate ceremonies. The structural stone temples with endowments for sensuous royal art performances at frequent temple festivals also came into vague. Rajarajesvara temple became the richest social unit of the time. The imperial Chola Emperors had a custom to crown themselves on more than one occasion in different places of their kingdoms. There were many Chola Emperors crowned in Chidambaram in addition to the first coronation at their capital city, because Chidambaram was considered as the religious capital of Chola rule. During the time of Vikrama Chola, the Nataraja of Chidambaram became virtually tutelary deity of the dynasty.[98] Yasushi Ogura stated that the increasing importance to the Sanskritised universal deities might meant the degradation of imperial temples as centres of worship in the empire.[99]

Usually, the king was the protector as well as the patron of the temple.[100] The king's dual responsibilities toward the temples distinguished from other wealthy donors.[101] The duty of the king was both a patron and protector of religion. As a patron, he endowed temples; and as a protector, he adjudicated disputes over honours and incomes. Sometimes he was even directly involved in religious rituals, acting as the sacrificer to the deity on behalf of the kingdom.[102] They received prestige and respect from the public in return for their patronage and service towards the temples. The temple functioned as a symbol or set of symbols.[103] Appadurai stated that the deity in India was conceived as a person and the religious images were ceremoniously vivified. The cycle of daily worship such as waking the deity, dressing and feeding, and putting on bed at night supported the belief, the God as a persona.[104] The interaction of the kings within a cultural environment was infused by a sense of the reality and meaningfulness of the sacred. Historical accounts showed that the king was sometimes honoured with ceremonies similar to those performed for the deity.[105] On the death of the devadasi, the temple deity to which she was associated with underwent a pollution.[106] The dead body of the devadasi was kept in front of the temple for short duration and the funeral pyre, sandal paste and other necessaries were brought from the concerned temple.

The association of devadasi with kings was respected for their special relationships to the divine and was, therefore, linked to the traditional worldview.[107] Frederique Apffel Marglin observed that the devadasis of Puri were known as *Calanti Devi* (walking Lakshmi) and the king was known as *Calanti* Vishnu (walking Vishnu).[108] The devadasis, as brides of Lord Jagannath, an incarnation of Vishnu, were interpreted as human representations of his consort Lakshmi. The kings of Orissa claimed to be partial incarnations of Vishnu. In South India, the Chola imperialism helped the extension of the devadasi system throughout the Chola domain. Rajarajan I and Rajendran I extended the system to its neighbourhood.[109]

Devadasis, who danced before the great god in a major temple, were 'married' to the ruling deity and they became the human embodiments of the god's consort. A king was homologous to the divine consort. Thus, devadasi was associated with kingship and was a symbol of royal sovereignty. The power of the divine consort (Sakthi) was the energy source of the male god as well as the king. As human embodiments of the goddess, devadasis were associated with Sakthi. Like kings, they were regarded as auspicious and associated with fertility and prosperity in general. Thus, devadasi could be substitute for the principal wives of a king in public rituals and they took place in seclusion. They had sexual intercourse with temple Brahmins. Since they were married to the god, they were not supposed to bear children. They could not marry a human; however, it was not uncommon for kings to have intimate relations with these symbols of his sovereignty.[110]

There were many kings who established the temples in their name. Vikramakesari Poothi constructed the temple under his name Vikramakesarichchuram.[111] Mahendravarman, the Pallava king named temple as Lalithangura Pallavachvarakkiraham.[112] In medieval period, temples were constructed for the remembrance of the dead and those temples were called as *pallippadai* (sepulchral temples). Parantakan I constructed a *pallippadai* for his father Adityan I in Kalahasti, a village of Tondaimanadu. In Tirunallam alias Konerirajapuram had a *pallippadai* of Kandaradityan was established by his queen Chembiyan Madevi. Rajarajan I constructed two sepulchral temples Arinjigaisvara temple at Melpadi and Kandalesvara temple at Tenneri for Arinjigai Chola and Uttama Chola respectively.[113] The image of the royal family was kept in the structural temples. It was believed to be the extension of the hero stones or memorial tablets that was practiced between the fifth and twelve century.[114] Nilakanta Sastry mentioned the worship of the Chembiyan Madevi image.[115] Rajendran I constructed the Panchamahadevisvara Temple in Ramanathan *koyil* for his stepmother, Panchavanmahadevi.[116] These acts signified that the temple service was the way of service of the royal household.

The Chola king Kochchengannan constructed seventy temples for Lord Siva.[117] The eleven verses of Sanskrit inscription praised the king Paramesvaravarman I for his construction of the temple for Lord Siva.[118] The early Chola rulers reconstructed thirty brick temples into stone.[119] During this period, most of the temples were converted into stone and all the stone temples were noted as *karrali*. The Mukthiswara temple of Kanchipuram was renewed into *karrali* by the Pallava queen, Dharma Madevi and the temple recruited forty nine *devaradiyar* for the ritual services.[120] Chembiyan Madevi, the mother of Uttama Chola renovated most of the Saiva temples (*padal perra sthalam*) into *karrali*.[121] She constructed the temples in Konerirajapuram (Tirunallam), Aduthurai, Tirukkodikaval, Kurralam, Tirunaraiyur, Kandarathithyam, Viruthachalam and Tiruvennainallur.[122] Chembiyan Madevi rebuilt the brick structure of central shrine of the Mahadeva temple at Tirukkodikaval in Nallarur Nadu into stone.[123]

Most of the inscriptions documented the recorded gifts to Brahmins and temples from wealthy and powerful persons and groups of a locality.[124] The Velvikkudi grant revealed that the Kali kings reestablished dharma by reviving land grants to Brahmin donors.[125] Pallavas and Pandiyas adopted Puranic and Sastric norms, institutionalised land grants to Brahmins and used Puranic cosmology and religion to promote the temple as an institution and integrative force.[126] The Pallavas and Cholas gave priority to the Brahmins for the ideological consolidation of the vast territories.[127] K.K. Pillai mentioned that after the invasion of Rajarajan I to the terrain of Nanchilnadu[128], the king provided gifts to Nancinattu Tiruccicindiram[129] (Suchindram temple) and Brahmins. He established the devadasi institution and insisted the practice of reciting the devotional hymns from Tevaram and Tiruvacakam. Rajarajan I popularised festivals and ceremonies to confine his temporal sphere of Rajarajan over the Nanchilnadu.[130] They even entered into the matrimonial relationship with royal families.[131]

The non-Kshatriya South Indian kings accommodated the Brahmins in comfortable and separate quarters and settled them exclusively in brahmanical villages called *brahmadeyam* for the sake of their royal legitimation through *yajnas* and *yagas*. The *brahmadeyam* which were the lands of the Brahmin were offered to separate quarters and settled exclusively as brahmanical villages which were granted by the non-Kshatriya South Indian kings. *Brahmadeyam* institution had great importance in the preservation and dissemination of brahmanical knowledge and religion.[132] Most of the *nadus* possessed at least one *brahmadeyam* where some forms of *sastric* learning and devotional worship of puranic deities.[133] These tax-free *brahmadeyam* lands were later denoted as *chaturvedimangalam*.[134] These *brahmadeyams* functioned mainly as an institution integrating pre-existing pastoral and agricultural settlements into a new agrarian order and as the disseminator and brahmanical ideology.[135] Sathianathaier asserts that the classical *brahmadeyam* was first developed in Tondaimandalam or whether the development occurred at the same time in both central southern parts of Tamil plain perhaps even in Venadu (modern Kerala).[136]

Brahmins were organisers and managers of production in the *brahmadeyam*. The elaborate arrangements for their upkeep were made by *sabhas* or assemblies of the *brahmadeyam* including their maintenance, repair, attention to sitting and control of water supply through accesses and specifying committees (*variyams*) for their supervision and administration.[137] In Brahmin households of *marudam* the cultivating groups in service of the Brahmins created new relations of production outside the existing framework on which all contemporary production activities were based. Such service groups were the beginnings of a new stratification into castes at later stage.[138] By the middle ages the Brahmins who propounded the Sacred Law might themselves be attached to temples with hundreds of prostitutes on their staffs.[139]

The decline of the Cholas by the end of the twelfth century placed the Hoysala occupation in the Tamil region. The establishment of the Vijayanagar Empire (1370) led the integration of the three cultural zones of Kannada, Telugu and Tamil. In later, Nayaka soothed the Telugu and Kannada settlement in the Tamil country. It was a great blow to the pre-exiting political structure of Tamil country. The fertile Cauveri delta attracted Telugu Brahmins, Reddi and Velamas, a dominant agricultural community of the arid northern zones of the Deccan plateau. It resulted a network of relations between wetland agricultural settlements and dry upland zones with a narrow resource base. These groups gradually became economically and politically powerful, and began impinging upon the pre-existing local power groups and their areas of control. The Telugu warriors claimed them as restorer of the tradition rather than innovators. They extended temple grants and donations. The new warrior class, subsequently known as the Mayors, emerged as the patron of temples and *mathas*.[140]

During the Vijayanagar period, Nayakas functioned as a feudatory of the great empire. The provincial chiefs were identified as *mandaleshvar* and *mahamandaleshvar*. The principalities were divided into seventy two *palaiyams*, which based on the Kakatiya model of seventy seven *padmanayakas*. However, later political development freed the Nayakas in Tamilakam.[141] The newly emerged kingdoms were centred in Madurai (1529-1736), Thanjavur (1532-1673) and Chenji (1640). Their kingship was differed from the earlier Pallavas, Cholas and Vijayanagar. The Nayaka rulers did not claim the *dharmic* ideologies, and preferred the *Sudra* pattern of kingship.[142] Nicholas Dirks, an anthropologist, mentioned that Vijayanagar and Nayakas subordination was articulated by the gifts and honors. The transaction between them was parallel transaction of *puja* and worship, and the emperor cast as deity.[143] The later Nayaka refashioned the political centre and established symbolic and organisational autonomy.[144] It influenced the sacred arena of temple and temple deities. Burton Stein detailed the large expansion of the temples centre after 1450.[145] However, the patronage to the Siva and Vishnu temple was decreasing in number and on the other hand minor deities like Amman and Ganesha was popularised.

The Nayakas entertained the concept of *annadana* (food donations) to Brahmin instead of land grants (*brahmadeyam*). It collapsed the dualistic model of Sanskrit kingship, the Kshatriya Brahmin alliance.[146] The period witnessed the shift in nature of patronage. In the second quarter of the sixteenth century, the state monetary endowment to the Tirupathi temple was dropped, and the local residents and merchants replaced it.[147] Velcheru Narayana Rao pointed out the decline of the temple inscriptions from the sixteenth century.[148] Nayakas widen their religious bases. They made land grants to Catholic churches in Nagappattinam. Acytappa Nayaka of Thanjavur granted a land to Nagore *dargah* of Sayyid Abdul Qadir Shah al Hamid (1520-1570).[149] During the Nayaka period, there was a new fortified political urban centre, and urban-based court in Tiruchirappalli, Salem, Dharmapuri, and Velur was established. It brought the new political centres apart from the traditional centres of earlier periods. During the Nayaka period, a constant conflict and competition occurred. In later part of their reign, the little kingdoms of Ramanathapuram and Pudukkottai emerged. It also became a new patron.

The role of king was of a master and lord. It imbibed the individualised semi-divinity of Nayakas.[150] The *quazi* divinity substantiated a palace into temple and temple into palace. The Nayaka court and temple became single world, which compare with their earlier empire sort of kingdoms. It blurred the boundary of courtesan and devadasi. According to Velcheru Narayana Rao, the culture of *bhoga*, of erotic longing and fulfillment, was one in which the boundaries between courtesans (*bhoga-stri*, *vesya*) and temple women that had become indistinguishable. Their new role as artists who performed at both temple and court allowed these women to be imaged as mistresses, wives, or even queens at the Nayaka court.[151] The Nayaka court produced a peculiar syncretic culture that integrated aspects of indigenous Tamil culture, Telugu literary material, the new Mughal style courtly practices from Maharashtra and the modernity of the European enlightenment.[152]

The *bhakti* tradition

The *bhakti* movement influenced the South Indian society. Elaine Craddock mentioned that the devotional movement contained an element of social as well as religious reform. It protested against the heterodox faiths of Buddhism and Jainism and favoured the brahmanical institution like temple, which was largely depended on the royal patronage.[153] The religious institutions gained a momentum with the concept of *bhakti*. The word *bhakti* meant loyalty.[154] Leslie Orr, a historian, noted that the Tamil *bhakti* ideologies of self-surrender and devotion to service had a great impact on the society.[155] The saints referred to them as *adiyar* or *thondar* (slaves) and they were indeed the slaves of the Lord. The *bhakti* age led to the proliferation of temples, multiplicity of deities and the growth of the *agamic* literature. Champakalakshmi said that the movement was able to synthesise the northern Sanskrit and the popular South Indian Tamil tradition.[156] Subramanian said that the new gods that were unknown or poorly known to the ancients became established pantheon.[157] The religious encounters between Sramanic and Vedic sects witnessed the propagation of new religious ideas. The Nayanmars and Alvars brought religion close to the people and popularised the temple rituals in South India. The *bhakti* movement preserved the brahmanical caste structure and fixed its enemy as Buddhism and Jainism.[158] Appar and Campantar praised the association of Brahmin and Vedic rites. They mentioned that they hailed from the sacred places where the Brahmins lived and performed Vedic sacrifices and the places, which were filled with Vedic chants and smoke of sacrifices.[159] Regularly the hagiographers and hagiographies belonged to the Brahmin caste and the royal household. The religious propagators like Nayanmar and Alvar came mainly from the upper strata.

Kesavan Veluthat, a historian, said that the *bhakti* movement demonstrated to have had direct links with the expression of agriculture and the formation of the state based on it.[160] This marked the new era in the temple preface. The period between 850 and 1200 witnessed the emergence of many new shrines in South India under the influence of *bhakti* saints.[161] The conscious efforts of the ruling family to adopt the *bhakti* ideal made it the dominant ideology in the formation of a powerful regional state under the Cholas.[162] Champakalakshmi considered Saivism was a deliberate choice by the Cholas. According to her, Saivism proved to be more efficacious instrument of acculturation for acquisition of a wider popular base of South Indian society and it easily incorporated parochial gods like Murukan and Korravai as Kanthan and Parvathi respectively. The conversion of local cult centres into shrines of Siva, through the identification of several local and popular forms as part of the Siva religious tradition.[163] It equated the phallic symbols or the aniconic lingam with the folk worship of the pillar and tree were the most significant factors in the elaboration of the popular base of Saivism. Saiva iconography evolved in direct relation to the specific requirements of the ideological needs of Cholas power.[164] The *bhakti* saints had a great impact on the state. In 29th year of Rajarajan I, ordered craftsmen to produce copper images of some of the important Saiva saints Nambi Arurar, Nankai Paravaiyar, Tirunavukkaracar and Tirunanacampantar.[165] Rajendran I conducted festivals in honour of the Saiva saints in Tiruvorriyur temple.[166] Kulottungan III in his 24th regal year made donations for the daily ritual worship of the images of the Nayanmars in a temple at Uttatur.[167]

The concepts such as self-surrender, sacrifice, dedication and destiny were deeply imbibed within the society. The metaphor for the human body as temple, apprehension of the divine through acts of devotion, provided the much needed justification of human existence, as against the Jain idea of self-mortification for salvation.[168] The poems of the *bhakti* saints repeatedly stress the inefficacy of penance involving fasting and bodily mortification; deep love and genuine surrender are necessary to reach the lotus feet of the Lord. Nayanmars and Alvars brought the *bhakti* strands together. The stories of the *bhakti* saints revealed the notions of complete surrender. Ciruthondar alias Paranjothi, the chief commander of Pallava was said to have sacrificed and cooked his five-year-old son when disguised Siva requested for cannibalistic meal. Iyarpakai Nayanmar was another Saiva saint from the *Vaishya Varna* who lived at Kaverippumpattinam in Chola country. *Tiruttondar Puranam*, the Saiva hagiography, praised him as the saint who could sacrifice everything to the god and his devotees.[169] According to the *Puranam*, the saint gave his wife to Brahmin mendicant for his desire. Later, he escorted them safely through the woods and assassinated his relatives who resisted the sacrifice of his wife.[170]

The kind of servitude or complete surrender was accepted through the concept of *bhakti*. Periyalvar mentioned that the vow of surrender as *nan adimai punden* which meant 'I surrendered'.[171] The post-Sangam epic, Chilappathikaram referred *adimaittiral* (group of slaves). The slaves were called *adiurai* and their status was *adimai* (slave). *Kalittokai*, the Sangam literature mentioned that slaves were being branded on their chest.[172] Tirumankai Alvar, the Vaishnavite referred him as 'becoming slave of God'.[173] The myth of Cundarar detailed that an old Brahmin suited a case against Cundarar regarding the slave agreement. It indicated that the slavery was common among all castes.[174] But no slave market existed. The hierarchical community system however reduced the lowest communities to the status of slave. The rigid division as master servant nature was a chief characteristic of the South Indian society.[175]

The *bhakti* movement helped to keep the rigid social stratification. The story of Nandanar,[176] the Paraiar saint demonstrated the hegemony of the caste system in society. The untouchable saint was born at Adanur near Chidambaram. His caste duties were slaughtering animals and preparing leather. He visited the Tirupunkur temple and worshipped Lord Siva. But he was unable to see the idol. Nandi, the vehicle of Siva was little moved and made him to experience the god's presence. After that, he constructed a pond and bathed. Here, it is evident that there were restriction of Nandanar to enter in the temple precincts and use of the public ponds. Later, the fascinated Nandanar was interested to see the god of the Chidambaram temple. But he could not enter the city of Chidambaram. The Brahmins and brahmanical ritual order posed the questions "purity". Nandanar's birth bothered him and he worried about his destiny. The Brahmins compelled him to cross the *velvi thee* (sacred fire). According to the myth, Nandanar entered into the fire and vanished. The Brahmins of temple mystified his murder and incorporated a myth of reaching the feet of God.

The concept, love was the central to the path of *bhakti* or devotion. George W. Spencer mentioned that the development of *bhakti* devotionalism and the infusion of popular Hinduism with the ideal of salvation through intense devotion to a personal deity is the most significant religious development in medieval South Indian history.[177] Love became an important element in the poems of *bhakti* saints. The concept was much expended genre of the Sangam Tamil literature. Subramaniam mentioned that the transmutation of *agam* into *bhakti* was the most functional and the most fortunate development in Indian's religion.[178] Tamil erotic tradition of *agaththinai*[179] transformed into emotional (*nayika-bhavu*) *bhakti* by the Vaishnava saints. It brought religious tradition of devotion a permanent element of ecstasy and eroticism.[180] *Bhakti* poetry in Tamil from the sixth century onwards drew much inspiration from this *agam* genre and in the case of *agam* poetry in particular.[181] The works of Nammalvar, Tirumankai, Kulacckara and Andal are classical examples of the transmutation of *agam* genre into the religious idiom. In general, the content was narrated in the first person singular. The chief moods of *bhakti* are union and separation resulting in *viraha* poetry expressing the anguish of unfulfilled love. Vijaya Ramasamy said that this was more closely associated with the feminine than with the masculine.[182] Both male and female saints take on a female personality. The *bhakti* saints personified them as lady love and God as lover. Vijaya Ramasamy pointed that the mystical union between the self as the bride and the supreme as the bridegroom was the basic of the *bhakti* tradition.[183] Periyalvar surrendered himself to Lord Vishnu. He further quoted that "...being marked, myself and everything I own, with sign of your."[184] Basava, the twelfth century saint, often referred himself as a woman whether as a loving bride or a cuckolding wife.

I am a married woman
Married to one am I.[185]

The emotional and sensuous character of worship (ecstatic singing and dancing) was propagated by the *bhakti* movement, which contrasted with its contemporary Sramanic religious tradition. The agamic tradition and the *bhakti* movement gave a ritual and religious orientation to the arts.[186] The dance of the Lord Siva was frequently praised.[187] Subramaniam explained that the performing arts could retain all their sensuousness under a religious umbrella because of the original and continuing erotic and romantic basis of *bhakti* to get the continuing support of the Hindu temple for centuries.[188] The music and dance were essentially cultivated as sensuous pursuits of pleasure. They were brought closer and integrated into religion as a byproduct of the rise of the *bhakti* movement in South India.[189] Appar praised the service, which was rendered by the temple girls as *thondu seidal, panikal pavilludal*.[190] The *bhakti* tradition provided an ideological base for the devadasi institution and their services.

The direct engagement of women in the bhakti tradition was less. Among the seventy five saints, only four were women Karaikkal Ammaiyar (Vaishya *Varna*), Mankaiyarkaraci (Kshatriya *Varna*), Andal (Brahmin caste) and Isainani Ammaiyar (Brahmin caste). Vijaya Ramasamy pointed that women who seem to reject the patriarchal structure at the worldly level continue to operate within the framework of patriarchy at the spiritual level.[191] Women, who abandoned their homes or rejected the ties of marriage, their devotional outpourings continue within the familial paradigm. The only difference was that, now the family consists of patriarchal gods as their husband such as Lord Siva and Vishnu.[192] The divine story of Karaikkal Ammaiyar (mother from Karaikkal) and Andal were the classical example of this nature. Their poems dwell in perpetual bliss with the omnipresent deities. In general, their poems mocked the worldly life, and considered God as their ultimate truth. They completely surrendered their soul and body.

Karaikkal Ammaiyar belonged to mid-sixth century. She was most probably the first poet saint who wrote hymns on Lord Siva. Her poetic composition was placed in the eleventh Saiva Tirumurai. According to the myth, the beautiful Punithavathi was born at Karaikkal in the Chola country. She married a merchant called Paramathaththa. She was an ardent devotee of Lord Siva. Her mystic experience separated her from her husband and led him to marry another woman. Then she left the worldly life and got a frail, bony ghost-like appearance. She started her pilgrims and stayed in Tiruvalankadu to compose poems on Lord Siva. She was interested in visiting Mount Kailash where Lord Siva was believed to be residing. However, the pious woman did not want to use her foot to claim the Himalaya, due to the sacredness of the mount. The impressed Lord Siva appeared and accepted her as his mother.[193]

The legend of Andal revealed an erotic expression of the *bhakti* cult. Her poems *Tiruppavai* and *Nachchiyar Tirumozhi* expressed her erotic love of the Lord Vishnu. She was an adopted daughter of Periyalvar, the Vaishnava saint. She madly loved the Lord Sriranganathar of Srirangam temple. She considered herself, as a ladylove of the God. She used to wear the garlands of god and loved her decked presence. Periyalvar annoyed with the activities of his daughter and insisted her to stop the different behaviours. The god became unhappy, and appeared before Periyalvar and exposed her divinity. Later, the deity accepted her as his bride. Andal adored like a bride, and entered into the temple sanctum and disappeared. Both these myths explained the abnormal lives of the women and their rejection of the worldly life. There was a kind of unrest in their personal lives. Karaikkal Ammaiyar was rejected by her husband, and Andal was an adopted daughter of the Brahmin of Srirangam temple. The stories ended with complete surrender to the god. The first one acknowledged God as a mother, and the later considered as a lover. The relationship between the god and women was strictly constructed within the domain of family.

Conclusion

The development of devadasi institution occurred due to the emergence of temple institution. The firm establishment of temple order in South India strengthened the devadasi system. The Brahmin-Kshatriya combination helped to preserve the patriarchal order in the society. The system had its consistence growth from the Pallava period onwards. The imperial Cholas improved the condition of devadasi system by the means of donation and protection. The *bhakti* movement provided an ideological base for the existence of the system. The medieval records detailed the role of devadasi in the temple. The nature of devadasi work was classified according to their social background. A kind of unequal hierarchy existed among devadasi women. The political intervention of the non-Hindus led a little setback in the system. However, the emergence of Vijayanagar brought back the old Vedic order in the Tamil country. The later medieval records and travelogues highlighted the public appearance of devadasi. It detailed the involvement of devadasi in physical relation in the profane places. The moral conduct of devadasi was continuously questioned by the later medieval text.

References

1. Jordan, Kay. K. *From Sacred Servants to Profane Prostitute: A History of the Changing Legal Status of the Devadasis in India, 1857-1947*. New Delhi: Manohar, 2003: p. 26.
2. Lerner, Gerda. *The Creation of Patriarchy*. New York: Oxford University Press, 1986: p. 7.
3. Mahalingam, T.V. *The South Indian Polity*. Madras: University of Madras, 1955: p. 11.
4. Subramanian, N. *History of Tamilnad*. Madurai: Koodal Publishers, 1978: p. 328.
5. *Ibid.*, p. 337.
6. *Ibid.*, p. 331.
7. *tudiyan panan paraiyan kadampanen; innan kallathu kudiyumillai*. (*Purananuru*. Song no. 335. ll. 7-8.)
8. Subramanian, N. 1978. *Op.cit.*, p. 330.
9. *Ibid.*, p. 331.
10. Champakalakshmi. R. and S. Gopal. *Trade, Ideology and Urbanisation, South India 300 B.C to 1300 A.D.* Delhi: Oxford University Press, 1996: p. 42.
11. Stein, Burton. *Peasant State and Society in Medieval South India*. Oxford: Oxford University Press, 1985: p. 4.
12. Subramanian, N. 1978. *Op.cit.*, p. 330.
13. Champakalakshmi, R. and S. Gopal. 1996. *Op.cit.*, p. 43.
14. Champakalakshmi, R. *Religion, Tradition and Ideology: Pre-Colonial South India*. New Delhi: Oxford University Press, 2011: p. 13.
15. *Ibid.*, p. 14.
16. *Ibid.*
17. Stein, Burton. 1985. *Op.cit.*, p. 9.
18. Subramanian, N. 1978. *Op.cit.*, p. 330.
19. Stein, Burton. 1985. *Op.cit.*, p. 9.
20. Subramanian, N. 1978. *Op.cit.*, p. 334.
21. Heitzman, James. *Gifts of Power: Lordship in an Early Modern State*. Delhi: Oxford University Press, 1997: p. 4.
22. Ramasamy, Vijaya. *Divinity and Diviance: Women in Virasaivism*. Delhi: Oxford University Press, 1996: 4.
23. Heitzman, James. 1997. *Op.cit.*, p. 4.
24. Veluththat, Kesavan. *The Political Structure of Early Medieval South India*. Hyderabad: Orient Longman, 1993: p. 156.
25. Marglin, Frederique Apffel. *Wives of the God-King: The Rituals of the Devadasis of Puri*. Delhi: Oxford University Press, 1985: p. 140.
26. *Epigraphia Indica*. Ed. H. Krishna Sastri. Vol. XVII. New Delhi: Archeological Survey of India, 1923-24 (Rpt. 1983): pp. 291-309.

27. Nagaswamy, R. *Studies in Ancient Tamil Law and Society*. Madras: The Institute of Epigraphy and Tamilnadu State Department of Archaeology, 1978: p. 5.
28. Champakalakshmi, R. 2011. *Op.cit.*, p. 13.
29. Veluthat, Kesavan. *The 'Early Medieval' in South India*. New Delhi: Oxford University Press, 2009: p. 61.
30. *Ibid.*
31. Sastry, Parabrahma P.V. *The Kakatiyas of Warangal*. Hyderabad: Government of Andhra Pradesh, 1978: p. 281.
32. Champakalakshmi, R. and S. Gopal. 1996. *Op.cit.*, p. 7.
33. Dehejia, Rajeev H. and Vivek H. Dehejia. "Religion and Economic Activity in India: An Historical Perspective." *American Journal of Economics and Sociology* 52, no. 2 (April, 1993): p. 145.
34. *Koyil* (The Temple) (in Tamil). 01/08/1926. *Kudi Arasu*.
35. Nagasamy, R and M. Chandramurthi. *Tamilakak Koyir Kalaikal* (The Inscriptions of Tamil Temple) (in Tamil). Chennai: Archaeological Department, Government of Tamilnadu, 1973. (Rpt. 2009): p. 2.
36. "Velvikkudi Copper Plates." *Epigraphia Indica*. XVII. 1923-24 (Rpt. 1983). *Op.cit.*, p. 306.
37. Sharma, R.S. *Early Medieval Indian Society: A Study of Feudalisation*. Kolkatta: Orient Blackswan Pvt Ltd, 2001 (Rpt. 2007): p. 18.
38. Narayanan, M.G.S. "The Role of Peasants in the Early History of Tamilakam in South India." *Social Scientists* 16, no. 9 (September, 1988): p. 25.
39. Sharma, R.S. 2001 (Rpt. 2007). *Op.cit.*, p. 19.
40. Narayanan, M.G.S. September, 1988. *Op.cit.*, p. 25.
41. Stein, Burton. 1985. *Op.cit.*, p. 64.
42. Pillai, K.K. *Thamizhaga Varalaru Makkalum Panpadum* (The History of Tamilnadu: People and Culture) (in Tamil). Chennai: International Institute of Tamil Studies, 2002: p. 197.
43. *South Indian Inscription* (*S.I.I.*) Vol. III, No. 205.
44. *S.I.I.* Vol. II. Part. 3. No. 66.
45. Sastri, K.A.N. *The Pandyan Kingdom*. Madras: Swathi Publications, 1972: p. 103. f.n 2.
46. Heitzman, James. 1997. *Op.cit.*, p. 1.
47. Champakalakshmi, R. "Ideology and the State in South India." *Mamimdipudi Memorial Lecture-I: Andhra Pradesh History Congress*, Srisailam, Session 33 (1989): p. 8ff.
48. *S.I.I.* Vol. XII. No. 103.
49. Stein, Burton. 1985. *Op.cit.*, p. 288.
50. Nagasamy, R and M. Chandramurthi. 1973. (Rpt. 2009). *Op.cit.*, p. 41.
51. Champakalakshmi, R. 1989. *Op.cit.*, p. 8ff.
52. Nagasamy, R and M. Chandramurthi. 1973. (Rpt. 2009). *Op.cit.*, p. 37.
53. These temples were in Mandakappattu, Mamandur, Pallavaram, Vallam, Tiruchirappalli, and Singavaram. (*Ibid.*, p. 35).
54. *Ibid.*, p. 39.

55. *Ibid.*
56. King of Tagadur-Adhiyar
57. Nagasamy, R and M. Chandramurthi. 1973. (Rpt. 2009). *Op.cit.,* p. 40.
58. *Ibid.*, p. 43.
59. *Ibid.*, p. 19.
60. Parasher, Aloka and Usha Naik. "Temple Girls of Medieval Karnataka." *Indian Economic and Social History Review,* 23, no. 1 (1986.): p. 73.
61. Subramanian, N. 1978. *Op.cit.*, p. 394.
62. Appadorai, A. *Economic Conditions in Southern India (1000-1500 A.D.)*. Vol. I. Madras: University of Madras, 1936 (Rpt. 1990): p. 277.
63. Parasher, Aloka and Usha Naik. 1986. *Op.cit.*, p. 73.
64. Stein, Burton. *All the Kings' Mana: Papers on Medieval South Indian History*. Madras: New Era Publications, 1984: p. 68.
65. Parasher, Aloka and Usha Naik. 1986. *Op.cit.*, p. 72.
66. Jeevanandam, S. "The Sacred Geography of Medieval Tamilakam- A Study of Distribution Pattern of Saiva and Vaishnava Temples." In Birendranath Prasad. Ed. *Monasteries, Shrines and Society: Buddhist and Brahmanical Religious Institutions in India in Their Socio-Economic Context*. New Delhi: Manak Publications, 2011: p. 247.
67. Karashima, Noboru. "Vijayanagar Nayakas in Tamil Nadu and the King." In Noboru Karashima. Ed. *Kingship in Indian History*. New Delhi: Manohar Publishers and Distributors, 1999: p. 152.
68. Champakalakshmi, R. 2011. *Op.cit.*, p. 71.
69. *Ibid.*, p. 92.
70. Appadurai, Arjun. *Worship and Conflict under Colonial Rule*. New Delhi: Orient Longman, 1981: p. 51.
71. *Epigraphia Indica*. Ed. N.P. Chakravarti. Vol. XXII. New Delhi: Archeological Survey of India, 1933-34 (Rpt. 1984): pp. 213-266.
72. Veluthat, Kesavan. 2009. *Op.cit.*, p. 67.
73. Basham, A.L. *The Wonder That Was India*. New Delhi: Rupa & Co, 1954 (Rpt. 2002): p. 185.
74. Appadurai, Arjun. 1981. *Op.cit.*, p. 21.
75. Minakshi, C. *Administration and Social Life Under the Pallavas*. Madras: University of Madras, 1977: p. 48.
76. Stein, Burton. 1984. *Op.cit.*
77. *S.I.I.* Vol. I. No. 24.
78. Veluthat, Kesavan. "Royalty and Divinity: Legitimisation of Monarchical Power in South India." *Proceedings of Indian History Congress 39th Session*. (1978): p. 243.
79. *Ibid.*,
80. Appadurai, Arjun. 1981. *Op.cit.*, p. 21.
81. Subrahmanian, N. 1989. *Op.cit.*, p. 15.
82. *Ibid.*
83. Veluthat, Kesavan. 1978. *Op.cit.*, p. 243.

84. Karashima, Noboru. 1999. *Op.cit.*, p. 153.
85. Minakshi, C. 1977. *Op.cit.*, p. 50.
86. Pillai, K.K. 2002. *Op.cit.*, p. 194.
87. *Ibid.*, p. 197.
88. *Ibid.*, p. 208.
89. Subramaniam, V. "Tamil Romantic Poetry and Bhakti Poetry in Relation to the Temple." In *Proceedings of the* 5th *International Conference-Seminar of Tamil Studies* Vol. I, edited by M. Arunachalam. Madras: International Association of Tamil Research, September, 1981: p. 7a-33.
90. Veluthat, Kesavan. 2009. *Op.cit.*, p. 67.
91. Subrahmanian, N. 1989. *Op.cit.*, p. 16.
92. Vellaivaranan, Ka. *Panniruthirumurai Varalaru* (The History of Twelve Tirumurai) (in Tamil). Vol. I. Annamalai Nagar: Annamalai University, Rpt. 1994: p. 262.
93. *thillaivazh anthanartham adiyarkkum adiyen. Tevaram Tirumurai*. 7. Song no. 39. l. 1.
94. Subramaniam, V. September, 1981. *Op.cit.*, p. 7a-36.
95. *Ibid.*, p. 7a-37.
96. Ogura, Yasushi. "The Changing Concept of Kingship in the Cola Period: Royal Temple Constructions." In Noboru Karashima. Ed. *Kingship in Indian History*. New Delhi: Manohar Publishers and Distributors, 1999: p. 126.
97. *South Indian Inscriptions: Tamil Inscriptions*. Ed. E. Hultzsch. Vol. II. (Parts 1 and 2). New Delhi: Archaeological Survey of India, 1991: pp. 1-21.
98. Ogura, Yasushi. 1999. *Op.cit.*, p. 129.
99. *Ibid.*
100. Jordan, Kay. K. 2003. *Op.cit.*, p. 29.
101. Arjun, Appadurai. 1981. *Op.cit.*, pp. 71-72.
102. Jordan, Kay. K. 2003. *Op.cit.*, p. 29.
103. *Ibid.*, p. 27.
104. Appadurai, Arjun. 1981. *Op.cit.*, p. 21.
105. Jordan, Kay. K. 2003. *Op.cit.*, p. 35.
106. *Ibid.*, p. 27.
107. *Ibid.*, p. 35.
108. Marglin, Frederique Apffel. 1985. *Op.cit.*, p. 112.
109. Sadasivan, K. *Devadasi System in Medieval Tamilakam*. Trivandrum: CBH Publications, 1993: p. 76.
110. Price, Pamela G. *Kingship and Political Practice in Colonial India*. Cambridge: Cambridge University Press, 1996: p. 69.
111. Nagasamy, R and M. Chandramurthi. 1973. (Rpt. 2009). *Op.cit.*, p. 44.
112. One of his pseudonym of Lalithanguran. (*Ibid.*, p. 20.)
113. Ogura, Yasushi. 1999. *Op.cit.*, p. 129.
114. *Ibid.*, p. 124.
115. Sastri, K.A.N. *The Colas*. Madras: University of Madras, 1955 (Rpt. 2000): p. 453.

116. Ogura, Yasushi. 1999. *Op.cit.*, p. 129.
117. Nagasamy, R and M. Chandramurthi. 1973. (Rpt. 2009). *Op.cit.*, p. 3.
118. *S.I.I.* Vol. XII. No. 20.
119. Srinivasan, K.R. "Chapters IV to VIII." In *Encyclopaedia of Indian Temple Architecture South India, Lower Dravidadesa 200 BC-AD 1324*, edited by Michael Meister. New Delhi: Manohar Publishers, 1991: p. 178ff.
120. *S.I.I.* Vol. IV. No. 827.
121. Nagasamy, R and M. Chandramurthi. 1973. (Rpt. 2009). *Op.cit.*, p. 45.
122. *Ibid.*
123. *S.I.I.* Vol. XIX. No. 292.
124. Stein, Burton. 1985, *Op.cit.*, p. 44.
125. *Epigraphia Indica.* XVII. 1923-24 (Rpt. 1983). *Op.cit.*, pp. 291-309.
126. Champakalakshmi, R. 2011. *Op.cit.*, p. 100.
127. Stein, Burton. 1985, *Op.cit.*, p. 340.
128. Nanchilnadu is the geographical location of modern Kanyakumari district of Tamilnadu.
129. *Travancore Archeological Series* (*T.A.S.*). Vol. VI. pp. 1-6.
130. Pillai, K.K. *The Sucindram Temple*. Madras: Kalashetra Publications, 1953: p. 26.
131. Champakalakshmi, R. 1996. *Op.cit.*, p. 42.
132. Stein, Burton. 1985. *Op.cit.*, p. 291.
133. *Ibid.*, p. 341.
134. Subramanian, N. 1978. *Op.cit.*, p. 332.
135. Champakalakshmi, R. 1996. *Op.cit.*, p. 17.
136. The statement of Sathianathaier was quoted in Stein, Burton. 1985. *Op.cit.*, p. 290.
137. Champakalakshmi, R. 1996. *Op.cit.*, p. 39.
138. *Ibid.*, p. 96.
139. Basham, A.L. 1954 (Rpt. 2002). *Op.cit.*, p. 186.
140. Dutta, Ranjeeta and Jamia Millia Islamia. "The Politics of Religious Identity: A Muslim Goddess in the Srivaisnava Community of South India." *Studies in History* 19, no. 2 (2003): p. 160.
141. The Talaikkottai battle (1565) between Vijayanagar and Bahmani Sultanate destructed the Vijayanagar rule. It led to establishment of many kingdoms in South India.
142. Narayana Rao, Velcheru; David Shulman and Sanjay Subrahmanyam. *Symbols of Substance: Court and State in Nayaka Period Tamilnadu*. Delhi: Oxford University Press, 1992: p. 57.
143. Dirks, Nicholas B. *The Hollow Crown: Ethnohistory of an Indian Kingdom.* Cambridge: Cambridge University Press, 1987: p. 99.
144. Narayana Rao, Velcheru; David Shulman and Sanjay Subrahmanyam. 1992. *Op.cit.*, p. 58.
145. Stein, Burton. "Temples in Tamil Country, 1300-1750 A.D." *Indian Economic Social History Review* 14, no. 11 (1977): pp. 11-45.

146. Narayana Rao, Velcheru; David Shulman and Sanjay Subrahmanyam. 1992. *Op.cit.*, p. 67.
147. Stein, Burton. "Economic Functions of a Medieval South Indian Temple." *The Journal of Asian Studies* 19, no. 2 (1960): pp. 163-176.
148. Narayana Rao, Velcheru; David Shulman and Sanjay Subrahmanyam. 1992. *Op.cit.*, p. 89.
149. *Ibid.*
150. *Ibid.*, p. 187.
151. *Ibid.*
152. Soneji, Davesh. "Introduction." In Davesh Soneji. Ed. *Bharathanatyam: A Reader*. New Delhi: Oxford University Press, ed. 2010: p. xv.
153. Craddock, Elaine. *Siva's Demon Devotee: Karaikkal Ammaiyar*. Albany: SUNY Press, 2010: pp. 1-2.
154. Hardy, Friedhelm. *Viraha Bhakti: The Early History of Krsna Devotion in South India*. Delhi: Oxford University Press, 1983: p. 460.
155. Orr, Leslie. C. *Donors, Devotees and Daughters of God: Temple Women in Medieval Tamilnadu*. Oxford: Oxford University Press, 2000: p. 22.
156. Champakalakshmi, R. 2011. *Op.cit.*, p. 36.
157. Subramanian, N. 1978. *Op.cit.*,
158. Champakalakshmi, R. 2011. *Op.cit.*, p. 66.
159. *Tevaram Tirumurai*. II. Song no. 312; *Tevaram Tirumurai*. V. Song no. 157. and *Tevaram Tirumurai*. VI. Song no. 216.
160. Veluthat, Kesavan. 2009. *Op.cit.*, p. 66.
161. Nagasamy, R and M. Chandramurthi. 1973. (Rpt. 2009). *Op.cit.*, p. 41.
162. Champakalakshmi, R. 2011. *Op.cit.*, p. 97.
163. *Ibid.*, p. 95.
164. *Ibid.*, p. 75.
165. *S.I.I.* Vol. II. Part. ii. No. 38.
166. *Madras Epigraphy Report (M.E.R.) (1913)*: inscr. 418.
167. *M.E.R. (1912)*: inscr. 506.
168. Champakalakshmi, R. 2011. *Op.cit.*, p. 66.
169. *mikka siradiyarkal yarenum vendum yavaiyum illaiyennnathe; ikkadarpadi nikala munkodukkum iyalpin niravar ulakiyar pagaiyar.* (Vellaivaranan, Ka. *Panniruthirumurai Varalaru* (The History of Twelve Tirumurai) (in Tamil). Vol. II Annamalai Nagar. Annamalai University, 1980 (Rpt. 1997): p. 1136.)
170. *Ibid.*, pp. 1135-1140.
171. *Nalayiranth Divya Prabhandam*. Tirumankai Alvar's *Periya Tirumozhi*. Song no. 1562. ll. 2-3.
172. *Kalittokai*. l. 247.
173. *emperu manukku enran; arumperu lunpu pukkit; dadimaipun duinthu ponen.* (*Nalayiranth Divya Prabhandam*. Tirumankai Alvar's *Tirukkuruntandakam*. Song no. 2036. ll. 2-4.) and *aththanin nadimai yallal; yathumon rariki lene.* (*Nalayiranth Divya Prabhandam*. Tirumankai Alvar's *Tirukkuruntandakam*. Song no. 2041. ll. 7-8.)

174. Subramanian, N. 1978. *Op.cit.*, p. 342.
175. *Ibid.*
176. Vellaivaranan, Ka. 1980 (Rpt. 1997). *Op.cit.*, pp. 1173-1176.
177. Spencer, George. W. "Religious Networks and Royal Influence in Eleventh Century South India." *Journal of the Economic and Social History of the Orient* 12, no. 1 (January, 1969): p. 46.
178. Subramaniam, V. September, 1981. *Op.cit.*, p. 7a-39.
179. *Agaththinai* is the literary genre in Sangam Tamil literature. It exclusively dealt with inner experience such as love, eroticism and etc…
180. Subramaniam, V. September, 1981. *Op.cit.*, p. 7a-33.
181. *Ibid.*, p. 7a-38.
182. Ramasamy, Vijaya. 1996. *Op.cit.*, p. 28.
183. *Ibid.*, p. 38.
184. *Nalayiranth Divya Prabhandam. Periyalvar Tirumozhi.* Section no. 5. Song no. 4. l. 1. and Section no. 1. Song no. 1. l. 7.
185. Ramasamy, Vijaya. 1996. *Op.cit.*, p. 12.
186. Sadasivan, K. 1993. *Op.cit.*, p. 157.
187. *thanki alari ularukattil thalsadai ettuth thisaiyumveesi; ankang kulirnthanal adumengal appan idantiru alankade.* (Karaikkal Ammaiyar's *Tiruvalankattu Muththa Tiruppathikam.* Section no. 2. Song no. 1. ll. 3-4.)
188. Subramaniam, V. September, 1981. *Op.cit.*, p. 7a-39.
189. *Ibid.*, p. 7a-38.
190. Appar Puranam. Song no. 169. l. 4; Song no. 170. l. 4; and Song no. 171. l. 3. Song no. 172 l. 1.
191. Ramasamy, Vijaya. 1996. *Op.cit.*, p. 28.
192. *Ibid.*, p. 29.
193. Vellaivaranan, Ka. 1980 (Rpt. 1997). *Op.cit.*, pp. 670-701.

Chapter – 3

Emergence and Growth of the Devadasi System: Pre-colonial Period

In history, reference to woman are minimum or even nill. They are marginalised and always kept in a subordinate position. Within the patriarchal structure, the multiple voices of women are subdued. Irrespective of caste and class, women are forced to face suppressions at different levels. In general, women are dominated by men across the culture, and patriarchy determined the future of women. However, women are the equal actor and agent in history, the recorded history does not provide a space for women. The recorded history has information of very few women. In South Indian history, the visibility of women occurred in three major areas, royal households, sacred centers and prostitution. The archival records of South India carried very little information on women who generally belonged to the above-mentioned categories. The inscriptions, *bhakti* literature detailed and praised the philanthropic activities of few royal women such as Mankaiyarkarci (wife of Pandiya king), Chembiyan Madevi (wife of Uttama Chola) and Kundavai (sister of Rajarajan I). These women generously endowed to the temples and other social activities. Though prostitution was common in history, the South Indian epigraphical records did not provide much detail about the prostitutes. In this context, the public appearances of devadasi was unique. Devadasi, the temple woman was visible throughout the history of South India. The devadasis were prominent women who shared the public domain and often played a prominent role in political and social events. They fulfilled several roles in parochial society.[1] They were employed in temples for multiple services, but their ritualistic performances such as dancing and singing were highlighted.

Devadasis in the medieval period

During the medieval period, devadasi became significant officiating dignitaries of the temple institution. The system was widely prevalent in the medieval period. The Pallavas, Cholas and Pandiyas were interested in the development of the devadasi system. An inscription dated 1203,[2] recorded that queen probably of Jatavarman Kulacekara I promoted the devadasi system in temple of Tirupattur[3] and the system was further extended in the Suchindram temple around same period.[4] The medieval temple inscriptions and other historical sources noted in different names for devadasi such as *devaradiyar*, *patiyilar*, *ishabattaliyilar*, *manikkam*, *nakkan* (Lord Siva), *nankai*, *talichcheri pendukal*, *thalaikkoli*, *devanar makal*, *rudraganikai*, *emperumanadiyar*, *sani* and etc. In general, the names of the medieval devadasis were prefixed with the word *nakkan*.[5]

Devadasi had a social recognition and exercised certain kind of privileges and rights in the religious institution as well as in society. An Annual Report of Indian Epigraphy (A.R.I.E.) mentioned that *Nankai* Paravai, was a famous devadasi of the reign of Rajendran I.[6] Her image was kept within the temple premises, with the image of the Chola emperor, Rajendran I (*See Appendixes*: - 4 and 5). Later, the images got ritual sanction, and even today, the temple priests conducted the rituals of the images. The personal communication with 'Padma Shri' P.R. Thilakam, the music teacher of Thanjavur and from the grand lineage of *kondi* tradition of the devadasi custom, revealed the establishment of temple for her ancestor Manickka Nacchiyar in the North Car Street of Thiyagarajar temple of Tiruvarur (*See Appendixes*: - 6 and 7).[7] According to the *kondi* tradition, devadasi received *parivattam* (special rights) from the temple of Thiyagarajar of Tiruvarur. So far, the tradition was continuing, and P.R. Thilakam received the special rights from the temple. During the temple procession, the temple car was halted for some time in front of the shrine to honour Manickka Nachchiyar and *kondi* lineage.[8]

In 1090, devadasi named Thillaivanamudaiyal Madavalli was specially mentioned as the sacred servant of the Siva temple of Tirumananjeri.[9] T.V. Mahalingam mentioned that the devadasi of medieval period was allowed to carry their flag and other paraphernalia.[10] Tiruvenkata *manikkam* of Tiruvenkatesvara temple of Tirupathi was permitted to use a palanquin.[11] Devadasis from Agastisvaram taluk had the hereditary rights in temple, with which they were associated.[12] The damaged record of 1474 said that Udaiyammal, a devadasi, was granted the privileges of *tiruvandikkappu* and *mudaladaivu*. According to that, she had the right to do her dance performance in the beginning, and she was entitled as *naluthikkum venra manikkam* (*manikkam* who conquered all the four directions).[13] In 1235, temple trustees recommended to name a village as Uravakkinanallur after the performance of the devadasi called Uravakkina *thalaikkoli*.[14]

The medieval sources highlighted the beauty and the characteristics of devadasi women. In general, the term *manikkam* meant ruby. The devadasis were popularly identified as *manikkam*. An inscription of Valisvara temple in

Tiruvalisvaram mentioned that the dancing girl Bhuvani Pandi is also called as Atkonda Naya*manikkam*.[15] The Pudukkottai State Inscription (P.S.I.) mentioned devadasi as *alagiapendir*, which meant exquisite beauty.[16] Another inscription noted devadasi as *alagilumalagiya*, which referred the devadasi as a beauty among the beauties.[17] Usually, the expert in the dance performance was titled as *thalaikkoli*. A 19th year inscription of Rajarajan III said that the Chola king Rajarajan III was pleased to watch the performance of Uravakkina*thalaikkoli* at Rajarajan *tirumanamandapam* (marriage hall) in Adhipurisvara temple.[18] Cundarar, a prominent Saiva saint, was attracted by the beauty and dance performance of the *rudrakanikai* called Paravai Nachchiyar of Tiruvarur temple.[19]

The dedication of devadasi to a deity or god did not meant that they had to live a life without the normal sexual pleasures and childbearing. The patriarchal family structure accepted devadasi as wife, mistress, ladylove and so on. The medieval records detailed the engagement of devadasi in a family as a wife, mistress etc. In feudal society, courtesans and slaves were the symbol of wealth. Therefore, many kings and nobles desired to hold devadasis as their mistresses.[20] The medieval Chola emperor such as Rajarajan I and Rajendran I had devadasi as their mistress. Elisaivallabhi and Theayagavalli were devadasis who became the consorts of Kulottungan I[21] and another inscription mentioned that one of the queens of Kulottungan I was *anukkiyar*, was a personal attendant of the God at Kanchipuram.[22] Paravai Nachchiyar of Tiruvarur temple and Sankili Nachchiyar of Tiruvorriyur temple were married the Saiva saint Cundarar.[23] An inscription of 1189, referred the marriage of a devadasi of Achyutamangalam.[24] An inscription 1049, Chatural Chaturi, a devadasi of Tiruvorriyur temple was the wife (*agamudaiyal* or *illal*) of one Nagan Perungadan.[25] Chokkatamdal, a *ganikai*, of the Tiru-vanaikka Temple became the wife and queen of Jatavarman Cundara-pandiyan.[26] An inscription of Ramalingesvara Velpuru temple stated that Kasadi Suramadevi as concubine of Kota Ketaraja.[27] Akkaranangai, *devanar makal* of Tiruvarur was the wife of Pillai Cheramanar, a confidant of a Chola king.[28] A Pandiya Chronicle recorded that Mavali Vanadhi Rayan, an illegitimate son of Maravarma Kulacekara I and Abhirami, a devadasi of the Tirupattur Kali *koyil* was chosen by the Vijayanagar generals as Pandiya ruler by 1400. After the fall of the Madurai Sultanate, these Mavali Vanadhi Rayan posed himself as a ruler of Madurai and started to rule the country for the time.[29]

The recruitment

The engagement of devadasi in the temple was considered as divine thing. The recruitment of devadasi occurred through various means such as presentation and purchase.[30] The medieval state, temple institutions and village assembly had the right to recruit and appoint the temple servants. The presentation was carried into two categories. Some women were gifted as an object and the other one was a voluntary dedication.[31] The extensive devotion, poverty, superstition and prayer were the chief factors for the volunteer dedication. Usually, the donor might be from the royal household, military generals, local chiefs, wealthy merchants and prominent devadasi. The legitimisation of the temple authorities or village assembly was required to become a temple servant. The parents of Sankili Nachchiyar were insisted upon to get the permission from the village assembly for their daughter to become a devadasi of Adhipurisvara temple.[32] The service of the temple women started from the very tender age. The Chebrolu inscription mentioned that the service of the devadasi starts from the age of eight.[33]

An inscription of the ninth century said that a girl named Mrugansetti was married to the deity of Parthibhasekharapuram.[34] Kulacekara Alvar married his daughter Cholakulavalli to Sriranganathar, the god of Srirangam temple.[35] An inscription of Keraladeva recorded that some girls voluntarily entered temple services.[36] Kamlavalli: (Uraiyur Nachchiyar) the daughter of Nandachola of Uraiyur was married to Sriranganathar and brought the dowry of 360 *kalams* of golden rice with dal, vegetables, other curry stuff, golden plates, containers and also a hundred maid servants were presented to the bride-groom.[37] *Tiruvidaimarudur Puranam* states that the Pandiya king Varakuna Pandiya dedicated his queen to Mahalingasami temple at Tiruvidaimarudur.[38] Uttama Chola presented eight trumpets and 24 fly whisks women to the image of Sribalideva in Adhipurisvara temple in his fifth regal year.[39] An another inscription of 1098-1099 mentioned that the Vellalar residents of Pandimangattuppaliyur, Jayakondachola mandalam's Amudan Velan, Amudan Pallikondan, Amudan Uyyavandan dedicated Angadi, her Perangadi and her descendants as *devaradiyar* to god Mahadeva in Tiruvakkarai Chandramulisvara temple[40] for service to temple.[41] In 948, a man from Nanthimangalam donated three women for fanning the idol for Tirukarrali Parameshvar Temple in Tiruchirappalli.[42] At Srikurmam Palakonda Sarvajni-deva (1471) presented two women, Sutasani and Saorasani to hold four *chamaram* in the morning and in the evening.[43] An inscription of Adhipurisvara temple recorded the dedication of five people by Tiruvegamudaiyan. The number included Periya nachchi, the daughter of Mari and her sisters Kavuthalviyai and Vadukalviyai.[44] An epigraph from Venkatachalapathi temple of Karisulndamangalam registered the consecration of certain persons, men and women as servants in temple of Thentiruvengadam alias Amararajapuri Chaturvedimangalam in Mulli *nadu*.[45] The epigraph further added that they had to do service in the *matha* (attached with the temple).[46] A record of 1453 mentioned that some six women including mothers, daughters and granddaughters entered the temple as a slave on the hereditary basis. The names of the women were Mallayi, daughter of Ulagudaiyanacchi, Ponnan, Alagapperumal, Venkatam and Thayuman.[47]

In the 29th regal year of Rajarajan I an order was issued to recruit temple servants to Rajarajesvara temple. The prolong inscription detailed the transfer of four hundred devadasis from other temples to the royal temple of Thanjavur.[48] During the 27th year of Kongu-Chola king Vikrama registered the appointment of girls to a temple.[49] Tirukkulichcharattu Alvar temple at Palkalam recruited five persons including one for beating the *segandigai* (gong) and two for blowing the *kalam* (trumpets).[50] An inscription of Tiruvalankadu mentioned the order of Kulottungan III for capture of girls.[51] They were transferred from other temple. Rajasundari, formerly serving in the temple of Jampai was transferred to the temple of Elavanasur.[52]

In 948, certain mediator named, Chandracekara of Nandivarma *mangalam* sold his three slaves to the temple of Vayalur.[53] A record of 1119, registered the hunters sold some of their family women as slaves to the temple of Tiruvallam.[54] Another record mentioned the sale of women for the temple service.[55] The inscription of 1218-1219, registered the sale of five women and their decedents.[56] A damaged inscription of Uttarapatisvara temple mentioned that the sale of four women as *devaradiyar* to the temple of Tiruvalangadudaiyar Nayanar for seven hundred *kasu*.[57] In Culamangalam, a kanakkar sold two of their slaves to the temples *alvilaip piramana isaivutittu*.[58] In 1208, Vayiradaran, a local chief sold thirty six of his slave to a person who were received in dowry.[59] The Uttarapatisvara temple mentioned that the sale of four women as *devaradiyar* to the temple of (Tiruva) langadudaiyar Nayanar, for seven hundred *kasu* during the 13th year of Rajadhirajan II.[60]

Duties of the devadasi

In the appointment of dancing girls, Rajarajan I drafted the rules for the temple services.[61] During the Chola period, an official supervision was strictly imposed on devadasi.[62] The Vaishnava saint Ramanujar introduced *Udaiyavar* Code (reforms) in the temple service of the Sriranganathar temple of Srirangam. According to that code, devadasis were listed in the third category and their duties were newly assigned. Later it enumerated in the canon of *Koyil Ozhugu*, the chronicle of Srirangam temple. It stated that devadasi would bath at dawn and adorn themselves and then they would visit the temple and stand well in sight of the deity.[63] The Kalattur inscription of Kulottungan III fixed the timings for the performance of each of the dancing girls in the temple of Cundara Cholisvara Udaiyar.[64] In Suchindram temple, devadasi were asked to dance at *Vadakkedam* when *diparadhana* happened and on the same time, other devadasis were engaged in a chorus of *kulavai* (making a sound with their tongue).[65] In 1370, an inscription stated that a devadasi was directed to conduct the daily worship of God in Narasimha temple at Chinnadasaripalli.[66] The temple of Suchindram mentioned that the devadasi of the temple participated in the reception of the ruling sovereign or members of the royal family and attended on them during their entire period of stay in the temple.[67] During the reign of Krishnadevaraya, Kuppayini was a devadasi of Tiruvengadam temple at Tirupathi accompanied the king to Tirupathi.[68]

The South Indian temples strictly conducted the regular ritual cycles in a day, week, month, season and year. Marco Polo, the thirteenth century Italian merchant traveller, mentioned that the king of Malabar region performed hundred and four prayers everyday morning and evening in honour of the deities.[69] K.K. Pillai, a historian, referred the duties of the devadasis in the Suchindram temple. According to the reference, on every Tuesday and Friday, devadasi of the temple cleaned and smeared the temple premises with water and cow dung.[70] Abbe Dubois, a French Catholic missionary, mentioned that in great temples, bringing water for the temple ritual was considered as an auspicious ceremony. Usually, water was brought on the back of elephants with the escort of Brahmins and other temple authorities. The procession was preceded by the musicians and dancers of the temple.[71]

In general, *pusai* (rite) was considered as the temple ritual. The *pusai* consisted of sixteen rites of adoration which directed to the deity such as *avakanam* (invocation), *stapanam* (fixing), *pattiyam* (water for the washing of the feet), *acamanam* (water for sipping), *arkkiyam* (water for hand washing), *apicekam* (bathing of the idol), *vastiram kantam cattutal* (dressing and perfuming), *puspancuttutal* (offering of flowers), *tupatipam camarpittal* (offering of incense and light), *naivettiyam* (offering of food), *pali* (sacrifice), *homam* (oblation through fire), *nityotsavam* (daily festival), *vattiyam* (music), *narttanam* (dancing), *utvacanam* (send-off).[72] The recruited devadasi had a multi-task within the temple institution. Their work covered all types of services. They had to participate in the daily cyclic of the temple worship from morning waking up to sleep time of the deities at night.

According to the custom, devadasis were well-trained and the division of labor was defined. Rekha Pande, a historian, classified the functions of temple girls in the sacred realm as ritualistic and non-ritualistic.[73] The ritualistic services were considered as dancing, performing *tirualatti* or *karpura alattai* (a mixture of turmeric, lime and camphor) and *tiruchulam* (the sacred trident)[74]. The non-ritualistic works were carrying lamp[75], maintaining perpetual lamp[76], bringing water for worship[77], fanning idol, husking paddy[78], cleaning rice[79] and kitchen vessels[80], washing clothes[81], decorating surroundings[82], waiting upon the Gods with fly whisk on occasions when she was stalled during the day[83] and prepared scented powder and burnt incense[84] and offering sacred flower and plant leaves.[85] Tiruvacakam, the Saiva canon, mentioned that garland making, sweeping, smearing and dancing were the duties of devadasis.[86]

The non-ritualistic services

Holding *chamaram* (fly whisk) in honour of the god was one of the important functions of devadasi.[87] Manickkavacakar, the prominent Saiva saint, pointed out to that devadasis who fanning the idol as *koyirppinap pillaikal*.[88] A copper plate probably 868 mentioned that a servant girl who was an expert in waving the *chamaram*.[89] An epigraph engraved on Chinthamaninathar temple at Vasudevanallur registered a gift of land to devadasis for waving the fly whisks.[90] Devadasi Pirainarusiradiyar of Vyaghrapurisvara temple at Tiruppulichchanam was granted the privilege of waving the *chamaram* during the car processions.[91] Konda Komati Pratapa Singa provided for holding of *chamaram* by two dancing maids named Nagadeva Gangasani and Bhudhi Singasani at Simhachalam temple.[92] Yasodadevi referred that Sutasani and Saorasani hold the *chamaram* from the morning and in the evening.[93] Usually, devadasis were tending flowers in temple gardens. The tradition was explicated in the life of Vipranarayanan, the famous Alvar saint, and Devadevi, his wife.[94] An Inscription of Tiruvallam temple detailed the engagement of devadasi in the making of flower garlands.[95] A bilingual inscription from Andhra Pradesh mentioned the allotment of a share of paddy to a devadasi for preparing garlands for the god.[96]

In Suchindram temple, devadasis lit the lamps in the shrines of the first *prakara* (premise) on the occasions of the evening *diparadhana* and accompanied the procession with lamps.[97] The inscriptions of Kachcha-pesvara temple mentioned the dedication of the two families of dancing girls to look after the lamps in the temple.[98] A record from Mantrapurisvara temple at Kovitur in the Thanjavur district registered an agreement by the dancing girls of the temple to burn a lamp in the shrine of Bhuvanapet Nachchiyar.[99] In 11-9 (?), an endowment of six *uttamangadamada* was entrusted to three hundred *sanis* of Kommauru for maintaining a perpetual lamp in the temple of Agastisvara.[100] In Tiruparkadal Bhattaraka temple at Kilimanur devadasis were ordered to carry the hand lamps for the god.[101]

Devadasis performed the duties such as pounding rice and turmeric, preparing scented powders and burning incense. In the temple of Tiruparkadal Bhattaraka devadasis were given rice offered to the temple for performing the work of pounding the paddy.[102] A record belonging to the reign of Chola Kulottungan III mentioned that the allotment of a share of the temple land to a devadasi in return of her services like pounding of rice.[103] A record of fifth century of Visvanathasami temple at Thenkasi mentioned that the appointment of some servants including devadasis for performing the works such as holding *chamaram*, pounding turmeric, burning incense, preparing scented powders, etc.[104] The 19th regal year of the Rajarajan, a Vayiradaran sold Thai and her four daughters for the husking of the paddy in Adhipurisvara temple in Tiruvorriyur.[105]

The ritualistic services

The ritual performance was one of the ancient phenomenon in South Indian history. The sources for the origin of the tradition traced from the literary records of ancient South Indian Tamils, particularly in *Tolkappiyam* and *Chilappathikaram*. The Tamil countryside, the Tamil *pan* or music, communal singing and dancing derived from the early indigenous rituals of worship at Murukan shrines.[106] The practice of ritual dancing performed by the ancient South Indian tribes such as the Maravar hunters, and the gradual transformation of it under the influence of the brahmanical religion, seems to point towards the probable inspiration for the system of temple dancing.[107] In Sangam literature, the dancing women and prostitutes are frequently mentioned. However, there was no evidence about the temple women. From the early medieval period onwards, the devotional literature of Alvars and Nayanmars (sixth to ninth century) were referred women as celestial and to offer them in the temple.

Normally, devadasis were good dancers and singers. Trivandrum Archaeological Series (*T.A.S.*) volume noted that the devadasis were expert in seven kinds of music.[108] They had undergone many rigorous training in dance and music.[109] Their songs and dance performance became a source of attraction for the lay worshippers and pilgrims.[110] Campantar, the notable Saiva saint, mentioned that dancing girls came round the temple singing and dancing.[111] K.K. Pillai recorded the dance performance of devadasis in the Suchindram temple.[112]

The temple festivals with dance and music concerts became an important event for the interaction between mass and temple.[113] The temple dancers performed music and dance recitals every day after the *puja* and temple festivals. In the 28th year of Kulottungan Chola, Sivan Thillainayakan *alias* Cirutthondanambi of Tannirkunram in Nenmali *nadu* made the following gifts to the temple of Mahadeva of Tirukkalar in Purangarambai *nadu* (a subdivision) of Rajendrachola *valanadu*, for the purpose of conducting the festival of Aravabharanadeva on the day of the new moon.[114] An Inscription in the time of Kulottungan III (1215) recorded that the king resumed fifty-six *tirunals* (sacred days) in the temple[115] and also revived some of the old practices found mentioned in some earlier records.[116] An inscription mentioned that the temple girls performed dance during the temple procession.[117] The 1486 inscription of Tirumalai temple executed the following *silasasanam* in favour of Valandi, daughter of Tiruvidhi *sani* Anaimadi, viz., Tiruvidhi *sani* and Anaimadi of the temple accompanied the processions of the deities through the streets with her set of pipers, drummers, dancers and dancing masters and exhibits her skill in dancing in the streets before the deities.[118] In Suchindram temple, devadasis staged the drama of *Sarangadhara* in *natakasala*.[119]

An epigraph engraved on Chinthamaninathar temple at Vasudevanallur registered gift of land to devadasis for performing dances.[120] In the sixteenth year of king Parakesarivarman, thirty *kalanju* of gold was used for the *nibanda* (expenses) for the *Chittirai tiruvila* (festival).[121] Out of thirty *kalanju* of gold, seven *kalanju* of gold was used for oil which required for the seven days of the festival, two *kalanju* of gold was used for flowers and scented sandal-paste and five *kalanju* of gold was utilized for food to serve the devotees whom form the *kotti* (*goshthi*).[122] During the festival, Sivan Thillainayakan of Tannirkunram made a provision for feeding the devotees (*devaradiyar*) of the god Mahadeva who had sprung at Tirukkalar in Purangarambai *nadu*, of Rajendrachola *valanadu*.[123] An inscription of second year of Vairamegavarman mentioned that Mullikkudaiyan Adittanali made the gift of land for conducting *tiruppali* (a ritual service) in the temple Tirukkulichcharattu-Alvar at Palkalam in Damar-kottam.[124]

A record dated 1235[125] of the time of Rajarajan III registered the presence of the king at the time of dance performance by a devadasi named Uravakkina*thalaikkoli* of the temple *mandapam*. On her performance, the king granted a village of sixty *veli*[126] of land to her.[127] The 17th year of Vikrama Chola's reign in 1135 made provisions for the recital of the songs in every Sunday at the Siva shrine of Elvanasur.[128] Devadasis had participated in the dramatic performances in the temples during the festival seasons and re-enacted various kinds of dance (*aryakkuttu*, *santikkuttu*, etc.) with meticulous care, devotion and dedication. These performances were held in the specific halls like *natakasalai* (drama hall), *nirutta mandapam* (dance auditorium) etc. For their performance they had received remuneration or *manya* (gift) or *jivita* (grants of allowances) which was granted by kings, nobles, temples, villagers and *sabhas*.[129] In course of the period, their artistic qualities became an iconic identity for them. Monier-Williams described that devadasi had no other duty but to dance before the shrine.[130] Altekar pointed out that the group of people visited temples not to respects the deities, but they intended to fulfill their love intrigues with the singing girls of the sacred shrines.[131]

During the festivals and trade fairs large amount of entertainments happened and the devadasis performed different rituals. An inscription mentioned that the temple girls performed dance during the temple procession.[132] In the temple at Suchindram, devadasis staged the drama of Sarangadhara in *natakasalai*.[133] In the 16th year of king Parakesarivarman, thirty *kalanju* of gold was used for the expenses (*nibanda*) for the *Chittirai tiruvila* (festival).[134] The out of thirty *kalanju* of gold, seven *kalanju* of gold was used for oil which required for the seven days of the festival, two *kalanju* of gold was used for flowers and scented sandal paste and five *kalanju* of gold was utilised for the food and presents to the devotees who form the *kotti* (*goshthi*).[135] In the 28th year of Kulottunga Chola, Sivan Tillainayakan *alias*

Chiruttondanambi of Tannirkunram in Nenmali *nadu* made the following gifts to the temple of Mahadeva of Tirukkalar in Purangarambai *nadu* (a subdivision) of Rajendra-chola *valanadu*, for the purpose of conducting the festival of Aravabharanadeva on the day of the new moon.[136] During the festival Sivan Tillainayagan of Tannirkunram made provision for feeding the devotees (*devaradiyar*) of the god Mahadeva who had sprung at Tirukkalar in Purangarambai *nadu*, (a subdivision) of Rajendrachola valanadu.[137]

An inscription of the time of Kulottungan III (1215) recorded that the king resumed fifty six *tirunals* (sacred festivals) in the temple[138] and he revived some of the old practices found mentioned in earlier records.[139] The process of the system further extended the system during period of Kulottungan III and Rajarajan III.[140] It is evident from two inscriptions dated 1204 and 1235.[141] It states that the system received royal support in Tiruvorriyur temple. Another inscription recorded that Rajarajan III seated in the Rajaraja *mandapam* in the temple, enjoyed the dance performance of a devadasi in the *Ani* festival.[142] During the 7th and 10th years of Partivarman, a devadasi named Kumaradi Nangai, daughter of Nanri Nangai donated ninety six sheep for perpetual lamp and the same devaradiyar donated ninety two *kalanju* of gold and ninety two *kadi* of paddy for the sacred expenses of the deity of Jalathesvara temple at Takkolam.[143]

Remuneration

The remuneration for the services of devadasis was provided in the form of house, land, food, tax exemption or remission, certain rights, etc. Most of the time, devadasis received the grant in a two or more combination of above. The rights included receiving tax, taking water from well, preference in the performance. Some of them were granted tax free lands and house sites for their service.[144] The kings and temple authorities had been granted village to devadasis. Based on their remuneration and rights, the service of the devadasi was drafted. The rights were issued to any individual devadasi or the group of devadasi. A number of records registered the sale of land[145] and house sites[146] to them and sale of villages to maintain them.[147] Frequently, devadasi was asked for a surety.[148] Usually, houses and lands were granted to devadasi. The living area of devadasi was generally called as *cheri*[149], *madaivilakam*[150] and land was situated around the temple complex. Protection by the king was considered an important one. The employees received their wages in terms of land, money or in kind, house-plot, paddy and food. The assembly (*ur*) of Palkalam entrusted the endowed land to Arayanichchingan, *uvaichchan* (drummer) residing in the village for the temple service.[151] According to the damaged record of 1474, devadasi Udaiyammal was taken into its establishment as the first devadasi and she was granted the privileges of *tiruvandikkappu* and *mudaladaivu* (the right to do the first dance service).[152]

In 1494, a record from the village of Kunrakkudi of Thennari *nadu* referred the gift of garden and house to a number of dancing girls for the service in the Kasivisvanathasami temple at Thenkasi.[153] In Rajarajesvara temple, the recruited women were allotted with one *veli* of land, which was calculated at hundred *kalam* of paddy and a house in the three quarters of the temple premises of North Street (191 houses), south street (184 houses) and west street (25 houses).[154] The Chebrolu inscription of Jaya, the famous general of Kakatiya Ganapatideva contains a list of the temple servants who were allotted their shares in lands. The list further detailed that each of the three hundred dancing girls of the temple.[155] A certain Varadarajan provided houses, lands and certain privileges to the newly appointed dancing girls for her service in the temple.[156] Another inscription from Tiruvalisvara temple also stated that a gift of house and land for the service of the dancing girls in the temple of Tiruvalakkoyiludaiya Tambiranar.[157] An epigraph of 1532 recorded some of the girls were granted house sites on both sides of a new street, called *bhogarajap perunthenruvu* which was close to the big tower of the temple.[158] In 1478, some dedicated girls were permitted to live in some houses in the north street of the Nachchiyar shrine near the *tirumadaivilagam* of a temple.[159]

In 1117, the Hoysala king Vishnuvardhana granted villages to the Chennakesava temple of Belur for conducting ceremonies, offerings and the livelihood of dancing girls, Brahmins and others in the temple.[160] An inscription from Narththamalai in Tiruchirappalli district mentioned that the authorities of Tirumalaikadambar temple assembled at the *tirumandapapam* (temple hall) and distributed one *ma* of land to ten devadasis for the service in the temple twice a day.[161] A fifteenth century record mentioned that devadasi of the Isvaran *koyil* was granted full freedom to live in the first house of the street.[162] A damaged inscription of Chennakesavasami temple stated the gift of three kuli land to the dancing girls in the temple of Ramesvara at Siripuram.[163]

A record of 1235 registered that the pleased king Rajarajan III ordered to grant a village of sixty *veli*s of land to devadasi.[164] An inscription of Mallikarjunadeva Maharaya referred the grant of some lands to devadasi. Besides other rights in full freedom (*devasimai suvandram*), devadasi was allowed to possess two hundred *kuli* land and water for cultivation from nearby well.[165] An inscription of 1498 mentioned the temple authorities granted full right over a grant of two *ma* (land measures) of tax-free lands and one *ma* of land in Kuttakkudi and rice *kuruni* (measure) paddy for three devadasis.[166] A record of 1208 stated that the temple authorities were pleased to grant the small village of Arumpulippadi as *jivita* to a devadasi.[167] A record of 958 of Kannaradeva registered the grant of land in Kodiyur to one Nrtta Vitanki, devadasi.[168]

Rajakesarivarman undertook to protect and feed Kana Kavirakurattiyar, a female disciple and follower of Guna Kirti Bhatara of Vidal (a) Madevi Annadimangalam on eastern side of Singapura *nadu*.[169] In 1168, temple of Tirupparkadal Bhattaraka at Kilimanur mentioned that the total daily offerings prepared with thirty-one *nali* and one *uri* of rice was to distribute among the temple servants, including the devadasi. According to it, devadasis who pounded the paddy and carried hand lamps was to receive two *nalis*.[170] At Suchindram temple, twelve *nali* of rice was granted to devadasi, Parapanada Perumal and her lineal descendants.[171] The king Kulottungan III gifted five thousand gold coins for the specific rituals such as the sacred bath for the images, twilight lamps and garlands silken clothes offerings of food.[172] The twelfth century. Tiruvalla Copper Plate mentioned that four devadasis received twelve measures of rice.[173] The record of 1496 registered the presentation of two *panams* to a devadasi for her services in the temple of Tirumalai.[174] The Rudramahesvaras (priest) of the temple were granted one *padakku* (measure) grain every day and two *panams* every month to the temple devadasi.[175] An epigraph of 1370 registered a gift to a devadasi for having conducted the daily worship in a temple.[176]

In general, tax remission and exemption was granted to devadasi. An inscription of Kampaharesvara Temple recorded the tax remission made on *puravari* to the temple servants.[177] The 1483 record stated an order of Narasa Nayaka, who exempting devadasi from the payment of certain taxes, which were not included in Koliyanallur simai.[178] An inscription of Srirangaraya referred one such remission of certain taxes on some lands of the Kaikkolas and devadasi of the temple of Tiruvennainallur.[179] The Koneriraja-puram inscription of Chembiyan Madevi mentioned that the temple servants who lived in the old tax free *devadana* land.[180] The 1582 inscription, registered the five musicians and *nattuvan* of Simhaputrinathasami temple of Melchittanur allowed to water their gifted lands from the *tangal* (northern tank) as *padijivitam* (livelihood).[181] A record from Achchiruppakkam dated 1361 referred to a gift of land to a monastery at Kanchipuram by Somappa and Koppanar.[182]

Gifts made by devadasi

History partially recorded the contribution of the devadasi women. Some temple women utilised their resources for charitable activities. Based on its nature, the endowments of devadasi was classified as secular and non-secular. The non-secular gifts included the dedication of people, livestock and other articles to temple[183] or other religious institutions. The secular gifts of devadasi were largely for the renovation and repair of the temple and other public domains.

In general, the donations were in kind land, money, livestock etc. A *thalaikkoli* gifted land by purchase to repair the sluice of a tank.[184] During the period of Kumara Kampana, certain Tiruppani Nachchiyar dug a pond called *Vengalamma-kuttai* in a village of Madam in Wandiwash taluk, Tiruvannamalai district.[185] The standing figures of the devadasis were sculptured on the eight pillars of the *natakasala* of Suchindram temple. K.K. Pillai interpreted them as donors of the *natakasala* of the temple.[186] An epigraph of 1533 recorded some of them deposited a sum of three hundred and thirty *narpanam* (gold coin) in the temple treasury as an offering to the God, which was invested for the improvement of the tanks and canals in the temple village and for increase in production.[187] The year 1486 inscription recorded the donation of three hundred *narpanam* by a devadasi to Tirupathi temple and they contributed their mite to the renovation and repair of the big tank in Tirupathi.[188] An inscription of 875 mentioned certain devadasi donated some amount of gold for a *nundavillakku* (perpetual lamp) to the God of Thenkilayattu Mahadeva.[189] A record of c. 1351-1352 from the temple at *Madam* registered the construction of *kalyana mandapam* (marriage hall) of the temple by a dancing girl of Kulandaiantavar temple.[190]

In 1495, a devadasi of Srirangam temple granted four *parivattam* for having sung the Ula of Kandadai Ramanujayyangar in the sanctum.[191] A devadasi donated to Guhanadesvarar temple, Kanyakumari in 1040.[192] A certain *kaikkolan* stole away the *pattai karai* (a kind of gold ornament) of the Goddesses of a temple, and he was unable to pay the fine of ten gold sovereigns. A generous devadasi remitted it on his behalf in the temple treasury and her deed was recorded. A devadasi also granted a gift to the maintenance of perpetual lamps in temples.[193] An inscription from the Saptarishisvara temple of Lalgudi stated that Vaidyanatha-*Manikkam*, a dancing-girl of the temple was presented a *kolgai* (ornament) of three hundred and sixty *varahan* to the god.[194] A gift of six *achchu* by the dancing girl Bhuvani Pandi alias Atkonda Nayamanikkam for the offerings to the god Alalacundara Nayanar set up in the same temple by a certain Kulacekara Bhatta and his consort Paravai Nachchiyar.[195]

Devadasis in the later medieval period

The devadasi system received a little setback during the later medieval period due to the decline of the imperial Chola and later Pandiya. The interlude of non-Hindus and the non-Tamils happened in the later phase of Tamilakam. It questioned the existence of devadasihood and later it influenced the characteristic changes in it. Frederique Apffel Marglin, an anthropologist, noted that the successive Muslim invasions and weak political authority must had lead the moral degradation on the part of *maharis* (was *a* word for devadasis in Odia).[196] The civil war between Sundara Pandiya and Vira Pandiya[197] led Malik Kafur, the army general of Ala-ud-din Khilji[198] into Tamil country. Ala-ud-din Khilji could not tolerate the temple women being a prostitute. Therefore, he ordered forcible marriage of the temple women.[199] Sadasivan mentioned that the institution of devadasi in Tamilakam suffered a hardship of sixty eighty years (1310-1378) due to political convulsions.[200] K.K. Pillai also pointed out that the invasion damaged the temple institution.[201] As in the case, the Muslim raid and plunder of South India would destroy the temple institution and it accelerated the decay of the devadasi system. The Telugu work Acharyasuktimuktavali[202] dealt the history of Srivaishnavism. It recounted the entry of the Muhammadan in the Srirangam temple and the vicissitudes of the idol of Sriranganathar. The work detailed the incident of how a dancing girl of the temple of Srirangam prevented the utter destruction of the temple by Muhammadan chief. According to the record, the military general was enamored by devadasi. She treacherously murdered him and threw him down from one of the tower of the temple and immediately she committed suicide. Her descendants are entitled to certain privileges in the temple of Srirangam even today in commemoration of this act of their ancestress.[203]

With establishment of the Vijayanagar Empire in the fouteenth century the Kannada and Telugu Nayakas emerged as a prominent patron of the temple institution. The emergence of the Vijayanagar rule in South India reformulated the system. Kumara Kampana, the chieftains of Vijayanagar emperor, restored the devadasi tradition and assured their safety.[204] Kumara Kampana restored the worship and services that had been discontinued since the non-Hindu began to rule over Madurai.[205] Krishnaswami Ayyangar, a historian, also mentioned that the restoration of the ritual practices of Srirangam temple by Kumara Kampana.[206] Tirumalai Nayaka (1625-1659) of Madurai and Ragunatha Nayaka of Thanjavur further extended their support to the religious endowments. The Vijayanagar rule faced political and cultural encounters with Muslims and Christians (as travellers). Therefore, Vijayanagar needed to construct its religious and cultural domain. Champakalakshmi mentioned the Vijayanagar rulers consciously promoted a high degree of Sanskriti-sation.[207] They created the Vedicization-Sanskrit 'cosmopolitan' culture for pan-Indian Vedic authentication.[208]

According to the epigraphical sources, Kumara Kampana was a person who restored the status of the devadasi.[209] An epigraph of 1368 recorded that Kumara Kampana appointed Kamarasa Vittappa of Anaigundi as his officer to enquire into the problems of devadasi.[210] In the 5th year of Rajanarayana Sambuvarayar, there was a disorder between *ishabattaliyilar* and *devara-diyar*.[211] The poor service condition and low remuneration are the reasons for the outbreak of the protest. The temple authorities of Adhipurisvara temple assembled in the *Vyakaranadana* hall under an *adhikari* (officer) called Tunaiyirunda nambi Kongarayar. The officer was able to settle the problem of the devadasis.[212] Kumara Kampana ordered his one subordinates to give material protection to the affected devadasi.[213] He appointed an officer called Mahapradhani to monitor the gifts to the temples and other religious institutions.[214] An inscription from Tittaikkudi mentioned his gift of the village of Attiyur to the temple.[215] An inscription of 1460 recorded a royal order as to the appointment of some devadasi to a temple.[216] In 1479, one Ettappa Nayaka left a number of maid servants as devadasi in the temple of Tirumalai Nayanar for the merit of Isvara Nayaka.[217] An incomplete inscription recorded the appointment of a certain Tentiruvengada-*manikkam* as a musician of the temple with her two brothers as a hereditary servants of the temple.[218]

Devadasi as property

Devadasis were treated as temple property, and they primarily served Brahmins and other patrons. The hierarchy existed within the devadasi institution. Usually, devadasis were divided according to their hierarchal gradation. According to their grade, their nature of work was determined. An inscription of 1208 elaborated the duties of the devadasi.[219] A Kopparam inscription of Andhra Pradesh[220] and Sudi inscription of Karnataka[221] detailed the hierarchy within the devadasi institution. In 1350, a kind of disagreement happened among devadasis of Tiruvorriyur temple due to the hierarchy. The *patiyilar* of the temple had high status than *devaradiyar* and *ishabattaliyilar*.[222] The *ishabattaliyilar* were to assist *patiyilar*. The *ishabattaliyilar* were also to perform dance but they were exempted from carrying the flywhisk during festivals. The *patiyilar* carried the superior social status to that of *devaradiyar* and that those in those turn were superior to *ishabattaliyilar*.[223]

An inscription of the period of Kumara Kampana recorded poverty, death and migration among the devadasi women.[224] The two inscriptions, which dated 1188 from Tamaraippakkam, recorded the self-immolation of two women who were probably devadasis. The first record stated that a woman musician usually accompanied a dancer of Tiruvagnisvara Mahadeva temple. When the dancer expired, the woman musician, out of her love for him, committed *sati*. It was recorded in the inscription as *udan pallikonda*.[225] The replacement of devadasi was immediately caused due to the incidents of the death and migration of any devadasi. In general, the immediate descendent or relative of the devadasi underwent the service of her predecessor. The failure of any qualified successor, the temple authorities had a right to appointment a qualified person.[226] According to the sources, the temple priests exploited the devadasi women. A 1239 record from Sivapuram registered the immoral behaviour of the two Siva Brahmins of the temple with the devadasis.[227]

The dedicated women were punch marked as a sign of life long servitude. An inscription stated the following phrase, "agreed to serve God as long as

Sun and Moon exist and therefore branded with the sacred symbols".[228] Sadasivan remarked that the symbol marked some significance to show the bondage of the women to the temple.[229] In general, women, slaves and animals were marked with sacred symbol of the respective temples.[230] The devadasis and cows were branded with the *sulam ilanchinai* (trident mark).[231] The branded devadasi could not enter the outside service, even in a royal household.[232] Usually, devadasis of the Siva temple were branded with the trident mark and those of Vishnu temples with *sanku* (shell) or *chakram* (discus) marks.[233] Siva devotees branded themselves with the *sulam* (trident), or *rishabham* (bull) mark. Appar, the prominent Saiva saint, had the impression of *sulam* or *rishabham* (bull symbol) on his body. Soundara Rajan mentioned that *chitrameli* (the plough) was used as a symbol for the devadasi of the Chola period.[234] Alvars refereed the process of *arakkilacchinai seithu* (the branding with sealing wax).[235] The damaged record of 1474 revealed that Udaiyammal, a famous devadasi was marked with the trident symbol on her body.[236] The 1119 Tiruvallam temple inscription noted a sale of *trisul* pierced *devaradiyar*.[237]

Devadasi in the seventeenth Century

The moral questions

According to the patriarchal norms, family is considered as sacred and the role of women was subordinate. The sexual code for women was strictly imposed, restricted and monitored. During the medieval period, the association of devadasi was considered auspicious. The social acceptance of the auspiciousness of devadasi made free from the strict restriction as compare to other Indian womenfolk. However, the later medieval records reflected the transcended condition of devadasi women. The later medieval records such as travelogues, hagiographies and other literary records highlighted the loose character of devadasi. The association of devadasi became an immoral act. An epigraph of seventeenth century from Vahesvarar temple at Malayadipatti provided us with some evidence of the immoral life of the devadasi. It stated that the *devidiyal* (devadasi) named Vadvulamangal was found with a Brahmin in an amorous way. The record runs thus *marupadiyumoru piramananai alaicchu vittille trundapadiyinale*.[238]

Travelers account

During the later medieval period, the foreign travelers such as Domingo Paes, Abraham Rogerius (1651), Francois Valentyn (1726), Bartholomous Ziegenbalg (eighteenth century) and Jacob Haafner[239] (nineteenth century) (*See Appendix*: - 8) recorded the devadasi tradition in their visit to South Asia, especially to the Indian sub-continent. Dutch pastor Francois Valentyn (1726) was the first one who mentioned the word *devadasikal* (plural form of devadasi) in his book *Oud en Nieuw Oost-Indien* (Old and New East India).[240] The Venetian jeweler Gasparo Balbi (1590) used the derogatory term *puttane del pagoda* (temple whore).[241] Della Valle referred that some of the dancers fanned the deities with flywhisks, and others were guided by a man who danced with them and was their masters.[242]

The seventeenth century Dutch Calvinist minister, Abraham Rogerius pointed out that devadasis as whores. His travelogue *De Open-Deure tot het Verborgen Heydendom* (The Doors an Open to the Hidden Heathendom) (1651) specifically pointed out that the lewdness of the women.[243] He criticised the attitude of Brahmin priests to encourage the dancing and singing of the women in the pure and sacred spaces like temple.[244] In his own words:

> It seemed a very strange affair, that while the Brahmins regarded the *Pagodas* (temples) as holy places, and the images were so holy that the Soundraes might not even touched them, that they also allowed such led women to serve their Gods. They let those women dance for them who were not only indecently clad, but whose lewdness was known to everyone.[245]

Pietro della Valle, a Italian traveler, mentioned them as 'public dancers' (*pubbliche ballatrici*) were prostitutes and that their songs and dances were lascivious.[246] Francois Bernier mentioned that the Brahmin priests of the Jagannath temple raped the young dancers after they were 'married' to the god. He pointed out that the selection of the beautiful girls as maiden of the God Jagannath by the priest. Further, he noted that the selected girls were accompanied the god to the temple with all the pomp and ceremony, in temple she remained the whole night, and having been made to believe that God will come and lie with her. The girl was commanded to inquire the god about the productive years. In the night, one of the impostors entered the temple through a small back door, enjoyed the unsuspecting damsel, and made them to believe whatever might be deemed necessary.[247]

Domingo Paes, a Portuguese traveler, detailed the general status of devadasi women in the Vijayanagar period. He referred the dancers of Vijayanagar as *baylhadeiras* or *bailadeiras* (female dancers).[248] He noted that devadasi had to perform dance during the feeding of idol in a regular basis[249], and during the festivals, the *bayaderes* were ordered to dance before the idol for long hours.[250] He referred the loose character of the devadasi. Further, he mentioned that the rich attirement of temple women, and their pleasure of shewing.[251] Devadasi in the Vijayanagar period were lived in the best streets in the city, and their streets carried the best rows of houses. Usually, they were desired to display her belongings, and they were much respected, and they classed amongst the honoured ones, who were the mistresses of the captains, and any respectable men might visit their houses without feeling shy.[252] He wondered that devadasis had a right to enter the palace, remained to stay, and could eat the betel with the aristocrats.[253]

Bartholomous Ziegenbalg was a Protestant Missionary, who reached Tranquebar (Nagapattinam district in modern Tamil Nadu) in 1706. The account of Ziegenbalg was considered as an important record in the history of South India.[254] The knowledge about the native language helped Ziegenbalg to refer authentic sources. His travelogue, *Malabarishes Heidenthum*[255] detailed the existence of thirteen kinds of temple servants. Among them, the *Gotterdienerinnen* (female servants of the Gods) was listed in the eleventh category. He detailed the temple services of devadasi and their special duty of dancing and singing in a separate complex. The travelogue mentioned that the devadasis had to learn to read and write. Ziegenbalg acknowledged their talent in the poetic genres. In general, the cleverest and finest maidens were selected as devadasi. They were insisted to carry a flawless body, and did not allowed getting married to a mortal. They adorned well, and could be easily recognised by their external appearance. The larger temples had a great number of devadasis, and some of the smaller temples did not have them. However, everyone considered them as whore, who had a privileged way of carrying their business, and thus, the Europeans called them as dancing whore.[256]

Ziegenbalg detailed the ceremonial marriage of devadasi. The temple priest carried out the dedication ceremony as a representative of God. The young girl was brought to the temple for the dedication. The priest bind devadasi to the gods with a bridal necklace, which was the sign of all those who were married. After the marriage ceremony, all the young married girls were given a marvelous procession around the streets.[257] He further emphasised that devadasis were free to prostitution with whomever they desire, and their houses became 'public brothels'. He mentioned that Europeans enjoyed watching the songs and dances of devadasi in the streets, and that many of them visited their houses. In his view, the devadasi system was a great shame and an insult to Christianity.[258]

Some of the indigenous literature reflected the condition of the later medieval period. The minor literary works such as *Virali Vitu Tutu* (messenger literature), ballad and *Thanippatar tirattu* (compilation work) focused the issues of the devadasi. The later medieval literatures did not have any ambiguity between the temple women and prostitutes. They were well aware of the uniqueness of the devadasi women. The works of Arunakirinathar and Kalamekam discussed the exploitative nature of the devadasi institution.

The literary work of Arunakirinathar revealed the encounter and love intrigues of a common person with the temple women.[259] Arunakirinathar was a fifteenth century mendicant who composed Tirupukazh, the sacred text on Lord Murukan. The life of Arunakirinathar was called as *Arunakirinathar Puranam*. He had a personal relationship with *dasis* of Annamalai temple.[260] The text *Arunakirinathar Puranam*, pointed out that devadasis were *ganikai* who married the deity of Lord Annamalai (Lord Siva).[261] It added that the *dasis* were born for a single mother and many fathers.[262] Kalamekam was a contemporary of Virupaksha Raya II (1466-1485), the emperor of Vijayanagar kingdom. The poet was known for his immoral life. He had a personal relationship with devadasis. His works praised, criticised and cursed the devadasi women. Especially, his work referred the affair of Mohananki, a devadasi of Tiruvanaikka temple. He converted from Vaishnavism to Saivism.[263] Somi of Arrur was another devadasi with whom Kalamekam lived for some time. He praised the beauty of Somi. According to him, the Lord Vishnu and Brahma were astonished to witness the beauty of *dasi* Somi.[264] He praised devadasis named Kuththal, her elder sister, her mother and grandmother at Madurai. He associated the eyes of Kuththal with sharp spear, her elder sister's with sapphire, her mother with lotus and grandmother with arrow.[265] In addition, another devadasi was known as Kamalatchi who had eyes like spear.[266] He visited Inchikudi (Tiruvarur) and had a physical relation with a devadasi named Kalaichi, and later he cursed her. He compared the breast of a *dasi* as a bitter guard, and her waist with pestle.[267] He criticised and mimics the language usage of Telugu *dasi*. He said that *emira ori, enthundi osthi*.[268] He blasphemy the voice of *dasi* of Nagappattinam. He stated that the voice of devadasi was a kin to a donkey.[269] His literary work, *Thanippadal Thirattu* addressed issues of devadasi and prostitute.[270]

Usually, the Tamil word *dasi* pointed out the temple women, and the word *veshi* referred prostitutes. He compared the prostitutes with monkey, betel leaf[271], coconut[272] and palm tree.[273] He mentioned that it was not easy to escape from them, and they always moved with us until the material vanished. They cheated everyone and did prank on others.[274] The *Udaiyar Kathai*, a sixteenth century Tamil ballad, referred the demoralised lives of devadasis of Nellaiappar temple (Tirunelveli) and Kasivisvananthar temple (Thenkasi). The ballad stated a quarrel of the devadasi of Nellaiappar temple to share a night with a rich Udaiyar.[275] The ballad further mentioned that the Udaiyar lived with Nallamangal, a *muraikkari* (devadasi) of the temple of Thenkasi.[276]

The *Virali Vitu Tutu* (the messenger poems) is one of the literary genres in Tamil literature, which extensively discussed about the relationship of devadasi and the composer. It was popular between 1600 and 1750. The genre is structured like a conversation between *virali* (messenger), who was a female messenger and the protagonist. Therefore, the particular genre of literature was called as the messenger poem. The content dealt with the morality and misconduct of devadasi. The text flooded with the sexual elements and extreme metaphors. The sexual activity of the devadasi women was vividly portrayed in the poems. Usually, the content of the poem is uniform. According to the literary genre, the educated pious Brahmin was the protagonist of the poems. In general, the protagonist had a quarrel with his family, especially with his wife, and then, he made pilgrimages. In the end of the travel, he was attracted by the performance of devadasi, and felt love for her. Later, he spent his entire earnings on her. After the economic drain, the family of devadasi, thrown out the protagonist form their house, but he refused to leave her. The annoyed protagonist complaint about the *dasi* in the village assembly, but his efforts were refused and mocked by the assembly. Subsequently, the protagonist started to criticise her, and met a local chieftain, who became his patron. Ultimately, he expressed his experience to the *virali* who could convince his wife and help him to reunite with his family.

Deivachchilaiyar *Virali Vitu Tutu*, Muvaraiyan *Virali Vitu Tutu*, Sethupathi *Virali Vitu Tutu*, Nannavur Sangamechuvara Sami Vedhanayaki Amman peril *Virali Vitu Tutu* and Kulappa Nayakkan *Virali Vitu Tutu* are the works, which are going to discuss. Deivachchilaiyar *Virali Vitu Tutu* is the oldest *tutu* literature.[277] Kumaraswami Avadani wrote the poem on Deivachchilaiyar of Krishnapuram near Tirunelveli. Tiruchchendur Nadalingappattan was the protagonist of the poem who lived with his wife and children. The family issues led him to pilgrim to Krishnapuram, Neiveli, Tiruvidaimaruthur, Brahmadesam, Papanasama and Punnaivanam. He watched the dance performance of Adhiruparattinam (devadasi of Rajasinga *mangalam*) on *Chithirai* festival in Punnaivanam temple. He desired her and vested his wealth on her. In the meantime, he built a friendship with Gothandan of Manur who was already exhorted by a *dasi* Mohavalli, a sister of Adhiruparattinam. After some time, the mother and sister of Adhiruparattinam abandoned Nadalinga-ppattan. He was confused and filed a complaint against her in the village assembly. The assembly refused the plea. The worried Nadalingappattan met Deivachchilaiyar of Krishnapuram, a chief of Tirunelveli province under Madurai Nayaka. The pleased chief gifted a huge amount. Later he met *virali* and asked to share his experience with his wife.[278]

The seventeenth century Muvaraiyan *Virali Vitu Tutu*[279] of Mallaiyur Chirampalak Kavirayar belonged to the period of Tirumalai Nayaka. Chanthai nagar Vasudeva *maraiyon* was a protagonist and his wives were named Abhirami and Mohavalli. The quarrel between the wives made him to flee and wandered to Tirupathi, Kalahasthi, Chidambaram, Tiruvarur, Tiruvaiyar, Tirupperunthurai, Kalaiyar *koyil*, Tiruppullani, Tiruppunalur, Rameshvaram, Kanyakumari and Srivilliputtur. The wandering Vasudevan met Indrani, the daughter of Kamakalavani of Srivilliputtur Vaishnava temple. He was curious to know about her. He was informed that the requirement of *dasi* was seven hundred to eight hundred *pon* (gold). It was interesting that the money was distributed to different categories such as hundred and twenty *pon* for a night with her, ten *pon* for *suganthankal*, ten *pon* for bed and twenty *pon* for brokerage. The admired Vasudevan agreed and spent his entire earnings. He praised her expertise in linguistic and dance skills.[280] After a while, she deserted him. Afterward, he met a philanthropist named Virai Venkatanathan of Muvarain, who secured his life.

Another *Virali Vitu Tutu* named, Saravana Perumal Kavirayar's Sethupathi *Virali Vitu Tutu* detailed an experience of Avathani, a Brahmin who had a personal relationship with a *dasi* called Inbavalli.[281] According to virali literary genre, Avathani met *dasi* in the Uttirakosamankai festival that led the quarrel in the family. He made pilgrimages and reached Tirumarudhur. There, he encountered Mohanamuthu, a *dasi*.[282] Avathani compared her with a deer and her eyes with spear. Further, he mentioned that her physical beauty completely charmed him.[283] After the separation, Avathani worried about her relationships, and noted that the money should be spent for charity works instead of satisfying her.[284] He criticised her as worst among all *dasi*.[285] Another *tutu*, Nannavur Sangamechuvara Sami Vedhanayaki Amman *Peril Virali Vitu Tutu* mentioned the story of Sodatha Avathani of Tirupathi who married the daughter of Timma *pattar*. The unhappy Avathani led to Tiruvorriyur, Chidambaram, Tiruvanaikka, Madurai and Palani. There he met Kamarasakkulikai, daughter of Manamalai who danced in Nrutta *mandapam* of Palani temple. As usual, he lost everything and met Punaladi Sangamechurar for a gift.[286] He worried that he gifted garlands, silks and pleasures to her, but in return, he received the disease alone.[287]

The eighteenth century Kulappa Nayakkan *Virali Vitu Tutu* of Supradeepak Kavirayar of Nilakottai dealt the life of Avathani of Srirangam. Punkavanam was his wife. He had an extra marital relationship with *dasi* of Chevvanthisar temple. It broke the family and he went away to Tiruvanaikka, Thenmadurai, Tirumaraikkadu, Muthukunram, Sivasamudram, Tirukkazhukunram, Avinasi, Chenkattankudi, Chidambaram, Tirukkulathi, Kasi, Alvartirunakari, Krishnapuram, Kurralam, Srivilliputtur, Tiruchuzhi, Tiruppuvanam and Cholaimalai. In Cholamai, an unknown saint warned the notorious activities of devadasi of Tiruvorriyur, and explained how the king Konthi lost his kingdom due to her. However, Avanthi did not listen the words of the saint and went to Minakshi temple of Madurai. There he met Madanapishekam, the daughter of Manikkamalai of Minakshi temple. Manikkamalai was not a dancer. She did the non-ritualistic performance in the temple, but her daughter became a notable temple dancer. The story revealed that the *dasi* used some medicine to mesmerised Avathani and later, he was thrown away from the house. The depressed Avathani encountered the Nilakottai Nagendra Bhoopathi and started working with him to earn wealth.[288]

All these minor literature carried out the similar elements. The bard was always losing his treasure to Brahmins. They had a personal problem in their family life and left for pilgrims to various brahmanical temples in the Indian subcontinent. They admired the beauty of *dasis* of any particular temple. The relative of *dasi*, especially her mother was powerful persona in the family. They lost their wealth to *dasis* and were thrown away from the house of *dasis*. The depressed bards launched a complaint in the public assemblies. However, the assemblies rejected their plea. The unnoticed bards attended the procession of any local chief. Usually, the local chief might be a philanthropist and donated a sound resource to the bard. Then the bard met a messenger and request for his reunion with the family.

Conclusion

The establishment of the devadasi system parallel with the temple organisation. During the medieval period, devadasi system was well established in South India. The Kings, nobles, and the temple institutions were liberal to give patronage the devadasi institution. In general, devadasis were recruited on voluntary and non-voluntary basis. The dedicated devadasi did ritualistic and non-ritualistic services in the temples as well as in the society. The devadasis were honoured with several titles such as *manikkam* (ruby) and *thalaikkoli* (an expert in the dance performance), etc. The functions of devadasi in the sacred realm were classified as ritualistic and non-ritualistic. The ritualistic services were considered as dancing, performing *tirualatti* or *karpura alattai* (a mixture of turmeric, lime and camphor) and *tiruchulam* (the sacred trident). The non-ritualistic works included carrying lamp, maintaining perpetual lamps, bringing water for worship, fanning idol, husking paddy, cleaning rice and kitchen vessels, washing clothes, decorating surroundings, etc. The historical remains exhibited the engagement of devadasi in the charitable activities.

The decline of the Chola emperor witnessed the degradation of devadasi system. The political instability of the later Pandiyas had worsened the condition of devadasi. Devadasi did not have any agency to communicate their problems and issues. However, the emergence of Vijayanagar revived the condition of devadasi. There was a strict code of conducts drafted and maintained by the state, caste and religious institution. The dedicated women were punch marked as a sign of lifelong servitude. The branded devadasis were not allowed to do the outside services. The later medieval records such as travelogues, hagiographies and other literary sources detailed the mischievous lives of devadasi women in the public domain.

References

1. Iyer, Latha and Kanakalatha Mukund. "Her story: Women in South India in the Seventeenth and Eighteenth Centuries," *Indica* 32, 1995: p. 38.
2. *Annual Report of Indian Epigraphy* (*A.R.I.E.*). of 1935-36. No. 190.
3. It is in the present day Ramanathapuram district of modern Tamil Nadu.
4. Pillai, K.K. *The Sucindram Temple*. Madras: Kalashetra Publications, 1953: pp. 287-289.
5. Ramachandran, K.S. "Some Observations on the Names Occurring in the Inscriptions of Rajaraja-I in the Brihadisvara Temple at Thanjavur, Tamilnadu." *Journal of The Andhra Historical Research Society* XXXVII, 1978: pp. 179-192.
6. *A.R.I.E.* of 1919. No. 680.
7. The information was collected through an in-depth interview with P.R. Thilakam at Thanjavur on March 15, 2011. The column of Sriram in *Sruti* magazine substantiated the details of the interview. (Sriram, V. "P.R. Thilagam: A Tiruvarur Kuravanji." *Sruti*. Issue. 255. (December, 2005): pp. 25-39.
8. *Ibid.*
9. *Pudukkottai State Inscription* (*P.S.I.*). No. 152.
10. Mahalingam, T.V. *South Indian Polity*. Madras: University of Madras, 1955: p. 336.
11. *Tirumala Tirupati Devasthanam Inscriptions*. (*T.T.D.E.S.*). Vol. II: p. 259.
12. *Census of India, 1901, Travancore*. N, Subramhanya Aiyar. Vol. XXVI. Part. 1. Trivandrum: Malabar Mail Press, 1903: p. 276.
13. *P.S.I.* No. 814. p. 553.
14. *A.R.I.E.* of 1912. No. 211.
15. *A.R.I.E.* of 1916. No. 345.
16. *P.S.I.* No. 553.
17. *P.S.I.* No. 533.
18. *A.R.I.E.* of 1912. No. 211.
19. Vellaivaranan, Ka. *Panniruthirumurai Varalaru* (The History of Twelve Tirumurai) (in Tamil). Vol. I, Annamalai Nagar: Annamalai University, Rpt. 1994: pp. 280-283.
20. Sadasivan, K. *Devadasi System in Medieval Tamilakam*. Trivandrum: CBH Publications, 1993: p. 149.
21. *Travancore Archeological Series* (*T.A.S*). Vol. VI: 14 20.
22. *Annual Report for 1921*. part. II. paragraph no. 33.
23. Vellaivaranan, Ka. Rpt. 1994. *Op.cit.*, pp. 280-321.
24. *A.R.I.E.* of 1925. No. 411.
25. *A.R.I.E.* of 1912. No. 147.
26. *A.R.I.E.* 1929-30. No. 269.
27. *South Indian Temple Inscription* (*S.I.T.I.*). Vol. X. No. 249.
28. *S.I.I.* Vol. XIX. No. 263.
29. *I.A.* Vol. XLIII. 1914. p. 10.

30. *A.R.I.E.* of 1916. No. 223.
31. *A.R.I.E.* of 1936-37. No. 49.
32. Vellaivaranan, Ka. Rpt. 1994. *Op.cit.*, p. 306.
33. *Epigraphia Indica*. Vol. V. No. 17.
34. *T.A.S.* Vol. I. p. 9.
35. *T.A.S.* 1924. Vol. V. Part. II. *Op.cit.*, p. 106.
36. *A.R.I.E.* of 1925. No. 76.
37. *Koil Ozhugu*. (Parthasarthi T.S. *The Koyil Olugu: History of the Srisangam Temple*. Tirupati: Tirumala Tirupali Devesthanam, 1954: pp. 7-8.)
38. Swaminathan, S. *The Early Cholas History, Art and Culture*. Delhi: Sharada Publicating House, 1998: p. 127.
39. *South Indian Inscriptions* (*S.I.I.*). Vol. III. Parts iii and iv. No. 143.
40. Tiruvakkarai Chandramulisvara temple is situated in Tiruvakkarai, Viluppuram taluk, South Arcot district.
41. *S.I.I.* Vol. XVII. No. 204.
42. Civacuppiramaniyan, A. *Tamizhakattil Atimaimurai* (Monograph of Slavery in Tamil Nadu) (in Tamil). Chennai: Kalachuvadu Pathppagam, 2005 (Rpt. 2010): p. 38.
43. Yasodadevi, V."The History of the Andhra Country (1000 A.D. to 1500)." *Journal of the Andhra Historical Research Society* XXVI, Parts. 1-4. (July, 1960-April, 1961): p. 27.
44. *S.I.I.* Vol. IV. No. 558.
45. *A.R.I.E.* of 1916. No. 564.
46. *Ibid.*
47. *P.S.I.* No. 793. pp. 541-542.
48. *S.I.I.* Vol. II. Part. 3. No. 66.
49. *A.R.I.E.* of 1922. No. 594.
50. *S.I.I.* Vol. XII. No. 114.
51. *A.R.I.E.* of 1926. No. 64.
52. *A.R.E.*, of 1906. No. 153.
53. *A.R.I.E.* of 1936-37. No. 149A.
54. *A.R.I.E.* of 1921. No. 230.
55. *A.R.I.E.* of 1913. No. 80.
56. *A.R.I.E.* of 1904. No. 499.
57. *A.R.I.E.* of 1913. No. 80.
58. *A.R.I.E.* of 1926. No. 94.
59. *Madras Epigraphy Report (M.E.R.)* of 1911. No. 296.
60. *A.R.I.E.* of 1913. No. 80.
61. Nagaswamy, R. *Studies in Ancient Tamil Law and Society*. Madras: The Institute of Epigraphy and Tamilnadu State Department of Archaeology, 1978: p. 64.
62. Sadasivan, K. 1993. *Op.cit.*, p. 82.
63. *Koyil Ozhugu*. *Op.cit.*, pp. 95-96.

64. Krishnamurthi, S.R. *A Study on the Cultural Developments in the Chola Period*. Annamalai Nagar: Annamalai University, 1966: p. 73.
65. *A.R.I.E.* of 1912. No. 274.
66. *A.R.I.E.* of 1938-39. No. 338.
67. Pillai, K.K. 1953. *Op.cit.*, p. 258.
68. Viraraghavacharya, T.K.T. *History of Tirupati: The Thiruvengadam Temple*. Vol. II. Tirupati: Tirumala Tirupati Devasthanams, 1954: p. 678.
69. Murray, Hugh. *The Travels of Marco Polo*. Edinburgh: Oliver and Boyd, 1847: p. 294.
70. Pillai, K.K. 1953. *Op.cit.*, p. 284.
71. Dubois, Abbe J.A. *A Description of the Character, Manner and Customs of the People of India*. Madras: J. Higginbotham, 1862: p. 294.
72. Appadurai, Arjun. *Worship and Conflict under Colonial Rule*. New Delhi: Orient Longman,1981: p. 22.
73. Pande, Rekha. 2006. *Op.cit.*, p. 498.
74. *P.S.I.* No. 162.
75. *S.I.I.* Vol. XIV. No. 132.
76. *A.R.I.E.* of 1906. No. 248.
77. *Koyil Ozhugu*. pp. 95-96..
78. *T.A.S.* Vol. V. pt. 1. No. 24.
79. *S.I.I.* Vol. VII. No. 458. and *A.R.I.E.* of 1912. No. 122.
80. *S.I.I.* Vol. VII. No. 485.
81. *A.R.I.E.* of 1916. No. 587.
82. Appadorai, A. *Economic Conditions in Southern India (1000-1500 A.D.)*. Madras: University of Madras, 1936 (Rpt. 1990). Vol. II. pp. 319-320.
83. *S.I.T.I.* Vol. I. No. 525.
84. *A.R.I.E.* of 1917. No. 519.
85. *S.I.T.I.* Vol. I. No. 525.
86. *Manickkavacakar's Tiruvacagam*. Section no. 5. l. 14.
87. Prasad, Awadh Kishore. "Functions and Gradations of Devadasis," *The Proceedings of the Indian History Congress* 45th session. Annamalai Nagar: Annamalai University (1985): p. 192.
88. *Tiruvempavai*. 10: 6.
89. *T.A.S.* Vol. XII. p. 192.
90. *A.R.I.E.* 1950-51. No. 363.
91. *Annual Report of South Indian Epigraphy* (*A.R.S.I.E.*). 1910. No. B. 313.
92. Yasodadevi, V. July, 1960-April, 1961. *Op.cit.*, p. 27.
93. *Ibid.*
94. Varadachari, K.C. *Alvars of South India*. Bombay: Bharatiya Vidya Bhavan, 1966 (Rpt. 1970): p. 80ff.
95. *S.I.I.* Vol. III. No. 93.
96. *S.I.I.* Vol. IV. No. 1384.
97. *A.R.I.E.* of 1916. No. 578.

98. *A.R.S.I.E.*, 1910. Nos. B. 312 and B. 313.
99. *A.R.S.I.E.*, 1909. No. B. 187.
100. *S.I.I.* Vol. X. No. 80.
101. *T.A.S.* Vol. V. No. 24.
102. *T.A.S.* Vol. V. No. 24.
103. *S.I.I.* Vol. IV. No. 1288.
104. *A.R.S.I.E.*, 1918. No. B. 519.
105. *Tiruvorri oorudaiya nayanarku ner kuru salaikku nerkurak konduvitta periyanachchiyaiyum ival makal mariyaiyum-ival thankai kavuththal viyaiyum ival Thanthai thirundaiyum ival thankai vadukalviyaiyum akap per ivaraiyum innayanar nerkuru salaikku ivarkalum ivvazhiyil ullarum santhirathiththavarai nerkuruvathavak kondu silalekai pannik kuduththen.* (*Kalvettu* (Inscription) (in Tamil). January, 1997. No. 4. p. 35.)
106. Champakalakshmi, R. *Religion, Tradition and Ideology: Pre-Colonial South India.* New Delhi: Oxford University Press, 2011: p. 67.
107. Singh, A.K. *Devadasis System in Ancient India.* Delhi: H.K. Publishers and Distributors, 1990: p. 24.
108. *T.A.S.* Vol. VI. pp. 14-20. Elisaivallabhi.
109. Ramachendrier, C. *Collection of the Decisions of the High Courts and the Privy Council on the Law of Succession, Maintenance and C (Applicable to Dancing Girls and their issues, Prostitutes not belonging to Dancing Girls' Community, Illegitimate Sons and Bastards and Illatom Affiliation up to December 1891.).* Madras: Scottish Press, 1892: p. ii.
110. Singh, A.K. 1990. *Op.cit.,* p. 12.
111. *Campantar Tevaram.* Part. 1. Tiruviyalur. 1.13. Song no. 130.
112. Pillai, K.K. 1953. *Op.cit.,* p. 284.
113. Kalarani, R. *Bharatanatyam in Tamilnadu (After A.D. 1200).* Madurai: J.J. Publications, 2004: p. 32.
114. *S.I.I.* Vol. III. Part. iv. No. 209.
115. *S.I.I.* Vol. VII. No. 11.
116. *A.R.I.E.* of 1912. No. 120.
117. *A.R.I.E.* of 1909. No. 370.
118. *T.T.D.E.S.* Vol. II. No. 86.
119. Pillai, K. K. 1953. *Op.cit.,* p. 234.
120. *A.R.I.E.* 1950-51. No. 363.
121. *S.I.I.* Vol. XIV. No. 128.
122. *S.I.I.* Vol. XIV. No. 128. The words *devaradiyar* and *kotti* may also be taken in the sense of dancing girls.
123. *S.I.I.* Vol. XIV. No. 210.
124. *S.I.I.* Vol. XII. No. 114.
125. *A.R.I.E.* of 1912. No. 211.
126. One *veli* of land is equal to 26,755 square meters.
127. This village is referred to earlier, was called Uravakkinallur.
128. *M.E.R. (1906-1907)*: 68, inscr. 165.

129. Sadasivan, K. 1993. *Op.cit.*, p. 8.
130. Williams, Monier. *Religious Thought and Life in India*. Part. 1. London: John Murray, 1885: p. 451.
131. Altekar, A.S. *The Position of Women in Hindu Civilisation*. Delhi: Motilal Banarsidass, 1959. (Rpt. 1983): pp. 182-183.
132. *A.R.I.E.* of 1909. No. 370.
133. Pillai, K.K. 1953. *Op.cit.*, p. 234.
134. *S.I.I.* Vol. XIV. No. 128.
135. *Ibid.*, The words *devaradiyar* and *kotti* may also be taken in the sense of dancing girls.
136. *S.I.I.* Vol. III. Part. iv. No. 209.
137. *S.I.I.* Vol. III. Part. iv. No. 210.
138. *S.I.I.*, Vol. VII. No. 11; *A.R.I.E.* of 1923. No. 396.
139. *A.R.I.E.* of 1912. No. 120.
140. Sadasivan, K. 1993. *Op.cit.*, p. 93.
141. *A.R.I.E.* of 1912. No. 122.
142. *A.R.I.E.* of 1912. No. 211.
143. *S.I.I.* Vol. III. Part. iii. No.184. and No.190. pp. 361, 366-367.
144. *P.S.I.* No. 870. p. 580.
145. *A.R.I.E.* of 1920. No. 467.; *A.R.I.E.* of 1929-30. No. 109.
146. *A.R.I.E.* of 1930-31. No. 207.; *S.I.T.I.* Vol. II. No. 1009.
147. *A.R.I.E.* of 1912. No. 153.
148. *P.S.I.* No. 176.; IA. Vol. XIII. (1884). p. 170.
149. *S.I.I.* Vol. II. Part. iii. No. 66.
150. *P.S.I.* No. 710. p. 490.
151. *S.I.I.* Vol. XII. No. 114.
152. *P.S.I.* No. 814. p. 553.
153. *A.R.I.E.* of 1917. No. 508.
154. *S.I.I.* Vol. II. Part. iii. No. 66.
155. *Epigraphia Indica*. Vol. V. No. 17.
156. *A.R.I.E.* of 1910. No. 289.; *Annual Reports* for 1911. part. II. paragraph no. 66.
157. *A.R.I.E.* of 1910. No. 292.
158. *A.R.I.E.* of 1921. No. 356
159. *P.S.I.* No. 817. pp. 554-555.
160. *Epigraphia Carnatica*. Vol. V. Belur 58.
161. *S.I.I.* Vol. XVII. No. 393.
162. *P.S.I.* No. 710. p. 490.
163. *S.I.I.* Vol. X. No. 77.
164. *A.R.I.E.* of 1912. No. 211.
165. *P.S.I.* No. 710. pp. 490, 496-497.
166. *P.S.I.* No. 718.
167. *A.R.I.E.* of 1937-38. No. 489.

168. *A.R.I.E.* of 1909. No. 370; *S.I.I.* Vol. V. No. 418.
169. *S.I.I.* Vol. III. Part. iii. No. 92. p. 224; Natural cave at Vidal (No. 84 of 1908).
170. *T.A.S.* Vol. V. No. 24.
171. *T.A.S.* Vol. IV. No. 21.
172. *M.E.R. (1912)*: inscr. 137.
173. Sreedhara Menon, A. *Cultural heritage of Kerala*. Kottayam: D.C. Books, 1978 (Rpt. 2008): p. 243.
174. *T.T.D.E.S.* Vol. II. No. 135.
175. *A.R.I.E.* of 1919. No. 229.
176. *A.R.I.E.* of 1938-39. No. 338.
177. *A.R.I.E.* of 1931-32. No. 61; *S.I.I.* Vol. IV. No. 133.
178. *S.I.I.* Vol. XVII. No. 220. *A.R.E.* of 1904. No. 198.
179. *A.R.I.E.* of 1921. No, 490.
180. *S.I.I.* Vol. III. Part. iii. No. 151A.
181. *S.I.T.I.* Vol. I. No. 29.
182. *A.R.I.E.* of 1901. No. 250.
183. *P.S.I.* No. 686. p. 475.
184. *S.I.I.* Vol. VIII. No. 169.
185. *A.R.I.E.* of 1919. No. 284.
186. Pillai, K.K. 1953. *Op.cit.,* pp. 141-142.
187. *T.T.D.E.S.* Vol. IV. No. 21.
188. *T.T.D.E.S.* Vol. II. No. 86.
189. *S.I.I.* Vo. XIII. No. 88.
190. *A.R.I.E.* of 1919. No. 265.
191. *T.T.D.E.S.* Vol. II. No. 134.
192. Perumal, A.K. *Thenkumariyin Kadhai* (in Tamil). (History of Kanyakumari). Chennai: United Writers, December, 2003: p. 234.
193. *P.S.I.* No. 867. pp. 578-579.
194. *A.R.I.E.* of 1928-29. No. 100.
195. *A.R.I.E.* of 1916. No. 345.
196. Marglin, Frederique Apffel. *Wives of the God-King: The Rituals of the Devadasis of Puri*. Delhi: Oxford University Press, 1985: p. 11.
197. Sundara Pandiya and Vira Pandiya were sons of Maravarma Kulasekara, the prominent later Pandiya king.
198. Ala-ud-din Khilji was the Sultan of Delhi.
199. Jaffer, S.M. *Some Cultural Aspects of Muslim Rule in India*. Delhi, 1972: p. 184.
200. Sadasivan, K. 1993. *Op.cit.,* p. 111.
201. Pillai, K.K. *Thamizhaga Varalaru Makkalum Panpadum* (in Tamil). Chennai: International Institute of Tamil Studies, 2009: p. 387.
202. Kesavacharya, Namburi. "Acharyasuktimuktavali". In S. Krishnaswami Ayyangar. Ed. *Sources of the Vijayanagar History*. Madras: University of Madras, 1919: p. 40.

203. *Ibid.* p. 41.
204. *A.R.I.E.* of 1916. No. 64.
205. Taylor, William. *Oriental Historical Manuscripts*. Vol. I. Madras: Charles Josian Taylor, 1835: p. 35.
206. Krishnaswami Ayyangar, S. Ed. *Sources of the Vijayanagar History*. Madras: University of Madras, 1919: p. 2.
207. Champakalakshmi, R. 2011. *Op.cit.*, p. 35.
208. *Ibid.*
209. *A.R.I.E.* of 1916. No. 64.
210. *A.R.I.E.* of 1912. No. 208.
211. *A.R.I.E.* of 1912. No. 212.
212. *A.R.I.E.* of 1912. No. 195.
213. *Annual Reports* for 1916. part. II. paragraph no. 33.
214. Krishnaswami, A. *The Tamil Country under Vijayanagar*. Annamalai Nagar: The Annamalai University, 1964: p. 49.
215. *A.R.I.E.* of 1903. No. 13.
216. *S.I.T.I.* Vol. I. No. 248.
217. *A.R.I.E.* of 1912. No. 401.
218. *A.R.I.E.* of 1916. No. 565.
219. *P.S.I.* No. 162.
220. *Epigraphia Indica*. Vol. XV. No. 6f.
221. *S.I.I.* Vol. X. No. 75cf.
222. *A.R.I.E.* of 1912. No. 212.
223. *S.I.T.I.* Vol. I. No. 525. p. 513.
224. *S.I.I.* Vol. IV. No. 318.
225. *Tamil Nadu Epigraphy*. 1972. Tamaraipakkam Inscription. No. 1.
226. Nagaswamy, R. 1978. *Op.cit.*, p. 65.
227. *A.R.I.E.* of 1927. No. 297. *Annual Reports* for 1927. part. II. paragraph no. 30.
228. *tiruvilaicchinaiyumittuch-chandradittavarai nerkkuruvadak kondu*. (*S.I.I.* Vol. VIII. No. 396.)
229. Sadasivan, K. 1993. *Op.cit.*, p. 48.
230. *A.R.I.E.* of 1922. No. 141; *Annual Reports* for 1921-22. part. II. Paragraph No. 19.; *A.R.I.E.* of 1921. No. 543.
231. *A.R.I.E.* of 1921. No. 543.
232. Sadasivan, K. 1993. *Op.cit.*, p. 50.
233. *A.R.I.E.* of 1921. No. 230. *Annual Reports* for 1921-22. part. II. paragraph no. 9.
234. Soundara Rajan. K.V. *The Art of South India: Tamilnadu and Kerala*. Delhi: Sundeep Prakashan, 1978: p. 18.
235. *pun pulavazhiyadaiththu arakkilanchinai seithu*. *Nalayira Divya Prapandam*. Tirumazhichai Alvar's Tirucchanda Viruththam. Song no. 76. L. 1.
236. *P.S.I.* No. 814. p. 553.
237. *A.R.I.E.* of 1921. No. 230.

238. *P.S.I.* No. 904. pp. 595-596.
239. Haafner, Jacob. *Reize in eenen Palanquim; of Lotgevallen en Merkwaardige Aanteekeningen op eene Reize langs de Kusten Orixa en Chroromandel* (in Dutch). Vol. I. Amsterdam: Johannes Allart, 1808: pp. 194-225.
240. Valentyn, Francois. *Oud en Nieuw Oost-Indien* (Old and New East India) (in Dutch). Vol. 5. Dordrecht and Amsterdam: Joannes van Braam and Gerard Onder den Linden, 1726: p. 54.
241. Bor, Joep. "Mamia, Ammani and Other Bayaderes: Europe's Portrayal of India's Temple Dancers." In Davesh Soneji. Ed. *Bharathanatyam: A Reader*. New Delhi: Oxford University Press, 2010: pp. 16-17.
242. *Ibid.*, pp. 17-18.
243. Rogerius, Abraham. *De Open-Deure tot het Verborgen Heydendom* (The Doors an Open to the Hidden Heathendom) (in Dutch). Ed. W. Caland. 's-Gravenhage: M. Nijhoff, 1651 (Rpt. 1915): p. 125.
244. *Ibid.*
245. *Ibid.*
246. Bor, Joep. 2010. *Op.cit.*, p. 17.
247. Bernier, Francois. *Travels in the Mogul Empire A.D. 1656-1668*. Archibald Constable. Tr. and V.A. Smith. Revised. London: Oxford University Press, 1916: p. 305.
248. Bor, Joep. 2010. *Op.cit.*, p. 15.
249. Sewell, Robert. 1982. *Op.cit.*, p. 241.
250. Sewell, Robert. *A Forgotten Empire (Vijayanagar)*. New Delhi: Asian Educational Service, 1982: p. 274.
251. *Ibid.*, p. 274.
252. *Ibid.*, p. 242.
253. *Ibid.*
254. *Malabarishes Heidenthum* was written in 1711.
255. The document was written in 1711 but it was published in 1926.
256. Caland, W. *Ziegenbalg's Malabarishes Heidenthum*. Amsterdam: Koninklijke Akademie van Wetenschappen, 1926: pp. 131-132.
257. *Ibid.*, pp. 228-229.
258. *Ibid.*, p. 229.
259. Sadasivan, K. 1993. *Op.cit.*, p. 150.
260. *Ibid.*, pp. 150-151.
261. *Ibid.*
262. *Ibid.*
263. *Abithana Chintamani: Tamil Kalaikazhanjiyam* (*Abithana Chintamani*: An Encyclopedia of Tamil Language) (in Tamil). A. Singaravelu Mudaliyar and A. Sivaprakasa Mudaliyar. Comp. Chennai: Seethai Pathippakam, 1899 (Rpt. 2004): pp. 260-261.
264. *aaraayum muththamil arruril somi azhakukandu; naaraa yanannedu maal aaki naan antha naan mukanum; orraa yirammadal oornthaanvil maaran uru alinthaan; per aana vaanavar konumkan aayiram perranane.* (Kalamekam. *Thanippadal Thirattu*. Song No. 46.)

265. *kooththaal vizhikal nedum koor velaam; kooththal than; muththaal vilikal muluneelam; - muththaal than; aaththaal vilikal aravintham; aaththaal than; aaththal vilikal irandu ambu.* (Kalamekam. *Thanippadal Thirattu.* Song no. 48.)
266. *murraatha kaanjiyinum mullaiyinum paalaiyinum; kaarraan pin chenra karunaimaal- perraan than; aalaip pathithaar alakaththi yatku ayanaar; velaip pathiththaar vizhi.* (Kalamekam. *Thanippadal Thirattu.* Song no. 181.)
267. *aintha thanankal irandumiru paakarkaai; vaainthaidai chekkuulakkai maaththirame- theinthakuzhal; mukkazhamchik kumpidikkum muthevi yaalkamalaik; kukkalichchik kumkalachchikku.* (Kalamekam. *Thanippadal Thirattu.* Song no. 38.)
268. *yemiraa ori enpaal enthundi vasthi enpaal; thaam iraach chonna ellaam thalaikadai therinthathu illai; pom irach choolum cholai poru kondaith thimmi kaiyil; naam irap patta padu naman kaiyil padu thane!.* (Kalamekam. *Thanippadal Thirattu.* Song no. 205.)
269. *vaazhththu thirunaakai vaaku aana thevadiyaal; paazhnththa kural eduththup paadinaal- nerruk; kazhuthaiketta vannaankan ten kanden enru; pazhuthai eduththu odivanthan paar.* (Kalamekam. *Thanippadal Thirattu.* Song no. 40.)
270. *Thanippadal Thirattu* is the collection of the poems of 15th century poet called Kalamekam.
271. *kollukaiyaal neeril kulikkaiyaal mel erik; killukaiyaal kattik kidakkaiyaal-thellu pagalch; chennra varai venra thirumalairaa yan varaiyil; verrilaiyum vesai aame.* (Kalamekam. *Thanippadal Thirattu.* Song no. 141.)
272. *paarath thalaivirikkum pannaadai melchurrum; chora ilaneer chumanthiruk-kum- nere mel; eri irankave inpamaam thennaimaram; koorum kanikai enre kol.* (Kalamekam. *Thanippadal Thirattu.* Song no. 140.)
273. *kattith thaluvuvathalaal kaalsera eruthalaal; ettip pannadai iluththalaal-muttap poi; aasaivaaik kallai arunthuthalaal appanaiyum; vesai enal aame virainthu.* (Kalamekam. *Thanippadal Thirattu.* Song no. 139.)
274. *ottam kadiyathaal ullavarai mevuthalaal; chettai evaridaththum seithalaal-naattamudan; kaaththirathththil kuttiyurak kattuthalaal thettuthalaal; koothiyarkku ner aam kuranku.* (Kalamekam. *Thanippadal Thirattu.* Song no. 143.)
275. Sadasivan, K. 1993. *Op.cit.*, p. 151.
276. *Ibid.*
277. Nagasamy, R. "Introduction." In *Muvaraiyan Virali Vitu Tutu*. Mithilaippattich Chitrampala Kavirayar. Chennai: Mahamahopaththiyaya Dr. U.Ve. Saminathaiyer Library, 1982: p. I.
278. Murugesan, C.S. *Varalaatril Devadasikal* (Devadasis in History) (in Tamil). Chennai: Kurinji, 2009: pp. 253-256.
279. *Muvaraiyan Virali Vitu Tutu*. Mithilaippattich Chitrampala Kavirayar. Chennai: Mahamahopaththiyaya Dr. U.Ve. Saminathaiyer Library, 1982.
280. *...senjchol; kalai ellam karruk kidanthal sankithu, nilalellam saathiththuk ninral- thulaiyaap; paravitham aththanaiyum paarththal.* (*Ibid.*, p. xxv.)
281. *Sethupathi Virali Vitu Tutu*. Sadhavathanam Saravanap Perumal Kavirayar. Karaikkudi: Ilakkiayap Pathippakam, 1947.

282. *Ibid.*, pp. v-vi.
283. *makanaka mandapathil vanthunirkum nirkum pothu kanden!; mohanamuth thennum orumoikulazhai- ekanuthal; vilazhakum painthavizhi vel azhakum kaal azhakum; sol azhakum malaiitta thol azhakum- pal azhakum; kai azhakum marpazhakum kathazhakum mookkazhakum mei azhakum kandavudan meimaranthen.* (*Ibid.*, p. ix.)
284. *sandalikku itta thanaththaiyellam ippadi orr; mandapaththaik kattiththaan vaiththoma?.* (*Ibid.*, p. xii.)
285. *selvattak kannanunth thevadimai thettuvenil; Melvattap penkalukku mirinaal: thevadimai thettunil-thevadiyar sampaththiyaththil, mikach chirantha penkalaiyum minchinaal.* (*Ibid.*, p. 24.)
286. *Nannavur Sangamechuvara Svami Vedhanayaki Amman peril virali vitu tutu.* Srirangam: SriVani Vilasa Achakam, 1969.
287. *malai koduththen; soolai vankinen; pattu koduththen; (santhu santhaik) kattu vankinen; moham koduththen; moham vankinen. Ibid.*, p. 10.
288. *Kulappa Nayakkan Virali Vitu Tutu*. n.d. Supradeepak Kavirayar. Karaikkudi: South India Press. (Murugesan, C.S. 2009. *Op.cit.*, pp. 273-288.)

Chapter - 4

The Devadasi System: The Colonial Period

This particular chapter discusses the changes in the devadasi institution during the colonial intervention and the course of nation building. The process of colonisation made a huge impact on the colonised countries. The period, eighteenth to early twentieth century witnessed a rift between traditionalism and modernity. The European renaissance and industrial revolution resulted in colonial power establishing colonies around the world. The European culture encountered the traditional Indian subcontinent. The dominant ideologies of the colonial state and the brahmanical social order discriminated and excluded the natives. The new social and economic changes questioned the existing social customs and practices of the local people. The introduction of the Christian missionaries criticised the superstitiousness of the brahmanical religion and practices. The monopoly of the colonial state resulted in the identity crisis among the colonised. The new market economy introduced new forms of production. It created a new power relationships. The newly emerged elites placed them in an important position in the colonial state.[1] The colonial modernity questioned the indigenous customs and social settings. It resulted a kind of thirst of historicity among the people. The traditional Indians started to search their identities and initiated the move of glorification of their ancient past. The orientalism provided a supportive base for it.

The institution of devadasi was not a discrete entity and it fused with the political economy of the society. The life of devadasi constantly shuttled according to the policies of state. The new social order questioned the place of women. The concepts such as morality, chastity, purity and sin became important denominators for the good women. This construction and reconstruction process questioned the existence of the devadasihood. The transition from the "sacred" to "secular" realm created a tension. The ritualistic roles of devadasi was overshadowed with the performing abilities. Their artistic qualities turn out to be popular. The colonial administrators recorded the public performances as *nautch* (dance). Generally, the *nautch* was performed by courtesans and devadasis. In South India, devadasis occupied a prominent position in the *nautch* performances. During the nineteenth century, "the sacred" identity of devadasis was lost and their *nautch* became the devadasi phenomena. Their artistic qualities became an iconic identity for them. Edgar Thurston in his book *The Caste and Tribes in Southern India* mentioned that *dasis* or devadasis as dancing girls who attached to the Tamil temples and who subsisted by dancing and music.[2] During the colonial period, the condition of devadasi was becoming critical and they were treated as prostitutes.

Devadasi in the Maratha court

The fall of Vijayanagar led the emergence of the new regional powers that were established on the basis of Madurai, Thanjavur and Chenji under Nayaka. During the reign of Nayaka, the boundaries between courtesans and temple women had become indistinguishable. It collapsed the homogenous identity of devadasihood.[3] Devadasis were assigned to a new role as an artist who performed both at the temple and court. Usually these women were allowed to be a mistress, wife, or queen at the Nayaka court.[4] The scattered and fragmentary references of the temple women, court dancers, and other public women only conjoined in the reign of Nayakas and following that the independent roles fully collapsed the identity of the devadasi.[5] In seventeenth century, Venkoji alias Ekoji-I (1676), the elder brother of Shivaji-I initiated the Maratha power in Thanjavur. The Maratha invasion brought the political changes in South India especially in the fertile region of Cauveri. The pan-Hindu ideas of Marathas continued the earlier practices.

The Thanjavur Maratha kings patronised music, dance and drama tradition. The Marathas were well-trained in art and were instrumental in the evolution of the different kinds of art forms. The period witnessed the fusion of western musical instrument in the Indian musical tradition such as harp. Thanjavur was considered as a seat of music and fine arts in dance and drama.[6] There are several records of Marathas that referred to the performance of *natyam* (dance) as *abinayam, adal, nadagam, natyam, baratham, sadhir* and *kelikkai*.[7] The temple dancers started to perform in the royal court, especially in the court of Serfoji II (1798-1832).[8] During the Maratha period, the dance of devadasi used to be called as *sadhir-attam* instead of *dasi-attam*. The Marathi word *sadhar* meant durbar (court). The dance which performed in the *sadhar* called *sadhar-attam* and later it became *sadhir-attam*.[9] The dance performances were held in dance auditorium in the palace, drama house, stages in temples, open auditorium, *sadhar* building in music *mahal, nattuvan chavadi* and stages of *kuravanchi*.[10] These dance performances were denoted as *sadhir* or *kelikkai* (enjoyment).[11] Hari Krishnan mentioned that the systemised and organised dance performance of devadasi dance forms was *sadhir kacheri*.[12]

The *sadhir* and *kacheri* were held in the palace auditoriums, drama houses, stages in temples, open auditoriums, *sadhir* building, *nattuvan chavadi* and music *mahal.*

There is a lot of evidence showing that the devadasi's performed in the palace. The official record detailed the participation of the devadasi in the *sadhir* and *kelikkai* (entertainment) performances in the palaces.[13] Usually the dance performance of *dasis* occurred in *pournami* (full moon) days in the palace. The Modi records mentioned the performance of dancing girls in the royal court on *pournami.*[14] Devadasi regularly performed in the palace of Amarasimmar in Tiruvidaimarudur.[15] Usually, the songs of Sahaji II, the Maratha king were performed with musical notes by dancers in the palace. The *Pancha Ratnap Pirabandam* and *Thyagaraja Vinotha Chitrap Pirabandam* mentioned about dance performance of the devadasis in front of Lord Siva.[16] Maratha court poets such as Vasudevakavi, Ramabharathy, Kirirajakavi and Sethraiyar composed songs in different languages in Tamil, Telugu and Sanskrit for the dance performance.[17] In 1801, devadasis Periya and Unnamalai did their performance in the Maratha court.[18] The Modi record stated the performance of dancing girls in the royal court and for that they received twenty three *cakrams* and five *panams.*[19] At the requisition made by ten dancing girls of Venugopalasami temple, twenty five *cakrams* were given to these *dasis* and the two dancing girls who had performed in the court on pournami were given five *cakrams.*[20]

During the Maratha period devadasis public appearance became visible. They performed sadhir on special occasions in temple, palace and other public places. The programs were regularly held during the festivals such as *Vinayakar sadhurthi*, *navrathiri*, *Saraswathi puja* and *dipawali* and other special occasions like government functions and marriages. According to Modi document, the *sadhir* performance on the *Navarathiri* festival was refereed as *navarathiri sadhir.*[21] *Tiruvidaimarudur Nondi Nadakam* of Ananda Bharathi Iyangar (1786-1864) referred the public appearance of the temple dancers and their different dance forms. The work detailed the temple dancers and their different *padas* (dance forms). It stated that the performance of the temple girls in the Tiruvudaimarudur *pusam* festival.[22] On *Saraswathi puja*, a special performance was done by *dasis* of Pancanada temple of Tiruvaiyar and the *melakkarurs* were given *inam* of five *cakrams.*[23] In 1797, during the festival of Kaman[24], several artists were invited from Tiruvaiyar, Tiruvarur, Kumbeshvara temple of Kumbakonam. They performed *sarangapani* and *lavani.*[25] Devadasis and *melakkurars* of Panchadiswara Sami temple of Tiruvaiyar were getting five chakras as *inam* for their temple service[26] and another record stated that the temple of Tiruvaiyar had eighty temple dancing girls.[27] The official records mention that in the marriage engagement of Tulaja II, four thousand six hundred and eighteen *cakrams* was spent[28] and *sadhir* and *kelikkai* dance performances were held in a palace.[29]

Marathas systematised the devadasi system. Tulaja II brought Mahadeva Annavi, a prominent *nattuvanar* from Tirunelveli and Subbaraya *odhuvar*[30] to Thanjavur to strengthen the art of dance. Tulaja II gifted a big house in upper-street and ten *veli* land to Mahadeva Annavi.[31] Subbaraya *odhuvar*, another *nattuvanar* also got a palace from Tulaja II.[32] In modern days, this place is popularly identified as *Nattuvachavadi*.[33] In the marriage of Rajashabayi (the daughter of Shivaji II), the Maratha king ordered that all the devadasis in the kingdom had to learn Hindustani and Carnatic dance. The Thanjavur Quartet[34] received an order and taught dance to all devadasis in the Maratha territory.[35] The dancing master or teacher received fifty to five hundred rupees with other presents for teaching a girl the usual dances. This generally was in the form of a contract which was greatly dependent on the wealth and position of the parties.[36]

The devadasis continued to have a predominant position in the medieval society. The seventeenth and eighteenth century historical evidences highlighted the decline in the position of the devadasi from the earlier state. During the seventeenth and eighteenth century period, devadasis were identified for their performing abilities. Interestingly, the Maratha documents did not carry the word 'devadasi'.[37] But the existence and engagement of devadasi was there. It was explicable through the documents which characterised the performance of women, their matrilineal identification and the association with a particular temple. A record mentioned that the five daughters of *dasi* Ramamani were given five *panams* and two *kalams* paddy each for every month by the court and they in turn were dedicated to Chidambaram temple by the palace authorities.[38] The record clearly stated that matrilineal claim and connection with a particular temple. According to Maratha documents and literature, Muthumangai, Muthupalani, Kaveri daughter Periya, Unnamalai, Chinnikkutty daughter Chellakkutty, Varalakshmi daughter Ramamani, Krishnaji daughter Nagarathnam, Kaveri daughter Krishna and Chandrap Piraba were the few *dasis* who performed in the Maratha palace.[39]

Muthupalani (1739-1790) was a prominent devadasi of the Maratha period. She was born in Thanjavur as a granddaughter of Thanjanayaki and daughter of Muthyalu. She was named after Lord Murukan of Palani temple. She was associated with the court of Pratapa Singh (1739-1763). Later she became a concubine of Pratapa Singh. The versatile Muthupalani was expert in Tamil, Sanskrit and Telugu. The semi-autobiographical poems *Radhika Santwanam* (Appeasing Radhika) revealed her ancestral lineages and her literary genius. The work used a different literary style called *saptapadam* which carried seven lines in a verse.[40] Her erotic poetry articulated the perspective of the courtesan's love and hinted the condition of the devadasi of the eighteenth century.[41] Bangalore Nagarathnam praised the work saying that it was filled with the elements of *shringara rasa* (erotic essence) which was written by a woman one who was born from the devadasi community.[42] The work highlighted the high status of the devadasi and also suggested that their intense knowledge in the fields of dance, music and literature.

The devadasi and the code of conduct

The Maratha court enforced a rigorous code of conduct for devadasi and the code severely punished the violators.[43] Usually, devadasi had to get an approval from the temple authority and government officials.[44] A temple street dancer from Kottai Ellaiyamman had a daughter named Krishna. She wanted to become devadasi but the temple authorities refused to admit her for more than two years. According to the source, she appealed to the king and pleaded for jobs at least in any other government departments for her livelihood.[45] In general, the girls were dedicated before their puberty.[46] The Maratha royal court and temple institutions purchased girls for temple service. The royal household purchased *dasi* Ramamani with five persons for Chidambaram temple. They were allowed to get five *panam* and two *kalam* of paddy per month.[47] In 1819, Muthambalpuram Kasivisvanathasami temple *dasi* Heera registered for usual ceremony called *pottu kattu*.[48] Few girls got some amount from the temple and they received monthly salary as well.[49] The particular temple devadasis were allowed to render their services to other temples.[50] Kamatchi Amman temple devadasi Kulivai (age tweleve) and Kambalayam (age ten) were transferred to the Rajarajesvara temple of Thanjavur.[51] The dancers were prevented to use palanquin except with prior permission from the court with royal order and seal. In general, there was a provision for the use of the palanquin only on two occasions such an occasion of the maiden performance and the case of illness. Devadasi Angu's daughter Nagu was asked to pay a fine of one *cakrams* and two *panams* as her bullock cart happened to cross the British resident's vehicle who had come to see the river in floods.[52]

In general, these women were distinguished from other women of their contemporary period and were respected for their learning and other accomplishments.[53] The Marathas made many rules and restrictions to control the sexuality of the devadasi. The records of the years 1820, 1846 and 1847 mentioned those rules and restrictions under the titles of *The Duties of the Dancers and Nattuvanars* and *Dress and Jewels which were restricted to the Dancers*.[54] These rules were strictly imposed on devadasi and *nattuvanar*. It distinguished devadasi from the other women. Devadasi should wake up at dawn and complete her bath and offer daily prayers. They were to perform a new peculiar service such as *kumbarati*, which was not evident from the earlier periods. Saskia Kersenboom-Story noted that the devadasis of Thanjavur court performed three significant functions such as accompanying king's processions, performing *kumbarati* and generated an auspicious atmosphere at the court by the performance of their song and dance.[55]Abbe Dubois noted that devadasi strictly performed the *arati* over idols in the morning and night, which avert the fatal influence of the looks and glances or evil minded persons.[56]

The God and king must be the theme of their dance performance. During the procession, devadasis were accompanied by *Miruthangam*, *Vina*, *Sarangi* and *Talam*. There was a kind of dress code that was followed. During *puja*, devadasis were permitted to wear shirt, sarees and *vijar* (*pyjama* kind of dresses). They were instructed to wear sarees with *sali* (kind of shawl). They were not allowed the embroidered blouses which were attached to the golden and *mahathabi* (silk) border. They were not allowed to use stitched grand tape (borders of saree, blouse, etc.) and *doomal* (handkerchief). Though they were allowed to use *dupatta*, but the colour should not be in white. The musicians who accompanied the procession were ordered to wear *muntasu* (a cloth which tied around forehead by men), shirts for their upper body, *nijar* for their waist and *dupatta* for their hip.[57]

Devadasi were restricted to put lengthy *kumkum* and *abir* on their forehead. They could not use the decorated silky ribbon for their hair decoration instead of that they were allowed to use golden ribbon. They must strictly avoid *salangai* (anklet), which was made out of pearl. They were restricted to use the *punki*, a musical instrument. They were instructed to use only *sisapani jarigai* (ornament) on their head but not the *nagathi jalar* (golden ornament for head). In some occasions they allowed to use *nagathi jalar* but strictly prohibited to use flowers on the occasions. They were permitted to use *kumkum*, golden ornaments and anklets during the processions only. Lemon was not kept for *pandi* (arrangement during the feasts). [58]

In spite of many restrictions, few devadasis, because of their personal relations had privileged position and enjoyed few concessions. The *Modi* records mentioned Sundari, a chief devadasi was one among them who was relieved from the restrictions which we mentioned earlier. She was a favourite of Serfoji II and she had a privilege to perform the first dance in the court during the celebration of four festivals of Gudyaca Padva, *Navarathiri*, *Dipawali* and *Sankranti*. She received fifteen rupees for every dance and twenty rupees on *Vijayadasami* festival along with a shawl. She was allowed to use palanquin.[59]

The *nautch* performances

In general, the devolution of royal cosmologies to lower levels of political organisation in South India occurred in the eighteenth century. The doctrine of lapses ended the independent rule of Marathas in Thanjavur to British in 1856. The newly emerged political power was settled in the entire region. The traditional pre-colonial governance was a complex one. The colonial officials had settled their power over the already functioning networks of the state and authority. The arrival of British and their impact was made on the temple institutions. Historically, the administration of the temple was state managed. The traditional kingship was much depended on the religious institution to retain their power structure. The colonisers understood the irrelevance of the temple patronage to sustain their imperial power over the natives. So they withdrew its support from the temple.

The withdrawal of patronage created a kind of vacuum. The Brahmin priests and other temple servants had to seek their new patrons. K.N. Panikkar pointed out the changing pattern of patronage structure in the eighteenth century.[60] The transformation of society required a new system of patronage. In the meantime, the introduction of the *zamindari* and *ryotwari* systems resulted in the creation of the new political lobby, who were frequently known as new elites in South Indian society. The traditional local chieftains were replaced by the new elites such as *zamindars*, *dubashis*[61] etc...The new elites functioned as mediator between the local and colonial administers. Gradually, they became powerful. Susan Neild-Basu detailed the influence of *dubashis* in Madras and addressed Madras as a city of *dubashis*.[62] The newly emerged new elites became new patrons to the powerful religious institutions. Interestingly, these new elites came from a different social background. Davesh Soneji mentioned that the Vellalar *dubashis* and other native elites such as *Smarta* Brahmins, Mudaliyars, Nayudus, and Chettiyars sponsored the performances of vocal music and poetry in their homes at the times of calendric festivals.[63]

The temples and other religious institutions came under the power of the local elites such as little kings, *zamindars*, *dubashis*, wealthy Brahmins and merchants. The local landlords started to patronise it by virtue of their socio-economic power. These patrons controlled and influenced devadasihood. It valued the character of the devadasis. The auspiciousness symbols of devadasi had become an important part of the ritual celebrations of non-royal elites.[64] In general, the 'Hindu' scriptures acknowledged the personal relationship of devadasi women with the worldly men. According to the 'Hindu' notion, any person or thing relating to a deity or temple is sacred, pure and incapable of polluting others. Usually, devadasi shared the domain of divinity in the living world. The body of devadasi was considered as 'pure'. The nobles believed that the association with that 'sacred body' was also sacred. There was no pollution in it. The powerful patriarch such as kings, little kings, *zamindars*, *dubashis*, wealthy Brahmins and merchants would like to become a patron of devadasi and desired to share the 'sacred body'.

The decline of temple economy led devadasi to lose temple patronage. Devadasi started to face the economic hardship and underwent through difficult circumstances. Largely, it led them in engaging in concubinage and prostitution to support their basic needs. Gradually, the activities of devadasi shifted from sacred to profane sphere. The sexual activities of devadasi were highlighted rather than their earlier ritual services. Most of the devadasis became an unskilled performer.[65] The temple staffs sent the daughters of devadasi to the palace after the vacancies filled in the temple.[66] Devadasi became the de facto concubines of the new elites. John Shortt, the Superintendent of Vaccination in the Madras Presidency mentioned that the devadasi were permitted to prostitute to any individual of an equal or superior caste to themselves and they lived as the professional of concubinage.[67] Frederique Apffel Marglin mentioned that originally the devadasis were chaste and associated with the temple only and not with the court. The later association with the court brought the custom of concubinage.[68] The disassociation from the ritual temples and association towards the worldly court would make them to depend on the new elites who were not necessarily patron of art would keep them as concubines. The Modern Rationalist weekly highlighted that the devadasis became an illegal life partner of the local elites who maintained their expenses by keeping them as their concubines.[69] Pamela G. Price mentioned the concubinage of devadasis in the royal court of Ramanathapuram.[70] The devadasis Ramamani and Kunjara were the concubines of the king of Ramanathapuram.[71] A *zamindar* in the North Arcot district maintained a large establishment of devadasi or *pagoda* (temple) dancers of Kalahasti temple who exclusively lived in concubinage. Their sons, who know no father, pass by the appellation of Nagari kunraradas, or sons of the country, and were slaves to the *zamindar*.[72]

The local elites funded and hosted professional performances of music and dance in the profane space. An account of the eighteenth century, Sanskrit work *Sarvadevavilasa* (sport of all divinities)[73] described the meeting of the patrons and scholars in the garden of Kalingaraya which was situated near Tiruvallikeni in modern Chennai. It stated that the patrons were the part of the management of the temples in Madras. The patrons came from social settings such as Brahmin and Mudaliar.[74] The devadasi one who associated with the particular religious institution came under the hold for the patronage. Venkatadri or Venkatachalam, the *dharmakarta* (temple trustee) of Tirunirmalai temple rebuilt the temple tower and car.[75] Devadasi became increasingly dependent.

Usually, devadasis participated in most of the palace ceremony such as coronation and festivals. But in the changed historical context, devadasis were made to dance in the private parties other than the ritualistic services which were regularly conducted in the temples and royal houses. During the colonial period, the private dance performance was called as *nautch* or *nautch* parties. So the dance performance of devadasi was also identified with that popular term *nautch*. John Shortt detailed in his account that the performance of dancing girls was well known and it was addressed as *nautch* or dance.[76] In general, the term *nautch* was a North Indian which was derived from Sanskrit word *natya* and it became a generic word for any dance.[77]

The dance performance of the traditional dancers was considered as a high honour to the guests. The service of devadasi was demanded outside the temple and huge amount was remunerated.[78] They travelled to different places to perform which was peculiar from the earlier custom of devadasihood. Here, the service was rendered to petty kings, *zamindars* and *dubashis* rather than the deities of the temple. Usually, devadasis were contracted for many days to perform in profane and the pleased masters were gifted with the valuables such as money, shawls, and other gold ornaments.[79] Arumuka Navalar (1822-1879), a Tamil scholar from Ilankai (modern Sri Lanka), referred the association of *nautch* with the kingdom of Ramanathapuram who had the practice of hiring devadasis to dance at major occasions.[80] Similarly, the *Madurai Mail* referred the *nautch* performance of the devadasi in the Ramanathapuram palace.[81]

The *nautch* was performed on the occasions of marriage, feast, and other public occasions. John Shortt noted that the *nautch* was a daily routine of little kings, *zamindars* and other new elites.[82] The expensive *nautch* performance was mostly held in either private houses or public assemblies.[83] John Shortt mentioned that the performance of the temple girls on the marriage occasions.[84] Ramachandram also referred the people's engagement with devadasi during the performing occasions such as festivals and marriages.[85] Ramachendrier, an assistant collector of Tiruchirappalli, mentioned that no marriage of a Hindu family of some position passes without the presence of dancing girls for four days.[86] E. Krishna Iyer, the Secretary of Music Academy of Madras, explained his experience that the rich families in Tirunelveli conducted a number of marriage functions in every summer. In those grandeur marriages were celebrated over four days and the wedding would not complete without music and dance performances. The *sadhir* performance was done by famous devadasi such as Muthurathnam Ammal.[87]

Often the dancing girls were also patronised by the Europeans. Throughout nineteenth century, the *nautch* performance was provided to English officials and elites.[88] After the settlement, British conceived India as their second home. They found themselves pitch forked overnight into unfamiliar and uncongenial surroundings. Biswanath Joardar pointed out that the separation from their kinsfolk of the British was racked and the dance performance of the native dancing girls provided a kind of entertainment. The *sahibs* and *memsahibs* were entertained to the *nautch* performance.[89] James Cordiner mentioned in his travel record that in the 1794, the an arrangement of the *nautch* programmes was a custom of the ladies and gentlemen for their friends who had visited their places.[90] Usually, Europeans compared the *nautch* performance with the European ballet.[91] Their taste towards the *nautch* was spectacle. Hunter in his journal highlighted the English presence in the *nautch* parties and used the word 'extraordinary' to note the performance of the dancing girls.[92] William Tennant pointed out the attendance of the *nautch* party was treated as a matter of courtesy.[93] From 1880 onwards, Europeans in India, especially the higher officials such as Viceroys, Governors, Collectors, District Magistrates and other law enforcing echelons used to attend the *nautch* parties.[94] The *nautch* performances were organised to honour the visit of the Prince of Wales (1875) and his son, Prince Albert Victor (1890) to British India.[95]

In general, the local elites, wealthy merchants and other eminent persons conducted the *nautch* parties. The *dharmakartas* in the temple regularly conducted *nautch* performance in the temple and invited high officials and friends for the occasions. *Sarvadevavilasa*, the Sanskrit work elucidated the relationship of *dharmakartas* and devadasi in the ninteenth century.[96] Devanayaka, a Sanskrit scholar was invited by the *dharmakarta* of Agastisvara temple in Nunkambakkam for the temple festival. A *dharmakarta* of Krishnan *koyil* in Coral Merchant Street was holding a performance on Sunday.[97] Vedachalam, a merchant, and *dharmakarta* in Madras invited his friends Kalingaraya, Sriranga and Devanayaka for the festival and the public performance of courtesans.[98] The work mentioned that there were three courtesans Narayani of Kumbakonam, Manga of Thanjavur, and Minakshi of Salem, who were renowned for their music and dance.[99] The document mentioned that Minakshi migrated to Madras to teach music to the daughters of *Pattanam* Subrahmanya Ayyar. These *dasis* were moved from their home town to Choolai, a place in modern Chennai. The patron, Vedachalam asked them to compose a *varna* (musical note) in Sanskrit and *kirtana* (psalmist) in Telugu on the god of Chidambaresvara and Agastisvara. The record highlighted the performance of an unknown Nachchiyar in the party of Venkatachalam. The work further documented the meeting of musicians and courtesans in the garden of Kalingaraya. The patrons such as Chinnaiah Mudaliar of Manali (patron of the Dikshitar's family) and Sundaresa or Sundara Mudaliar of Kovur (patron of Vina Kuppier) were also engaged in the gathering.[100]

Devadasi system and the colonial state

The following section is going to discuss about the various issues which were related to the institution of devadasi which happened under the direct control of British rule. The ninteenth century India was in the process of transformation in all spheres. The European Renaissance and industrial revolution widened the colonial power over its colonies. The European culture had encountered with Indian intelligentsia. The rapid growth of Christian missionaries highlighted the superstitious of the brahmanical religion and the colonial modernity questioned the existing Indian system. The orientalist substantiated the colonial conditioning. The new Indian society was looking for its glorious past. These changes influenced indigenous people to search their new purified social identities and also it encountered the problem of glorification of their past. The newly 'enlightened' Indian intelligentsia critiqued superstitiousness in the brahmanical religion. The reformers engaged in the abolition of sati, child marriage, purdah system, etc. The reformers did not question the religion but they worked for its revival. In general, these reforms did not happen in the lower level and also it did not question the widely existed practices such as caste. With regards women, freedom, education and single or unmarried life was completely denied to 'good' women in the country.[101] In the meantime, British authenticated the native practices and legalised some of the Indian beliefs. The brahmanical rituals became a Hindu code of conduct and it universalised to all natives.

The question of morality

Though the British were interested in attending the *nautch* parties, missionaries and few other colonial officials regularly voiced their opinion against the *nautch* performance and participating in it. They believed *nautch* and devadasi system were symbol of degradedness. The attending or witnessing *nautch* was considered as stigma. Kimiko Ohtani, an art historian, revealed the degradation of the standard dance performances and the expectation of the audiences transferred to view the beauty of dancers rather their performance.[102] P.N. Appusvami expressed his hesitation to watch the dance performance of devadasi because of their vulgar gestures.[103] Sarada, a noted dancer, recollected her childhood memory about the restriction to see the dance performance. But she used to hide and watch the performance behind a pillar when she visited temples.[104] Parthasarathy also looked upon devadasi dance as 'vulgar and indecent'.[105]

In ninteenth century, there was a series of problems in the engagement with tradition and modernity. The period witnessed the displacement of rural sector leading towards a miserable life for the lower strata of the society.[106] Kumkum Sangari and Sudesh Vaid mentioned that the colonial intervention in the agrarian economy generally intensified the oppression of the majority of rural women.[107] Janaki Nair noted that the transformation of the colonial economy produced series of realignments in the nature of family and in gender relations.[108] At the end of the ninteenth century, the process of the nation building played a key role in the construction of the Indian culture and Indian womanhood. The colonial modernity as much as the traditions it supplanted or incorporated, continued to be the bearer of patriarchal ideologies.[109] The evolution of the national consciousness was very relevant in the transformation of the devadasi tradition.

The Indian intelligentsia, especially middle class started to acquire the Victorian morals and ethics, especially after 1858.[110] K.N. Panikkar illustrated that the familiarity with European history, institutions and languages and the concomitant influence of the European ideas of liberty, rationalism and humanism made Indians critical of their own institutions and consequently led them to reform.[111] The Indian intelligentsia thirsted on their historical antiquity and retrieved their past. It became an important agenda of the anticolonial project. It provoked a kind of cultural superiority and then they started to criticise the superstitious elements in the society. The historical consciousness was being reshaped to construct their 'superior' culture. Women became a part of the reformist agenda. The women's question became important. The reformers voiced their concerns on *sati*, child marriage and widow remarriage. The characters such as coarse, vulgar, loud, quarrelsome, devoid of superior moral sense and sexual immorality were questioned and simultaneously the national consciousness developed the notions of womanly virtues as chastity, self-sacrifice, submission, devotion, kindness, patience and the labours of love. Partha Chatterjee mentioned that the entire phase of the national struggle was to protect, preserve and strengthen the national culture.[112] The 'national' morality was constructed on a woman's body. These ideas led into the image of submissive women, service-minded wife and glorified mother.[113] Ramachendrier mentioned that freedom, education and single or unmarried life had been denied to any family or caste women in this country.[114] They are kept in utter ignorance of the art of singing and dancing, as it was believed erroneously that most of those who sing lead necessarily a loose life.[115]

The entire arguments of the reformers were placed on the core of the revival of the Hindu tradition otherwise super ego of their indigenous culture. They voiced for social purity rather than liberation and empowerment of human being, particularly on the issues of women. Usually, these reformers did not interrogate with the fundamental attitudes of religion. They wanted to hold the caste Hindu social order. Lata Mani argued that the activity of the early colonial reformers had been just an attempt of reformulating Indian tradition, specifically Hinduism.[116] The tradition was reconstituted under colonial rule. Sumit Sarkar also questioned the inception of the colonial modernity.[117] Lata Mani stated that women and brahmanical scripture became interlocking grounds for the colonial articulation.[118] The concept of Aryan women occupied the centre stage in the recounting of the past. Uma Chakravarti said that the amalgamation of the Brahman and Kshatriya and Aryan values was an ideology for the reconstruction of a new identity for Indian womanhood.[119]

Kumkum Sangari and Sudesh Vaid mentioned that the early constellation of the Aryan women was an elitist concept in class and caste. The Vedic model became a popular consciousness and organised reform.[120] The nineteenth century reformers portrayed women as *pativrata* (chaste woman).[121] An idea of temperance, social purity, an ascetic like tendency of self-denial, vegetarianism and sexual abnegation were invoked to create the modern Hindu women.[122] Their primary issue was on to retain the 'purity' of their culture.

Partha Chatterjee in his article, the *Nationalist Resolution of the Women's Question* discussed the concept of the domain of culture as 'material' and 'spiritual' sphere.[123] The dichotomy between outer and inner, home and world, spiritual and material, feminine and masculine was the basic argument. The material domain lied outside and spiritual was inner. The new patriarchal institution placed men in the outer domain which meant material and the female was in the spiritual inner world. The inner otherwise home was the principal site for expressing the spiritual quality of the national culture and women were instructed to take the main responsibility of protecting and nurturing quality of it. The external conditions of life for women must not lose their essentially spirituality.[124]

The Hindu womanhood was constructed through the Orientalist scholarship of the Indian past.[125] It was this very blend of eroticism and devotional worship that shocked the missionaries.[126] India's temple dancers and singers have a long history in European travel literature.[127] Marco Polo was the first European to provide a lengthy account of India's temple dancers.[128] He mentioned the dedication of the young girls in the temples of Malabar.[129] Jan Huyghen van Linschoten mentioned that the existence of the practices such as *sati* (in Goa) and *Balliadera*. In Portuguese language, *Bailadeira* meant *Nautch* girls or dancing girls.[130]

The reformers articulated a notion of 'true' womanhood and restricted women within the family. The female sexuality was controlled and marriage became essentialised. The subsuming of all Indian womanhood to the idealised Indian middle class women translated in legal terms into instituting a brahmanical patriarchal family from with its reproductive sexual economy at the centre.[131] The colonial discourse on Indian womanhood identified devadasi as aberrations, archipelagos of un-Hindu practices.[132] The placing of devadasi was a big question. In general, devadasi were educated, independent and shared the public space in the patriarchal structure. The non-conjugal sexuality of devadasi became problematic. These changes constructed the devadasi as a prostitute.

A section of reformers believed that the degradation of the society was mainly caused by devadasi women. Their arguments were more on safeguarding the purity of Hindu religion and accused devadasi as a cause for the institutional failure of Hindu religion. In general, they shared the view of the fundamentalist principle of Hindu orthodoxy. They concerned for the 'pure' religious sphere which the body of devadasi would be polluted the sacred sphere of the Hindu religion. Yande mentioned that the attainment of salvation of the soul or emancipation from the worldly misery requires man to be pure in word, thought and deed.[133] Yande stressed the importance of social and moral purity of the Hindu Pantheon.[134] R.B. Sarma, the author of *Pottukkattum Vazhakkam Ikkalaththirkup Poruthuma?* (Is the *pottu* ceremony relevant for this age?) stated that the Hindu religious custom was not responsible for the illegal activities of temple women and the abolition of the *pottu* ceremony could purify the human society and help the South Indian woman to empower.[135] Ramachandram in his monograph *The Devadasi* noted that these women of ill fame ruined the country with their shameless trade.[136] Further, he opined that the system was the creation ground for the devils.[137]

In 1927, M.K. Gandhi visited South India and Sri Lanka. During the visit, he engaged in series of conversation with devadasi and addressed the issues of devadasi in the public and private gatherings in Mayavaram, Chidambaram, Madras, Trichur, Ernakulam, Coimbatore and Yalpanam (modern Jaffna, Sri Lanka). He was grieved to hear about devadasi and asked society to help them to recover their lives.[138] In Ernakulam, Gandhi clarified that there was no credit in the institution of devadasi and warned the society that the existence of devadasi would disgrace every young man.[139] He warned the people calling them as devadasi would insult God under the sacred name of religion.[140] He further mentioned that the institution of devadasi was a shame[141] and their occupation would be immoral[142] and inhuman[143]. He advised people to get rid of the disgraceful and immoral institution.[144] Thiru.Vi. Kalyanasundaram was a social reformer, who was popularly known as Thiru.Vi.Ka. presided over many conferences which were related to devadasi and voiced for their resurrection. He noted that they could not accept the degraded tradition of devadasi which was practiced in the name of Hindu religion.[145] He was concerned about that the cultural epicenter such as temples which were functioned and known for its immoral activities and he specified that the main functions of devadasi was selling their body.[146]

The *Naik-Maratha Mandal* reported that devadasis invariably carried the most nefarious trade of prostitution.[147] Sarma questioned the misconduct of devadasi as a prostitute. Further, he highlighted that devadasi system was the cultivating ground for the young prostitute.[148] Kalyanasundaram criticised the temple institutions in India as the place of production of devadasis.[149] He further stated that the duty of devadasi caste was prostitution, but the prostitution was not only restricted to *patiyilar* community.[150] Ramachandram pointed out that the system of devadasi was a institution of prostitution which was attached to the temple.[151] The dedicated women had to closely associate with a priest and secretary of the temples. Their relationship made them go into immoral life. In modern times, the term servant of the Gods now denoted as a prostitute and prostitution.[152] It mentioned that this custom of dedication of girls to the gods had been responsible for bringing into existence and perpetuating these castes of hereditary prostitutes.[153] Gandhi worried about the temple being a brothel house. In a public meeting at Karaikkudi, Gandhi quoted

> ...not every structure made of brick and mortar labeled temple is necessarily a temple. There are, I am sorry to say, many temples in our midst of this country which are no better than brothels.[154]

Purification of the Hindu religion

Usually, reformers endorsed Hindu religion and acknowledged the ancient glory of the temple women. They considered the devadasi custom would pollute the Hindu religious order. Parthasarathy pointed out that the dancers appealed to the baser instincts of men and brought disrepute to the Hindu society.[155] In Madras, Gandhi stressed the purification of Hindu religion and asked people to remove the custom of devadasi.[156] He marked devadasi as persons who transferred temples into brothels.[157] Ramachandram stated that the devadasi women who once lived an ascetic life, whom generally prayed and danced with deep devotion to God and their mind too centred on the God alone. But now those women devotees were in out of temples and most of them survived a debauchery and it rendered the abominable situation of the temple institution.[158] Further, he quoted

> Alas! Our houses of prayer and worship have been perverted into dens of debauchery and vice and our holy shrines are a nursery of men and children of shame.[159]

Sarma expressed the similar ideas. He stated that once devadasi were *rudraganikai* whom practiced the strict moral conduct and well received by the devotees due to their asceticism.[160] But the loss of their asceticism led devotees to disrespect the community.[161] Sarma suggested that the system could be retained when the dedicated women became pious like ancient one.[162] Kalyanasundaram noted that there were many myths and histories that existed regarding the origin of the custom. The myths revealed that the women were dedicated from each family to the particular deity for the temple service and those women believed, god as their husband and led a mendicant life. But later, these women led indiscipline life.[163] Kalyanasundaram considered that few devadasis had a relationship with many men because of their sexual pleasure rather than monetary benefits.[164] According to him, men and wealth were the prime causes of the existence of the devadasi custom.[165]

Yande stated that the holiness of the life was the prime condition and unchastity and voluptuousness were reckoned as extreme sin.[166] He further recommended that those who indulged in them were threatened with all sorts of terrible punishment in a future existence.[167] In the Women's Meeting at Coimbatore, Gandhi expressed his idea of the Ramarajya and stressed women to live like Sita[168]. According to him, Sita was purified in her heart and body.[169] In another meeting, he referred that the beauty of a virtuous woman did not consider in the fineness of external appearance, but it was in the possession of a pure heart and virtuous life.[170]

The reformers placed their arguments within the religious context. They tried to establish that the devadasi custom was not an integral part of the Hindu tradition. Kalyanasundaram had an assumption that the Indian rulers resembled the ancient Greek tradition of dedication of the women to the deity.[171] Yande explained that the dancing women were not mentioned in the Hindu text.[172] Sarma stated that there was no truth that the *Vedas* and *Sastras* insisted the dedication and on the other hand it brought bad names to the religion.[173] Yande detailed that the custom was not at all sanctioned by our Hindu religion which had been based on *Vedas*.[174] And he explained that there were no records in Sanskrit and Prakrit legends which existed regarding the idols which were supposed to require service of such dedicated prostitutes and the custom was entirely against the genius of all religious cults which have their root in Vedic teachings.[175] *Manusmriti* had not the least conception of this most baneful and irreligious custom. The Hindu laws strictly prohibited in all kinds of immoral conduct and enjoined purity of thought, speech and conduct.[176] Yande mentioned that *puranam* or religious legends taught and inculcated the importance and sublimity of pure life.[177] He mentioned that this was as ungodly affair "for the nearer the temple, but farther from God." People were not caring for the culture of the moral being.[178] Yande detailed that there was no god who claimed any sanctity would brook such highly insulting and utterly unholy services of prostitutes, and own them as maid servants or wives as they were usually made out to be by means of the ceremony of dedication.[179]

The reformers glorified womanhood. C.S. Lakshmi noted that Kalyanasundaram worshipped the divinity in each woman and he visualised motherhood as the centrality of femininity.[180] Kalyanasundaram frequently referred women as Goddesses.[181] He clarified that the some of the highly cultured persons unfortunately hesitate to pronounce their honest verdict against the custom, because of the fact that it is associated with a phase of religious worship.[182] He stated that the sisters (devadasi) of ours serve our lust. There was no evil in their eyes, they were capable of fine perceptions and as pure feelings as any other woman in the world.[183] The false idea that theirs was the ideal religion and it needs no reform; and think that all those who propose any reform in it are atheist and deserve to be despired and hate.[184]

In Jaffna Student Congress, Gandhi worried that the ancient tradition and laws had been degraded. He warned that against being misled into wrongdoing under the name revival of ancient culture. Perhaps, you would understand the significance of this warning coming as it did from a man who was himself not only a lover of ancient culture but endeavouring in his own life...ancient practices might have been perfectly good and perhaps absolutely necessary at the time when those practices were adopted, but they might be entirely out of date with modern needs such as untouchability, the devadasi institution, drunkenness and sacrifice of animals.[185]

In general, the social reformers believed that the engagement of the state and some individuals could stop these social problems like devadasi system. Kalyanasundaram gave a solution that men had to give opportunity to women to get rid of this evil practice.[186] He mentioned that it was impossible to expect the custom to disappear of its own accord, for it would take a long time for education and enlightenment to reach the lowest strata of our society.[187] The people pursued pleasure of the devadasi women and would not be prepared to get rid of it.[188] The devadasis led an immoral life to their ignorance. The men should teach the values of the womanhood.[189] He mentioned that the few good women also existed among the devadasi community. They should marry and lead moral life. Male should selflessly and even dare to accept those kinds of women.[190] *Naik-Maratha Mandal* noted that the law alone would free our society for this most immoral highly injurious and greatly unjust custom.[191] It further stated that the government was perfectly justified to prevent such superstitious and self-interested persons from sacrificing the well being of their innocent girls.[192] Sarma mentioned that the government has the responsibility for the moral conduct of its subjects.[193] Ramachandram also shared the same idea that the government should appeal to help the reformer to much needed reform.[194]

Kalyanasundaram stated that every Indians should think that they all are their brothers and sisters.[195] It was not that much easy to reform devadasis. The moralist should establish a rescue home for them and provide food, education, vocational training and they could make them marry.[196] Gandhi suggested two basic things before the enactment of the bill in the Public Meeting at Coimbatore. According to him, the young or old men who are making unlawful use of these dear sisters refrain from making them the object of their lust. Then he welcomed everyone to join in the crusade against the existence of this system, whether it is by legislation or by creating an active enlightened public opinion against the evil.[197] He continually stressed that the sexual union with a prostitute would spoil the health.[198] God and its mercy would bless for the reform of the devadasi system.[199]

In 1891, however, the Vrittanita Chintamani, echoing the fears that were voiced in the Madras press, conceded that the concern for the abolition of the devadasi system was rooted in fears of female empowerment within the new colonial dispensation. Thus, it noted that some dancing girls' of Madras were very rich, lived in large houses, kept carriages and paid large amounts of municipal taxes; this entitled them to vote in municipal committees. The paper suggested that these rights be withdrawn to reduce the embarrassment faced by respectable gentlemen who had to beg these 'low women' for their vote.[200]

Within this context, the entire colonial debate questioned the existence of devadasi women. In general, devadasi could not be compartmentalised within the inner sphere which meant spiritual because devadasis were vibrant, educated and possessed property which was not common for other women. The reformers, however wanted to bring devadasi women into the private domain of a 'home', through marriage.[201] Marriage and family were recommended as a solution to the plight of women and this is required for them to be placed under the security of *pati* (husband). The status of the wife respect to her husband in the opinion of reformers like Veerasalingam was that the husband was to be held as God, since he provided all comforts and caters to the pleasures of the wife; and hence she should dedicate herself to his service, if need be, tolerate his anger, abuse and patiently endured even beating and physical violence...the wife should not wear flowers and jewels and should not laugh loudly when the husband was away.[202]

The nationalist flagged the concept of the Indian motherhood and compared the nation with mother. They visualised the morality of a country soulfully depended on the character of the Indian women.[203] The concepts such as purity, righteousness and discipleship played a key role in nation making.[204] Venkataratnam Naidu mentioned the dignity was the high and solemn relationship of the human being which distinguished human from animals.[205] They stressed the social purity was important for the national growth.[206] According to them, the social purity meant chastity in body and mind.[207] The masculine ideas of the nation initiated the process of constructing the Indian womanhood. R.G. Bhandarkar praised the land which was cultivated the noble qualities of women.[208] These characters were the backbone of the nationalist ideologies and questioned the existence of the devadasi on the basis of morality, purity, and chastity, etc. The devadasis universally discouraged the notion of strict purity. They insisted the moral values were not more important than art and pleasure.[209] It was insisted for the devadasis that moral value was more important than art and pleasure and they should lead a life accordingly. Ananda Charlu, a member of the Imperial Legislative Council, opinioned that the Hindu temples could not improve unless the dancing girls were removed from the religious premises.[210] R.G. Bhandarkar mentioned that patronising devadasi was debasing effect on the morality of men and women of the country. He considered that attending or conducting *nautch* parties would spoil the boys and girls of the family.[211]

There was a series of engagement on the issue of *nautch* performance of devadasi women. In Madras Presidency, the purity and the *anti-nautch* movements found their chief advocates. The Purity Movement, the Indian National Social Conferences (1885) and Madras Hindu Reform Associations (1892) marked the significant beginning in the Indian social reform activities. It actively campaigned for the *anti-nautch* movements.[212] In 1894, Venkataratnam Naidu introduced a resolution in the National Social Conference in Madras to condemn *nautches*.[213] The campaigners were against the *nautch* on the basis of morality, not on their aesthetic values. Even they were not ready to accept the concept that devadasis were the remains of the medieval nunnery.[214] Their aim was not mere elegant breeding, but pure living.[215] They raised the questions on the principles of the system and favoured Indian nation would compete in morals.[216] According to them, the *nautch* was a form of impurity which destroyed the glory of the nation. They perceived devadasis were the national weakness. They contempt employing the dancing girls' entertainment was to disapprove open impurity wherever it was found.[217] M.G. Ranade critiqued the system that *nautches* in our temples were the chief cause for impurity.[218] Annie Besant worried about the shameful association of devadasi and the music.[219] Venkataratnam Naidu also said that no woman can by custom be a musician in calling, unless she was also a public woman by profession. It was her fallen condition that made her eligible for that occupation.[220] He further worried that the Indian music, rich in devotional and unfortunately pretty full in the amorous element, will have to be considerably improved on the purely social side.[221] M.G. Ranade[222], Justice N. G. Chandavarkar[223] also supported these arguments.

The British were trying to implement various laws to ensure the moral progress in the Indian subcontinent.[224] There were recurrent demanded to the officials to shun the *nautch* parties given by the wealthy Indians.[225] The participation of Prince Albert Victor in the *nautch* performances was criticised by some of the English settlers and Indian elites. Ralph Johnson, the Bishop of Calcutta, condemned the prince participation and mentioned it as an immoral.[226] But British officials stated that the participation in the proceedings had been perfectly decorous.[227]

In the meantime, William Miller (1838-1922), the founder of Madras Christian College, expressed his disappointment with the *nautch* parties. In 1893, he organised a meeting with the help of the Indian elites to discuss the issues which was related to the *nautch*. Subramaniya Aiyar, the editor of *The Hindu* daily, played a key role in the meeting. The public gathering drew a memorial and dispatched to Lord Wenlock, the Governor of Madras Presidency, and Lord Lansdowne, the Viceroy of India, to shun receptions at which *nautch* girls were to dance.[228] Both the Governor of Madras and the Viceroy of India hesitated to interfere with the religious susceptibilities of Indians.[229]

Lord Wenlock official reply politely rejected the campaigners' plea. Lord Wenlock and Lord Lansdowne considered that they did not see any impropriety in the *nautch* performances. Further, they mentioned that the performance was their professional exhibition of their skills as dancers and it in accordance with the customs of the country.[230] *The Hindu* daily severely commented on their reply to the *nautch* campaigners.[231] *Madras Mail* also supported the *anti-nautch* campaign and advised Europeans to favour it.[232] In a letter to the *Madurai Mail* (May 5, 1894), Baskara Sethupathi, the ruler of Ramanathapuram, explained his noninvolvement in *nautch* parties which was organised by Virasamy Naidu.[233] And in 1894, Baskara Sethupathi barred the participation of devadasi in the *Navarathiri* festival.[234] *Naik-Maratha Mandal* condemned the government responsible for continuing of the custom.[235] It mentioned that the trade of prostitution brings some lucre and incurring to get better facilities to carry it, and hence they secure better patronage than other ordinary prostitutes. It further mentioned that they made large gains by singing and dancing.[236]

The civilising role of the colonial government

The colonial intervention by the devadasi system in the Indian sub-continent made a great impact. The social and economic changes affected the life of the devadasis. The 'sacredness' of the devadasi was questioned and they were forced to search their identity. The colonial officials struggled to differentiate the public women of the West and the religious women of the East. Abbe Dubois compared the devadasi and their alluring demeanor with lascivious European women.[237] Frederique Apffel Marglin mentioned that the cultural meaning of the feminine has been profoundly altered for both Indian and non-Indian eyes by colonialism.[238] These brought up to the profession of dancing.[239] Throughout their regime, they had problems in the policymaking issues with regard prostitution and devadasi system.[240] The establishment of the colonial settlement and introduction of the colonial administration initiated the new economic policies of the British which were influenced the devadasi customs in a multiple way. In general, the coloniser was not able to distinguish between the devadasi and prostitutes. Most of the colonial officials compared devadasi and prostitutes. Abbe Dubois pointed them as prostitutes.[241] Edgar Thurston mentioned that the *dasis* or devadasis were practicing the oldest profession in the world which meant prostitution.[242] They believed that the system was a corrupted one.[243] Alice Van Doren worried and stated that *karma* (destiny) condemned devadasi to a life of religious prostitution.[244] Priyadarshini Vijaisri pointed that the fluidity on lack of links with the temple and economic pressures resulted in their cultural marginalisation.[245] The exodus of outcaste sacred prostitutes to the metropolis, especially cantonment areas as commercial sex workers was a marked feature during this period. Some of them also worked as labourers or coolies in factories.[246]

The unmarried soldiers, slavery, concubinage, polygamy, prostitution and drunkenness were the prominent issues in the colonial period.[247] Philippa Levine mentioned that in every cantonment after dusk, the vicinity of the European lines was haunted by women of the lowest and poorest class who, though not prostitutes by professions, were willing to prostitute them for an even smaller sum than is claimed by the regular courtesan.[248] Further, she pointed out that the shortage of European women was made to foray the every spinster and widow irrespective of their physical charms. In addition, devadasi became an easy prey to them.[249] The age old 'sacred prostitution' with trained 'professional lewdness' had been marked to sell sex. The expansion of the vice was such that 'dancing girls and prostitutes' levied a tax of the soldiers who were suffering from diseases. This practice was proposed in Madras as well.[250]

The evidence of the child trafficking in the colonial period was witnessed. During famine, agents were sent out to purchase girls to recruit as the dancing girl.[251] Eamalingum Moodelly of Wallajapetis (modern Taluk in Vellore district of Tamil Nadu), two little daughters while they were playing in the street went missing. The parents launched a complaint and police ascertained a woman, who crossed the river towards Arcot with two little girls. The police inspector found the girls and the woman, who kidnapped the girls. The woman confessed that the girls were kidnapped to recruit as a dancing girl in Chittoor (modern district in Andhra Pradesh). The woman was convicted five years imprisonment by the magistrate of Chittor.[252]

The nineteenth century account of Abbe Dubois's *A Description of the Character, Manner and Customs of the People of India* detailed the lewdness attitudes and upbringing of devadasi women. According to the document, devadasi were the performers who were supported out of the revenues and considerable share from the temple. The document highlighted their profession as dissolute. It further added that in order to stimulate more briskly the passion which their lewd employment was intended to gratify that they had recourse to the same artifices as were used by persons of their sex and calling in other counties. Shameless as the dancing girls of India appeared to be, they would not venture, upon any occasion, to stop a man in the streets, or to take any indecent liberty in public. And, on the other hand, a man who would take such liberties, even with a prostitute, far from being applauded, or joked with, by the spectators, as happens in some other countries, would be obliged to hide his head in shame, and would be treated with marks of indignation.[253] These women used perfumes, elegant and attractive attire, particularly of the head, sweet scented flowers intertwined with exquisite art about their beautiful hair, multitudes of ornamental trinkets adapted with infinite taste to the different parts of the body, a graceful carriage and measured step, indicating luxurious delight; such are the allurements and the charms which these enchanting syrens display to accomplish their seductive designs.[254] The dancers in the temples were the most decently clothed. They are so nice in covering every part of the body, as to have the appearance of being affectedly precise, or as if they intended, by the contrast with the more open attire of other dames, to excite more strongly the passion which they wished to inspire, by carefully veiling a part of the charms which it covets.[255]

The description mentioned that these women were instructed from infancy to the various modes of kindling the fire of voluptuousness in the cold hearts; and they would know how to vary their arts and adapt them to the particular disposition of those whom they wish to seduce.[256] Abbe Dubois pointed them as prostitutes who were the only females in India who may learn to read, to sing and to dance. Such accomplishments belonged to them exclusively, and were, for that reason, held by the rest in the same profession in such abhorrence, that every virtuous woman would consider the mention of them as an affront.[257] As soon as a girl attained maturity, her virginity, if not debauched by the temple Brahmins, was sold to outsiders in proportion to the wealth of the party seeking the honour, if such it might be termed, after which she led a continuous course of prostitution.[258]

John Shortt was the one who differentiated prostitute and devadasi by using the vernacular terms such as *dasi* (to note temple women) and *veshi* (common prostitute).[259] He mentioned that the one of the worst institutions connected with Hinduism and the poor unfortunate women being the victims of such a system.[260] The first they executed with grace, though with lascivious attitudes and motions. Their chanting was generally confined to the obscene songs which related to some circumstance or other of the licentious lives of their god.[261] They were also obliged to assist at all the public ceremonies, which they enlivened with their dance and merry song. As soon as their public business was over, they opened their cells of infamy, and frequently converted the temple into a stew house.[262] They were bred to this profligate life from their infancy. Joardon mentioned that the missionaries in India focused their attention on the *nautch* as one of the moral issues. In fact, a section of missionaries felt that the practice of *nautch* was growing among European Christians and increased anti-Christianity feeling.[263]

Legal issues

An important task of the early nineteenth century colonial government was that to document the 'native' religious practices. In 1861, the Indian Penal Court (IPC) was formulated and the Indian High Courts Act of 1861 established the high courts in Madras, Bombay and Calcutta. The coloniser made an effort to universalise the legal code in the Indian subcontinent. The colonial administration structured 'tradition' through the agency of the courts, serving to equalise structurally unequal people.[264]

The process of universalisation benefited the Brahmin community in the Indian society. The process authenticated the brahmanical textual tradition and its culture as universal. Their caste customs and religious practices became the law for all. In 1864, a substantial body of Hindu legal texts had been translated into English. The newly emerged native law officer such as Brahmins were able to officiate their religious principles as the basis of the vast and diverged culture like India.

The homogenisation of Indian law had a problem in addressing the indigenous cultural and religious practices such as family law, inheritance, child marriage, property rights, etc. There was a contestation raised on the basis of the Dravidian ideology. A non-Brahmin Justice Devadoss arbitrated that *srutis* and *smrithis* were applicable only to the Aryans and it did not make any impact on other races that inhabited the country. In his judgment, he established the concept of Dravidian and the incapability of the uniform legal code on the basis of religious principle. According to him, the laws, especially which were related to family relations, succession and inheritance were based on Manu, Yajnavalkya and Vignaneswara. According to Manu, the term *sudra* was used to define a section of people who were different from Aryan like the word 'native' from Europeans. So fundamentally those laws were applicable to Aryan not to all the people in the society.[265]

There was a tension between the traditional and modern legal systems. The colonisers preferred to implement the British model of public law and Indian mode of private law. Kay. K Jordan mentioned that the Anglo-Indian legal system recognised inheritance, marriage, and adoption based on religious laws and customs linked to a uniform criminal code based on foreign secular sources which complicated the legal status of the devadasis.[266] The coloniser believed that the judicial decisions had silently promoted the cause of female emancipation and progress.[267]

The patriarchal Hindu law is constructed on the sexual role of women. Kunal Parkar noted under new patriarchy marriage instantiated itself in law.[268] Marriage was absolutely indispensable for the Hindu women and it became the source for all legal status and rights. The sexual activity outside the marriage was considered as sin and designated as 'un-chastity', 'incontinence' or prostitution. It was severely punished as incontinence. The Hindu community was organised around marriage. The Hindu law conditioned women's property rights upon their chastity.[269]

The colonial judicial law established the rights of the temple women and it recognised the institution. The High Court observed that the dancing girls was a separate community and had no caste, or belonged to any caste, and that consequently they could adopt a girl from any caste or no caste.[270] In 1888, the Madras High Court Justice Muttusami Iyer in the case of *Venku vs*

Mahalinga (1888) observed that the existence of dancing girl's connection with temples was according to the ancient established usage of the country, and this Court would, in our opinion be taking far too much upon itself to say that it is so opposed to 'the legal consciousness' of the community at the present day as to justify the court in refusing to recognise existing endowments in connection with such an institution.[271] In the case of *Vengamuthu* vs *Pandaveswara Gurukal* (1883) explained that the plaintiff, dancing girls brought offerings according to custom and placed them before the god when he came to the Raja mandapam in the temple on the seventh day of the *Chittrai Vasantha Vizha* (April 21, 1880) and asked the defendants to present the offerings to the god, burn incense, and then distribute them; the defendants refused to take the offering on the ground that the plaintiff had gone to a Komati's house to dance. She sued for damages, for the rejected offerings and for loss of honour, and a perpetual injunction against the defendants to allow the plaintiff to perform, according to custom, the *mantapa padi* (placing god) in the Raj Mandapam in the seventh day of the *Chithirai Vasantha Vizha*. Turner CJ delivered the following Judgment that the members of a sect were entitled, subject to the rules made by the duly consisted authorities of the sect, to take part in the public worship of the sect, and if any one of them was wrongly prevented from so doing, he was entitled to seek from the Civil courts such remedies as they could afford him. If the Judge finds that on an occasion when public worship was being carried on the appellant was entitled to take part in it, but was wrongly prevented from doing, she would be entitled to some relief.[272]

The colonial judicature occupied a central position in disputes over temple honours and rituals. Devadasi had some laws and special rights which were not applicable to the common womenfolk of the Indian subcontinent. The dancing woman was recognised by the Hindu law. According to the law, a woman who should marry or unmarried were not allowed to perform in a stage as an actress or a songstress, however they were chaste and virtuous. The violation of the particular law led them an outcaste.[273] But this particular law was not applicable to devadasi. On the other hand, they had some other special provisions such as adoption and inheritance.

The colonial law recognised the adoption rights of the dancing girls which was an immemorial custom. The introduction of Penal Code in 1861 showed that a dancing woman may make an adoption of a girl, carrying with it civil rights for purposes of inheritance and collateral succession, and that such right was to be adjudicated upon, in the absence of a positive rule of law to the contrary, with reference to the custom of the caste, and the analogies of Hindu law as a pointed out in *Kamakshi* vs *Nagarathnum* (1870).[274] John Shortt mentioned that the dancing girls could adopt a daughter with the permission of the authorities of the temple to which she belonged.[275] In general, devadasi could not adopt a son and it was not possible to transfer the property to the adopted son. On the other hand, the adopted girl had right to relish her mother's property after her lifetime when she was an heiress. The Madras High Court recognised a custom of adaptation in the *Venku* vs *Mahalinga* (1888) case.[276] In April 1856, three judges of the Sudder Dewanny Adawlut addressed the case of *Venkatachellum vs Vencatasawmy,* (Special Appeal No. 6 of 1856) opinioned that it was irrelevant to point out that the girl was adopted either by purchase or in any other manner by dancing girls. It questioned the formalities for the adaptation and recognised adopted girl as a daughter.[277] In the case of *Narasanna* vs *Gangu* (1890), a girl who was not formally adopted, but introduced into the temple by one of two sisters from the dancing girl was recognised as the adopted daughter of that sister.[278]

Inheritance

The colonial judiciary relied on the Hindu law and the patriarchal law sanctioned the rights to property to devadasi women. The Bombay High Court insisted in the case of *Tara Naikin* vs *Nana Lakshman* (1890) that the incumbent of the nomination of the successor by devadasi to inherit her rights in the temple endowment. It further refused the involvement of the court of law in the custom which was recognised by the country.[279] There was case between *Muttukannu* vs *Paramasami* (1889) regarding the inherit property of the adoptive mother. The son of the adopted daughter and the second adopted daughter filed a case for the adoptive mother. The second adopted daughters succeeded the rights of the adoptive mother.[280]

During the colonial period, most of the cases were registered for the inheritance of the property. There was a case in the Madras High Court between *Narasanna* vs *Gangu* (1890) regarding the property. The property was divided between the two brothers and sisters. The two sisters shared each on fourth and lived as dancing women. After the death of one sister, a dispute arose on an heir. The brother claimed her property, but his right was denied by her niece. Even though she was not formally adopted by the dead sister, she was introduced as her hereditary successor. The Madras High Court acknowledged the claim of the niece.[281] Had she lost the case, the property of the dancing girl would have reverted back to the temple to which she was attached.[282]

In a case of *Chinna Ummayi* vs *Tegarai Chetti*[283] in 1876 stated that dancing woman who was attached to a temple filed a case against the *dharma-karta*'s right by custom to veto the introduction of a new dancing girl into the temple. The court opinioned that the right claimed was that of an association of dancing women to enjoy a monopoly of the gains of prostitution held that a Court of Justice could not countenance such a right. But in 1878, in the case of *Kamalam* vs *Sadagopaswami* (I.L.R., 1, Mad, 356), the court recognised the right, observing that it was necessary to inquire into the existence of such right as it would affect the question whether the plaintiff had sustained injury by the defendant's interference. This case was distinguished from the former on the ground that there was no allegation of any endowment attached to the office. Justice Muttusami Iyer observed that if the custom which was the source of the hereditary right to the office was an immoral custom and one to monopolise the gains of prostitution, the existence of an endowment makes a difference and removed the legal taint in the source of the right.[284]

The controversy regarding the right age for dedication

On some occasions, the Anglo-Indian courts expressed hesitation in recognising specific legal claims made by dancing girls.[285] From the 1860s, temple dancing girls, temple servants and others were convicted under the IPC. The colonial writers consistently essentialised temple dancing girls as 'prostitutes'.[286] Whitley Stokes in his *The Anglo-Indian Codes* mentioned that the crimes peculiar to India, such as thuggee, professional sodomy, dedicating girls to a life of temple harlotry, human sacrifices, exposing infants, burning widows, burying lepers alive, gang-robbery, torturing peasants and witnesses, sitting *dharna*.[287] The IPC prohibited the adoption of minor girls as dancing women. The IPC sections 372 and 373 preventing the dedication of minor girls and adoption of infant girls by dancing women for the purpose of making them devadasis as such treated as penal offences. The IPC section 372 mentioned that whoever sell, hire, or otherwise disposes of any minor under age of sixteen years with intent that such minor shall be employed or used for the purposes of prostitution, or knowing it likely that such minor would be employed or used for such purpose, shall be punished with imprisonment of either description for a term which extended to ten years and shall be liable to fine.[288] It was insisted that they obtain a Medical Officer's certificate if the girl was above sixteen years before adopting and dedicating them.[289] The prescribed age limit is insufficient.[290] But the Act of 1924, Chapter XVIII raised the age limit of the dedication to eighteen.

Arunachalam worked as a servant in the house of a dancing girl and lived in the same household. He was interested to dedicate his minor daughter to the temple service. In 1876, Madras High Court upheld the conviction of a father for arranging the dedication of his daughter to temple service while she was under the age of sixteen. The High Court opinioned that the dedication ceremony did not carry any violation because there was no specific evidence which proved that the adoptee would be prostituted.[291] In 1891, the Madras High Court underwent a trial against Basava, a father who was dedicating his minor daughter to the god. Justice Parker considered that the dedication was equivalent to disposing a girl for the purpose of prostitution. But the customary law provided rights to the devadasi to have promiscuous intercourse with any men.[292] The Bombay High Court convicted Tippa, for dedicating his five or six years age of daughter to the temple service. The case exhibited the sexual exploitation of the minor girl and the convicted father found guilty. But the verdict was lenient.[293] There was a case (*Queen Empress* vs *Ramanna*) against the temple trustee for the dedication of the minor girls and their involvement in the prostitution. As per the case, the adopted daughter of a devadasi was dedicated to the temple when she was under sixteen years and she also was employed as a prostitute.[294]

Subsequently, a devadasi adopted a second girl from her caste. The devadasi and the parents were charged under the IPC Sections of 372 and 373. The accused were convicted by the Deputy Magistrate. Later, the Session Court Judge reversed the conviction on the appeal with respect of the similar caste affiliation of the girl's parents and devadasi. The Session Judge further observed that the adopted minor girl's economic position was not worse than that which she was before the adoption and that the Section of IPC could not apply to adoption among the dancing women class themselves which do not alter for the worse the status of the child.[295] On the revision of the judgment, Justice Parker opinioned that the session judge had not determined the circumstances of the case and its intension of the adoption either it was for sexual service or her obsequies or hereditary property. Justice Muttusami Iyer observed that there was no offense if the intension should be an inheritance of the lineage and he added that the girl should be brought up as a daughter until a maturated state and she was allowed to select either married life or the profession of her prostitution mother.[296]

Prostitution

Kunal Parker mentioned that the growth of urban society engendered a new urban prostitution, with Hindu women as its principal practitioners.[297] In general, prostitutes were chiefly deserted women, abandoned widows and orphans.[298] According to Hindu Law, they were all considered as outcastes and they did not exist as a separate community like devadasi. The state struggled to differentiate devadasi from prostitutes. And somehow, the government recognised the civil rights of dancing girls because the Hindu law considered devadasi as a separate class.[299]

In nineteenth century, the British Government enacted Contagious Disease (CD) Acts of 1864, 1866 and 1869 in England to safeguard the health of the British soldiers from the venereal diseases such as syphilis and gonorrhea. The British Government protected the health of soldiers through the control of the female body.[300]According to the act, female prostitute were instructed to undergo a regular checkups and treatment in health centres. Later the act was extended to all its Colonial courtiers. In 1868, the Indian Contagious Diseases Act (Act XIV of 1868) was enacted with similar provisions for the supervision, registration, and inspection of prostitute women in major Indian cities and seaports.[301] The colonial government was required to keep registers and issue the licenses to prostitutes. The examining hospitals were infamously called Lock Hospitals.[302] The process excluded the dancing girl community from its provisions. In many cases devadasi were exempted to attend the Lock Hospital for examination and certificate due to their religious status.[303] Ramachendrier noted that the government recognised somewhat their status by not classing them with the common whores and prostitutes who were actually brought under the act and compelled to attend the Lock Hospital for examination and certificate.[304]

Another major issue that arose in this period was the conflict between the personal and private law. If the government agreed to continue with the institution of the devadasis which was recognised in personal law, this would violate the spirit of the public law which blamed prostitution, child marriage, *nautch* performance, etc. The government kept strict accordance with the personal law of devadasi who were frequently violated the spirit of the public law. Yande mentioned that the duty of the colonial government was believed as to prohibit persons who set apart their girls for prostitution.[305] The colonial law did not recognise the hereditary lineage among the prostitutes. Ramachendrier said that the courts had made no distinction between the dancing girls and other common prostitute in the application of the rule of succession to the extent that prostitute daughters succeed to the estate of their prostitute, mothers to theirs.[306] *Mathura Naikin* vs *Esu Naikin* (1880) an adopted daughter of a professional prostitute like a dancing woman sued for a share of property from her adoptive mother. But the Justice West dismissed the suit on the grounds that professional prostitution tainted the custom of the caste on which the claim was based.[307]

In general, reformers believed that the engagement of state and individuals would end up the social problems such as devadasi system. Reformers understood that the immoral life of devadasi continued because of their ignorance. So reformers stated that it was impossible to expect the custom to disappear of its own accord, for it would take a long time for education and enlightenment to reach the lowest strata of our society.[308] People pursued pleasure of the devadasi women and would not be prepared to get rid of it so easily.[309] Kalyanasundaram mentioned that there also existed the 'good' women in the devadasi community and requested men to help devadasi to get rid of the evil practices. He further appealed that the selfless men should marry those women.[310]

Naik-Maratha Mandal noted that the law alone would free our society for this most immoral highly injurious and greatly unjust custom.[311] It further stated that the government was perfectly justified to prevent such superstitious and self-interested persons from sacrificing the wellbeing of their innocent girls.[312] Sarma mentioned that the government had the responsibility for the moral conduct of its subjects.[313] Ramachandram appealed government to help the reformer to the much needed devadasi reform.[314]

The abolition acts

In early twentieth century temple dancing girls had been criminalised.[315] The movement of the abolition of the devadasi system occurred since 1868 Onwards. In 1906 and 1907 the World Conferences seriously discussed the abolition of the devadasi institution.[316] The government of British India had its serious interest in the reform bill. The abolition discourses occurred in two different spaces such as in the British India and the princely states of the Indian subcontinent.

The *nautch* parties were banned on the arrival of Prince of Wales in 1905. In 1906, people of Bombay appealed the Governor to ban the custom. Butler, the home secretary of British India, circulated a letter in March 3, 1911 to get opinion about the sections of the IPC, 372 and 373. Narayana Iyer, the magistrate of Madurai court, replied that the devadasi were the women who traditionally protected the chastity of the married household women. He further added that the poverty forced them into prostitution.[317] The magistrate reasoned the lack of invitation to the public performance, such as marriage due to the reform activity and the famine of 1876 were the causes of the degenerated condition of devadasi women. He suggested various measured to deal with the devadasi such as isolation of prostitutes, frequent monitoring, severe punishment and the prohibition of adaptation.[318]

In 1912, three prominent persons Kanammani Gajjitha Bhai, Mudholkar, Metkith of the Imperial Law Assembly worked for the abolition of the custom and introduced three different Bills. The government of British India sent the Bill into the presidencies to know their opinion. Based on the recommendation, the colonial government enacted a Bill in September 1913. Further, the content was sent to the expert committee to review the Bill. In March 1914, the reviewed report was circulated for the public opinion. The Bill was most appreciated by the public, but some of the primary issues such as protection of the devadasi women created a lot of uproar and the Bill failed.

Later 1922, H.S. Gour carried the Bill in the Imperial Legislative Council and recommended the banning of *nautch* and the tightening of the IPC provision in the adoption of minors. The parliament members discussed the issue. But the Bill failed by a huge margin on the basis of the public opinion. In 1924, the Bill was passed and it revised the sections IPC 372 and IPC 373. On January 1, 1925, the law was enacted. The Bill banned the dedication of the girl after fourteen years, because the Hindu doctrines mentioned that the dedication of the girls should be held before their puberty. The Bill was contradictory in its nature with the earlier Bills. According to IPC, the marriage of the minor was illegal. The Bill did not address the greedy nature of society who could dedicate the children for profit. The reformers criticised the Bill.

Sarma mentioned that the prevention of the dedication of the girls to the temple was for the sake of the goodness of the humanities.[319] Muthulakshmi Reddi mentioned that the training of the devadasi was cruel to Indian society. There should be no objection from the religious doctrines to the enactment of the abolition law. She questioned the fundamentalist notion and criticised the practice of public opinion in the enactment of the law. In 1924, the first Act (XVII of 192) was passed by the Central administration to stop the dedication and introduced two amendments in the IPC section 373. In 1927, the Madras Legislative Council (MLC) passed a resolution which recommended the Madras Government to intervene to prevent the dedication. V.R. Pantulu mentioned in the Central Legislature that the devadasi issue was regionally based. Muthulakshmi started to campaign against the custom and she helped to convene and addressed several conferences by members of the devadasi community to debate the issue.

Following the event, in 1928, a Bill for the Suppression of Brothels and Immoral Traffic was passed in the Legislative Council. The Bill raised the issue of inclusion of the devadasi women under this particular act. The rationalist argued that the conviction that it was the only institution of the devadasis that encouraged prostitution in the country.[320] It further stated that the dedication of the girls to temples has attracted bigger crowds to these places, and consequently the profession has extended to other communities also. The rationalist considered that there was no distinction between devadasi and prostitute. According to them, devadasis earned from the temples, but it was undeniable that they earn through the temples. This was the special advantage which the devadasis had over the prostitutes, hence the greater necessity for wiping out the former.[321] Ramamirtham pointed out that the law should be very rigorous and should come into force immediately because the dedication of devadasi for religious reasons would be very narrow. The temple trustees and wealthy people trafficked the children for prostitution with the support of the religion. The dedication of girls to prostitution in the name of religion should be abolished by means of strict legislation.[322] In 1928, an amendment to the Hindu Religious Endowments Act of 1926 enfranchised devadasis ‘freeing’ from service in temples, and granting the lands to them permanently. In 1930, the Act of 1930 restricted the *pottu* ceremony in the temple.[323] According to the Act, the dedication of the women in the name of *pottu* and *gejja puja* (anklet ceremony) in the temple premises and the other prayer hall was considered illegal. The Law further warned that the participation and performance in the *pottu* and *gejja* ceremony was punishable up to one year and fined. The Act permitted and recognised the marriages of the earliest dedicated women.

The prevention of devadasi in princely states

In 1909, Mysore Presidency ordered to stop the *gejja puja* and later in the same year the state completely abolished the devadasi institution. The government further allowed devadasi and her family to enjoy the allotted grants.[324] Muthulakshmi appreciated the Mysore princely state for setting a good example.[325] Janaki Nair mentioned that the abolition of the custom in the Mysore State was not merely as a protector of dharma but restorers of purity.[326] Subsequently, the officials of the Pathmanabha temple stopped the dedication of the Nayar girl at Suchindram temple in 1909.

The Pudukkottai Princely State in Tamil country disseminated a memorandum to its assembly member to opinion about the devadasi system in March 1914. Seventeen, out of the thirty members replied. Among those seventeen, eight favoured for the prohibition of devadasi practices. The five argued for the continuation of the custom with certain conditions and three insisted for the perpetuation of the existing practice and one felt that the importance of the consultation of the *sastras*. Finally, the Princely State hesitated to completely prohibit the devadasi service in the temple and also disagree with the performance of the devadasi girl in the temple. The State was ready to accept the IPC sections of 372 and 373 which restricted the minor girls in the temple service. The Divan of the State ordered to prohibit the *pottukattuthal* ceremony. The State took some measures to safeguard the minors in the state. According to it any women from the devadasi community who were dedicated to the temple either single or married nor widowed should be accomplished in the performing arts. It restricted the dedication of the minor girls who were not less than sixteen and it were exempted those who already dedicated.

In 1926, the regency of the Sethulakshmi Bai (1924-1931) of Travancore Princely State issued the proclamation to stop the dedication of the girls in the temples. The proclamation was well received by the reformers. Gandhi appealed the Princely States in Kerala to stop the customs and referred the process of devadasi abolition in Mysore State in 1909.[327] *Kudi Arasu*, the newspaper of Self-Respect Movement, welcomed the efforts of the Princely State of Travancore for the abolition. It commented that the abolition act could abandon the prostitution in the state.[328] During the Virudhunagar Women Conference, Indirani Balasubramanian (the member of Self-Respect Movement) praised the State for the banishment of the devadasi tradition in the Kerala temples and highlighted that the ruler of the Travancore Princely State as women, so she could clearly understood the problems.[329] Further, the Conference appealed to the rest of the Princely States such as Baroda for the enactment of laws to prevent the devadasi.[330] On different occasions, Nilavathi (the activist of the Self-Respect Movement) appreciated and welcomed the efforts of the brahmanical Travancore Princely State for the abolition of the devadasi institution in the state.[331]

Apart from the State, some of the individuals initiated and made their personal efforts to prevent the customs from the temple institutions. E.V. Ramasami, the leader of the Self-Respect Movement, was one among them. He served as a secretary and head of the Temple *Devasthana* Committee between the years of 1904-1927.[332] During his tenure, he made some of the progressive initiation to improve the condition of devadasi. He was considered as one of the earlier person, one who stopped the process of selling girls to the temple. He declared that the transfer of title was invalid and he mentioned that devadasis sold their title for the amount of rupees fifteen to ninety. Further, E.V. Ramasami stated that the title was purchased by fallen women who were economically depressed and misused the titles. He ordered to restrict the recruitment of new *dasis* in the temple and also banned that the continuation of the heirless *dasis* in the temple.[333] Like E.V. Ramasami, a Nattukottai Chettiyar who had taken the management of some of the temples, agreed that they should have the goodness to remove the dancing women from our sacred temples.[334]

Hence, if we look at the past, we see a continuous deterioration in the status and position of the devadasis. In the early period of the system the devadasis were very popular and had a great reputation. After the imperial Cholas and later Pandiyas the position of the devadasis faced a setback, but the emergence of the Vijayanagar revived the devadasis tradition. The position during the reign of the Thanjavur Marathas and Nayakas of Madurai identified devadasis with their dance performance. The terms such as *sadhir*, *kelikkai* was associated with them. After the colonial intervention the identity of the devadasi shifted to the *nautch*. The 'sacredness' of the devadasi was questioned. The colonial discourse on morality and aesthetic questioned the very existence of the devadasi system.

References

1. Chatterjee, Ratnabali. "The Queens' Daughters: Prostitutes as an Outcast Group in Colonial India," *CMI Report for Chr. Michelsen Institute Department of Social Science and Development* 8. (December, 1992): pp. V-VI.
2. Thurston, Edgar and K, Rangachari. *Castes and Tribes of Southern India*. Vol. II. Madras: Government Press, 1909: pp. 125-126.
3. Soneji, Davesh. *Unfinished Gestures: Devadasis, Memory and Modernity in South India*. Chicago: The University of Chicago Press, 2012: p. 30.
4. Narayana Rao, Velcheru, David Shulman, and Sanjay Subrahmanyam. *Symbols of Substance: Court and State in Nayaka Period Tamilnadu*. New Delhi: Oxford University Press, 1992: p. 187.

5. Soneji, Davesh. 2012. *Op.cit.*, p. 30.
6. Venkatramaiah, K.M. *Administration and Social Life under the Maratha Rulers of Thanjavur* (in Tamil). Thanjavur: Tamil University, 1984: p. 483.
7. Arivudai Nambi, M.S. *Fine Arts Under the Marathas of Thanjavur A.D. 1676-1855* (in Tamil). Puducherry: A. Kirija, 2006: p. 244.
8. Radhika, V.S. "Development of Sadir in the Court of Raja Serfoji-II (1798-1832) of Tanjore" PhD diss., University of Hyderabad, November, 1996: p. 26.
9. *Ibid.,* p. 73.
10. Arivudai Nambi, M.S. 2006. *Op.cit.*, p. 240.
11. *Ibid.*
12. Krishnan, Hari. "Inscribing Practice: Reconfiguration and Textualisations of Devadasi Repertoire in Nineteenth and Early Twentieth century South India," In Indira Viswanathan Peterson and Davesh Soneji. Ed. *Performing Pasts: Reinventing the Arts in Modern South India*. New Delhi: Oxford University Press, 2008: p. 74.
13. *Saraswati Mahal Modi Records*. Bundle No: 2c and Sub Bundle 23. (Venkatramaiah, K.V. *Thanjai Marattiya Mannar Modi Avanath Tamilakkam Kurippuraiyum* (The Translated notes of the Modi Records of the Thanjavur Maratha Kings) (in Tamil). Vol. II. Thanjavur: Tamil University, 1989)
14. *Saraswati Mahal Modi Records*. Bundle No. 123 (C): 26. 1811 (Venkatramaiah, K.V. *Thanjai Marattiya Mannar Modi Avanath Tamilakkam Kurippuraiyum* (*The Translated notes of the Modi Records of the Thanjavur Maratha Kings*) (in Tamil). Vol. I. Thanjavur: Tamil University, 1989. pp. 130-147.)
15. Arivudai Nambi, M.S. 2006. *Op.cit.*, p. 240.
16. *Ibid.,* p. 234.
17. *Ibid.*
18. *Sarasvati Mahal Modi Tamil Translation* (S.M.M.T.). MS. 1. p. 7. 1801.
19. *Saraswati Mahal Modi Records*. Bundle No. 315. p. 19. 1817.
20. *Saraswati Mahal Modi Records*. Bundle No. 123 (C). p. 36. 1811. (Venkatramaiah, K.V. 1989. *Op.cit.*, Vol. I. pp. 130-147.)
21. *Saraswati Mahal Modi Records*. Bundle No. 31 (C). 1807.
22. Arivudai Nambi, M.S. 2006. *Op.cit.*, p. 236.
23. *Saraswati Mahal Modi Records*. Bundle No. 123 (C). p. 11. 1811. (Venkatramaiah, K.V. 1989. *Op.cit.*, Vol. I. pp. 130-147.)
24. According to Hindu mythology Kaman means god of love.
25. *Saraswati Mahal Modi Records*. Bundle No. 123 (C). p. 14 and 35. 1811. (Venkatramaiah, K.V. 1989. *Op.cit.*, Vol. I. pp. 130-147.)
26. *Saraswati Mahal Modi Records*. Bundle No. 123 (C). 1811. (Venkatramaiah, K.V. 1989. *Op.cit.*, Vol. I. pp. 130-147.)
27. Arivudai Nambi, M.S. 2006. *Op.cit.*, p. 239.
28. Bundle No: 138c/ 1776.
29. *Saraswati Mahal Modi Records*. Bundle No. 2c Sub Bundle No. 23. (Venkatramaiah, K.V. 1989. *Op.cit.*, Vol. II. pp. 414-419.)
30. Nattuvanar of Thulaja II court and father of Chinnaiah, Ponnaiah, Sivanandam and Vadivelu. They popularly known as Thanjai Nalvar (Thanjai's Four).

31. Arivudai Nambi, M.S. 2006. *Op.cit.*, p. 237.
32. *Ibid.*
33. *Ibid.*
34. Thanjavur Quartet is the famous brothers Chinnaiah, Ponnaiah, Vadivel and Sivanandam. They were exponent in performing art especially in dance. They belonged the Isai Vellala community of south India. They are considered as the chief architects of Indian classical performance of sadhir, which is popularly known as Bharatanatyam of modern day.
35. *Saraswati Mahal Modi Records*. Bundle No: 160C/1844. (Venkatramaiah, K.V. April, 1989. Vol. I. *Op.cit.*, p. 414.
36. Shortt, John. "The Bayaderes; or, Dancing Girls of Southern India". *Council of the Anthropological Society of London* III (1870.): p. 188.
37. Soneji, Davesh. 2012. *Op.cit.*, p. 28.
38. *Sarasvati Mahal Modi Tamil Translation (S.M.M.T.)*. MS. 6. p. 418. 1819 C.E.
39. Arivudai Nambi, M.S. 2006. *Op.cit.*, p. 238.
40. Mulchandani, Sandhya. Tr. *The Appeasement of Radhika: Radhika Santawanam*. New Delhi: Penguin Books, 2011: pp. ix-xv.
41. Narayana Rao, Velcheru and David Shulman. *Classical Telugu Poetry: An Anthology*. Berkeley: University of California Press, 2002: p. 293.
42. Tharu, Susie J. and K. Lalita. Ed. *Women Writing in India 600 B.C. to the early 20th Century*. Delhi: Oxford University Press, 1993: p. 2.
43. Soneji, Davesh. Ed. *Bharathanatyam: A Reader*. New Delhi: Oxford University Press, 2010. p. xiii.
44. Venkatramaiah, K.M. 1984. *Op.cit.*, p. 323.
45. *Saraswati Mahal Modi Records*. 22-24. (Venkatramaiah, K.V. September, 1984. *Op.cit.*, pp. 323-324).
46. Venkatramaiah, K.M. 1984. *Op.cit.*, p. 322.
47. *Saraswati Mahal Modi Records*. 6-418; Venkatramaiah, K.M. 1984. *Op.cit.*, p. 322.
48. *Saraswati Mahal Modi Records*. 9-18.
49. Venkatramaiah, K.M. 1984. *Op.cit.*, p. 322.
50. *Ibid.*
51. *Saraswati Mahal Modi Records*. 6-19; Venkatramaiah, K.M. 1984. *Op.cit.*, p. 323.
52. *Sarasvati Mahal Modi Tamil Translation* (S.M.M.T.). MS. 5. p. 8. 1825.
53. *Ibid.*, p. 117.
54. *Saraswati Mahal Modi Records*. Bundle No. 2c Sub Bundle No. 17. (Venkatramaiah, K.V. 1989. *Op.cit.*, Vol. II. pp. 414-419.)
55. Kersenboom- Story, C. Saskia. *Nityasumangali*. Delhi: Motilal Banarsidas, 1987: p. 64.
56. Dubois, Abbe J.A. *A Description of the Character, Manner and Customs of the People of India*. Madras: J. Higginbotham, 1862: p. 297.
57. *Saraswati Mahal Modi Records*. Bundle No. 2c Sub Bundle No. 17. (Venkatramaiah, K.V. 1989. *Op.cit.*, Vol. II. pp. 414-419.)

58. *Ibid.*
59. *Ibid.*
60. Panikkar, K.N. *Culture, Ideology, Hegemony: Intellectuals and Social Consciousness in Colonial India*. Madras: Tulia, 1995: p. 38.
61. The word 'dubash' or 'dubashi', literally meant a man of two languages. In Colonial Madras, they were interpreters, translators, secretaries, supervisors and mediators. They also functioned as a kind of advisor, guide, broker, and inevitably moneylender for the colonial masters.
62. Neild-Basu, Susan. "The Dubashes of Madras," *Modern Asian Studies* 18, no. 1 (1984): pp. 1-31.
63. Soneji, Davesh. ed. 2010. *Op.cit.*, p. xvi.
64. Price, Pamela G. *Kingship and Political Practice in Colonial India*. Cambridge: Cambridge University Press, 1996: p. 69.
65. Thiruchandran, Selvy. *The Spectrum of Femininity: A Process of Deconstruction*. New Delhi: Vikas Publishing House Pvt Ltd, 1998: p. 31.
66. Shortt, John. 1870. *Op.cit.*, p. 188.
67. *Ibid.*, p. 182.
68. Marglin, Frederique Apffel. *Wives of the God- King: The Rituals of the Devadasis of Puri*. Delhi: Oxford University Press, 1985: p. 11.
69. *The Modern Rationalist*. February, 1992. Vol. XVIII. No. 2. p. 31.
70. Price, Pamela G. 1996. *Op.cit.*, p. 35.
71. *Ibid.*, pp. 69-70.
72. *Ibid.*, pp. 187-188.
73. *Sarvadevavilasa* is a Sanskrit work which was written in 18th century. The meaning of the word *Sarvadevavilasa* is the sport of all divinities. The work was identified and translated by V. Raghavan, an eminent musicologist.
74. Raghavan, V. "Some Musicians and their Patrons About 1800 A.D. in Madras City," *The Journal of the Music Academy* XVI, Parts. I to IV. (1945): p. 136.
75. *Ibid.*, p. 134.
76. Shortt, John. 1870. *Op.cit.*, p. 189.
77. Ohtani, Kimiko. "Bharata Na□yam", Rebirth of Dance in India." Studia *Musicologica Academiae Scientiarum Hungaricae* 33, Fasc. 1/4. (1991): p. 302.
78. Shortt, John. 1870. *Op.cit.*, p. 193.
79. *Ibid.*
80. Price, Pamela G. 1996. *Op.cit.*, p. 154.
81. *Madurai Mail*. 05/05/894.
82. Shortt, John. 1870. *Op.cit.*, p. 193.
83. Percival, Spear. *The Nabobs*. London: Curzon Press, 1932. (Rpt. 1980): p. 34.
84. Shortt, John. 1870. *Op.cit.*, p. 189.
85. Ramachandram, M. *The Devadasi*. Conjeeveram: S.K.B. Press, 1900: p. 4.
86. Ramachendrier, C. *Collection of the Decisions of the High Courts and the Privy Council on the Law of Succession, Maintenance and C (Applicable to Dancing Girls and their issues, Prostitutes not belonging to Dancing Girls' Community,*

Illegitimate Sons and Bastards and Illatom Affiliation up to December 1891.). Madras: Scottish Press, 1892: p. ii.

87. Krishna Iyer, E. *Centenary Issue. Chennai: Music Academy,* August 9, 1997: p. 16.
88. Ballhatchet, Kenneth. *Race, Sex and Class under the Raj.* New Delhi: Vikas Publishing House Pvt Ltd, 1979: p. 157.
89. Joardar, Biswanath. *Prostitution in Nineteenth and Early Twentieth Century Calcutta.* New Delhi: Inter- India Publications, 1985: p. 43.
90. Cordiner, James. *A Voyage to India.* Aberdeen: A. Brown and Co, 1820: p. 120.
91. Ballhatchet, Kenneth. 1979. *Op.cit.*, p. 35.
92. Percival, Spear. 1932. (Rpt. 1980). *Op.cit.*, p. 35.
93. Tennant, William. *Indian Recreations.* Vol. I. C. Stewart: London, 1804. pp. 55- 56.
94. Joardar, Biswanath. 1985. *Op.cit.*, p. 44.
95. Ballhatchet, Kenneth. 1979. *Op.cit.*, p. 157.
96. Raghavan, V. 1945. *Op.cit.*, pp. 127-136.
97. *Ibid.*, p. 134.
98. *Ibid.*, p. 132.
99. *Ibid.*
100. *Ibid.*, p. 136.
101. Ramachendrier, C. 1892. *Op.cit.,* p. ii.
102. Ohtani, Kimiko. *Op.cit.,* p. 301.
103. *Ibid.*, p. 302.
104. *Ibid.*
105. The article of Kimiko (Ohtani. 1991. *Op.cit.,* p. 302).
106. Thirumali, Inukonda. 2005. *Marriage, Love and Caste: Perceptions on Telugu Women During the Colonial Period.* New Delhi: Promilla and Co., Publishers, 2005: p. 23.
107. Sangari, Kumkum Ed. *Recasting Women Essays in Colonial History.* New Delhi: Kali for Women, 1989: p. 8.
108. Nair, Janaki. *Women and Law in Colonial India: A Social History.* New Delhi: Kali for Women, 1996: p. 49.
109. Nair, Janaki. "The Devadasi, Dharma and the State." *Economic and Political Weekly* 29, no. 50. (December. 10, 1994): p. 3158.
110. Ohtani, Kimiko. 1991. *Op.cit.,* p. 301.
111. Panikkar, K.N. 1995. *Op.cit.,* p. 3.
112. Chattejee, Partha. "The Nationalist Resolution of the Women's Question," in Kumkum Sangari and Sudesh Vaid. Ed. *Recasting Women: Essays in Colonial History.* New Delhi: Kali for Women, 1989 (Rpt. 2010): pp. 238-239.
113. Thirumali, Inukonda. 2005. *Op.cit.,* p. 138.
114. Ramachendrier, C. 1892. *Op.cit.,* p. ii.
115. *Ibid.*

116. Mani, Lata. "Contentious Traditions: The Debate on Sati in Colonial India." In Kumkum Sangari and Sudesh Vaid. Ed. *Recasting Women: Essays in Colonial History*. New Delhi: Kali for Women, 1989 (Rpt. 2010): pp. 88-126.
117. Sarkar, Sumit. "The Women's Question in Nineteenth Century Bengal." In Kumkum Sangari, and Sudesh Vaid. *Women and Culture*. Bombay: SNDT Women's University, 1985: pp. 157-172.
118. Mani, Lata. 1989 (Rpt. 2010). *Op.cit.*, p. 89.
119. Chakravarti, Uma. *Everyday Lives, Everyday Histories: Beyond the Kings and Brahmanas of 'Ancient' India*. New Delhi: Tulika books, 2006: p. 4.
120. Sangari, Kumkum and Sudesh Vaid. Ed. 1989. *Op.cit.*, pp. 9-10.
121. Thirumali, Inukonda. 2005. *Op.cit.*, p. 106.
122. Ballhatchet, Kenneth. 1979. *Op.cit.*, p. 157.
123. Chatterjee, Partha. 1989 (Rpt. 2010). *Op.cit.*, pp. 233-253.
124. *Ibid.*, p. 243.
125. Kannabiran, Kalpana. "Judiciary, Social Reform and Debate on 'Religious Prostitution' in Colonial India." *Economic and Political Weekly* 30, no. 43. (October 28, 1995): p. WS59.
126. Bor, Joep. "Mamia, Ammani and Other Bayaderes: Europe's Portrayal of India's Temple Dancers". In Martin Clayton and Bennett Zon. *Music and Orientalism in the British Empire, 1780s-1940s: Portrayal of the East*. Hampshire: Ashgate Publishing Ltd, 2007: p. 48.
127. *Ibid.*, p. 39.
128. *Ibid.*, p. 40.
129. Polo, Marco. *The Travels of Marco Polo*. L.F. Benedetto. Tr. and Sir E. Denison Ross and Eileen Power. Ed. New Delhi: Asian Educational Trust, 1931 (Rpt. 1994): pp. 304-306.
130. van Linschoten, Jan Huyghen. *The Voyage of Jan Huyghen Van Linschoten to the East Indies*. Arthur Coke Burnell. Tr. Vol. 1. London: The Hakluyt Society, 1885: p. 264.
131. Nair, Janaki. 1996. *Op.cit.*, p. 37.
132. *Ibid.*
133. Yande, D.S. *Dedication of Girls to Gods: Plea for Prohibition by Law by Naik-Maratha Mandal*. Bombay: V.P. Vengurlekar, (n.d.): p. 7.
134. *Ibid.*, p. 8.
135. Sarma, R.B. *Pottukkattum Vazhakkam Ikkaluththirkup Poruthuma?* (Is it Relevant the pottu ceremony for this Age?) (in Tamil). Madras: C. Munisawmy Mudaliar and Sons, (n.d.): pp. 2-5.
136. Ramachandram, M. *The Devadasi*. Conjeeveram: S.K.B. Press, 1900: p. 1.
137. *Ibid.*, p. 4.
138. *The Hindu*, 15/09/1927. *The Collected Works of Mahatma Gandhi (June-September 1927)*. Vol. 34. New Delhi: Ministry of Information and Broadcasting Division, 1969: pp. 530-531.
139. *The Hindu*, 15/10/1927. *The Collected Works of Mahatma Gandhi (September 1927-January 1928)*. Vol. 35. New Delhi: Ministry of Information and Broadcasting Division, 1969: p. 38.

140. *The Hindu*, 15/09/1927. *The Collected Works of Mahatma Gandhi (June-September 1927)*. Vol. 34. New Delhi: Ministry of Information and Broadcasting Division, 1969: pp. 530-531.
141. *Ibid.*
142. *The Hindu*, 19/10/1927. *The Collected Works of Mahatma Gandhi (September 1927-January 1928)*. Vol. 35. New Delhi: Ministry of Information and Broadcasting Division, 1969: p. 149.
143. *The Hindu*, 10/09/1927. *The Collected Works of Mahatma Gandhi (June-September 1927)*. Vol. 34. New Delhi: Ministry of Information and Broadcasting Division, 1969: p. 503.
144. *The Hindu*, 13/09/1927. *The Collected Works of Mahatma Gandhi (June-September 1927)*. Vol. 34. New Delhi: Ministry of Information and Broadcasting Division, 1969: p. 521.
145. Rasagopalan, Sarala. *Thiru.Vi.Ka. Pennurimaich Chinthanaigal* (The Feminist Thoughts of Thiru.Vi.Ka) (in Tamil). Chennai: Olip Pathippakam, 2007: pp. 134-135.
146. Kaliyanasundaranar, Thiru.Vi. *Pennin Perumai allathu Vazhkkaiththunai* (The Pride of Women and the Partner) (in Tamil). Chennai: Saratha Pathippakam, 2006: p. 266.
147. Yande, D.S. n.d. *Op.cit.,* p. 1.
148. Sarma, R.B. n.d. *Op.cit.,* p. 5.
149. Rasagopalan, Sarala. 2007. *Op.cit.*, p. 128.
150. *Ibid.*, p. 133; Raghavan, A. *Jeevakarunyach Chamayam Mahalir Urimaiyai Marukkuma*? (Did the religion which preach love as its principle would restrain the women's rights?) (in Tamil). 08/11/1931. *Kudi Arasu.*
151. Ramachandram, M. June, 1900. *Op.cit.*, p. 1.
152. Kaliyanasundaranar, Thiru.Vi. 2006. *Op.cit.,* p. 266.
153. Yande, D.S. n.d. *Op.cit.*, p. 1.
154. *The Hindu*, 27/09/1927. *The Collected Works of Mahatma Gandhi (September 1927-January 1928)*. Vol. 35. New Delhi: Ministry of Information and Broadcasting Division, 1969: p. 37.
155. Ohtani, Kimiko. 1991. *Op.cit.,* p. 302.
156. *The Hindu*, 10/09/1927. *The Collected Works of Mahatma Gandhi (June-September 1927)*. Vol. 34. New Delhi: Ministry of Information and Broadcasting Division, 1969: p. 497.
157. *The Speeches Delivered by Indirani Balasubramanian in the Second Self-respect Conference which held at Virudhunagar*. 09/08/1931. *Kudi Arasu.*
158. Ramachandram, M. 1900. *Op.cit.*, p. 2.
159. *Ibid.*
160. Sarma, R.B. n.d. *Op.cit.,* p. 6.
161. *Ibid.*, p. 7.
162. *Ibid.*
163. Kaliyanasundaranar, Thiru.Vi. 2006. *Op.cit.*, p. 264.
164. *Ibid.*, p. 273.
165. *Ibid.*, p. 274.

166. Yande, D.S. n.d. *Op.cit.*, p. 7.
167. *Ibid.*
168. Sita was a mythical figure in Ramayana. Generally the figure represents submissive, pure and chastity.
169. *The Hindu*, 19/10/1927. *The Collected Works of Mahatma Gandhi (September 1927-January 1928)*. Vol. 35. New Delhi: Ministry of Information and Broadcasting Division, 1969: p. 148.
170. *The Hindu*, 27/09/1927. *The Collected Works of Mahatma Gandhi (September 1927-January 1928)*. Vol. 35. New Delhi: Ministry of Information and Broadcasting Division, 1969: p. 38.
171. Kaliyanasundaranar, Thiru.Vi. 2006. *Op.cit.*, p. 265.
172. Ramachandram, M. 1900. *Op.cit.*, p. 4.
173. Sarma, R.B. n.d. *Op.cit.*, p. 3.
174. Yande, D.S. n.d. *Op.cit.*, p. 7.
175. *Ibid.*
176. *Ibid.*, p. 14.
177. *Ibid.*, p. 8.
178. Ramachandram, M. 1900. *Op.cit.*, p. 3.
179. Yande, D.S. n.d. *Op.cit.*, p. 8.
180. Lakshmi, C.S. "Mother, Mother-Community and Mother-Politics in Tamil Nadu." *Economic and Political Weekly* 25, no. 42/43. (October 20-27, 1990): p. WS74.
181. Kaliyanasundaranar, Thiru.Vi. 2006. *Op.cit.*, p. 266.
182. Yande, D.S. n.d. *Op.cit.*, p. 5.
183. *The Hindu*, 15/09/1927. *The Collected Works of Mahatma Gandhi (June-September 1927)*. Vol. 34. New Delhi: Ministry of Information and Broadcasting Division, 1969: pp. 530-531.
184. Yande, D.S. n.d. *Op.cit.*, p. 5.
185. *The Hindu*, 01/12/1927. *The Collected Works of Mahatma Gandhi (September 1927-January 1928)*. Vol. 35. New Delhi: Ministry of Information and Broadcasting Division, 1969: p. 154.
186. Kaliyanasundaranar, Thiru.Vi. 2006. *Op.cit.*, p. 267.
187. Yande, D.S. n.d. *Op.cit.*, p. 4.
188. *Ibid.*
189. Kaliyanasundaranar, Thiru.Vi. 2006. *Op.cit.*, p. 267
190. *Ibid.*, p. 272.
191. Yande, D.S. n.d. *Op.cit.*, p. 6.
192. *Ibid.*
193. Sarma, R.B. n.d. *Op.cit.*, p. 6.
194. Ramachandram, M. 1900. *Op.cit.*, p. 6.
195. Kaliyanasundaranar, Thiru.Vi. 2006. *Op.cit.*, p. 275.
196. *Ibid.*, p. 278.
197. *The Hindu*, 18/10/1927. *The Collected Works of Mahatma Gandhi (September 1927-January 1928)*. Vol. 35. New Delhi: Ministry of Information and Broadcasting Division, 1969: p. 154.

198. Kaliyanasundaranar, Thiru.Vi. 2006. *Op.cit.*, p. 268.
199. *Ibid.*, p. 279.
200. Nair, Janaki. (December 10, 1994). *Op.cit.,* p. 3159.
201. Thirumali, Inukonda. 2005. *Op.cit.*, p. 106.
202. Ramalakshmi, R. "Dissent, Protest and Movement Against Patriarchy: Women's Writings in Modern India." Presidential Address. Modern Andhra Session. *A.P. History Congress Proceedings*. Hyderabad. (2001): p. 7.
203. Naidu, R. Venkataratnam. "Social Purity and Anti-Nautch Movement." in C. Yajnksvara Chintamani. Ed. *Indian Social Reform*. Part I. Madras: Thompson and Co, 1901: p. 266.
204. Naidu, R. Venkataratnam. 1901. *Op.cit.*, p. 257.
205. *Ibid.*, pp. 258-259.
206. *Ibid.*, p. 259.
207. *Ibid.*
208. *Ibid.*, p. 277.
209. *Ibid.*, p. 278.
210. *Ibid.*, p. 263.
211. *Ibid.*, p. 277.
212. *Ibid.*, p. 270.
213. Ballhatchet, Kenneth. 1979. *Op.cit.*, p. 159.
214. *Ibid.*
215. *Ibid.*
216. *Ibid.*
217. *Ibid.*
218. "Justice Ranade Speeches on the Eleventh Social Conference, Amraoti." In C. Yajnksvara Chintamani. Ed. *Indian Social Reform*. Part II. Madras: Thompson and Co, 1897: p. 94.
219. Naidu, R. Venkataratnam. 1901. *Op.cit.*, p. 276.
220. *Ibid.*
221. *Ibid.*, p. 278.
222. Yajnksvara Chintamani, C. 1897. *Op.cit.*, p. 51.
223. Chandavarkar, N.G. "On Social Reform." In C. Yajnksvara Chintamani. Ed. *Indian Social Reform*. Part IV. Madras: Thompson and Co, 1901: p. 314.
224. Ballhatchet, Kenneth. 1979. *Op.cit.*, p. 123.
225. *Ibid.*
226. *Ibid.*, p. 157.
227. *Ibid.*
228. Shortt, John. 1870. *Op.cit.*, p. 158.
229. *Lansdowne to Wenlock*. 16/05/1893, 20/05/1893. MSS Eur D 558/24.
230. *The Hindu*. 09/10/1893.
231. *The Hindu*. 09/10/1893.
232. *Madras Mail*. 10/05/1893.
233. *Madurai Mail*. 05/05/1894.

234. Price, Pamela G. 1996. *Op.cit.*, p. 159.
235. Yande, D.S. n.d. *Op.cit.*, p. 2.
236. *Ibid.*, p. 3.
237. Dubois, Abbe J.A. 1862. *Op.cit.*, p. 295.
238. Marglin, Frederique Apffel. 1985. *Op.cit.*, p. 12.
239. Shortt, John. 1870. *Op.cit.*, p. 182.
240. Levine, Philippa. "'A Multitude of Unchaste Women:' Prostitution in the British Empire." *Journal of Women's History* 15, no. 4 (Winter, 2004): p. 160.
241. Dubois, Abbe J.A. 1862. *Op.cit.*, p. 295.
242. Thurston, Edgar and K, Rangachari. 1909. *Op.cit.*, pp. 125-126.
243. Dubois, Abbe J.A. 1862. *Op.cit.*, p. 296.
244. Van Doren B. Alice. *Lighted to Lighten: The Hope of India.* Massachusetts. The Central Committee on The United Study of Foreign Missions, 1922: p. 25.
245. Vijaisri, Priyadarshini. *Recasting the Devadasi Patterns of Sacred Prostitution in Colonial South India.* New Delhi: Kanishka Publishers, Distributors, 2004: p. 135.
246. *Ibid.*, p. 135.
247. Dalrymple, William. *White Mughals: Love and Betrayal in Eighteenth Century India.* New Delhi: Viking, 2002: p. 25.
248. Levine, Philippa. "Orientalist Sociology and the Creation of Colonial Sexualities." *Feminist Review.* no. 65. (Summer, 2000): pp. 5- 21.
249. Levine, Philippa. Summer, 2000. *Op.cit.*, pp. 5-21.
250. Ballhatchet, Kenneth.1979. *Op.cit.*, pp. 26, 28, 29.
251. Shortt, John. 1870. *Op.cit.*, p. 187.
252. *Ibid.*, pp. 186-187.
253. Dubois, Abbe J.A. 1862. *Op.cit.*, p. 296.
254. *Ibid.*, p. 295.
255. *Ibid.*, p. 296.
256. *Ibid.*, p. 295.
257. *Ibid.*
258. Shortt, John. 1870. *Op.cit.*, p. 185.
259. *Ibid.*, p. 182.
260. *Ibid.*, p. 194.
261. Dubois, Abbe J.A. 1862. *Op.cit.*, p. 295.
262. *Ibid.*
263. *The Harvest Fields.* September, 1888. Vol. IX: 99. (Joardar, Biswanath. 1985. *Op.cit.*, p. 44.)
264. Nair, Janaki. 1996. *Op.cit.*, p. 25.
265. *Viswanatha Mudali And Anr. vs Doraiswami Mudali And Anr.* on 12 February, 1925. (1925) 49 M.L.J. p. 684.
266. Jordan, Kay. K. *From Sacred Servants to Profane Prostitute: A History of the Changing Legal Status of the Devadasis in India, 1857- 1947.* New Delhi: Manohar, 2003: p. 37.

267. The statement attributed to Justice West of the Bombay High Court in Indu Prakash, 14 March 1887, quoted in Sudhir Chandra, "Whose Laws?: Notes on a Legitimising Myth of the Colonial Indian State." *Studies in History* 8, (1992): pp. 187, 210.
268. Parker, Kunal M. "A Corporation of Superior Prostitutes' Anglo- Indian Legal Conceptions of Temple Dancing Girls, 1800- 1914." *Modern Asian Studies* 32, no. 3. (July, 1998): p. 562.
269. *Ibid*., p. 566.
270. Ramachendrier, C. 1892. *Op.cit*., p. 9.
271. *Venku v. Mahalingai*. (1888). I.L.R. Mad. 393. (Ramachendrier, C. 1892. *Op.cit*., p. 7.)
272. *Vengamuthu v. Pandaveswara Gurukal*. (1883). I.L.R. 6 Mad. 151. (Ramachendrier, C. 1892. *Op.cit*., p. 4.)
273. Ramachendrier, C. 1892. *Op.cit*., pp. ii-iii.
274. *Kamakshi v. Nagarathnam*. (1870). 5 M.H.C.R. 161. (Ramachendrier, C. 1892. *Op.cit*., p. 4.)
275. Shortt, John. 1870. *Op.cit*., p. 185.
276. *Venku v. Mahalinga*. (1888). I.L.R. Mad. 393. (Ramachendrier, C. 1892. *Op.cit*., p. 7.)
277. Ramachendrier, C. 1892. *Op.cit*., p. 8.
278. *Narasanna v. Gangu*. (1890). I.L.R. 13 Mad. 133. (Ramachendrier, C. 1892. *Op.cit*., p. 8.)
279. *Tara Naikin v. Nana Lakshman*. (1890). I.L.R. 14 Bom. 90. (Ramachendrier, C. 1892. *Op.cit*., p. 7.)
280. *Muttukannu v. Paramasami*. (1889). I.L.R. 12 Mad. 214. (Ramachendrier, C. 1892. *Op.cit*., p. 8.)
281. *Narasanna v. Gangu*. (1890). I.L.R. 13 Mad. 133. (Ramachendrier, C. 1892. *Op.cit*., p. 9.)
282. Ramachendrier, C. 1892. *Op.cit*., p. 9.
283. *Chinna. Ummayi v. Tegarai Chetti*. I.L.R. 1 Mad. 168.
284. Ramachendrier, C. 1892. *Op.cit*., p. 3.
285. Parker, Kunal M. (July, 1998). *Op.cit*., p. 580.
286. *Ibid*., p. 562.
287. Stokes, Whitley. Ed. *The Anglo-Indian Codes*. Vol. I. Oxford: The Clarendon Press, 1887: p. 71.
288. Cranenburgh, D.E. *The Indian Penal Code Being Act XLV. of 1860 Annotated with Rulings of the High Courts in India up to July 1894*. Calcutta: Law-Publishing Press, 1894: pp. 355-359.
289. Ramachendrier, C. 1892. *Op.cit*., p. v.
290. Yande, D.S. n.d. *Op.cit*., p. 13.
291. *Regina Vs. Arunachellam*. I.L.R. 1. Mad. 1876. (Cranenburgh, D.E. 1894. *Op.cit*., pp. 356-357.)
292. *Queen Empress v. Basava*. I.L.R. 15. Mad. 1891. (Cranenburgh, D.E. 1894. *Op.cit*., p. 357.)

293. *Queen Empress v. Tippa*. I.L.R. 16. Bom. 1892. (Cranenburgh, D.E. 1894. *Op.cit.*, pp. 357-358.)
294. Cranenburgh, D.E. 1894. *Op.cit.*, p. 358.
295. Ramachendrier, C. 1892. *Op.cit.*, p. v.
296. *Ibid.*
297. Parker, Kunal M. (July, 1998). *Op.cit.*, p. 578.
298. Ramachendrier, C. 1892. *Op.cit.*, p. 12.
299. Devadasis should be exempted as they are following the profession in accordance with the Hindu customs. Another has stated that they follow the Gandharva system of Hindu marriages, and hence should not be classified as prostitutes. Perhaps these witnesses hold that the Devadasis being the mistresses of "the heavenly father" will not stoop to be so low as to entice ordinary mortals. Fanciful indeed! Let not the advocates of Hinduism try to establish their reputation in this sphere also. (*Revolt*. 17/04/1929.)
300. Levine, Philippa. "Venereal Disease, Prostitution, and the Politics of Empire: The Case of British India." *Journal of the History of Sexuality* 4, no. 4. (April, 1994): p. 583.
301. *Ibid.*, p. 581.
302. The 'lock' hospital was originally for the housed lepers. But later it became an exclusive institution for venereal diseases. (Levine, Philippa. April, 1994. *Op.cit.*, p. 583.)
303. Ramachendrier, C. 1892. *Op.cit.*, p. ii.
304. *Ibid.*
305. Yande, D.S. n.d. *Op.cit.*, p. 15.
306. Ramachendrier, C. 1892. *Op.cit.*, p. vii.
307. *Mathura Naikin v. Esu Naikin*. (1880). I.L.R. 4 Bom. 545, 565. (Ramachendrier, C. 1892. *Op.cit.*, p. 5.)
308. Yande, D.S. n.d. *Op.cit.*, p. 4.
309. *Ibid.*
310. Kaliyanasundaranar, Thiru.Vi. 2006. *Op.cit.*, pp. 267-272.
311. Yande, D.S. n.d. *Op. cit.*, p. 6.
312. *Ibid.*
313. Sarma, R.B. n.d. *Op.cit.*, p. 6.
314. Ramachandram, M. 1900. *Op.cit.*, p. 6.
315. Parker, Kunal M. (July, 1998). *Op.cit.*, p. 560.
316. *Devadasi Ozhippuch Chattam* (The Abolition of the Devadasi Act) (in Tamil). 23/03/1930. *Kudi Arasu*.
317. *Krishnapatrika*. 15/05/1911. It was rendered from Kannabiran, Kalpana. "Judiciary, Social Reform and Debate on 'Religious Prostitution' in Colonial India." *Economic and Political Weekly* 30, no. 43. (October 28, 1995): p. WS64.
318. *Ibid.*
319. Sarma, R.B. n.d. *Op.cit.*, p. 2.
320. *Revolt*. 17/04/1929.
321. *Ibid.*
322. *Ibid.*

323. *The Abolition of the Pottu ceremony in the Hindu temples in Madras Presidency* (in Tamil). 30/03/1930. *Kudi Arasu.*
324. Yande, D.S. n.d. *Op.cit.*, p. 6.
325. *Stri Dharna*, Vol 13, December 1929, Nos. I and 2.
326. Nair, Janaki. (December 10, 1994). *Op.cit.*, p. 3163.
327. *The Hindu*. 17/10/1927. *The Collected Works of Mahatma Gandhi (September 1927-January 1928)*. Vol. 35. New Delhi: Ministry of Information and Broadcasting Division, 1969: pp. 137-138.
328. *Iniyavathu Puththi Varuma*? (Will awareness come after this?) (in Tamil). 05/10/1930. *Kudi Arasu.*
329. *The Speeches Delivered by Indirani Balasubramanian in the Second Self-respect Conference* which held in Virudhunagar. 09/08/1931. *Kudi Arasu.*
330. *Ibid.*
331. Nilavathi, S. *Devadasi Arppanamum Tirvithankore Samaththanamum* (The Devadasi Dedication and the Princely State of Travancore) (in Tamil). 24/08/1930. *Kudi Arasu*; The Speeches Delivered by Indirani Balasubramanian in the Second Self-respect Conference which held in Virudhunagar. 09/08/1931. *Kudi Arasu*; Nilavathi, S. *Penn Makkalum Swedesha Samasthanangalum* (Princely States and Women) (in Tamil). 02/08/1931. *Kudi Arasu.*
332. *Samayach Sirthirutham.* (The Religious Reform) (in Tamil). 23/10/1927. *Kudi Arasu.*
333. *Devadasi Olippu Murai* (The Abolition of Devadasi Custom) (in Tamil). 31/08/1959. *Viduthalai.*
334. Ramachandram, M. 1900. *Op.cit.*, p. 6.

Chapter - V

The Twentieth Century Debate on Devadasi System

Towards the end of nineteenth century, reformers lead the first phase of *anti-nautch* and anti-dedication campaign. Usually, the reformers were nationalist and they believed in Brahmanical doctrines. Their primary concern was on social purity and they wished to construct a 'pure' nation. But in early twentieth century a section of reformers brought different arguments for the abolition of devadasi system which was centred on radicalism. The second phase got its momentum with emergence of the Self-Respect Movement in South India. There was a significant difference between the groups of reformers regarding the reasoning for the abolition of the system in the society. The radicals understood the religious nature of the system and criticised it, because they envisaged that the degraded devadasi system could entertain the subordination, trafficking and sexual exploitation of women.

Among the reformers, Muthulakshmi Reddi was a prominent personality who tirelessly argued for devadasi abolition. Ideologically she had a complex position. It was a mixture of two phases of the reforms. On one hand, she was concerned about the puritan Hindu religion but on the other side she argued for the abolition of the system for the empowerment of womanhood. Interestingly, the campaign of Muthulakshmi was supported by the rational arguments of the Self-Respect Movement. The effort of reformers were able to create awareness among the people. Following these development, in 1930, Madras Legislative Council (MLC) passed a resolution to prevent the dedication of devadasi.

In general, reformers were engaged in arguments with the revivalist who were generally nationalist and conservatives. The revivalist could not encounter the strong radical questions of reformers. But in the early 1930s, the revivalist entered into a different political move to revive the cultural dance of devadasis which was popularly known as *sadhir attam* and *dasi attam*. The 'Renaissance' process stigmatised and renamed the dances of devadasi as 'Bharatanatyam' and positioned it in a 'sacred space'. The entire twentieth century devadasi discourse raised the multiple voices from the society. This particular chapter tend to be located in this particular historical context and attempts to bring out the different discourses on the issues of devadasi. This chapter extensively used the records of the contemporary writings of devadasi, activist and revivalist in different newspapers, magazines and journals such as *Kudi Arasu*, *Ananda Vikatan*, *Sudesamitran*, *Navasakthi*, *New India*, *The Hindu* and the *Journals of Music Academy*.

The twentieth century reformers and the devadasi discourse

Muthulakshmi Reddi

Muthulakshmi Reddi (July 30, 1886-July 22, 1968) was a prominent woman who actively engaged in the abolition discourse and pioneered the women's movement in India (*See Appendix*: - 9). She was inspired by the efforts of Josephine Butler who questioned the Contagious Diseases (CD) Acts in England and its colonies in 1885.[1] Pudukkottai born Muthulakshmi was a daughter of devadasi called Chandrammal and Narayanasami. In her life Muthulakshmi broke many hurdles of orthodox-patriarchal-caste society. She joined as a physician in the Egmore Government Hospital, Madras as a Women and Children's specialist. Later, she was chosen as a Legislative member (1926-1930) of Madras Presidency and became the Deputy President of the Assembly. She always gave her primary concern for the welfare of children and women.

As a first woman legislator, Muthulakshmi brought out two important bills such as abolition of devadasi system and removal of brothel houses in the Madras Presidency. She strongly criticised devadasi practice and worked for the abolition of the tradition. She considered that the system was a great piece of injustice, a great wrong, a violation of human rights and a practice of immorality.[2] In her autobiography, she noted that the acts for the suppression of brothels and immoral traffic were the most important legislation of her career.[3] She stated that the eradication of the evil practice should be done for the interest of humanity.[4] She acknowledged Women's Association and MLC for the support of her efforts in women's issues in the Local Council.[5] She was worried about the party members in the MLC who would not recognise her social works but was happy that her medical and educational work were acknowledged.[6]

Muthulakshmi firmly believed in the institution of the State. According to her, the State should have a responsibility and power to rescue the young girls from treachery and deceit. She stated that the state ought to guard the morals of the individual and the society. She suggested that the State should understand the evils which sanctioned the practices, thus encouraged the immoral trafficking of women.[7] In general, Muthulakshmi compared the devadasi system with the institution of prostitution.[8] On the basis of the brothel house report, she urged the government to take immediate steps to remove the minor girls from brothels to a safe custody and separated the minor girls from the prostitute mothers. She further stressed the inclusion of the prostitute devadasis within the purview of the bill.[9] Muthulakshmi referred to the earlier order of the colonial state which rescued women from the treachery. She recalled Lord William Bentinck as a good governor because of his strict measures and his orders in the eradication of social evils which severely punished the culprits. She also criticised her contemporary government for its failure in the enactment of the important acts such as Sarda Act and the prohibition of the dedication of minor girls as devadasis into Hindu temples.[10]

Muthulakshmi understood the regional variation of the devadasi custom which was largely practiced in Indian Subcontinent.[11] During the MLC debate, she established facts that devadasis were recruited from various castes among the Hindus and having different names in different districts.[12] She doubted if the liberation of the country would benefit the devadasi women. She was aware that there was no guarantee that the self-governed Indian state could secure the Indian women from all the disabilities such as the custom of early marriage, purdah, unequal marriage laws, unjust inheritance laws, etc...[13]

The life of young devadasi

Muthulakshmi was much concerned about the childhood of devadasi girls. She mentioned that the custom was a great wrong and injustice to the innocent young of the country.[14] She highlighted the contradiction within the Indian Legal framework. According to Indian Penal Code, the dedication of girls of tender age under eighteen years was prohibited. But the Law indirectly permitted parents or guardians to dedicate the children after the age of eighteen.[15] In this particular circumstance, Muthulakshmi established the fact of the incapability of young girls in decision making about their career. She stated that the childhood of the devadasi children were tutored and advised by the actions of both perditions and orthodox relations (*See Appendix*: - 10).[16]

Muthulakshmi mentioned that the concepts such as caste duty or *dharma* could not force the young girls for training and practice of the wicked custom. She mentioned that the training for the immoral trade began for these girls from their childhood when they even could not think and act for themselves.[17] In her words, it was a little tender, innocent child in the hands of a wicked power when the fashioning process began.[18] In general, the innocent girls, both adopted and legitimate children of *dasis* were taught music, dancing and all other fine accomplishments to make them attractive to vice. Such unhealthy and superstitious notions were constantly imbibed into the minds of young girls during their young age. So after their matured state, they could not think rationally.[19] The parallel ideas were shared by Thiru.Vi. Kalyanasundaram and Gandhi. Kalyanasundaram, who is popularly known as Thiru.Vi.Ka. and was concerned about the daughters of devadasi who were also identified as devadasi or *dasi*.[20] Gandhi referred to the devadasi system as an institution of trafficking children. He recommended law to punish such wicked people who traded upon the souls and bodies of children.[21]

Muthulakshmi mentioned that these women do not belong to the brothel class and they were only victims of tradition, custom or mistaken religious fervour.[22] She specified about the *pottu* ceremony that prohibited the girls from lawful marriage and gave a license for promiscuity. She understood that ignorance, superstition and poverty were the chief causes for the continuation of devadasi tradition. She mentioned the unhealthy and superstitious notions were constantly dinned into the minds of girls in their very impressionable age. So the girls even after their maturity could not choose on their free will and it led them a life of shame.[23] Further, the fear of God and punishment would create a panic in the minds of the young girls that God would curse them if they were not married to the Almighty.[24] She recommended the persuasive method and educative propaganda work among those illiterate to recover from the evil customs. The custom prevalent among the unenlightened of the community and who with their persuasive methods and educative propaganda work among those illiterate.[25]

Muthulakshmi's dilemma

Muthulakshmi established a fact that the institution of devadasi was not a universal practice of Hindu religion. She provided an example that the custom of practice was largely restricted within South India.[26] She pointed out that the customs were introduced into the Hindu society during the turbulent period of the Indian history for the safety and protection of its women, but still allowed to exist through the ignorance and illiteracy of the masses and the neutrality of the government towards social evil.[27] She felt that the association of caste and religion were the main reasons for the existence of the system.[28] She referred as to how one could tolerate young innocent girls to be trained in the name of religion to lead a life of promiscuity, a life leading to the disease of the mind and the body.[29]

Muthulakshmi had a dilemma while placing the Hindu religion and devadasi system. She was concerned with Hindu religion. She believed in Hinduism, hindu life and ritual tradition. She added that the exploitation of women in the society led her to move the resolution otherwise reform was not needed.[30] According to her, the system affected the morality, health and wellbeing of the Hindu society at large, makes it communal in nature and this made it a question of national importance and interest.[31] In MLC meeting, she addressed that without civilising the Hindu community it was not possible to boast of any culture or civilisation.[32]

Muthulakshmi mentioned that the existence of the system was not only degrading the Hindu society, it was a greater curse to Hindu religion. She said that a woman who manipulated religion and god for this profession they were cheaper than any one else.[33] The Hindu temples, holding out *inams* or salaries for dedication, created an impression in the minds of the ignorant people that impurity and immorality in a particular caste were no sin, no crime so long they underwent the ceremony of dedication.[34] Her conservative positions were criticised by the rationalist especially her decision regarding the importance of the religious education in the schools.[35] E.V. Ramasami, (September 17, 1879-December 24, 1973) the founder of the Self-Respect Movement, criticised the approach of Muthulakshmi towards the abolition of the system. He mentioned that the intention of Muthulakshmi was not to abolish prostitution, but her primary concern was on the revival of the Hindu religion because she believed that the devadasi system was a symbol of degradation of the Hindu religion.[36]

Muthulakshmi was quite concerned about the concept of chastity and morality. She stated that chastity in women had been looked upon as the supreme virtue of womanhood.[37] She spoke about her mother in *My Experience as a Legislator* as a person who was an example of piety, purity and truth.[38] She gave much importance to sexual purity and believed it was the highest ideal of human character. According to her, the height of spirituality could be attained through morality.[39] Muthulakshmi in her monograph, *Why Should the Devadasi Institution in the Hindu Temples be abolished?* illustrated the Hindu mythology of Viswamitra and Ahalya.[40] The myths suggested that an immoral life would ruin the character of the human being. She further perceived the structure of devadasi system as a system of social injustice, moral mon-strosity and a religious crime, but not as a social hygiene.[41] She believed that the system could affect the morality, health and well-being of the Hindu society. So these reforms would strengthen the moral tone of the society.[42]

Muthulakshmi condemned the criticism of the Hindu religion. In November 4-5, 1933, Muthulakshmi delivered a presidential address at *the Seventh Andhra Provincial Women's Conference* at Ellore. In her address, she opposed the works which were critical of the Hindu religion and society. She said:

> I have come across books, purposely written to slander the Hindu society and to say to the world that the Hindus are a worthless race of people, are unfit to associate with and are unfit for any self-rule or self-government and to wield any responsibility.[43]

Muthulakshmi shared the platforms of nationalist, reformers, radicals and revivalist. She had a great respect for the nationalist Gandhi and

Annie Besant. She praised Annie Besant (1847-1933). She mentioned that Besant had made a valuable contribution to the causes of the Indian women.[44] She also participated in the Self-Respect Movement under the leadership of E.V. Ramasami (*See Appendixes*: - 11 and 12). She presided *the Second Self-respect Women's Conference*, which was held on May 11, 1930 at Erode. The Conference honoured Muthulakshmi for her tireless efforts towards women's liberation through legislative, public media that changes the attitudes of patriarchy.[45]

The Self-Respect Movement and devadasi question

Suyamariyathai Iyakkam (The Self-Respect Movement) was initiated in 1925.[46] The Movement did not possess a singular moment of origin.[47] The Movement voiced the concern of marginalised sections of the society and questioned the hereditary monopoly of Brahmins in the caste society.[48] The Movement criticised the existing caste structure and cultural hegemony of Brahmanism. Geetha and Rajadurai have mentioned that the movement was mounted on a radical opposition to Brahmins and Brahmanism.[49] There was a huge difference between the earlier reformers and later reformers who were generally called Self-Respecters.[50] In general, the radicals came from the Self-Respect Movement, who chiefly advocated for universal brotherhood, anti-Brahmanical and anti-ritualistic society. It gave much priority to the self-respected life of the common people.[51] The social engagement of Self-Respecters was unique. E.V. Ramasami, always insisted on people not to accept his words blindly, he asked them to understand and analyse the content in it.[52] They argued that rationality, self-respect were the birth right of all human beings.[53] They established the irrelevance of devadasi custom and proved the exploitative nature of religion on the female body.

Women's liberation was one of the prominent aims of the Self-Respect Movement.[54] The rationalist mentioned that the liberation of country was depended on women's liberation.[55] The Self-Respecters did not bother about political freedom but about social freedom. In 1929, *the Women's Conference* declared that 'Self-Respect' was the birth right of every one rather than 'Self-Rule'.[56] According to them, self-rule was only a secondary right.[57] They did not give any relevance to the nation state in reform activities. E.V. Ramasami stated that social reforms were not an agency for the regeneration of the nation.[58] They announced that the liberation of woman was one of the primary concern for the empowerment of the society.[59] In *the Sree Narayana Dharma Paripalana* (S.N.D.P.) *Conference*, the woman Self-Respecter Alarmelmangaiyath Thayammal stressed the importance of the women's liberation.[60] E.V. Ramasami believed that the liberation of women would not only liberate women's body, but it could even create a huge impact on the society.[61] The liberation could resolve problems such as widowhood.[62] The Self-Respecters worked for gender equality and the gender sensitisation of the society.

Women understood the relevance of the Self-Respect Movement for the process of women emancipation.[63] *The Women's Conference* of 1929 signified equal rights for men and women.[64] The Movement voiced the reformation of the resurrected women.[65] The Self-Respecters insisted that the devadasi system was a danger to the 'self-respect' and 'discipline' of human society.[66] The Movement provided a space for women to express their ideas. Geetha and Rajadurai stated that the women self-respecters were the active historical agents who made and re-made their everyday lives and therefore history.[67] Nilavathi[68], Jnanammal[69], Lakshmi Ammal[70], Ramamirtham, Rukmani Ammal, Alarmelmangaiyath Thayammal, Janaki, Jothi, Saraswathi Ammal, Lakshmirathan Bharathi[71], Sivakami Chidambaranar[72] were a few women writers of the Self-Respect Movement who continuously raised women's question in the patriarchal society.[73]

E.V. Ramasami, was the chief campaigner of the Movement. The Self-Respect Movement largely owed its ideas and concepts to He.[74] Usually, his conceptions critiqued ignorance, superstitions, fundamentalism, meaningless customs and baseless manners in the society. E.V. Ramasami questioned Brahmin Nazism and introduced the Self-Respect Movement and was instrumental in various other movements such as the Non-Brahmin Movement in Tamilnadu (1925), Temple Entry Movement (1924-1925), Anti-Hindi Movement (1935).

E.V. Ramasami is popularly known as 'Periyar' or 'Thanthai Periyar'. There was a political move behind the name of E.V. Ramasami which is quite interesting and relevant to the particular historical context. According to the caste tradition, generally caste name was affiliated with the personal name. So he was usually called E.V. Ramasami Naicker. As a rationalist, E.V. Ramasami condemned the custom of using the caste name. From December 25, 1927 onwards he started to write his name as E.V. Ramasami and became a model for others. But people were hesitant to call him by name due to respect. So they used to address him as '*Periyar*' which meant 'Elder'. In 1938, *the Women's Conference* of Tamilnadu passed a resolution to call him as *Periyar* for his service towards women and their empowerment.[75]

Kudi Arasu, the rational newspaper

The radicals, strongly believed education would liberate the people from their social clutches. *Kudi Arasu*, the radical newspaper of the Self-Respect Movement, mentioned that education brought knowledge, culture, discipline, and good character.[76] E.V. Ramasami understood the prominence of the media.

Geetha and Rajadurai referred the understanding of Self-Respecters about the power of media. They noted that the concern of the Self-Respecters was that the single most secular index of Brahmin power in these modern times was due to the newspapers.[77] The Self-Respecters were so convinced of interlinks between the power of words (newspaper) and the authority of the Brahmins that they began newspaper and weeklies of their own whenever they could.[78] The Self-Respecters considered print media as a prime tool for the propagation of the ideas of the Self-Respect Movement.[79] They considered that the popularity of the press was laid in its principle.[80] The Self-Respecters believed that the newspapers were generally established as a guiding factor of the society's growth, human solidarity and national development. It should enlighten layman.[81] E.V. Ramasami insisted, especially the non-Brahmin to read the magazines[82] such as *Kudi Arasu* (The Republic), *Dravidan*, *Justice* and *Nava Sakthi*.[83] Through the newspaper, the Self-Respecters were continuously engaged in the criticism of the fundamental ideas which was propagated in magazines such as *Swadesamitran*, *Suyarajya* (Self-Rule) and *Tamilnadu*[84] and *Ananda Vikatan*.[85] An intellectual debate between the bipolar ideologies took place in the newspaper. Therefore, they were interested in establishing a Parallel media.

In 1922, E.V. Ramasami and Va.Mu. Thanga Perumal Pillai had a discussion in Coimbatore prison to establish a newspaper for the propagation of ideas of Self-Respect, brotherhood and socialism.[86] On May 2, 1925, *Kudi Arasu* was started from Erode by Thanga Perumal and E.V. Ramasami.[87] Until July 1925, they were the editors of the newspaper. After the death of Thanga Perumal (March 6, 1926), E.V. Ramasami became the sole editor.[88] Usually, E.V. Ramasami wrote a column and expressed his opinion towards multiple social issues. Frequently, he wrote columns under the pseudonym of *Chitraputtiran*. In general, *Kudi Arasu* was accepted as the official newspaper of the Self-Respect Movement. It brought out the multiple voices and ideas of Non-Brahmin, women and religious minorities. It carried substantial rational arguments of Non-Brahmin thoughts especially on the social issues such as reservation, Brahmanism and women. It further questioned patriarchy, child-marriage, prostitution, devadasi system, brahmanical marriages.[89] *Kudi Arasu* continually engaged for the reformation of the resurrected women.[90] It encouraged the Non-Vedic and inter-caste marriages[91] and also campaigned for the widow marriages.[92] Along with news of political non-Brahmanism and the Self-Respect Movement, it carried articles on contemporary politics, social reform and carried regular columns on science, religion, and atheism.[93]

Generally, *Kudi Arasu* engaged with a series of discussion with the arguments of revivalist. It condemned the promotion of caste ideologies, caste order and concealing caste atrocities, through its magazines.[94] It opposed the attitude and content of fundamentalist magazines, journal. On June 19, 1927, *Kudi Arasu* wrote a column, *Itharku Yen Mounam? Parppanappath-thirikkaikalin Purattu* (Why there is silence? the twist of the brahmanical magazines) detailed the double standards of the Brahmanical newspapers on social issues.[95] Another column revealed how the newspapers a published news without any ideologies and used the opportunities for their political advantages.[96] *Kudi Arasu* carefully countered the superstitiousness and anti-feminist ideas of prominent leaders such as Gandhi, Anne Besant[97], Sathyamurthi, Srinivasa Iyangar[98], Krishnamachchariyar, etc. The *Revolt* questioned the statement of Gandhi that a women was queen in her home.[99] *Kudi Arasu* condemned the criticism of the Justice magazine on the resolutions of *the Women's Conference* about the equal rights for both sexes.[100]

Questioning patriarchy

The Self-Respect Movement was aware that patriarchy and religion were the prime causes for the continuation of the devadasi practice and the reason for other problems such as women's subordination in the society. Lakshmi Ammal mentioned that irrational religion and patriarchal religious doctrines were the root causes of the social evils.[101] The Self-Respecters understood that the general condition of women was the worst.[102] E.V. Ramasami said that the position of women in society was worse than even that of untouchables. Self-Respecters believed that the empowerment of women would improve the general condition of the society. He requested women to believe in their selves, act boldly and move forward to break their bonds and get rid of the servitude.

The Self-Respect Movement questioned the patriarchal system of society. It stated that in a patriarchal structure, women were treated as sexual object and property[103] and the society treated women as a child bearing machine and equated women with animal.[104] Nilavathi criticised the notions that delivering girl child was a curse.[105] Kunjitham, a Self-Respecter, stated that women were morally and spiritually subjugated and their world restricted to the kitchen and that they were kept out of the public domain.[106] *The South Indian Social Reformers Conference* passed resolutions to abolish distinctions on the bases of birth. It recommended the establishment of equality between sexes and suggested the rights of widow to inherit the entire property of their husband.[107]

Deconstruction of masculinity

The Self-Respecters were critical towards various issues such as masculinity, marriage, property rights, *purdha*, divorce, child-marriage, devadasi system, prostitution, language and contraception.[108] The Self-Respecters were much concerned with the subjugation of women bodies. They deconstructed myths which were imposed on women's bodies. E.V. Ramasami said that the servitude of women made them 'mobile corpse'.[109] The Self-Respecters believed that the real liberation of women would happen after the abolition of masculinity. The society should work hard to abolish the notion of masculinity, then only women would be empowered.[110]

E.V. Ramasami critiqued the concept of *anmai* (masculinity). According to him, the term *anmai* itself harassed womanhood. As long as the concept of masculinity existed in the society women would not get any liberation and emancipation.[111] The Self-Respecters were critical towards the linguistic politics on women body. E.V. Ramasami commented on the word *vibachari*, meaning prostitute which was widely used to refer to women who engage in prostitution. He stated that there was no equivalent word in Tamil for a man who was involved in prostitution and also he referred a word *vibacharan* to the Tamil etymology to point to a male prostitute.[112] In the same way, he depoliticised the word *karpu* (chastity) and gave rational arguments for it.[113]

In general, chastity was believed to be the foremost duty of womanhood. E.V. Ramasami mentioned the importance of the deconstruction of the word *karpu* for a gender sensitive society. He stressed that the concept of *karpu* should be uniform to both the male and female body.[114] He stated that the concept of *karpu* was embedded in the slavery which was imposed by the Brahmin patriarchy in the South Indian society and he further stated that there were no word or any equivalent concept had been used to define the male body.[115] He reasoned that the masculinity of the language was the basis for the unavailability of such words.[116] Lakshmi Ammal also criticised the religious theories which did not mention any *dosha* (stain) for men practicing prostitution.[117]

The Self-Respecters understood the construction of caste on women body and so they encouraged love marriages, choice marriages and inter-caste marriages which could deconstruct the caste structure in the society.[118] They argued that love marriages would eradicate casteism in the society.[119] They propagated Self-Respect Marriages which excluded brahmanical rituals.[120] Usually, *Kudi Arasu* popularised Self-Respect Marriages.[121] On November 21, 1926, *Kudi Arasu* reported the Self-Respect Marriage of a Baljiya Naidu in Thathampatti village, near Salem.[122] In 1929, a marriage was held between Gurusamy of Mudaliyar caste and Kunjitham of *Isai Vellalar*.[123] However, Self-Respecters were critical about the marriage institution. They did not believe that marriage was only system which could rescue a woman. Kunjitham stated that the social customs of India brought up girls for getting married. As marriage became a prime goal, there were no women who escaped from its clutches.[124]

Women's Choice

The Self-Respecters understood the potential of women and acknowledged the credibility of women's choice. They were reluctant to let men take decisions on women's issues. The Self-Respecters strongly believed that women's liberation could never happen in the hands of men.[125] *Kudi Arasu* mentioned that the main reason for the subjugation of women was their dependence on men.[126] Kunjitham noted that women alone could understand their rights, difficulties and capacities.[127] A wife of Venkatasubba Rao stated that women should no longer leave men to decide what was best for them. The downtrodden condition of women all over the world was occurring due to the fact that they were governed by 'man' made laws.[128] According to the Self-Respecters, the participation of men in the women's liberation movement did not give any freedom to women. It condemned women into being slaves forever. E.V. Ramasami used metaphors to signify the issue, such as, "the fox will not liberate the goat and chickens."[129] So, *Kudi Arasu* advised women to take decisions for themselves.[130] Nagalingam wrote that the independence of women was in their mental freedom and in free expression of their thoughts.[131] *Kudi Arasu* stated that women were the real obstacle for themselves rather than their male counterparts because women still did not considered themselves as worthy of being liberated.[132]

Women's education was seen as an important criteria for women's liberation.[133] A column *Woes of Indian Womanhood* in *Revolt* detailed how women were denied access to certain rights such as education.[134] In a column *Kulanthaikaludan Manamakkal Thirumanam* (The Marriage among Children) insisted that education should not carry any partiality towards male or female.[135] In 1928, *the South Indian Social Reformers Conference* passed resolutions on the compulsory elementary education for all irrespective of caste, creed and sex. It insisted on a special provision for the children of depressed classes of school-going by providing free boarding, books and other materials.[136] *The Second Self-Respect Conference* (1930) declared that illiteracy was the source for women's subordination.[137] It mentioned that the deplorable position of Indian women was due to the lack of education.[138] It stressed the importance of the free education for both sexes at least till sixteen years.[139]

Lakshmi Ammal said that the property rights for women and the right to choose a marriage partner were the two important concerns for women's subordination.[140] E.V. Ramasami argued for women's choice in motherhood. He established the fact of subordination of womanhood in the form of motherhood. He appealed to women to stop giving birth and further stated that women should understand that they were not responsible for the reproduction of the human society. So, even if it caused a reduction in the population, there was no reason for women to worry.[141] The rationalist thought that *sati* was far better than child marriages. They considered the sorrow of *sati* was for only one day but child marriages made women suffer much longer.[142]

The Self-Respect Movement argued for the economic empowerment of women. It also voiced the property rights for women.[143] *The Second Self-Respect Conference* welcomed equal rights for males and females in property, guardianship, adoption.[144] The Conference welcomed the Divorce Act.[145] It emphasised on the importance of property rights to women.[146] Ramamirtham, the Self-Respecter, stressed the usage of the *swadesi* (indigenous) goods for economic prosperity and women's empowerment.[147] The conference gave much importance to the vocational education of women and also encouraged women to do social work such as maintaining orphanages.[148]

The Self-Respecters de-mystified various metaphors which were related to women subservience. They questioned the concept of beauty which was associated exclusively with women. E.V. Ramasami pointed to the irrelevance of having long hair.[149] When it came to love marriages, E.V. Ramasami encouraged them but questioned the myths related to the concept of love. He pointed out that the concept of love was a constructed one and he recommended the society to discontinue those beliefs.[150] He criticised the phrases such as *love is forever and it cannot be changed* and *love at first sight*. His rationality questioned exaggeration and longevity of love.[151]

E.V. Ramasami mentioned that in society, no one had the right to construct or even discuss an individual's affection, desire, love, lust, companionship, passion etc.[152] The concept of love did not carry any greatness in it. It was just as like other feelings such as affection, ignorance, lust, friendship, sorrow etc. Every relationships and bonds was made for human satisfaction alone. So it was nothing extraordinary and did not mean anything more than that.[153] The word made people mad. The exaggerated concept of love could ruin the harmonious life of individuals. It would be a burden for spouses. According to him, woman was bound to live with an annoying man forever in the name of love. He believed that love was not a natural feeling and argued that if love was natural then why the feelings should occur only between male and female bodies.[154] The material reality instigates the feeling of love. Otherwise it could not occur between men and women or women and men.[155] E.V. Ramasami condemned that the negligence of real love in the name of chastity and so on. He argued for the abolition of religion and its customary law which promoted patience and chastity for women. A woman should have the rights to divorce and the right to choose partner for herself.[156]

E.V. Ramasami did not have faith in the institution of marriage, but he overwhelmingly encouraged the Self-Respect and inter-caste marriages. He criticised the arranged and forced marriages and he believed that these kinds of marriages were the prime causes for the women subjugation and servitude. According to him, the marriage institution was an incalculable harm for the womanhood. E.V. Ramasami believed that the marriage institution was nothing but the institution of female slavery.[157] He criticised the 'sacredness' of the marriages. He stated that if marriage was sacred then why did conjugal murders and crimes occur? He said that marriage was nothing but a convenient bond between men and women for a better life.[158] He opined that marriages were unnatural. The restriction of the sexual freedom of the women, the marriage system and its rituals symbolised the bondage of woman to a particular man.[159]

The Self-Respecters believed that the servitude of womanhood was caused due to their ignorance. E.V. Ramasami stated that the long process of socialisation had made woman to acknowledge 'the superiority' of masculinity and trained them to observe the masculine structure in the society.[160] The Self-Respecters questioned the notion of curse and sin. A column in Revolt stated the construction of the society in seeing women as sin and even crossing shadow of women was crime. In general, women were compelled to do household duties. So, the columnist recommended Indian women to give their attention to their social problems and attain freedom.[161]

Devadasi system and the Self-Respect Movement

Based on their views on women and her liberation the Self-Respecters strongly believed that the abolition of the devadasi system was desirable and important.[162] E.V. Ramasami considered that the abolition of the *dasi* system and child marriage would lead to women's empowerment.[163] The rationalists considered devadasi system as a system of professional prostitution.[164] Indirani Balasubramanian said that in the initial stages, the dedicated ones believed that they were slave to the *Devas* and served God. But in later days these slave women became prostitute, it was clearly understandable from the word *devaradiyal* or *devadasi*.[165] She mentioned that people considered devadasi as a profession.[166] In 1929, *the Women's Social Conference* strongly condemned the continuation of devadasi system in the Hindu Temples.[167] *Kudi Arasu* worried that the devadasis had to dance in temple throughout the day and then have sex with priests at night.[168] It further stated that devadasi institution was a danger to the disciplined and self-respected life of the human society.[169] It questioned that devadasis were dedicated to temple for performing dances, but they dressed well and exposed their body and invited devotees to their houses and looted their money. All these notorious things happened in the name of the Hindu pantheon.[170]

Devadasi and prostitution

E.V. Ramasami understood that the *pottu* ceremony was a license for prostitution in the name of God.[171] He raised questions such as why the Hindu temples needed *dasis* or prostitutes?; why did service to God need prostitutes? and what is a need for prostitutes in temple? He perceived that these prostitutes were kept to attract the devotees. He mentioned that in our country none of the devadasis were ready to accept the reason that poverty was the cause for their entry in this profession. He added that it was believed that they were in the profession due to the gods' desire.[172] In these days, even the *nautch* party was not considered as disciplined act. In the meantime, they said that the dance was needed by god and it was a religious matter.[173]

The Self-Respecters were able to understand the differences between prostitution and devadasihood. They opined that prostitution could be a cause for other social evils such as murder, robbery, and etc.[174] *Kudi Arasu* used the Tamil term *vesi* to refer to prostitute and *dasi* to denote devadasi. An article in *Kudi Arasu* mentioned that devadasis were cursed as *dasi* as well as *vesi* too.[175] A Column, *Vibachcharam Oliyuma* (Will prostitution be eradicated?) reasoned that the prostitution occurred due to male chauvinism and the concepts such as 'chastity' and 'chaste wife'. The social restriction on love, widow marriage, lack of choice in selecting life partner, property rights were prime causes which made women become prostitutes.[176] The term *vesi* (prostitute) was coined by men to hide their role and blame the woman.[177] The term prostitute was referred to women being slaves to men.[178] There was no term to identify men as prostitutes. The rules and regulations in our country were mostly against the nature and humanity. It only gave rise to slaves.[179]

In some occasions, reformists considered that prostitution was the profession of devadasis. *The S.N.D.P Conference* of Calicut (modern Kerala) mentioned that the devadasis considered prostitution as their duty by birth.[180] Nilavathi remarked that the devadasi institution was comparable to prostitution and also worse than any other social evil.[181] She pointed out that the revival of the *pottu* tradition would encourage prostitution in our society.[182] She criticised that the life of the devadasi was to sell their chastity for their livelihood and further added that no other country practiced such custom.[183] In 1930, *the Women's Conference* commented on that devadasi sisters practicing dancing and singing and thus propagating the degraded profession of prostitution.[184]

E.V. Ramasami stressed the importance of the abolition of the *dasi* system and considered as it a profession.[185] He appreciated the Mysore state for abolishing devadasi system in their temples and freeing their deities from prostitution.[186] Raghavan, a Self-Respecter, wrote that religion gave license to prostitution in the name of *pottu* ceremony.[187] He further stated that many devotees made pilgrimages to visit devadasi and satisfy their lust through them.[188] The religious rituals and festivals which the devotees performed were indirectly popularised as notorious characteristics of the Hindu pantheon.[189]

Hindu Saiva religions encouraged prostitution in the name of dedication.[190] The priest kept the belongings of devotees who brought materials for *puja* in order to keep for their *dasis*.[191] *Kudi Arasu* mentioned that Rameshwaram, Madurai, Tiruchendur, Chidambaram, Srirangam, Palani, Kasi and Ghaya were the places where the practice of religious prostitution was common among the people.[192]

All these debates made the common people also interested in engaging in the process of social reform. The letters to the editor of *Kudi Arasu* showed the eagerness of the people to participate in the process. Minatchi, a reader of *Kudi Arasu,* commented that prostitution was only the job of *dasis*. It had been in existence since the medieval period. She further stated that in modern times, upper caste women were competitive and women of a particular castes were devadasi.[193] Another reader, Thandapani also wrote that prostitution had existed among *dasis* from the medieval period onwards and the *dasis* conference were worried about the dominance of the other caste women in prostitution. So at the conference they decided to do marriage for their girls in order to move away from this custom.[194] During *the Second Women's Self-Respect Conference*, Ramamirtham suggested devadasi sisters to break the tradition of *pottu* and marry a person in whom they were interested.[195] A reader from Nagercoil appreciated the activities of *Kudi Arasu* and mentioned that during those days *Kudi Arasu* was actively involved in the process of eradicating social evils, for instance prostitution, that were prevalent in the Hindu temples in the name of religion. He further complained about the prolonged performance of devadasi in the temple premises following the religious sermons.[196]

Writings of the devadasi

The Self-Respect newspapers gave special attention to the issues of devadasi. Devadasi and other activists of the Self-Respect Movement frequently wrote columns in the newspapers. On June 17, 1928, Masilamanip Pillai wrote a column *Devadasikalukkor Vendukol: Namathu Nokkam* which meant *An Appeal to Devadasis: Our Intention* in *Kudi Arasu*. The content mentioned that the burning of the *pottu* would resurrect the life of women.[197] According to him, all the hardships of devadasi women occurred due to the *pottu* ceremony. He stated that women lost their lives because of this ceremony. A column in *Kudi Arasu, the Abolition of the Pottu Ceremony in Hindu Temples of Madras Presidency* noted that after the *pottu* ceremony, devadasis, prostitution and even concubines would accept prostitution as their next profession.[198] Masilamanip Pillai stated that people from the devadasi community possessed better-clothes, ornaments and other luxurious goods according to their social and economic status. So the ignorant parents tried to imitate other and brought up their children in a superstitious ambiance.

The young minds did not understand the truth that the custom would degrade their future. Even within their families, the dedicated women were not considered to be as good as others. Their children were humiliated as *vesi mahane* which meant son of a prostitute.[199] Masilamanip Pillai mentioned that these actives naturally denied the self-respecting life of the young girls.[200]

A column in *Kudi Arasu, Naan Vilaimagala*?[201] (Am I a prostitute?) detailed the woes of devadasihood. The letter was written by an anonymous author under the identity of Devadasi. The column mentioned:

> She (Devadasi) could not marry and led an ordinary life because she was born to a devadasi community and brought up for dedication. The *pottu* was the one ornament which made her discernible from others. The *pottu* was a tag, it indicated that she could be purchased like materials in a shop and that they could have control over her body. Other girls like her were married, and society considered them 'family girls' and treated them well. Those girls had a good family life with love, care and affection. But her condition was pathetic. Even though she had gone to school with them, the society now labelled her as a 'prostitute'. In the name of tradition, she had to control her desires and sell her body. The society controlled her completely and made her carry the burden caused by it. She tried to carry the heavy burden but lost her conscience. It was a violation of the law. Her 'responsible' mother and society kept her in an unreturned hell. If even her caretakers behaved like this, where could she find shelter? The society savored her misery.

The columnist raised the question of rescuing the life of devadasi. They further pointed out that the epics, religious doctrines, religion, tradition witnessed the existence of the notorious custom as it became the duty to the particular community. She worried about the redemption of the girl. According to her, her own community and the country put heavy weight on the little minds. The unbearable weight made them 'slave' for centuries. She compared the *pottu* with the 'poisonous snakes'. The fundamentalist poisoned the people regarding the reformers. Though reformers considered the evil practices and tried to eradicate them. But the fundamentalist criticised them as atheist and portrayed them as religious traitor and further that the reformers wanted to protect the people to get their salvation. She mentioned the statement of Mayo and replied of the fundamentalist. Mayo stated that in India, traditionally, young girls in the particular families sold their chastity. The revivalist counters that the Indian traditions has faith in truth and kept the young girls with chastity as ornaments. She wrote that these selfish fundamentalist did not allow them to live a decent life. She strongly believed that the future would be eclipsed. She welcomed the upper caste women to take care of their 'divine professional' and provided rest to them because the devadasi tradition was established and protected in the name of God. The small section in the society kept the particular group for exploitation.[202]

Religion and the devadasi institution

The Self-Respecters stressed the importance of religious reforms in the society.[203] A column, *Swamikalum Devadiyalkalum* (Gods and the Slaves of God) stated that all the social evils in the society occurred in the name of religion alone.[204] Self-Respecters strongly believed that religion was the root causes of social evils.[205] They sarcastically referred that the mythologies of the Hindu Gods were known for their mischievous activities and prostitution.[206] An article, *Pengal Viduthalaikku Je! Je! Je!* (Hail! Women's Liberation) mentioned the same that in India all miserable events occurred in the name of religion.[207]

E.V. Ramasami believed that religious sentiments were the root causes for all social evils. The deities of our country were the markers for all the notorious activities.[208] He considered the Hindu Gods and Goddesses to be the greatest guiding factor of gambling, treachery, falsehood, theft, deceit, prostitution, concubine, murder, and life torture were the partially otherwise more or less completely symbolise the Hindu pantheon. He questioned how people could be disciplined under such a God and how they could hope for justice.[209] E.V. Ramasami insisted that religion was not considered for the disciplined way of life it was instructed for rituals alone.[210] He said that he wondered whether God should protect the people or the people should protect the God.[211] He said that the people would understand God as the reason to love their neighbours and to lead a disciplined life. It was for this that they established religion too.[212] But Hindu religion did not have any control and made one slave.[213] E.V. Ramasami said that the God themselves made women as prostitutes.[214]

The Self-Respecters strongly condemned the prostitution in the name of religion.[215] E.V. Ramasami criticised the Hindu religion for considering the establishment of the devadasi system as one of the thirty two *dharmas* of the Hindu religion.[216] All the suppression happened if in the name of religion meant that we should destroy the religion.[217] E.V. Ramasami mentioned in *the Tirunelveli Conference* that the existence of devadasis in the name of god and religion was shameful to the Hindu society. So he recommend people to stop the custom.[218] Nilavathi referred that the reformation of religion was more important rather than the abolition of it. Further, she requested for the removable of corruptions in religion and its institution.[219] Nilavathi said that if religion faded away from our country then only the country would prosper.[220] She said that the abolition of devadasi system was laid in the abolition of the religion and the abolition of the religion would free the innocent women.[221]

The Self-Respect Movement questioned religion for the continuation of the devadasi custom. A column in *Kudi Arasu, Iniyavathu Puththi Varuma*? (Will awareness come after this?) mentioned that the prostitution occurred with the support of the temple institution.[222] Lingam, a columnist of *Kudi Arasu,* insisted that the devadasis should be sent away from the temple institution and leave the God without any worldly wife or concubines.[223] *Kudi Arasu* criticised that the establishment of the rituals which insisted that the gods keep their concubines with them and insisted on devadasis in temples. The devotees visited temple in the name of *bhakti* to see these girls and make an arrangement.[224] A column in *Kudi Arasu* stated:

> in politics we worked hard to eradicate social evils. But it was not fruitful. We understood that the religious doctrines were root causes for all these evils. After that we planned to work remove the superstitions of the society.[225]

The Self-Respecters strongly condemned the exploitative nature of the priests. *Kudi Arasu* in an article stated that the trustees of the village temple and their children decided the life of the beautiful devadasis and rest were left to the devotees, the ones who visited the temple.[226] In major temples, it was mostly the priests who acted as pimps for the devadasis. They destroyed the lives of the youngsters. Most of the temples witnessed that they were places for harlotry[227] and the most of the priests took devadasis with them even during their travels.[228] Even if they themselves could not go, they would dispatch their *dasis* for that work (prostitution).[229] Nilavathi mentioned that the members of the dominant caste and priests acted as pimps and encouraged the devadasi institution.[230] During festival times, the houses of most priests functioned as brothels.[231] For the sake of religious service to the deity, women were made devadasis but in the name of service the priests would exploit them and make them sell their bodies for their livelihood.[232]

The Self-Respecters were critical of the superstitious attitudes of the devadasi institution. Indirani Balasubramanian questioned the dedication practice of devadasi to fulfill their wishes.[233] Raghavan, a rationalist, criticised devadasi women for considering that their dedication would lead them to heaven. He added that the notion increased the number of devadasis in the country. The devotees also supported prostitution in the name of God and religion. The devotees were pleased to keep devadasis in the temples and inviting them for their household functions such as marriages, puberty and other functions. Sexual union with devadasis was considered a prestigious issue to the elite.[234] The social recognition of the devadasis also encouraged others to enter this evil profession. The immoral life led them to suffer from venereal disease. It was also communicable to their male partners. It would then spread all over the families of these men. And later, the entire country would become sick.[235]

E.V. Ramasami stated that even going to hell was a better option than being a slave.[236] According to the rationalist Raghavan, the Gods whom men worshipped were themselves a symbolic representation of the patriarchy of the society. Religion and scholars stood for prostitution instead of abolition of the devadasi system.[237] In a column in *Kudi Arasu*, the rationalist mentioned that one section of the people married god in the name of religion and were considered as divine wives, but they were later molested by the priests and then everyone used their bodies and it was through this that they earned money.[238] He also noted how the Hindu gods were depicted as having their wives on their hands, tongues or shoulders. People did not learn chivalry from their Gods and did not treat their women with decency. It resulted in the servitude of women and children. The socialisation process encouraged the slavery and the whole country became enslaved. If these kinds of systems were made by Gods, then those Gods should be destroyed.[239] E.V. Ramasami sarcastically stated that it was a great pity that such a great burden should be foisted upon the head of poor God. He explained that Hindu religion considered that women were created to be prostitutes and so had to be kept under surveillance. He hence believed that the Hindu religion would not give any freedom or liberation to women.[240]

State and devadasi system

In 1927, Muthulakshmi initiated a motion regarding the dedication of girls to temples. Muthulakshmi forwarded the legal enactment for the abolition of the devadasi system. She believed that the introduction of the bill would rescue thousands of young innocent children from a life of immorality and vice, from suffering alone throughout their lives, and from disease and death resulting from being infected with venereal disease.[241] She was a little disappointed with the legislative process regarding the abolition of the devadasi system. She mentioned that the prevention process went back to 1868, but still, the Central Government was interested in receiving the opinion of the Local Government where the evil practice was quite prevalent.[242] She urged the government to stop the custom immediately.

In the MLC debate on the devadasi issue, Muthulakshmi recommended the Government of India to implement the Abolition Act to stop the practice of dedicating young girls and women to Hindu temples for immoral purposes under the pretext of caste, custom or religion.[243] She worked hard to pass the resolution in the MLC. In the Council meeting, she attempted to justify the need for the bill:

> I beg to move this resolution which stands in my name in response to the wishes of all the women's associations in this Presidency who feel this practice of dedicating young girl or young women to temples for immoral purposes as a slur on Indian womanhood and a great wrong and

> injustice done to the innocent young of the country… in deference to my own personal conviction that in the cause of humanity and injustice, we can no longer delay this piece of beneficial legislation, a reform by which we can rescue thousands of young innocent children from a life of immorality and vice, from life-long individualism, suffering disease and death resulting from infection with venereal disease.[244]

In general, the historicity of devadasi was highlighted by the revivalist group who argued for the preservation of devadasi tradition. They believed the devadasi system was of divine origin and so the abolition would question the religious faith and customs of the Hindus. In 1932, *the Brahmin Conference* was held in Thanjavur. It made decisions for the continuation of child marriages and orthodoxi principles. It also sought the removal of the act of abolition of the devadasi system.[245] The Conference criticised *the Women's Conferences* and mentioned that these kinds of conferences would break traditional Indian values such as family, unity, art, etc.[246] According to them, the *Women's Conference* violated the norms of the Hindu doctrines.[247] C. Vijaya-raghavachchari, a revivalist, pointed out that the devadasi custom was a sacred one.[248] Muthulakshmi replied to this argument and stated in the assembly of MLC:

> … aged devadasis often bought girls from other caste, Hindu and so. Of late, there has been an unnecessary quarrel in the Press about the origin of this class because the different communities disown these people, but I may inform the honorable. Members that however much the other communities might try to disown them, still none can deny the fact that the devadasis are one of us, and our own kith and kin and are not descended from heaven nor imported from foreign countries to the Hindu temples.[249]

The introduction of the Bill received a mixed response. Muthulakshmi mentioned that the vested interests became alarmed at the move and tried with all their influence to dissuade her from moving the resolution but she was adamant and almost took a vow that she would not rest till she got this pernicious custom eradicated.[250] A section of the devadasis appreciated the effort of Muthulakshmi and invited other devadasi women to join the protest against the illegal custom.[251]

There was a strong criticism of Muthulakshmi's efforts on devadasi issues. Muthulakshmi stated that people did not have courage to oppose her directly. She understood the ignorance of women folk who opposed the bill.[252] Her opponents began to attack her through the press, both the vernacular and the English.[253] A section of the public began underhand activities and set up one or two bogus associations to write petitions to government and distribute unworthy literature to the public to prevent the bill from becoming law. She therefore had to use all the resources at her command to counteract such evil propaganda.[254] She compared women who were opposed the Hindu reform to frogs in a well.[255] In response to Sathyamurthi[256] who claimed that the Devadasi system was a divine one, Muthulakshmi said that then the priests and their castes should themselves allow their sisters to dance and sing in temple rituals and earn fortunes.[257]

Munusamy Naidu, an MLC member, said that the introduction of the bill was unnecessary and he was clear in not casting his vote.[258] Sulthana pointed out that the implementation of the bill would not make any difference.[259] On the other hand, Kalyanasundaram welcomed the bill initiated by Muthu-lakshmi.[260] R.K. Shanmugam spoke for the abolition of the devadasi system in the Delhi Legislative Assembly.[261] Anjaneyalu stated that the general condition of devadasis was not satisfactory, and that the introduction of the devadasi bill was important for the improvement of the community. He further praised Muthulakshmi in the MLC meeting for introducing the devadasi bill.[262] Somayajalu was worried that the bill had been introduced rashly without any further debate.[263] Kotti Reddy favoured the bill and stated that the main aim of the bill was to ban the devadasi dance and songs.[264]

The revivalist was trying to establish the importance of the dance in the ritual tradition of Hindu religion. The fundamentalist compared the system of devadasi with Christian nuns. During the discussion in the house of Sami Venkatachalam, Sathyamurthi compared devadasi with the Christian nuns.[265] Sathyamurthi worried that the claim of abolishing the *pottu* ceremony would entitle others to question the other Hindu values such as removing the priest from the temple services also.[266] On another occasion, a *dasi* claimed that they are not prostitute but *devaradiyar* and served the deity for life.[267]

The arguments of reformers concerned the livelihood of devadasi women. Yande stated that the law should ensure that the devadasis enjoyed the lands which had originally been granted to them.[268] Muthulakshmi stated that the temples had been allotting lands to these families which they had been enjoying from the time immemorial as an inheritance in lieu of their service in the temples.[269] She further stated that devadasi women were going to the extent of buying girls from other communities for dedication to ensure the benefits of their lands and other rights.[270] The princely state of Mysore understood the issue and ordered the confirmation of the *inams* which had been specifically granted to devadasi under Rule VII, Clause F of the *Inam* rules.[271]

The speaker replied to the debate that the bill had been discussed well for nearly three times before being introduced.[272] Initially, the bill had not been passed. Only seventeen votes had been in favour of the bill and forty two votes had been against it.[273] Muthulakshmi worried that the Justice Party MLC members had cast their vote in favour of the public opinion on the issue. The reformists were shamed by the attitudes of the Justice Party members in the assembly.[274] Muthulakshmi criticised the government machinery and its authorities for their lackadaisical attitudes towards prohibiting the dedication of minor girls to Hindu temples as devadasis.[275]

During the discussion on the bill, the fundamentalists and some devadasis protested against the initiation of Muthulakshmi. The conservative devadasis stated that the abolition of the system would make their lives miserable.[276] In 1927, Duraikkannu and Parvathi from the devadasi community wrote a letter to the members of the MLC requesting the prevention of the abolition of the devadasi act.[277] Their appeal stated that the passing of the act would question the livelihood of devadasis and affecting the harmonious life of household women, because it was widely believed by devadasis themselves that their community was preventing the world from the practice of prostitution.[278] Muthulakshmi was pained to observe that the upper-caste people did not help the devadasi community in their efforts to reform.[279] She wrote a letter to Gandhi asking for his support in the Abolition bill. In it, she mentioned that the most of the Congress men opposed her reform measures and defended the infamous institution.[280] Gandhi replied saying that he appreciated her efforts and noted that her proposal was mature enough and wished her the support of the lovers of purity in religious and general social life. [281] Regarding the efforts of Muthulakshmi, Gandhi appreciated her works in Legislative Council and advised her not to adopt completely western methods.[282]

The Women's Social Conference appealed to the government, the Hindu Religious Endowment Board, temple committees and trustees for the prohibition of the dedication ceremony of girls within the premises of any temple or any other place of worship. It supported the Prevention of Dedications Bill. The Conference called on the local legislature and the government to enforce the Brothel Bill as a law on the lines drafted by the Madras Vigilance Association, with ample provision by the State for the moral and mental training of minor girls up to the age of twenty one on the lines of the Madras Borstal School system.[283] *The South Indian Social Reformers Conference* passed resolutions on the demand of abolition of the devadasi institution. This Conference strongly condemned the attitude of the members in the legislature who opposed the measure incorporating this reform.[284]

With respect to the abolition of the *pottu* ceremony, the Madras government asked for public opinion. The Self-Respecters supported Muthulakshmi and criticised the government move for wanting to know the public opinion regarding the abolition of the devadasi act. It mentioned that the act of the government was foolish. In this country, women were dedicated to temples in the name of God and religion. It made a certain kind of public legitimisation on prostitution. In the beginning, the custom was common among all castes but currently it was restricted to a particular community.[285]

In a letter in *Kudi Arasu*, E.V. Ramasami mentioned that the *pottu* ceremony of the Hindu women in the Hindu temples led them into prostitution. For the sake of money, devadasis performed prostitution. So their lives moved against nature and they were made to lead shabby lives. They often fell victim to venereal diseases.[286] He claimed that Muthulakshmi was not trying to prevent prostitution, but her efforts were only to close down the main entrance to prostitution.[287] He was aware of the problems in abolishing prostitution in a colonial country like British India. He noted the inability of the western countries in the prevention of prostitution. But he opined that the practice of prostitution in the name of religion should be stopped in the country.[288] Further, he stated that the system of dedicating girls after eighteen years did not prevent them from entering prostitution as they were trained in dance, music and prostitution in the name of custom and religion since childhood. Usually, young girls were tempted by concepts such as heaven after death and also because it was an easy way of making money.[289] So, he recommended the government to enact the prohibition of the prostitution in Madras Presidency to prevent parents from their daughters who were considered children as their future profit.[290] He also pointed out that arguments such as the endurance of the custom 'in the name of religion' were unacceptable and he cited the ineffectiveness of the earlier enactment of the abolition of minor girls as devadasis.[291] E.V. Ramasami clarified that the religious doctrines did not support the dedication of the girls after their puberty. Further, he sarcastically remarked that the desired act of Muthulakshmi would revive the Hindu religion. So, the government and the legislators had nothing to worry about in enacting the devadasi abolition bill, as it would not affect the Hindu religion.[292]

Vijayaraghavachchari, the revivalist, pointed out that the custom was a sacred one. But *Dravidian*, the Self-Respecter's newspaper, explained to him about the functioning of Hindu temples as brothels.[293] The content criticised the establishment of the rituals which insisted that the Gods keep their concubines with them and insisted that devadasis remain in the temples. Devotees visited temples in the name of *bhakti* to exploit these girls by establishing physical relationships with them. These acts affected ordinary household women as well.[294] The column mentioned that the colonial rulers had received help from the Brahmin caste in continuing their rule in India. So, they had been reluctant to carry out any social reforms. But in modern times, people had the power to criticise or even appreciate the government, and so the government must heed the words of the reformers.[295]

The Self-Respecters understood the importance of the legal engagement of the Colonial Government on the abolition of devadasi system. They spread awareness among the public about the legal action against the devadasi institution. Nilavathi worried about the ignorance of the people and relevance of the legal sanction in creating awareness among the ignorant people.[296]

E.V. Ramasami favoured the abolition of the devadasi system and wrote a letter to the Secretary of Madras Presidency.[297] *The Self-Respect Conference of Tirunelveli* appreciated the efforts of Muthulakshmi. It condemned the activities of Sathyamurthi and the fundamentalists in supporting the system due to their ignorance.[298] *Kudi Arasu* vehemently condemned Sathyamurthi's statements such as that the dedication of girls to the temples was religious and a matter of honour and hence the custom should continue to exist.[299] It stated that the religious fanatics did not allow either reforming the mutt or abolishing prostitution in order to protect their religion and its principles.[300] Nilavathi mentioned that the members of the MLC questioned the future of women in order to retain their caste and religious rites in the society.[301]

Kudi Arasu expressed its sadness at the ineffectiveness of the Act in the abolition of the *pottu* ceremony. Even after the legal enactment strongly insisted on by Muthulakshmi, the system did not function properly.[302] *The Second Self-Respect Conference* condemned the attitudes to the dedication of young girls and the profits made from their dancing and singing. It also welcomed Jeyakkar's raising the issue of the abolition of the *pottu* ceremony in the Indian Parliament and the efforts of Muthulakshmi in the abolition of the *pottu* ceremony in Madras Legislative Assembly.[303] *Kudi Arasu* mentioned that the Sengunthar[304] organisations and the Legislative Assembly worked for the abolition of the system.[305] *The Chidambaram Youth Conference of Isai Vellalar* made a decision that the birth and work of people should not make them to be considered as low. There should be free education to youngsters and *pottu* ceremony should be abolished completely.[306]

When the Government of Madras sought public opinion on the abolition the devadasi act, it welcomed the notion and instructed people to support the bill.[307] There were many public gatherings to oppose devadasi dedication and welcome the bill implemented by Muthulakshmi Reddi.[308] *The Isai Vellalar Conference* which was held in 1930 at Nagappattinam condemned the dedication of women to temples as an uncivilised act.[309] There was a meeting held in Tiruvarur on March 5, 1930 to support Muthulakshmi Reddi's abolition of the devadasi act and it also condemned the dedication young girls in the name of religion and leading them into evil life.[310] It stressed that all the self-respected women should marry as it was for their salvation from a miserable life.[311] Indirani Balasubramanian condemned the obstacles created by the legislative members in the enactment the abolition of the devadasi act.[312]

Bharatanatyam, the dance tradition of devadasi

Usually, devadasi and their artistic performance were inseparable. The livelihood of the devadasi largely depended on their performing ability. Frederique Apffel Marglin stated that the dance was very close to devadasi.[313] But the process of abolition and stigmatisation questioned the existence of the devadasi women. The strong protest against the devadasi system established a public opinion against the performance of devadasi women. The reformers, radicals, missionaries, doctors, journalists and social workers regarded the custom as a serious problem to the society and its community too. Sundar Kaali, the art historian, mentioned that an moral and sexual economies of nationalist modernity could not accommodate either *dasi* or her art. In consequence, *dasi* was pushed to the cultural margins of South Indian society.[314]

The Self-Respecters did not bother about the aesthetic values of the devadasi dance performance. More than that, they considered the exploitative and the submissiveness nature of the female body through the performance. *Kudi Arasu* mentioned that the performance of devadasi during the *puja* hours would disturb the minds of the devotees.[315] Kuppusami, a columnist in *Kudi Arasu,* mentioned that younger *dasis* were singing songs and danced during the marriage procession for money. But they did not consider modesty and public discipline and their performance tried to seduce the audience.[316] *Kudi Arasu* criticised the attitude of devadasi. It mentioned that devadasis were dedicated to temples for performing dances, but they dressed well and exposed their body to invite the devotees to their houses and looted their money.[317] These kind of performance seduces our young students and created a bad name for the country.[318]

The Self-Respect Movement propagated for the restriction of the performance of devadasi women. In 1928, *the Youth Conference of Isai Vellalar* at Chidambaram passed resolutions that the musical system of devadasi was degraded and recommended for reform.[319] In 1930, *the Women's Conference* asked the devadasi performers to leave their degraded profession, such as prostitution and it appealed to the people not to engage in *nautch* parties.[320] *The Musical Conference* of Erode in between May 12 and 13, 1930 advised the musician and other performers to maintain dignity.[321] These kinds of performance defame our country and seduce our young students.[322] In the name of the God women became prostitutes.[323]

The term, Bharatanatyam

Historically, the dance tradition of devadasi was popularly known as *sadhir attam*, *dasi attam* and *kurnatakam*. Since the dance used small drum orchestra was called as *china melam* (small troupe) which was opposed to *periya melam* (big troupe). The *periya melam* was performed in the outdoor engagements and generally included the musical instruments like *Natha-swaram* and *Tavil*.[324] *Ananda Vikatan*, a Tamil weekly, mentioned that on the basis of the time spent, they were well paid. They earned nearly hundred to two hundred rupees for their public performances.[325] In late 1920s, the processes of revival started to misinterpret the history of devadasi's dance.

They renamed *sadhir attam* as Bharatanatyam.[326] T.J.S. George, the biographer of M.S. Subbulakshmi, called the revival process as Brahminisation of music and dance.[327] Anand, a columnist in Outlook magazine, used the phrase that the total hijack of the South's rich classical arts into airless Brahmins monopolies and stifling its genuine growth.[328]

There was a huge discussion on renaming of devadasi's dance. It is difficult to find the exact person who coined the word Bharatanatyam. Kimiko Ohtani, an art historian, mentioned that the term Bharatanatyam was used only sixty years ago.[329] She assumed that the term Bharatanatyam began to be used around 1935 and by 1940 it had already become common.[330] In general, the revivalist claimed its credit. Rukmini Devi, V. Raghavan (musicologist) and E. Krishna Iyer were the leading personalities in the process. In earlier articles, often the dance performance of Rukmini Devi was called as Indian classical dance and the word, Bharatanatyam was seldom used.[331] However, Gowri Rama-narayan wrote that Rukmini Devi was the one who began to use it. According to her, at first, E. Krishna Iyer called his dance Natya, which means drama. The meaning of Bharata, as Rukmini Devi explained, was a combined word that was *bha* from *bhava* (emotion), *ra* from *raga* (melody) and *ta* from *tala* (rhythm).[332] Rukmini Devi authenticated her role in the process of renaming the devadasi dance tradition. She mentioned that so far as she knew that she was the first person, who began to dance in the early 1930's, to give the (new) name to the dance and since then the word Bharatanatyam had been acceptable in common use.[333] However, Sarada, a close associate of Rukmini Devi, did not know whether Rukmini Devi was the first one to use the name, Bharatanatyam.[334]

Ramasubramaniam wrote that the term was first coined by E. Krishna Iyer in the twenties of this century to honour the mythical name of *Bharata*, the author of the *Natya sastra*.[335] In 1932, *the Madras Music Conference* of the Music Academy passed a resolution to renaming of *sadhir* into Bharatanatyam. The idea was to remove the unsavory connotations of the priory existing names like *sadhir*, *dasi attam*, etc. The 'depraved' *sadhir* entered a 'respectable' home of Brahmin elites. The *Centenary Issue* of Krishna Iyer mentioned that it had been given a new lease of life under a new name just like girl given in marriage.[336] It was obvious that the new name helped tremendously to de-associate dance from its old image.[337] V.K. Narayanan Menon, president of Sangeet Natak Akademi, mentioned that term Bharatanatyam was coined by Raghavan to give the dance respect and a change of outlook about it.[338] Further, *Sruti* magazine stated that Raghavan used the word Bharatanatyam for the first time in his article (1933) which was titled *Bharatanatya Classical Dance-South Indian Nautch (In the Background of the Controversy over the Art)* and it was published in the journal *Sound and Shadow*, Madras, Vol. II, Issue 6, 1933.[339]

The revival of devadasi's dance

The revivalist had a strong disagreement with the reformers. C.N. Muthuranga Mudaliar criticised the reformist in *the Madras Music Conference, 1932*. He said that an object of the *anti-nautch* party was to abolish prostitution which was common among the class who were practicing the art.[340] He further stated that the reformers were working hard to eradicate it. But the abolition process did not prevent the custom of prostitution. So it clarified that prostitution had nothing to do with the practice of dance.[341] The pressure from the colonisers and radicals made the conservatives to resist the reform activities. The Brahmin, revivalist and other conservatives worked for the revival of their cultural and religious elements. Their arguments were largely supported by the ideologues of the Theosophical Society and Music Academy of Madras.[342]

The colonial politics on the devadasi practices renamed the dance art of devadasi as Bharatanatyam. Usually, revivalist claimed that the art of devadasi was 'sanitized' and 'revived'. Kaali Sundar noted that the so called respectable upper caste-well-read Brahmin men and women took up the task of reviving the devadasi dance tradition.[343] Davesh Soneji, an art historian, stated that the practice and politics of Bharatanatyam make tangible both realist and utopian visions of culture, nation, religion and aesthetics.[344] The devadasi figure stood at the centre of Bharatanatyam discourse.[345] Frederique Apffel Marglin mentioned that the view of the devadasis as morally degenerate women, and of the royal courts and the kings as the instruments of this degeneration solved a contradiction for the nationalist elite who were concerned with the 'revival' of Indian arts, a contradiction created by the West.[346]

Rukmini Devi (1904-1986)

Rukmini Devi was one of the prominent women in the process of the renaming Bharatanatyam. *Ananda Vikatan* praised Rukmini Devi as a reviver of Bharatanatyam.[347] Rukmini Devi was born into a Brahmin family to an engineer father in Madurai. During her teenage, her family shifted to Madras because of their parents' involvement in the activities of the Theosophical Society. She was interested and worked for Annie Besant, the president of the Society. There she met George Sydney Arundale (1878-1945), an English theosophist who had become the president of the Society after the death of Annie Besant.

In 1920, George Sydney Arundale married Rukmini Devi. The marriage provided her an international exposure and the opportunity to witness the performance of famous Russian dancer Anna Pavlova at Covent Garden, London in 1924. The performance of Anna inspired Rukmini Devi to meet her in Australia and learn dance steps from her troop. Anna advised Rukmini Devi to concentrate on the revival of the art forms of her country.[348] Rukmini Devi learnt *sadhir attam* from devadasis and *nattuvanars.*[349] Maylapore Gauri Amma (?-1970), a devadasi, was the first *sadhir* teacher of Rukmini Devi. Later, she learnt from Minakshi Sundaram Pillai (1869-1954), the famous *nattuvanar* of Panthanainallur.[350] But Minakshi Sundaram was reluctant to teach a girl from other communities. However, with the help of Krishna Iyer, she managed to persuade him to accept her as a student in 1934.

Rukmini Devi's first performance was held in December 1935 at the Adyar theatre within the compound of the Theosophical Society (*See Appendix*: - 13). She claimed that the performance was a part of the convention of the Society rather than a private function. It drew large public attention. The particular performance of Rukmini Devi was considered as the first public presentation of Bharatanatyam.[351] The dance was performed in a big hall in front of diverse audience such as whites and black, Judges, Lawyers, Secretaries, Nationalist, Government employees, and children. The huge crowd witnessed the changing scenario in relation to Bharatanatyam.[352]

R. Krishnamurthy[353] (September 9, 1899-December 5, 1954), who was popularly known as Kalki, wrote a column *Adal Padal* (Dancing and Singing) in Ananda Vikatan stated that the performance of Rukmini Devi was the great momentum of the revival of the ancient tradition.[354] The journals of Theosophical Society encouraged Rukmini Devi and published her dance activities between 1936 and 1937. But her Guru Minakshi Sundaram was not satisfied with her immediate *arangerram* (first public stage performance). Minakshi Sundaram in his article *Bharatha Natyam* questioned the talent of the modern performers who were generally performing the traditional dance and criticised the changes in the dance style. He mentioned that the changes were unwanted and there was no need to incorporate this in the traditional dance style of the devadasi tradition. He was concerned about the improper training and their selection of western dress and ornaments.[355]

Immediately after her *arangerram*, Rukmini Devi established an institution called the *International Academy of Arts*. It was officially registered in January 1936 under the Charitable Societies Act.[356] Initially, the institution recruited the students from the members of the Society and friends. Later, she renamed the institution as *Kalakshetra*. Until 1945, Kalakshetra was financially supported by the Theosophical Society.[357]

The revivalist and dances of devadasi

The revivalist undervalued the traditional techniques of devadasi dance. Rukmini Devi criticised the performance of devadasi as a stunt. According to her, the dance performance of devadasi did not have any soul.[358] Avanthi

Meduri mentioned that Rukmini Devi and others of her 'high social class' considered that the existing dance forms as being too crude and literal.[359] In an interview with Kimiko Ohtani, Sarada Hoffman, an associate of Rukmini Devi, shared her *Kalakshetra* experiences. In the interview, she said that Rukmini Devi instructed her students to forget the dance techniques which were taught by the early teachers, because she believed that the traditional dance steps were not correct.[360]

Geetha and Rajadurai discussed about the arguments of Self-Respecters on political Brahmanism.[361] Rukmini Devi was ambiguous to substantiate her position. She was not from a traditional dancing community and so, she critiqued the traditional methods of learning dance. She stated that a creative artist expressed the Divine Genius, so nobody could teach something which was related to divinity. The expressions must come from the inner-self, as something no one could help to express.[362] She further stated that in the modern day performances, *psyche* played a predominant role rather than the body.[363] There were differences between the acrobatic steps and dance movements. There was no need for dancer to do the tricks of acrobats. The real dancer could make just a few gestures with a higher knowledge.[364]

Rukmini Devi stressed that the body could fulfill its highest dharma not only by giving to the world an expression of physical grace with an embodiment, an expression, of the cosmic being.[365] The essential elements of the dance was a joy, the inner bliss which was a deep experience.[366] Rukmini Devi said that art could be one of the greatest achievements of humanity. The dance transcended the physical with the body as a vehicle and lifted humanity into a world of the higher emotion of joy and the pure intellect or wisdom.[367] On the other hand, she mentioned dance was an expression of the physical body. The physical expression was both dangerous and magnificent instruments. The weakness of the physical body was its coarseness and vulgarity.[368] There was no place for vulgarity in dance.[369] The sensual and vulgar expressions which were introduced into life were always a sign of deterioration of civilisation.[370]

The queen of Travancore addressed in *the Madras Music Conference, 1930* of the Music Academy. There, she expressed that the need for an organised and sustained effort for the revival of art by conserving and developing its beauties and removing its excrescences.[371] The critical Rukmini Devi, made many changes in the dance tradition, especially in music, background and presentation.[372] She blended *sadhir attam* with the new and old forms. During the dance performance, *nattuvanars* were traditionally accompanied by devadasi. In general, the audiences were distracted by the gestures of *nattuvanars*.[373] Rukmini Devi replaced *nattuvanars* by *Kalakshetra* singers in the dance performance and seated them in the corner of the stage.[374]

Krishnamurthy appreciated these changes in his column *Adal Padal*.[375] But in late 1920s, E.V. Ramasami was critical of Brahmin attempts at appropriating all honours in the field of music to themselves. He had, then argued that non-Brahmin musicians were deliberately undervalued, denied respect and honours and humiliated while their Brahmin peer, even if younger in years and lacking talent, had been encouraged by the Brahmin press.[376]

Usually, *shringara* (love or eroticism) was considered as the chief element of the traditional dance. Krishnamurthy mentioned that the beauty of Bharatanatyam was based on the element of *shringara*.[377] Rukmini Devi believed that the portrayal of *shringara* was "ordinary and low".[378] Kalyanasundaram, a *nattuvanar*, mentioned about his personal experience of his hesitation to explain the meaning of a text or movement to young girls.[379] Rukmini Devi also felt that expressing *shringara* movements in the profane area would not suit her and the students. So, Rukmini Devi and other Brahmin elites thought to differentiate the so called vulgarity from sublime.[380] She selected her repertoire carefully. She choose *bhakti* (devotion) as a concept and used songs which were based on religious theme.[381] Kimiko Ohtani mentioned that Rukmini Devi discarded eleven *padams* whose main theme was on *shringara* and introduced *kirtana* which had not been part of the traditional devadasi dance form.[382]

Rukmini Devi approached the dance reforms through body control, mind and awareness. In a typical Brahmanical manner, she focused on ritual, style and form. She considered form as a revealing content and perceived it as a dynamic thing.[383] She visualised the process of reform as a secularisation of the devadasi dance.[384] She gave much attention to the personal experience of the dancer rather than the perspective of the audience.[385] According to her, the creative spirit (dance) did not mean always new ideas and everything must be done differently. She believed the person who had the creative genius could do the same movements a hundred times, but it seemed different because each time the concerned person perceived it new.[386]

Rukmini Devi believed that the Indian dance was ruined due to the savagery of war like the destruction of magnificent monuments of ancient culture.[387] She further stated that the Indian art forms were not just meant for merely showing off to others.[388] In ancient India, art forms were part of the everyday life.[389] But in modern times, there was no creative art in modern performances.[390] So she suggested the modern dancer could change and adapt the ancient art to suit the modern needs.[391] Especially, Bharatanatyam needed such combination of old and new styles. She wished that the glorious traditional dance should not be stopped by telling in the following ways:

> Wherever God has left His work comparatively undone, we must finish it. We must carry on His Beauty and if we want to be expressive and creative, we must add and not subtract.[392]

Rukmini Devi mentioned the incapability of Indians to discover the ancient treasures such as dance.[393] According to her, the great personalities usually discover the greatness and bring out that greatness to the foreground.[394] Art in the West was the Parthenon of Greece. It was in a ruined state, but the enormous efforts were made to reconstruct the Art. The reconstruction happened because of the beauty of the art and it could inspire the society for thousands of years.[395] Rukmini Devi stated a following story about the conservation of the ancient culture:

> An old bronze had been kept for years in a brass shop. The material was considered as neglected and unwanted one. But later, sometimes a person came with the aim of collecting the beautiful brass from the shop. The shopkeeper got surprised and then replied that the material was very old and nobody liked it. So he sold it for a cheap price. On the other hand, the visitor was extremely happy and wondered the ignorance of the shopkeeper who possessed the bronze material.[396]

Nationalism

As a Theosophist and a Brahmin, Rukmini Devi was interested to continue the age old Hindu practices especially, the dance tradition. She considered that dance was an ancient culture and religion.[397] Many Indologists and nationalist historians advanced the claim that Bharatanatyam was a direct descendant of the arts of the Tamil Sangam age.[398] Minakshi Sundaram Pillai addressed that Bharatanatyam was ancient and it could explain the mythical history.[399] The upper class Brahmin elite claimed the dance form from the age old Sanskrit tradition. The veteran musicologist, Raghavan acknowledged the term *sadhir* during his discussions on the dance traditions of South India.[400] Raghavan mentioned that the music of ours had been age old and it was the outcome of our spiritual and religious fervour.[401] He considered Bharatanatyam as an authentic Indian dance art. He traced its antiquary from the *Rig-Vedic* hymns, *Mahabharata* and *Chilappathikaram*.[402] He stated that the Bharatanatyam was same dance that Arjuna taught the *Virata* princess in the *Mahabharata* and also it was the same dance that Malavika danced in the play of Kalidasa and Madhavi did in *Chilappathikaram*.[403]

Theosophical society had great respect for the Hindu tradition and for the devadasi institution. Annie Besant stated that the dancing class woman of temple were established to exonerates the ancestors from any such evil motives and was worthy of their earnest attention. Further, she mentioned that the devadasis were a band of pure virgin devotees who attached to the ancient

Hindu temples and used to preach religion to the common place that resort to the temple for their daily worship. She further noted that in ancient times they were held in high esteem and had a respect and very well looked after. They would spend their time in doing religious service to the Gods and the devotees of the temple as the word *dasi* itself signifies. They would follow the procession of Gods addressed in the simplest *sanyasi* garbs and singing pious hymns suitable to the occasion.[404]

Sathyamurthi spoke about the importance of the musical revival of India, especially South India. He insisted that music has always played a larger role in helping the achievement of freedom to other countries.[405] He recommended that Indian National Congress should use the new spirit which emerged among Tamils with regards to music and dance for Indian nationalism.[406] Hence, the Music Academy was established to fulfil the national dreams.[407] Sathyamurthi mentioned that one of the aims of the music academy was to rescue the South Indian music from the stagnation into which it had fallen at the present day.[408] He worried that the South Indian music could be considered as normal feature of every home.[409] The Music Academy assimilated all the rich musical elements of the non-Brahmin traditions of South India.

In the nineteenth and early twentieth century aestheticians and scholars involved in formulating the history of Indian dance, attempting to compensate for its progressive "degradation", elevated dance to a new high.[410] Annie Besant mentioned that the 'native' culture was superior to that of the colonizers.[411] Krishnamurthy stated that nationalism was the chief causes for the revival of the dances and music in South India.[412] In a public gathering, Rukmini Devi mentioned that the self-rule would not occur unless the Indian art forms were revived.[413] Krishnamurthy recommended that Indian National Congress should use the new spirit which emerged among Tamils with regards to music and dance for Indian nationalism.[414] In 1935, Kothai Nayaki presided the Music Conference in Nagappattinam and it, passed a resolution that all women would learn music and Bharatanatyam.[415]

Religious spirit

The revivalists placed the dance and music within the religious context. They stressed the importance of spirituality in dance performance. The *Madras Music Conference of 1930* mentioned that music was divine origin because it communicated the divine qualities such as healing, soothing and softening the distressed human minds and bodies.[416] The Madras Music Academy recommended the Hindu Religious Endowments Boards to revive the tradition of reciting *Tevaram* and *Prabandham* and performances of Bharatanatyam and Nathaswaram as a part of the daily offerings to the God in all temples.[417] In 1927, Conference of the Indian Music Club was held in Tiruchirappalli. The Conference extensively discussed about the dance performance of devadasi and passed resolution under P.G. Sundaresu Sastry. The resolutions that stressed the importance of the revival of dance tradition in Madras Presidency. According to it, dance was one among the sixteen *upachchara* of Vedic agamas and dance of woman was considered as a part of the *Asvamedha yagna*. Further, it stated that the reformers were ignorant, so the temple institution should not remove *natyam* (dance) during the *aradhana* (puja).[418] *Kudi Arasu* condemned the resolution of the Conference of the Indian Music Club and questioned the supporters of the resolution and asked if they would dare to make their wives dance in temples with devotional rapture.[419]

The revivalist voiced for spirituality. Raghavan mentioned that the temples had rare ragas and forms of composition and it serve art as well as the moral and spiritual regeneration of the people.[420] Rukmini Devi stressed the importance of the religious spirit in the dance and she noted that the elements and inspiration of dance should be influenced by the religious values alone.[421] She admitted that Indian dance was merged with the rhythmic movement with music, philosophy and spiritual ideals and these elements could not be separated.[422] In *Annual Music Conference*, G.N. Balasubrahmanyam mentioned that the modern music was the highly evolved development of our ancient music.[423] He stressed that the music of the West is mainly secular, orchestral, recitative, and collective as against ours which is spiritual, vocal, interpretative and individual. It was mainly as a means for uplifting the human spirit towards Godhead.[424]

The revivalist believed that the problem of modern civilisation was based on its thought processes.[425] Except among the purest classical dancers, the body was the chief instrument of ugliness. But they concealed this ugliness through their dance performances. They conceived that the dance performance in the music halls, night clubs and other entertainments would not only degrade the dance but also womanhood.[426] According to them, in the entire world India alone had a perfect system of dancing which the ancient classical text revealed and showed that the dance had the highest conception of beauty in their respective age.[427]

Rukmini Devi mentioned that in earlier days Indian art was performed because of its unconscious efforts, but nowadays people were trying to do it consciously.[428] The revivalist gave much attention to the real experiences.[429] Rukmini Devi stated that dancers while performing the themes from the religious books should feel the spirit of Radha in everyday life while performing the story of Sri Krishna and Radha.[430] The beauty of the argument was the witness of the soul rather than of the mind.[431] Further, she stated that the Indian dance was the magnificent conception of Lord Natarajar, the divine dancer, and who was considered as the father of all arts, the teacher and the great *yogi*. The world got salvation not only through His meditation but also

His dance. So, the dancer should understand the spirit of Natarajar and the pure essence of the Art.[432]

The revivalist condemned the approach of criticising the Indian *nautch* and mentioned that it was a fashion in modern times to question the Indian *nautch*. Inadequately, they pointed out that the condemnation was least deserved. The performance of Krishna Bhagavatar of Thanjavur of Harikatha exposed the unworthiness of the criticism. The performance altered the public opinion and properly placed the concept of *abhinayam* in a modern dance tradition.[433] Following these developments, the Academy invited Srimati Gowri to dance in its Annual Conference on January 3, 1932 with the musical accompaniment of Balaraman of the Nadamuni Band.[434]

The decisive discussion on the fate and future on dance was held on the sixth day of the *Sixth Annual Conference* of the Music Academy. The venue was a special *pandal* erected for the occasion to the north of the Ripon Buildings in the then People's Park. The *pandal* was circular in shape and very spacious. It easily could accommodate two thousand persons. A big dais was also erected for the artists who were to give model performances every evening. A huge gathering of prominent people attended the conference and many took part in its deliberations. Several dignitaries attended the conference.[435]

The Music Academy of Madras

The relationship between the Music Academy and Bharatanatyam was inseparable. Stan Harding supported the Academy for its initiation towards dance.[436] The Music Academy was considered as one of the early premier Music Academies in South India. The history of the Academy went back to mid-twenties. In 1928, the Music Academy was established and it addressed *nautch* question.[437] The well-wishers and music lovers were interested to establish an organisation to stimulate the concentration of a musical culture in South India. The *All-India Music Conference* was held in 1927 at Madras, while following the Conference of the Indian National Congress. The All-India Music Conference recommended the formation of a Music Academy in Madras for the preservation and encouragement of the traditional arts. Later, the organisation played an important role in the revival of Indian classical dance form.

Srividya Natarajan mentioned that the Music Academy was an important institution for the promotion of classical music and dance.[438] Usually, the members of the Music Academy were part of the cultural wing of the Indian National Congress who was projecting devadasi as performer of Bharatanatyam and identified themselves as the 'pro-art progressives'.[439] Avanthi Meduri mentioned that the institution of Music Academy was involved in the political reformulation of Bharatanatyam which actually helped to make the dance more respectable.[440] Sathyamurthi praised the Academy for the restoration of Bharatanatyam to its pristine honourable place.[441] *Centenary Issue of E. Krishna Iyer* explained that the executive and academic works of the Academy laid the foundation for rescuing Bharatanatyam from its danger of extinction and reviving.[442]

The Academy played a key role in the revival of devadasi dance. *The Centenary Issue of E. Krishna Iyer* stated the Music Academy of Madras and E. Krishna Iyer acted as knight in shining armor, stepped into the battle to help save the dance in distress and assist the transfiguration of the sullied *sadhir* into blessed Bharatanatyam significantly.[443] The formation of the Music Academy was in the interest of India. The Academy was established to promote the Brahmanical art tradition of South India. It primarily concentrated on the encouragement and promotion of the Hindu tradition. The Brahmin elites and orthodox Hindus would like to construct the national art. Nationalism was the chief causes for the revival of the dances and music in South India.[444] Krishnamurthy noted the performance of *sadhir* in the Congress sessions.[445] Mostly these performances were held in the premises of the Congress.[446]

E. Krishna Iyer (August 9, 1897-1968)

E. Krishna Iyer played a decisive role in the renaissance of *sadhir* dance into Bharatanatyam. He was born in Tirunelveli as one of the fourteenth children of Kailasa Iyer and Ananthalakshmi. He was a trained musicians and dancer. Since 1925, he learnt *sadhir* from Madurantakam Jagadambal, a celebrated devadasi and later Melatur Natesa Iyer taught him a dance.[447] As a Law graduate, he was active member in the Home Rule League under the leadership of Annie Besant.[448] Later, he engaged with the several political movements which were initiated by Gandhi. As a freedom fighter, he was jailed in 1930 and 1932, He became an associate-editor of the Free Press News which was the young nationalist news agency in the 1930s.[449] After that he was more deeply engaged in journalism and he also became an art critic of newspapers such as *The Mail* and the *Indian Express*. However, art activities dominated his later life. [450] He favoured the devadasi abolition but concerned for the revival of the dance forms. E. Krishna Iyer considered the effort of reformers to discourage the devadasi custom as reasonable.[451] He fought vigorously with the *anti-nautch* troop. He did not defend the system. He accepted the evils of the system but he made out a persuasive case for preserving the art of dance.[452] He fought against the *anti-nautch* campaign through performance, writing, lectures, and encouraged and helped other dancers. In 1932, Krishna Iyer fought a crucial battle in the press with Muthulakshmi Reddi over the abolition of the devadasi system.

E. Krishna Iyer, was one of the Secretaries of the Academy who was interested in including *sadhir* programmes in the Academy.[453] He invited devadasis to perform in the Academy. According to the *Centenary Issue of E. Krishna Iyer*, the executives of the Academy were keen to understand the development of dance discourse and willing to rescue the traditional *sadhir* dance. They strongly condemned the efforts of the reformers which regarding the abolition of the devadasi and their performances. Mrs. Harding forewarned in her speech that the ritual dances should not be transplanted (to the secular stage) because it had struck roots deep already; and that only tender shoots could easily be transplanted, not trees.[454] V. Varaha Narasimhcharlu, member of the Academy Experts' Committee, criticised that if there was any defect in the morals of these persons (devadasi), steps should be taken to remedy that defect but to destroy the art itself on that ground is neither an effective remedy not a wise step.[455]

Diwan Bahadur N. Pattabhirama Rao Pantulu gave an illustration of 'ghee'. He mentioned that everyone admitted that ghee as a necessary nutrition diet. If ghee got spoiled by being stored in a brass or copper vessel, people did not even think of giving up the use of ghee. But they tried to secure it purity by taking care to see that it was store in a better vessel.[456] His argument was supported by P.G. Sunderasa Sastriar of National College, Tiruchirappalli. He said that it was true that ghee would be spoiled if kept in a brass or copper vessel. But there was a remedy for it; it was to provide a coating to the vessel. Similarly, if we teach respect to the people who are already practicing this art, there can be no fear of immorality creeping in.[457] Further, he stated that this was like 'giving a dog bad name and hanging it'. So it was most unfair that just because somebody wrote something in the papers about dancing, we should let the art die once for all.[458]

Srinivasa Raghava Ayyangar, noted authority of Tyagaraja's compositions, said that the immediate task of the art lovers should be to encourage the fine arts, particularly among the reclaimed members of the devadasi class, as their heredity in the art, it was enough, for the present they were induced to cultivate a sympathetic and an appreciative attitude towards it. Time will work out the rest.[459] Stan Harding accepted the immemorial history of dance tradition and she mentioned that the disassociation of the dance from the temple would be like uprooting an old tree. Further, she argued for the irrelevance of the modern costumes changes of devadasis.[460]

The new stage of devadasi

The Music Academy's attention towards dance was at its peak during the period between 1930 and 1935. The Music Academy made an effort to revive the devadasi dance tradition. The Music Academy started to organise the dance performances of devadasi. The academy noted that it has almost become a fashion nowadays to condemn the Indian *nautch* and look askance at it. They felt that this condemnation was least deserved. They hoped that in the days to come public opinion will veer round and give unto *abhinayam* its proper place.[461] Later, the *Annual Music Conference of Music Academy of 1932* marked the significant event in the revival of *sadhir attam*. The sixth day (December 28, 1932) of the Conference was devoted to the discussion on the *Nautch* Question. E. Krishna Iyer prepared a resolution on the dance.

The resolutions favoured and encouraged the art of Bharatanatyam. It stated that Bharatanatyam was a great and ancient art which was unexceptionable. It appealed to the public and art associations for the necessary attention to encourage Bharatanatyam. The conference requested the Music Academy to take steps to disseminate correct ideas regarding the art and to help the public to a proper appreciation thereof. It agreed to initiate the move with women's organisations who should give a proper training in the art, by instituting a course of instruction. It suggested that to make dancing respectable it was necessary to encourage public performances before respectable gatherings.[462] The resolution was intended to reform devadasis and suggested the importance of an alternative profession.[463] Krishnamurthy public opinion for softening the desirability of saving sadhir dance with its good qualities.[464]

The executive functionaries of the Academy continued to encourage the art of dance under its new name of Bharatanatyam. The academy provided a space for the dance performance and the Academy allowed the dancer to perform their dance. In a decade between 1930 and 1940, a significant number of devadasi performed in the Academy. The Academy helped to stage dances by outstanding devadasi. The Music Academy organised its first performance concerts of Kalyani daughters of Thanjavur in March 1931.[465] The performance drew a small crowd but marked a significant event in the history of dance in South Indian culture.[466] During the concert, the academy instead tried to move public opinion against the condemnation of the Indian *nautch* and it focused on the performance and the grandeur of the art.[467] Further, the note welcomed the changing notions of the public towards the dance.[468]

E. Krishna Iyer reported that the renaissance of the Bharatanatyam might be said to have begun on January 1, 1933, the date of the second recital of the Kalyani daughters at the Academy.[469] The *Annual Conference of the Music Academy, 1934* witnessed the intention of the Academy for dance reforms. Sathyamurthi praised the Academy for its efforts towards the restoration of Bharatanatyam to its pristine honourable place.[470] Artists from families which considered dance as a hereditary profession dominated the stage until 1936. The first non-professional dancer at the Academy was Balachandra, a Brahmin girl about whom not much information is available and danced in December 1938.[471] After the 1935, a new factor emerged in the South Indian dance tradition. A group of Brahmin women who were associated with the Theosophical Society started to learn the dance.[472] These Brahmin dancers had infused their 'upper' caste values to the dance.[473] The Music Academy provided a platform for these 'new' dancers. The participation of the devadasi's performance in the Academy started to decrease. Douglas M. Knight Jr referred that from the formation of Music Academy there were twenty-one dance performances that were held by the end of 1940. He enumerated between 1931 and 1937, thirteen dance performance of devadasi occurred but the period between 1938 and 1940 witnessed the growing number of the performance of non-devadasi.[474]

Conclusion

The two decades 1920's and 1930's were significant in the history of devadasi system. In 1920's, the devadasi system was in for abolition. Muthulakshmi and Self-Respecters from the Self-Respect Movement argued, worked and campaigned for the abolition and propagated the irrelevance of the custom in the name of 'sacredness' and 'divine duty'. The hard work of Muthulakshmi and Self-Respecters was able to create a public opinion against the practices and passed the resolution of the devadasi dedication in the MLC in 1930. Following the historical event, the revivalists who generally accepted Brahmanical ideas initiated the move of reviving the dance of devadasi. They renamed devadasi dance as Bharatanatyam. The Theosophical Society and Music Academy of Madras helped the initiatives of Rukmini Devi and E. Krishna Iyer. They made some of the changes in the traditional dance for the convenient. In the 1930's, the dance of devadasi was staged in the so-called secular and 'prestigious' stages of Music Academy. In the mean time, some of the Brahmin girls started to learn dance from the traditional *nattuvanars* and gradually occupied the stages of devadasi and questioned the cultural economy of the devadasi community. Hence, by the end of twentieth century the devadasis lost their dance tradition.

References

1. Muthulakshmi Reddi, S. *Why Should the Devadasi Institution in the Hindu Temples be Abolished?*. Madras: Central Co-operative Printing Works, Ltd, 1927: p. 4.
2. Muthulakshmi Reddy, S. *My Experience as a Legislator*. Madras: Current Thought Press, 1930: p. 56.
3. *Ibid.*, p. 59.
4. *The Proceedings of the Madras Legislative Council: Second Session of the Third Legislativle Council*. Vol. XXXVIII. October 31-November 5, 1927: p. 415.
5. Muthulakshmi Reddy, S. 1930. *Op.cit.*, p. 227.
6. *Ibid.*, p. 58.
7. Muthulakshmi Reddy, S. 1927. *Op.cit.*, p. 4.

8. *The Proceedings of the Madras Legislative Council: Second Session of the Third Legislative Council*. Vol. XXXVIII. October 31-November 5, 1927: p. 415.
9. Muthulakshmi Reddy, S. 1930. *Op.cit.*, p. 59.
10. Muthulakshmi Reddy, S. *The Presidential Address of Dr. (Mrs.) S. Muthulakshmi Reddi*. Delivered at the Seventh Andhra Provincial Women's Conference held at Ellore. November 4-5, 1933: p. 6.
11. Muthulakshmi Reddy, S. 1927. *Op.cit.*, p. 2.
12. *The Proceedings of the Madras Legislative Council: Second Session of the Third Legislative Council*. Vol. XXXVIII. October 31-November 5, 1927: p. 416.
13. Muthulakshmi Reddy, S. 1930. *Op.cit.*, p. 232.
14. Muthulakshmi Reddy, S. 1927. *Op.cit.*, p. 1.
15. *Ibid.*, p. 2.
16. *Ibid.*, p. 3.
17. *Ibid.*, p. 2.
18. *Ibid.*
19. *The Proceedings of the Madras Legislative Council: Second Session of the Third Legislative Council*. Vol. XXXVIII. October 31-November 5, 1927: pp. 416-417.
20. Kaliyanasundaranar, Thiru.Vi. *Pennin Perumai allathu Vazhkkaiththunai* (The pride of women and the partner) (in Tamil). Chennai: Saratha Pathippakam, 2006: pp. 263-264.
21. *Young India*, 29/08/1929. *The Collected Works of Mahatma Gandhi (June-October1929)*. Vol. 41. New Delhi: Ministry of Information and Broadcasting Division, 1970: p. 337.
22. Muthulakshmi Reddy, S. 1927. *Op.cit.*, p. 8.
23. *Ibid.*, p. 2-3.
24. *Ibid.*, p. 2.
25. *Ibid.*, p. 1.
26. *The Proceedings of the Madras Legislative Council: Second Session of the Third Legislative Council*. Vol. XXXVIII. October 31-November 5, 1927: p. 415.
27. Muthulakshmi Reddy, S. 1930. *Op.cit.*, p. 232.
28. Muthulakshmi Reddy, S. 1927. *Op.cit.*, p. 6.
29. Muthulakshmi Reddy, S. 1930. *Op.cit.*, p. 56.
30. *The Proceedings of the Madras Legislative Council: Second Session of the Third Legislative Council*. Vol. XXXVIII. October 31-November 5, 1927: pp. 416-417.
31. *The Proceedings of the Madras Legislative Council: Second Session of the Third Legislative Council*. Vol. XXXVIII. October 31-November 5, 1927. p. 415.
32. *Ibid.*, pp. 416-417.
33. Muthulakshmi Reddy, S. 1927. *Op.cit.*, p. 10.
34. *Ibid.*, p. 9.
35. *Thirumigu Muthulakshmi Ammalin Thermanam* (The Decision of Muthulakshmi Ammal) (in Tamil). 27/05/1928. *Kudi Arasu*.

36. *Pottukkattu Niruththum Chattam* (The Prevention of *Pottu* Ceremony Act) (in Tamil). 30/03/1930. *Kudi Arasu.*
37. Muthulakshmi Reddy, S. 1927. *Op.cit.,* p. 10.
38. Muthulakshmi Reddy, S. 1930. *Op.cit.*
39. *Ibid.,* p. 10.
40. *Ibid.,* p. 13.
41. *Ibid.,* p. 10.
42. Muthulakshmi Reddy, S. 1927. *Op.cit.,* p. 13.
43. Muthulakshmi Reddy, S. 1933. *Op.cit.,* p. 6.
44. Muthulakshmi Reddy, S. 1930. *Op.cit.,* p. 232.
45. *The Welcome Speeches of Mrs. Lakshmi Ammal in the Second Self-respect Women's Conference* (in Tamil). 04/05/1930. *Kudi Arasu.*
46. *Thoughts of Periyar E.V.R.: Publisher's Introduction.* Compiled by V. Anaimuthu. Chennai: Periyar E.V. Ramasamy-Nagammai Education and Research Trust, 2009: p. 45.
47. Geetha, V and S.V. Rajadurai. *Towards a Non-Brahmin Millennim: From Iyothee Thass to Periyar.* Calcutta: Samya, 1998: p. 302.
48. *Ibid.,* p. 312.
49. *Ibid.,* p. 308.
50. The word 'Self-Respecters' indicated the activists who were largely engaged in the social filed and intellectual sphere to propagate the rational ideas of the Self-Respect Movement.
51. *Samayach Sirthirutham.* (The Religious Reform) (in Tamil). 23/10/1927. *Kudi Arasu.*
52. *Ibid.*
53. The speech was delivered by E.V. Ramasami in 14th Sengunthar Community Conference which held at Chennimalai, Coimbatore. (Ramasami, E.V. *Pirappurimaiyum Athan Thadaikalum* (The Birth Rights and its Obstacles) (in Tamil). 09/01/1927. *Kudi Arasu.*)
54. *Periyar Kalanchiyam: Kudiyarasu-Puratchi.* (*An Encyclopedia of Periyar: Kudi Arasu and Puratchi*) (in Tamil). Vol. 18. (1935- I). K. Veeramani. Com. Chennai: The Periyar Self-respect Propaganda Institution, 2010: p. 308.
55. Sakthidas. *Pengal Viduthalai* (The Women Liberation) (in Tamil). 29/06/1930. *Kudi Arasu.*
56. *Sthirikal Mahanadu* (The Women's Conference) (in Tamil). 08/12/1929. *Kudi Arasu.*
57. *Kudi Arasu.* 30/07/1927.
58. Presidential address of E.V. Ramasami at the *South Indian Social Reformers' Conference* held on 26/11/1928 at Madras. *(Revolt.* 05/12/1928 and 12/12/1928.
59. *Devadasi Olippu Murai* (The Abolition of Devadasi Custom) (in Tamil). 31/08/1959. *Viduthalai.*
60. *S.N.D.P Yogam Endru Sollappadum Thiyar Mahanadu* (The Conference of Thiyar which was popularly known as *S.N.D.P Yogam*) (in Tamil). 08/06/1930. *Kudi Arasu.*
61. *Ibid.*

62. *Kulanthaikaludan Manamakkal Thirumanam* (The Marriage among Children) (in Tamil). 21/09/1930. *Kudi Arasu.*
63. *S.N.D.P Yogam Endru Sollappadum Thiyar Mahanadu* (The Conference of Thiyar which was popularly known as *S.N.D.P Yogam*) (in Tamil). 08/06/1930. *Kudi Arasu.*
64. *Sthirikal Mahanadu* (The Women's Conference) (in Tamil). 08/12/1929. *Kudi Arasu.*
65. *Vibhachcharath Thadaich Chattam* (The Prostitution Prevention Act) (in Tamil). 01/05/1932. *Kudi Arasu.*
66. *Engum Suyamariyathai Sathyakirakam* (In Everywhere, the Non-Violence Protests for Self-Respect). 06/11/1927. *Kudi Arasu.*
67. Geetha, V. "Gender and Political Discourse." *Economic and Political Weekly* 26, no. 7. (February 16, 1991): p. 388.
68. Nilavathi. *Indhu Madha vizhchchikkum Idhara madha Valarchchikkum Udhavi Purivathu- Pazhum: Thindamaiyum-Vidhavaikalin Thuyaramume*! (Helping for the growth of other religions and degrading the Hindu religion make dissolute: The sorrows of widows and unsociability) (in Tamil). 09/03/1930. *Kudi Arasu.*
69. Jnanammal. *Pengalukku Vendiya Seethanam Yathu?* (The gift which women needed?) (in Tamil). 06/04/1930. *Kudi Arasu.*
70. *The Welcome Speeches of Mrs. Lakshmi Ammal in the Second Self-respect Women's Conference* (in Tamil). 04/05/1930. *Kudi Arasu.*
71. Bharathi, Lakshmirathan. *Hinthu Vithavaikal Nilamaiyum, Avarkal Marumanathirkkuch Chatta, Samugath Thadaikalaum* (The condition of the Hindu widows and the social cum legal obstacles for their remarriages) (in Tamil). 15/03/1931. *Kudi Arasu.*
72. Chidambaranar, Sivakami. *Pengal Nilamai: - Angalaivida Pengal Ilivanavarkala?* (The condition of women: Are Women more ignominy than men) (in Tamil). 18/10/1931. *Kudi Arasu.*
73. *S.N.D.P Yogam Endru Sollappadum Thiyar Mahanadu* (The Conference of Thiyar which was popularly known as *S.N.D.P Yogam*) (in Tamil). 08/06/1930. *Kudi Arasu.*
74. Srilatha, K. *The Other Half of the Coconut: Women Writing Self-Respect Moment.* New Delhi: Kali for Women, 2003: p. 3.
75. Anaimuthu, V. 2009. *Op.cit.,* p. 46.
76. Jnanammal. *Pengalukku Vendiya Seethanam Yathu?* (The gift which women needed?) (in Tamil). 06/04/1930. *Kudi Arasu.*
77. Geetha, V and S.V. Rajadurai. 1998. *Op.cit.,* p. 314.
78. *Ibid.,* p. 315.
79. Kunjitham, S. *Kudi Arasum Namathu Iyakkamum* (*Kudi Arasu* and Our Organisation) (in Tamil). 15/05/1932. *Kudi Arasu.*
80. *Ibid.*
81. *Swadeshamitranaum Sriman Kirshnamachariyarum* (Swadeshamitran and Mr Krishnamachari) (in Tamil). 04/12/1927. *Kudi Arasu.*
82. *Puratchi*, the Tamil weekly, was established in November 26, 1933, and in March 26, 1934, The Tamil weekly *Paguttharivu* was established. E.V. Krishnasami,

the brother of E.V. Ramasami, became the editor of the both the Tamil weeklies. on November 7, 1928, E.V. Ramasami established *Revolt,* The English weekly. It became the first English language weekly to be published by the Self Respect Movement, and it was edited by E.V. Ramasami. *Viduthalai*, the bi-weekly, was published from June 1, 1935 for Justice Party, later it became daily.

83. *Swadeshamitranaum Sriman Kirshnamachariyarum* (Swadeshamitran and Mr. Krishnamachari) (in the Tamil). 04/12/1927. *Kudi Arasu* and The decisions which made were under the leadership of E.V Ramasami in Tirunelveli Self-respect Conference. 11/12/1927. *Kudi Arasu.*
84. *Errukkondom* (Accepted) (in Tamil). 08/04/1928. *Kudi Arasu.*
85. *Naan Alakkum Moottai* (The bag which I am measured) (in Tamil). 08/04/1928. *Kudi Arasu.*
86. Anaimuthu, V. 2009. *Op.cit.,* p. 38.
87. The office of *Kudi Arasu* was inaugurated by Tiruppathirip Puliyur Sivashanmuga Meingana Sivachchariyar Samikal alias Gnaniar Samikal in April 18, 1925. Usually, the newspaper was published from Erode. But a short time, between June 16 and December 15, 1929 the newspaper was published from Chennai. The newspaper was banned by the colonial Government in 1934, 1941 and 1942. As a newspaper *Kudi Arasu* was published between May 2, 1925 and November 5, 1949. From November 5, 1949 onwards *Kudi Arasu* became weekly.
88. After the arrest of E.V. Ramasami for anti-Hindi agitation E.V. Krishnasami became an editor. After the release E.V. Ramasami regained its position as editor of the *Kudi Arasu* until 1949.
89. *Brahmaniya moliththa Thirumanmum Nankodaiyum* (The marriage and gift that abolish the Brahmanism) (in Tamil). 18/09/1927. *Kudi Arasu.*
90. *Vibhachcharath Thadaich Chattam* (The Prostitution Prevention Act) (in Tamil). 01/05/1932. *Kudi Arasu.*
91. *Ibid.*
92. *Oru Vidhavaippenn Thevai* (A widow wanted) (in Tamil). 13/01/1929. *Kudi Arasu.*
93. Geetha, V and S.V. Rajadurai. *Revolt: A Radical Weekly from Colonial Madras.* Chennai: Periyar Dravidar Kazhagam, (n.d.): p. 8.
94. *Swadeshamitranaum Sriman Kirshnamachariyarum* (Swadeshamitran and Mr Krishnamachari) (in Tamil). 04/12/1927. *Kudi Arasu.*
95. *Itharku Yen Mounam? Parppanappaththirikkaikalin Purattu* (Why there is silence? the twist of the brahmanical magazines) (in Tamil). 19/06/1927. *Kudi Arasu.*
96. *Hindhumadha Pirachcharam* (Propagation of the Hindu religion) (in Tamil). 15/04/1928. *Kudi Arasu.*
97. *Srimathi Besantammaiyar* (Ms. Besant) (in Tamil). 20/11/1927. *Kudi Arasu.*
98. *Srinivasaiyangarum Mirattalum* (Srinivasa Iyangar and his threat) (in Tamil). 11/12/1927. *Kudi Arasu.*
99. Balan, K.M. *Woes of Indian Womanhood.* 27/10/1929. *Revolt.*
100. *Vivaha Rathu* (Divorce) (in Tamil). 29/12/1929. *Kudi Arasu.*
101. *The Welcome Speeches of Mrs. Lakshmi Ammal in the Second Self-respect Women's Conference* (in Tamil). 04/05/1930. *Kudi Arasu.*

102. Natarajan, Srividya. "Another Stage in the Life of the Nation: Sadir, Bharathanatyam, Feminist Theory". PhD diss., University of Hyderabad, 1997: p. 13.
103. *Pengal Viduthalaikku J! J! J!* (Hail! for women liberation) (in Tamil). 24/11/1929. *Kudi Arasu.*
104. Nilavathi, S. *Penn Makkalum Swedesha Samasthanangalum* (The Princely States and Women) (in Tamil). 28/06/1931. *Kudi Arasu.*
105. *The Self-Respect Women's Conference*, Salem district (in Tamil). 15/05/1932. *Kudi Arasu.*
106. Kunjitham, T.S. *The Position of Indian Women.* 06/10/1929. *Revolt.*
107. *Revolt.* 11/12/1928.
108. *Penngal Munnetra Mahanadu* (The Womens' Progressive Conference) (in Tamil). 24/11/1929. *Kudi Arasu.*
109. Periyar. *Pen Yen Adimaiyanal?* (Why women became enslaved?) (in Tamil). Chennai: Periyar Self Respected Propaganda, 1992 (Rpt. 2004): p. 64.
110. *Pengal* (Women) (in Tamil). 12/08/1928. *Kudi Arasu.*
111. Periyar. 1992 (Rpt. 2004). *Op.cit.*, pp. 74-79.
112. *Thoughts of Periyar E.V.R.: Speeches and Writings of Periyar E.V. Ramasamy.* Vol. 1, Part. 2. V. Anaimuthu. Comp. Chennai: Periyar E.V. Ramasamy-Nagammai Education and Research Trust, 1974 (Rpt. 2009): pp. 258-262.
113. *Ibid.*, pp. 208-211.
114. *Ibid.*
115. *Ibid.*, pp. 211-218.
116. *Ibid.*, pp. 258-262.
117. *The Welcome Speeches of Mrs. Lakshmi Ammal in the Second Self-respect Women's Conference* (in Tamil). 04/05/1930. *Kudi Arasu.*
118. *Mahalir Urimai* (Women's rights) (in Tamil). 01/12/1929. *Kudi Arasu.*
119. Raghavan, A. *Jeevakarunyach Chamayam Mahalir Urimaiyai Marukkuma?* (Did the religion which preach love as its principle would restrain the women's rights?) (in Tamil). 08/11/1931. *Kudi Arasu.*
120. The Self-Respect Marriages are nothing but the marriage which is happened without any rituals and waste of time. (*Kulanthaikaludan Manamakkal Thirumanam* (The Marriage among Children) (in Tamil). 21/09/1930. *Kudi Arasu.*)
121. *Suyamariyathai Thirumanam* (The Self-Respect Marriage) (in Tamil). 29/06/1930. *Kudi Arasu.*
122. *Parppaniyaththai Ozhiththa Kalyanankal* (The Marriages that abolished Brahmanism) (in Tamil). 21/11/1926. *Kudi Arasu.*
123. Rasagopalan, Sarala. *Thiru.Vi.Ka. Pennurimaich Chinthanaigal* (The Feminist Thoughts of Thiru.Vi.Ka) (in Tamil). Chennai: Olip Pathippakam, 2007: p. 147.
124. Kunjitham, T.S. *The Position of Indian Women.* 06/10/1929. *Revolt.*
125. *Pengal* (Women) (in Tamil). 12/08/1928. *Kudi Arasu.*
126. *Vaithiga Veri* (The Religious Mania) (in Tamil). 07/02/1932. *Kudi Arasu.*
127. Kunjitham, T.S. *The Position of Indian Women.* 06/10/1929. *Revolt.*
128. *Revolt.* 24/11/1929.

129. Periyar. 1992 (Rpt. 2004). *Op.cit.*, pp. 74-79.
130. *Vivaha Rathu* (The Divorce) (in Tamil). 29/12/1929. *Kudi Arasu.*
131. Nagalingam. *Matharum Samuga Sudhanthiramum* (Women and their social independence) (in Tamil). 10/11/1925. *Kudi Arasu.*
132. *Pengal* (Women) (in Tamil). 12/08/1928. *Kudi Arasu.*
133. Sakthidas. *Pengal Viduthalai* (The Women's liberation) (in Tamil). 29/06/1930. *Kudi Arasu.*
134. Balan, K.M. *Woes of Indian Womanhood.* 27/10/1929. *Revolt.*
135. *Kulanthaikaludan Manamakkal Thirumanam* (The Marriage among Children) (in Tamil). 21/09/1930. *Kudi Arasu.*
136. *Revolt*, 11/12/1928.
137. *The Welcome Speeches of Mrs. Lakshmi Ammal in the Second Self-respect Women's Conference* (in Tamil). 04/05/1930. *Kudi Arasu.*
138. *Penn Kalvi* (Women's Education) (in Tamil). 03/06/1928. *Kudi Arasu.*
139. *Mathar Mahanattil Niraiveriya Thermanangal* (The Decisions which made in the Womens' Conference) (in Tamil). 18/05/1930. *Kudi Arasu.*
140. *The Welcome Speeches of Mrs. Lakshmi Ammal in the Second Self-respect Women's Conference* (in Tamil). 04/05/1930. *Kudi Arasu.*
141. Periyar. 1992 (Rpt. 2004). *Op.cit.*, pp. 74-79.
142. Kaivalyam. *Udankattai Eruvathu Oru Naal Thukkam, Baliya Vivaham Palanaal Thukkam* (Sati is the one day sorrow but child marriage is everyday sorrow) (in Tamil). 21/09/1930. *Kudi Arasu.*
143. *Iniyavathu Puththi Varuma*? (Will awareness come after this?) (in Tamil). 05/10/1930. *Kudi Arasu.*
144. *Mathar Mahanattil Niraiveriya Thermanangal* (The Decisions which made in the Womens' Conference) (in Tamil). 18/05/1930. *Kudi Arasu.*
145. *Ibid.*
146. *Ibid.*
147. *Ibid.*
148. *Ibid.*
149. Singaravelu, Ma. *Pothuvudaimaiyum, Pengalum* (Socialism and Women) (in Tamil). 15/11/1931. *Kudi Arasu.*
150. Anaimuthu, V. 1974 (Rpt. 2009). *Op.cit.*, pp. 309-315.
151. *Ibid.*
152. *Ibid.*
153. Periyar. 1992 (Rpt. 2004). *Op.cit.*, p. 22.
154. Anaimuthu, V. 1974 (Rpt. 2009). *Op.cit.*, pp. 309-315.
155. *Ibid.*
156. *Ibid.*
157. Periyar. 1992 (Rpt. 2004). *Op.cit.*, p. 32.
158. Anaimuthu, V. 1974 (Rpt. 2009). *Op.cit.*, pp. 309-315.
159. Periyar. 1992 (Rpt. 2004). *Op.cit.*, p. 12.
160. *Ibid.*, pp. 309-315.

161. Balan, K.M. *Woes of Indian Womanhood*. 27/10/1929. *Revolt*.
162. *The Abolition of the Pottu Ceremony in the Hindu Temples in Madras Presidency* (in Tamil). 30/03/1930. *Kudi Arasu*.
163. *Sriman Nayakkar Alachanthapurathil 20-03-1928-il Nigalthiya Chorpolivin Charam* (The highlights of the E.V. Ramasami's speech which delivered at Alachandapuram) (in Tamil). 15/04/1928. *Kudi Arasu*.
164. *Revolt*, 11/12/1928.
165. *The Speeches Delivered by Indirani Balasubramanian in the Second Self Respect Conference which held in Virudhunagar* (in Tamil). 09/08/1931. *Kudi Arasu*.
166. *Ibid.*
167. *Revolt*, 24/11/1929.
168. *Avarkal Enna Pesukirarkal?* (What are they speaking?) (in Tamil). 19/08/1928. *Kudi Arasu*.
169. *Engum Suyamariyathai Sathyakirakam* (In Everywhere, the Non-Violence Protests for Self-Respect). 06/11/1927. *Kudi Arasu*.
170. *Ibid.*
171. *Swamikalum Devadiyalkulum* (Gods and Prostitutes) (in Tamil). 04/09/1927. *Kudi Arasu*.
172. *Ibid.*
173. *Engum Suyamariyathai Sathyakirakam* (In Everywhere, the Non-Violence Protests for Self-Respect). 06/11/1927. *Kudi Arasu*.
174. *Vibachcharam Oliyuma* (Will the prostitution be eradicated?) (in Tamil). 29/05/1932. *Kudi Arasu*.
175. *Kulanthaikaludan Manamakkal Thirumanam* (The Marriage among Children) (in Tamil). 21/09/1930. *Kudi Arasu*.
176. *Vibachcharam Oliyuma* (Will the prostitution be eradicated?) (in Tamil). 29/05/1932. *Kudi Arasu*.
177. Chidambaranar, Samy. *Sivanesarkalin Seikai* (The Activities of Saiva Saints) (in Tamil). 02/11/1930. *Kudi Arasu*.
178. *Ibid.*
179. *Ibid.*
180. *S.N.D.P Yogam Endru Sollappadum Thiyar Mahanadu* (The Conference of Thiyar which was popularly known as *S.N.D.P Yogam*) (in Tamil). 08/06/1930. *Kudi Arasu*.
181. Nilavathi, S. *Penn Makkalum Swedesha Samasthanangalum* (The Princely States and Women) (in Tamil). 12/07/1931. *Kudi Arasu*.
182. Nilavathi. *Saratha Sattam* (The Sarada Act) (in Tamil). 10/08/1930. *Kudi Arasu*.
183. Nilavathi, S. *Penn Makkalum Swedesha Samasthanangalum* (The Princely States and Women) (in Tamil). 12/07/1931. *Kudi Arasu*
184. *Mathar Mahanattil Niraiveriya Thermanangal* (The Decisions that made in the Womens' Conference) (in Tamil). 18/05/1930. *Kudi Arasu*.
185. *Sriman Nayakkar Alachanthapurathil 20-03-1928-il Nigalthiya Chorpolivin Charam* (The highlights of the E.V. Ramasami's speech which delivered at Alachandapuram) (in Tamil). 15/04/1928. *Kudi Arasu*.

186. *Swamikalum Devadiyalkalum* (Gods and prostitutes) (in Tamil). 04/09/1927. *Kudi Arasu.*
187. Raghavan, A. *Jeevakarunyach Chamayam Mahalir Urimaiyai Marukkuma*? (Did the religion which preach love as its principle would restrain the women's rights?) (in Tamil). 06/12/1931. *Kudi Arasu.*
188. *Ibid.*
189. *Swamikalum Devadiyalkalum* (Gods and prostitutes) (in Tamil). 04/09/1927. *Kudi Arasu.*
190. Raghavan, A. *Jeevakarunyach Chamayam Mahalir Urimaiyai Marukkuma*? (Did the religion which preach love as its principle would restrain the women's rights?). 06/12/1931. *Kudi Arasu.*
191. *Alaya Archakar* (The temple priest) (in Tamil). 05/02/1928. *Kudi Arasu.*
192. *Kovil* (The Temple) (in Tamil). 23/10/1927. *Kudi Arasu.*
193. *Vedikundukal* (Bombs) was a column for the readers in *Kudi Arasu*. Minatchi. *Vedikundukal* (Bombs) (in Tamil). 30/07/1927. *Kudi Arasu.*
194. Thandapani. *Vedikundukal* (Bombs) (in Tamil). 30/07/1927. *Kudi Arasu.*
195. *Mathar Mahanattil Niraiveriya Thermanangal* (The Decisions that made in the Womens' Conference) (in Tamil). 18/05/1930. *Kudi Arasu.*
196. *Kanam 'Kudi Arasu' Paththirathipar Avarkatgu* (Letters to *Kudi Arasu* editor) (in Tamil). 18/12/1927. *Kudi Arasu.*
197. Masilamanippillai. *Devadasikalukkor Vendukol: Namathu Nokkam* (An Appeal to Devadasi: Our Intension) (in Tamil). 17/06/1928. *Kudi Arasu.*
198. *The Abolition of the Pottu Ceremony in the Hindu Temples in Madras Presidency* (in Tamil). 30/03/1930. *Kudi Arasu.*
199. Masilamanippillai. *Devadasikalukkor Vendukol: Namathu Nokkam* (An Appeal to Devadasi: Our Intension) (in Tamil). 17/06/1928. *Kudi Arasu.*
200. *Ibid.*
201. *Naan Vilaimagala*? (Am I a prostitute?) (in Tamil). 21/12/1930. *Kudi Arasu.*
202. *Ibid.*
203. *Swamikalum Devadiyalkalum* (Gods and Prostitutes) (in Tamil). 04/09/1927. *Kudi Arasu.*
204. *Ibid.*
205. Nilavathi, S. *Penn Makkalum Swedesha Samasthanangalum* (The Princely States and Women) (in Tamil). 28/06/1931. *Kudi Arasu.*
206. *Sivalinga Ragasiyamum Thamil Makkalin Ariyamaiyum.* (The secret of Siva Liga and the Ignorance of Tamil people) (in Tamil). 24/02/1929. *Kudi Arasu.*
207. *Pengal Viduthalaikku Je! Je! Je!* (Hail! for Women's Liberation) (in Tamil). 24/11/1929. *Kudi Arasu.*
208. *Swamikalum Devadiyalkalum* (Gods and Prostitutes) (in Tamil). 04/09/1927. *Kudi Arasu.*
209. *Ibid.*
210. *Madhaththai Parriya Vibaretham* (The Perversity of the Religion) (in Tamil). 18/09/1927. *Kudi Arasu.*
211. *Ibid.*
212. *Ibid.*

213. *Sriman Nayakkar Alachanthapurathil 20-03-1928-il Nigalthiya Chorpolivin Charam* (The highlights of the E.V. Ramasami's speech which delivered at Alachandapuram) (in Tamil). 15/04/1928. *Kudi Arasu.*
214. *Chiththira Puththiran.* (in Tamil). 02/03/1930. *Kudi Arasu.*
215. *Thirumigu Muthulakshmi Ammalin Thermanam* (The Resolution of Muthulakshmi Ammal) (in Tamil). 27/05/1928. *Kudi Arasu.*
216. *Vidhava Vivakam* (The Widow Remarriage) (in Tamil). 27/10/1929. *Kudi Arasu.*
217. *Sriman Nayakkar Alachanthapurathil 20-03-1928-il Nigalthiya Chorpolivin Charam* (The highlights of the E.V. Ramasamy's speech which delivered at Alachandapuram) (in Tamil). 15/04/1928. *Kudi Arasu.*
218. *The decisions which made were under the leadership of E.V Ramasami in Tirunelveli Self-respect Conference* (in Tamil). 11/12/1927. *Kudi Arasu.*
219. Nilavathi, S. *Penn Makkalum Swedesha Samasthanangalum* (The Princely States and Women) (in Tamil). 28/06/1931. *Kudi Arasu.*
220. Nilavathi, S. *Penn Makkalum Swedesha Samasthanangalum* (The Princely States and Women) (in Tamil). 12/07/1931. *Kudi Arasu.*
221. *Ibid.*
222. *Iniyavathu Puththi Varuma*? (Will awareness come after this?) (in Tamil). 05/10/1930. *Kudi Arasu.*
223. Lingam, S.V. *Varungal! Ini Seiyappovathu Enna?* (Come on! what is our next act?) (in Tamil). 04/05/1930. *Kudi Arasu.*
224. *Kovil* (The Temple) (in Tamil). 09/10/1927. *Kudi Arasu.*
225. *Samayach Sirthirutham.* (The Religious Reform) (in Tamil). 23/10/1927. *Kudi Arasu.*
226. *Swamikalum Devadiyalkalum* (Gods and Prostitutes) (in Tamil). 04/09/1927. *Kudi Arasu.*
227. *Ibid.*
228. *Kurukkalin Purattu* (The distorted facts of the priest) (in Tamil). 25/09/1927. *Kudi Arasu.*
229. *Ibid.*
230. Nilavathi, S. *Penn Makkalum Swedesha Samasthanangalum* (The Princely States and Women) (in Tamil). 12/07/1931. *Kudi Arasu.*
231. *Kovil* (The Temple) (in Tamil). 09/10/1927. *Kudi Arasu.*
232. *Mathathin Kodumai* (The Religious Attrocity) (in Tamil). 26/10/1930. *Kudi Arasu.*
233. *The Speeches Delivered by Indirani Balasubramanian in the Second Self-respect Conference which held at Virudhunagar* (in Tamil). 09/08/1931. *Kudi Arasu.*
234. Raghavan, A. *Jeevakarunyach Chamayam Mahalir Urimaiyai Marukkuma*? (Did the religion which preach love as its principle would restrain the women's rights?) (in Tamil). 06/12/1931. *Kudi Arasu.*
235. *Ibid.*
236. Anaimuthu, V. 1974 (Rpt. 2009) *Op.cit.*, p. 237.
237. Raghavan, A. *Jeevakarunyach Chamayam Mahalir Urimaiyai Marukkuma*? (Did the religion which preach love as its principle would restrain the women's rights?) (in Tamil). 06/12/1931. *Kudi Arasu.*

238. *Ibid.*
239. *Ibid.*
240. Periyar. 1992 (Rpt. 2004). *Op.cit.,* pp. 9-79.
241. Muthulakshmi Reddy, S. 1927. *Op.cit.,* p. 1.
242. *The Proceedings of the Madras Legislative Council: Second Session of the Third Legislative Council.* Vol. XXXVIII. October 31-November 5, 1927: p. 414.
243. *Ibid.,* p. 415.
244. *Ibid.*, pp. 415- 416.
245. Nilavathi, S. *Penmakkalae Elungal* (Arise Women) (in Tamil). 03/07/1932. *Kudi Arasu.*
246. *Ibid.*
247. *Ibid.*
248. *Kovil* (The Temple) (in Tamil). 09/10/1927. *Kudi Arasu.*
249. *The Proceedings of the Madras Legislative Council: Second Session of the Third Legislative Council.* Vol. XXXVIII. October 31-November 5, 1927: p. 416.
250. Muthulakshmi Reddy, S. 1930. *Op.cit.,* p. 56.
251. Masilamanippillai. *Devadasikalukkor Vendukol: Namathu Nokkam* (An Appeal to Devadasi: Our Intension) (in Tamil). 17/06/1928. *Kudi Arasu.*
252. *Ibid.,* p. 58.
253. *Ibid.,* p. 59.
254. *Ibid.,* p. 58.
255. *Ammamikal Azhukural* (The cry of the middle aged Women) (in Tamil). 14/01/1945. *Dravida Nadu.*
256. Sathyamurthi was an active Congress person, nationalist and conservative in Madras Presidency.
257. Raghavan, A. *Jeevakarunyach Chamayam Mahalir Urimaiyai Marukkuma*? (Did the religion which preach love as its principle would restrain the women's rights?) (in Tamil). 06/12/1931. *Kudi Arasu.*
258. *Chennai Sattasabhai Devasthana Sattathirutha Masotha* (The Hindu Religious Endowment Bill of Madras Presidency) (in Tamil). 02/02/1929. *Dravidan.*
259. *Ibid.*
260. Kalyanasundaram, Thiru.Vi. *Thiru. Vi.Ka Vazhkkaik Kurippukal* (A Biographical Notes of Thiru.Vi. Kalyanasundaram) (in Tamil). Saiva Siddanta Kazhakam, 1982: p. 603.
261. *The Speeches Delivered by Indirani Balasubramanian in the Second Self-respect Conference which held at Virudhunagar* (in Tamil). 09/08/1931. *Kudi Arasu.*
262. *Chennai Sattasabhai Devasthana Sattathirutha Masotha* (The Hindu Religious Endowment Bill of Madras Presidency) (in Tamil). 02/02/1929. *Dravidan.*
263. *Ibid.*
264. *Ibid.*
265. *Yaar Poiyar*? (Who is the liar?) (in Tamil). 20/11/1927. *Kudi Arasu.*
266. *Orvambu* (Gossips) (in Tamil). 06/11/1927. *Kudi Arasu.*

267. *Ibid.*
268. Yande, D.S. *Dedication of Girls to Gods: Plea for Prohibition by Law by Naik-Maratha Mandal*. Bombay: V.P. Vengurlekar, (n.d.): p. 6.
269. Muthulakshmi Reddy, S. 1927. *Op.cit.*, p. 8.
270. *Ibid.*
271. *Ibid.*
272. *Chennai Sattasabhai Devasthana Sattathirutha Masotha* (The Hindu Religious Endowment Bill of Madras Presidency) (in Tamil). 02/02/1929. *Dravidan*.
273. *Ibid.*
274. *Devadasi Ozhippoch Chattam* (The Devadasi Abolition Act) (in Tamil). 23/03/1930. *Kudi Arasu*.
275. Muthulakshmi Reddy, S. *The Presidential Address of Dr. (Mrs.) S. Muthulakshmi Reddi*. Delivered at the Seventh Andhra Provincial Women's Conference held at Ellore. November 4-5, 1933: pp. 5-6.
276. *Pottukkattu Niruththum Chattam* (The Prevention of *Pottu* Ceremony Act) (in Tamil). 30/03/1930. *Kudi Arasu*.
277. *Devadasi Vinnappam* (An Appeal of Devadasi) (in Tamil). 30/10/1927. *Kudi Arasu*.
278. *Ibid.*
279. *Young India*, 29/08/1929. *The Collected Works of Mahatma Gandhi (June-October1929)*. Vol. 41. New Delhi: Ministry of Information and Broadcasting Division, 1970: p. 338.
280. *Ibid.*, p. 337.
281. *Ibid.*, p. 338.
282. *The Hindu*, 10/09/1927. *The Collected Works of Mahatma Gandhi (June-September 1927)*. Vol. 34. New Delhi: Ministry of Information and Broadcasting Division, 1969: p. 497.
283. *Revolt*. 24/11/1929.
284. *Revolt*. 11/12/1928.
285. *Devadasi Ozhippoch Chattam* (The Devadasi Abolition Act) (in Tamil). 23/03/1930. *Kudi Arasu*.
286. *Pottukkattu Niruththum Chattam* (The Prevention of *Pottu* Ceremony Act) (in Tamil). 30/03/1930. *Kudi Arasu*.
287. *Ibid.*
288. *Ibid.*
289. *Ibid.*
290. *Ibid.*
291. *Ibid.*
292. *Ibid.*
293. *Kovil* (The Temple) (in Tamil). 09/10/1927. *Kudi Arasu*.
294. *Ibid.*
295. *Devadasi Ozhippoch Chattam* (The Devadasi Abolition Act) (in Tamil). 23/03/1930. *Kudi Arasu*.

296. Nilavathi, S. *Innum Penn Pavam Erpathu Nanro*? (Is it still good that women accept sin?) (in Tamil). 14/02/1932. *Kudi Arasu.*
297. *Pottukkattu Niruththum Chattam* (The Prevention of *Pottu* Ceremony Act) (in Tamil). 30/03/1930. *Kudi Arasu.*
298. *The decisions which made were under the leadership of E.V Ramasami in Tirunelveli Self-Respect Conference.* 11/12/1927. *Kudi Arasu.*
299. *Dasikalum Sathiyamoorthikalum* (The Dasis and Sathyamurthis) (in Tamil). 06/11/1927. *Kudi Arasu.*
300. *Ibid.*
301. Nilavathi, S. *Antho Pennulakamae*? (Ah! the world of women?) (in Tamil). 13/03/1932. *Kudi Arasu.*
302. *Parpanarallathor Katchi Sattasabhai Memberkalukkor Echarikkai* (A Warning to the Legislative Members of Non-Brahmin Party) (in Tamil). 11/12/1927. *Kudi Arasu.*
303. *Mathar Mahanattil Niraiveriya Thermanangal* (The Decisions that made in the Womens' Conference) (in Tamil). 18/05/1930. *Kudi Arasu.*
304. Senguthar is one the backward caste in Tamil Nadu.
305. *Engum Suyamariyathai Sathyakirakam* (In Everywhere, the Non-Violence Protests for Self-Respect). 06/11/1927. *Kudi Arasu.*
306. *Isai Vellala Ilainarkal Manadu* (*The Youth Conference of Isai Vellalar*) (in Tamil). 04/11/1928. *Kudi Arasu.*
307. *The abolition of the Pottu ceremony in the Hindu temples at Madras Presidency* (in Tamil). 30/03/1930. *Kudi Arasu.*
308. *Srimathi Muthulakshmi Masothavukku Atharavu* (A Support for the Bill of Mrs. Muthulakshmi) (in Tamil). 30/03/1930. *Kudi Arasu.*
309. *Ibid.*
310. *Thiruvaruril Pottukattuththadai Masodhavukku Atharavu Koottam* (A gathering for the support of Abolition of the Devadasi System in Tiruvarur) (in Tamil). 13/04/1930. *Kudi Arasu.*
311. Masilamanippillai. *Devadasikalukkor Vendukol: Namathu Nokkam* (*An Appeal to Devadasi: Our Intension*) (in Tamil). 17/06/1928. *Kudi Arasu.*
312. *The speeches delivered by Indirani Balasubramanian in the second Self-Respect conference which held at Virudhunagar* (in Tamil). 09/08/1931. *Kudi Arasu.*
313. Marglin, Frederique Apffel. *Wives of the God-King: The Rituals of the Devadasis of Puri.* Delhi: Oxford University Press, 1985: p. 28.
314. Kaali, Sundar. "Disciplining the Dasi: Cintamanai and the Politics of a New Sexual Economy." *Bioscope* 4, no. 1. (2013): p. 52.
315. *Swamikalum Devadiyalkalum* (Gods and Prostitutes) (in Tamil). 04/09/1927. *Kudi Arasu.*
316. Kuppusami, P. *Bharathamadhavin Puththirikal Nam Sagotharikalallaraa*? (The daughter of our mother country are they not our sister?) (in Tamil). 14/04/1929. *Kudi Arasu.*
317. *Engum Suyamariyathai Sathyakirakam* (In Everywhere, the Non-Violence Protests for Self-Respect). 06/11/1927. *Kudi Arasu.*

318. Kuppusamy, P. *Bharathamadhavin Puththirikal Nam Sagotharikalallaraa*? ((The daughter of our mother country are they not our sister?) (in Tamil). 14/04/1929. *Kudi Arasu*.
319. *Isai Vellala Ilainarkal Manadu* (*The Youth Conference of Isai Vellalar*) (in Tamil). 04/11/1928. *Kudi Arasu*.
320. *Mathar Mahanattil Niraiveriya Thermanangal* (The Decisions which made in the Women's Conference) (in Tamil). 18/05/1930. *Kudi Arasu*.
321. *Tamil Mahana Sangita Mahanadu Thermanangal* (The Resolutions that made in the Tamil regional Music Conference) (in Tamil). 01/06/1930. *Kudi Arasu*.
322. Kuppusamy, P. *Bharathamadhavin Puththirikal Nam Sagotharikalallaraa*? ((The daughter of our mother country are they not our sister?) (in Tamil). 14/04/1929. *Kudi Arasu*.
323. *Iniyavathu Puththi Varuma*? (Will awareness come after this?) (in Tamil). 05/10/1930. *Kudi Arasu*.
324. Natarajan, Srividya. 1997. *Op.cit.,* p. IX.
325. Periyar. 1992 (Rpt. 2004). *Op.cit.,* p. 12.
326. Meduri, Avanthi. "Bharatha Natyam- What Are You?." *Asian Theatre Journal* 5, no. 1. (1988): p. 13.
327. George, T.J.S. *MS: A Life in Music*. New Delhi: Harper Collins Publishers, 2007 (Rpt. 2010): p. 87.
328. Anand, S. "Cauvery in a Puddle." *Outlook*. January 21, 2002.
329. Ohtani, Kimiko. "Bharata Nâm□yam', Rebirth of Dance in India." *Studia Musicologica Academiae Scientiarum Hungaricae* T. 33, fasc. 1/4. (1991): p. 305.
330. *Ibid*., pp. 305-306.
331. *Ibid.,* p. 306.
332. Ramnarayan, Gowri. "Rukmini Devi: A Quest for Beauty." Part. 1. *Sruti*. Issue. 8. (June, 1984): pp. 17-29.
333. "The Renaming of an Old Dance: A Whodunit Tale of Mystery". *Sruti*. Issue. 27/28. (December, 1986-January, 1987): p. 30.
334. The personal communication of Kimiko Ohtani with S. Sarda in 1989. (Ohtani, Kimiko. 1991. *Op.cit.,* p. 20.)
335. Ramasubramaniam, V. "'Anti-Nautch Movement'." *The Bulletin of the Institute of Traditional Culture*. Reports of Seminars: Problems facing Bharata Natyam. (1967): p. 300
336. *Krishna Iyer, E. Centenary Issue*. Chennai: Music Academy, August 9, 1997: p. 11.
337. Ohtani, Kimiko. 1991. *Op.cit.,* p. 306.
338. "The Renaming of an Old Dance: A Whodunit Tale of Mystery". *Sruti*. Issue. 27/28. (December, 1986-January, 1987): p. 30.
339. *Ibid.,* p. 31.
340. "The Madras Music Conference 1932." *The Journal of the Music Academy* IV, no. 1-4. (1933): p. 121.
341. *Ibid.*

342. Natarajan, Srividya. 1997. *Op.cit.,* p. 14.
343. Kaali, Sundar. 2013. *Op.cit.,* p. 52.
344. Soneji, Davesh. Ed. *Bharathanatyam: A Reader*. New Delhi: Oxford University Press, 2010: p. xi.
345. *Ibid.,* p. xiii.
346. Marglin, Frederique Apffel. 1985. *Op.cit.,* p. 29.
347. *Adal Padal* (Dance and music) (in Tamil). March 22, 1936. *Ananda Vikatan*. p. 30.
348. Ramnarayan, Gowri. "Rukmini Devi: A Quest for Beauty." Part. 1. *Sruti*. Issue. 8. (June, 1984): pp. 17-29.
349. *Nattuvanars* are the dance teachers. They are belonged to the devadasi community.
350. Ramnarayan, Gowri. "Rukmini Devi: A Quest for Beauty." Part. 1. *Sruti*. Issue. 8. (June, 1984): pp. 17-29.
351. *Ibid.*
352. *Adal Padal* (Dance and music) (in Tamil). 22/3/1936. *Ananda Vikatan*. pp. 27-28.
353. Krishnamurthy was a prominent Brahmin novelist, journalist, nationalist. He was actively engaged in the discourse of dance and music. Usually, Krishnamurthy wrote columns in *Ananda Vikatan* under the pseudonym of *Adal Padal*.
354. *Adal Padal* (Dance and music) (in Tamil). 22/3/1936. *Ananda Vikatan*. pp. 27-28.
355. Pillai, Meenakshisundaram. "Bharatha Natyam." 28th *Conference Souvenir*. Madras: The Music Academy, 1954: p. 14.
356. Ramnarayan, Gowri. "Rukmini Devi: A Quest for Beauty." Part. 1. *Sruti*. Issue. 8. (June, 1984): pp. 17-29.
357. George Arundale was died in 1945.
358. Devi, Rukmini. *The Creative Spirit*. Adyar: The Theosophical Publishing House, (n.d.): p. 1.
359. Meduri, Avanthi. 1988. *Op.cit.,* p. 9.
360. Ohtani, Kimiko. 1991. *Op.cit.,* p. 306.
361. Geetha, V and S.V. Rajadurai. 1998. *Op.cit.,* p. 320.
362. Devi, Rukmini. *The Creative Spirit. Op.cit.,* p. 1.
363. *Ibid.,* p. 2.
364. *Ibid.,* p. 14.
365. Devi, Rukmini. *Dance and Music*. Adyar: Theosophical Publishing House, (n.d): p. 5.
366. *Ibid.,* p. 6.
367. *Ibid.*, p. 8-9.
368. Devi, Rukmini. *Dance and Music. Op.cit.,* p. 5.
369. *Ibid.*, pp. 5-7.
370. *Ibid.*, pp. 7-8.

371. "The Madras Music Conference, 1930". *The Journal of the Music Academy* II, no. 1. (1931): p. 70.
372. Devi, Rukmini. "The Late Sri Pandanallur Meenakshisundaram Pillai." 28th *Conference Souvenir*. Madras: The Music Academy, 1954: p. 20.
373. *Adal Padal* (Dance and music) (in Tamil). 22/3/1936. *Ananda Vikatan*. p. 28.
374. Ohtani, Kimiko. 1991. *Op.cit.,* p. 307.
375. *Adal Padal* (Dance and music) (in Tamil). 22/3/1936. *Ananda Vikatan*. p. 28.
376. *Kudi Arasu*, 20/04/1930.
377. *Adal Padal* (Dance and music) (in Tamil). 3/11/1935. *Ananda Vikatan*. pp. 20-21.
378. Ramnarayan, Gowri. June, 1984. *Op.cit.,* p. 23.
379. The personal communication of Kimiko Ohtani with *nattuvanar* Kalyana-sundaram in 1989. (Ohtani, Kimiko. 1991. *Op.cit.,* p. 307).
380. Meduri, Avanthi. 1988. *Op.cit.,* p. 11.
381. Ohtani, Kimiko. 1991. *Op.cit.,* p. 306.
382. *Ibid.,* p. 306.
383. Meduri, Avanthi. 1988. *Op.cit.,* p. 11.
384. *Ibid.,* p. 13.
385. Devi, Rukmini. *The Creative Spirit. Op.cit.,* p. 5.
386. *Ibid.,* p. 13.
387. Devi, Rukmini. *Dance and Music. Op.cit.,* p. 8.
388. Devi, Rukmini. *The Creative Spirit. Op.cit.,* p. 6.
389. *Ibid.,* p. 6.
390. *Ibid.,* p. 5.
391. *Ibid.,* p. 9.
392. Devi, Rukmini. "The Indian Dance." In George S. Arundale. Comp. *Principles of Education*. Adyar: Theosophical Publishing House, 1926: p. 2.
393. *Ibid.,* p. 10.
394. *Ibid.,* p. 11.
395. *Ibid.*
396. Devi, Rukmini. *The Creative Spirit. Op.cit.,* p. 9.
397. Devi, Rukmini. *Woman as Artist*. Adyar: Theosophical Publishing House, (n.d): p. 13.
398. Soneji, Davesh. 2010. *Op.cit.,* p. xiii.
399. Pillai, Meenakshisundaram. 1954. *Op.cit.,* p. 13.
400. Raghavan, V. "Bharatha Natyam-Ilakkiyam." (A Grammar for Bharatanatyam) (in Tamil). *25th Conference Souvenir*. Madras: The Music Academy, 1951: pp. 11-16.
401. Raghavan, V. "Musical Traditions of the South". *30th Conference Souvenir*. Madras: The Music Academy, 1956: p. 21.
402. Raghavan, V. 1951. *Op.cit.,* p. 9.
403. Raghavan, V. "Bharatha Natya". 23rd *Conference Souvenir*. Madras: The Music Academy, 1949: p. 9.

404. Muthulakshmi Reddi referred the statement in her speech. (Muthulakshmi Reddi, S. 1927. *Op.cit.*, p. 5.)
405. Satymurthy, S. "Greetings and Messages." *The Journal of the Music Academy*. Vol. 1. No. 1. (January, 1930): p. 74.
406. *Adal Padal* (Dance and music) (in Tamil). 19/1/1936. *Ananda Vikatan*. p. 19.
407. The history of the Music Academy is goes back to 1920's. The idea got a definite shape in 1927 when the All-India Music Conference was held in Madras.
408. "The Madras Music Conference, 1930". *The Journal of the Music Academy* II, no. 1. (1931): p. 71.
409. *Ibid.*
410. Meduri, Avanthi. 1988. *Op.cit.*, p. 8.
411. Natarajan, Srividya. 1997. *Op.cit.*, p. 31.
412. *Adal Padal* (Dance and music) (in Tamil). 19/1/1936. *Ananda Vikatan*. p. 19.
413. *Adal Padal* (Dance and music) (in Tamil). 22/3/1936. *Ananda Vikatan*. p. 30.
414. *Adal Padal* (Dance and music) (in Tamil). 19/1/1936. *Ananda Vikatan*. p. 19.
415. *Adal Padal* (Dance and music) (in Tamil). 03/11/1935. *Ananda Vikatan*. pp. 18-21.
416. "The Madras Music Conference, 1930". *The Journal of the Music Academy* II, no. 1. (1931): p. 69.
417. "School of Dancing." *The Journal of the Music Academy* V, no. 1-4. (1934): p. 121.
418. *Orvambu* (Gossips) (in Tamil). 06/11/1927. *Kudi Arasu*.
419. *Ibid.*
420. Raghavan, V. "Musical Traditions of the South". *30th Conference Souvenir*. Madras: The Music Academy, 1956: p. 21.
421. Devi, Rukmini. *The Creative Spirit*. *Op.cit.*, p. 12.
422. Devi, Rukmini. 1926. *Op.cit.*, p. 1.
423. Balasubrahmanyam, G.N. "Thirty Second Conference Presidential Address of Vidwan G.N. Blasubrahmanyam." *The Journal of the Music* Academy. (1958): pp. 25-26.
424. Balasubrahmanyam, G.N. 1958. pp. 25-26.
425. Devi, Rukmini. *Woman as Artist*. *Op.cit.*, p. 17.
426. Devi, Rukmini. *Dance and Music*. *Op.cit.*, p. 2.
427. *Ibid.*, p. 3.
428. Devi, Rukmini. *The Creative Spirit*. *Op.cit.*, p. 17.
429. *Ibid.*, p. 20.
430. *Ibid.*, p. 19.
431. Devi, Rukmini. *Woman as Artist*. *Op.cit.*, p. 5.
432. Devi, Rukmini. 1926. *Op.cit.*, p. 2.
433. *Krishna Iyer, E. Centenary Issue*. August 9, 1997. *Op.cit.*, p. 4.
434. *Ibid.*
435. *Ibid.*, p. 5.
436. "School of Dancing." *The Journal of the Music Academy* V, no. 1-4. (1934): p. 120.

437. Natarajan, Srividya. 1997. *Op.cit.*, p. 14.
438. *Ibid.*
439. *Ibid.*, p. 13.
440. Meduri, Avanthi. 1988. *Op.cit.*, p. 12.
441. "The Seventh Session of the Madras Music Conference, 1934." *The Journal of the Music Academy* VI-VIII. (1935-1937): p. 150.
442. *Krishna Iyer, E. Centenary Issue*. August 9, 1997. *Op.cit.*, p. 11.
443. *Ibid.*, p. 1.
444. *Adal Padal* (Dance and music) (in Tamil). 19/1/1936. *Ananda Vikatan*. p. 19.
445. *Ibid.*, p. 17.
446. *Ibid.*
447. Venugopal, S.V. "Facts about the Renaissance in Bharata Natya." *Sri Krishna Iyer's Shashtiabdapurthi Commemoration Volume*. Madras: Bharathiar Sangam, 1957: p. 22.
448. *The Shashtiabdapurthi Celebration Committee. Sri E. Krishna Iyer's Shashtiabdapurthi Commenoration Volume*. Madras: Bharathiar Sangam, 1957: p. 19.
449. *Ibid.*, p. 20.
450. *Ibid.*
451. *Krishna Iyer, E. Centenary Issue*. August 9, 1997. *Op.cit.*, p. 5.
452. *Ibid.*, p. 18.
453. E. Krishna Iyer was functioned as the Secretary of the Music Academy during years of 1928-1932 1934-1935 and 1937-1939.
454. *Krishna Iyer, E. Centenary Issue*. August 9, 1997. *Op.cit.*, p. 13.
455. "The Madras Music Conference 1932." *The Journal of the Music Academy* IV, no. 1-4. (1933): p. 116.
456. *Ibid.*, p. 121.
457. *Ibid.*, p. 122.
458. *Ibid.*
459. *Krishna Iyer, E. Centenary Issue*. August 9, 1997. *Op.cit.*, p. 10.
460. "School of Dancing." *The Journal of the Music Academy* V, no. 1-4. (1934): p. 120.
461 "The Academy's Concerts." *The Journal of the Music Academy* II, no. 1. (1931): p. 78.
462. "The Madras Music Conference 1932." *The Journal of the Music Academy* IV, no. 1-4. (1933): 113, p. 123.
463. *Krishna Iyer, E. Centenary Issue*. August 9, 1997. *Op.cit.*, p. 5.
464. *Ibid.* p. 18.
465. "The Academy's Concerts." *The Journal of the Music Academy* II, no. 1. (1931): p. 78.
466. *Krishna Iyer, E. Centenary Issue*. August 9, 1997. *Op.cit.*, p. 4.
467. "The Academy's Concerts." *The Journal of the Music Academy* II, no. 1. (1931): p. 78.
468. *Ibid.*

469. *Krishna Iyer, E. Centenary Issue*. August 9, 1997. *Op.cit.*, p. 11.
470. "The Seventh Session of the Madras Music Conference, 1934." *The Journal of the Music Academy* VI-VIII. (1935-1937): p. 150.
471. *Krishna Iyer, E. Centenary Issue*. August 9, 1997. *Op.cit.*, p. 13.
472. Natarajan, Srividya. 1997. *Op.cit.*, p. 14.
473. *Ibid.*
474. Knight Jr, Douglas M. *Balasaraswathi: Her Art and Life*. Chennai: Tranquebar Press, 2010: pp. 117-118.

Chapter - 6

The Life Stories of Some Selected Devadasis of South India

In 1969, Carol Hanisch published an article in Shulamith Firestone and Anne Koedt edited *Notes from the Second Year* on "The Personal is political". These papers detailed on how personal problems are associated with political problems. They explained that there was nothing called personal. The personal experiences are always a political experience. The content stressed the importance of 'experience'. So the 'personal' experience or problem of a woman is not only a problem of a particular women, it is collective issues of womanhood. The life of devadasi was much intertwined with society and it was an integral element of South Indian history. It helps us to understand the real conditions of the devadasi women during early twentieth century. Here, this particular chapter focuses the lives of some selected devadasis from South India, especially the lives of Muvalur Ramamirtham, Bangalore Nagarathnam, Balasaraswati and M.S. Subbulakshmi.

There is a rationale behind the selection of these women. All the four women were from the devadasi community and they belonged to the period, when the abolition of devadasi discourse was at its peak. The lives of these women directly or indirectly reflect the developments related to the abolition of the system in the twentieth century Indian society. Also, these women represented the different discourses of the devadasi issue. Bangalore Nagarathnam was from Mysore who voiced her opinion for the continuation of the devadasi system. Muvalur Ramamirtham was firmly against the devadasi custom and intensively worked hard for the abolition of the system. She became a social reformer and close associate of E.V. Ramasami of the Self-Respect Movement. Balasaraswati came from the strong devadasi lineage of Vina Dhanam of colonial Madras. She questioned the Sanskritisation of devadasi dance tradition and, represented the devadasi's dance to the modern world. On the other hand, M.S. Subbulakshmi, the musical legend from devadasi community, signified the transition of the autonomous devadasi woman to a submissive woman of modern patriarchal society.

Writing live story is a complicated process. Sidonie Smith and Julia Watson mentioned that the axes of subject's identifications and experiences are multiple, because locations in gender, class, race, ethnicity and sexuality complicate one another and are not merely additive.[1] In this way, writing live story of devadasi or women from the devadasi community was much complicated process, because the association of social stigma with devadasi woman caused a serious damage to the personal life of devadasi women. Hence, it was difficult even to get basic information about the concerned women. In modern times, usually devadasis were hesitant and reluctant to reveal and share their life. In the transformed social setup, family members of devadasi did not encourage the discussion and the process of documentation of a woman from her family. B.M. Sundaram, a musicologist, and compiler of the book *Marbu Thantha Manikkankal* (The Gifts of the Tradition) mentioned in his field experience that Tirukkokarnam Pakkiri Ammal, a devadasi, deliberately misguided the author with regard to her identity.[2]

Jeevasundari, the biographer of Ramamirtham, faced a problem with the family members of Ramamirtham while writing and publishing a book on Ramamirtham. In her personal communication, she explained that the family members of Ramamirtham considered it a humiliation on researching the life of the ardent Ramamirtham.[3] T.J.S. George, the biographer of M.S. Subbulakshmi, has mentioned in his preface the absence of any kind of records about M.S. Subbulakshmi's life and the fortress erected around by her husband, Thiyagaraja Sadasivam.[4] He further explained that the first was a familiar problem of not preserving paper, maintaining records and having a sense of history and second was non-negotiable Sadasivam who controlled all access and all information. He stated that nothing was ever known that Sadasivam did not want known.[5] He pointed out that Sadasivam made sure that he was the only source of information about himself and M.S. Subbulakshmi. And he further stated that there was no choice for any interviewers.[6]

Muvalur A. Ramamirtham (1883-1962)

Muvalur A. Ramamirtham (*See Appendix:* - 14) was a pioneer woman in South India who initially shared the public sphere in the Congress and began her political career in the 1920's. Later she, joined the Self-Respect Movement and became a leading campaigner of the movement. In her fifty years of political career, she worked hard for women empowerment and the values of the advocated Self-Respect Movement. Kunjitham Gurusami, the Self-Respecter, has mentioned in the preface of Ramamirtham's novel *Dasikal Mosavalai alladhu Mathipetra Minar* (*Dasis web of deceit or enlightened playboy*) that Ramamirtham was the first among the women who staged a public meeting and campaigned for the cause.[7] Jeevasundari also mentioned that the writings and sources for Ramamirtham were available only from the printing press of the Self-Respect Movement.[8] Here her life history was largely derived from the sources of the magazines of the Self-Respect Movement and other pamphlets. Unfortunately, she was not recognised like Muthulakshmi Reddi for her contributions against the devadasi tradition by the historians.

Ramamirtham was born in Tiruvarur and brought up in Muvalur near Thanjavur district in modern Tamil Nadu. Her parents were Krishnasami and Chinnammal. Her family lineage was traced from Paravai Nachchiyar, a medieval *bhakti* saint women. Her childhood was miserable. Her father was depending for his survival on his devadasi sisters Chayavathi and Thangappappu. The sisters were interested in Ramamirtham following the tradition of the devadasis. Though her parents belonged to the devadasi community, they hesitated to dedicate their only daughter. Because according to tradition, the daughter of a male member was generously not given as a devadasi.[9] However, the furious sisters threw them out of the house. In her fourth year, they migrated to Muvalur, the home of Chinnammal. Later, due to poverty, her father abandoned his family and moved to Madras. The destitute mother worried about the life of Ramamirtham and sold her for an old sari and ten rupees to a wealthy *dasi* Achchikkannu.[10] The unexpected child started to cry when she saw that her mother had disappeared. The *dasi* provided some jewellry and new clothes to her. The innocent child Ramamirtham was quite happy. Ramamirtham had a respect for her adopted mother and she used to write her name as Muvalur A. Ramamirtham. The initial 'A' signified Achchikkannu.[11]

Achchikkannu arranged a teacher to teach different languages such as Tamil, Telugu and Sanskrit to Ramamirtham. Within three years, she had a good command over the languages. Then she started to learn music. These advantages helped Ramamirtham to forget her parents. It was customary that learning music was necessary to become a *dasi*.[12] She learnt dance from *nattuvanar* 'Peralam' Suyambup Pillai. At the age seven, she underwent a *gejja* puja (anklet ceremony) and at the age of ten, she became an expert in artistic skills. In the meantime, Ramamirtham's real parents became economically prosperous in Madras. But they were reluctant to accept their daughter because of their social status.[13] The educated Ramamirtham had a discourse on religion with the field experts and enriched her knowledge. *Dasi* Achchikkannu decided to conduct *pottu* ceremony for Ramamirtham at the age of seventeen. The other *dasis* did not agree for this dedication and they argued that Ramamirtham belonged to a daughter of the male member of the *dasi* caste.

The distressed Achchikkannu tried to make money from other ways. A local merchant aged sixty five years old was interested in the teenager

Ramamirtham. The *dasi* insisted her to marry the old merchant. Ramamirtham decided to leave her adopted mother. She worried about her future shelter. Then, she decided to marry her teacher Suyambup Pillai and expressed her interest towards him. Initially, Suyambup Pillai was hesitant and later he accepted her. The simple marriage was performed without any rituals in Valuvur temple, near Mayiladuthurai in modern Tamil Nadu. They had three children, but the first two died of illness. Chellappa was the only survived son of the couple. But the marriage was rejected by the society. In the course of time, the hatred Achchikkannu reconciled and she nominated Ramamirtham as her heir of Achchikkannu bequeathed his entire property to Ramamirtham and it made her financially stable. Later, she invited her parents from Madras.

The public life of Ramamirtham

At the age of thirty five, Ramamirtham was impressed by Gandhi, especially his views towards the issues of devadasi. She started to propagate the ideology of Gandhi in the streets of Madras Presidency. She started to wear *khaddar* dresses and actively involved in the *khaddar* campaign and the Non-Cooperation Movement. She campaigned for women's liberation, anti-liquor, education and widow marriage. She was against untouchability and child marriage. She helped untouchables to wear *dhoti*. She influenced many devadasi women to use *khaddar* and sold it and she was imprisoned for this. On the demand of Gandhi, Ramamirtham started to live a simple life in a hut. Once the *khaddar* materials were stollen and it was found that a poor woman had stollen it to wear. Ramamirtham was very much moved by this incident and she asked the judge to free her.[14] Ramamirtham mentioned that she joined Congress at the age of thirty eight and initially she was happy. She believed that Congress provided a space for *dasi* and for the abolition of the custom. The Congress members praised her and she became very popular.[15] She participated in her maiden Congress Conference at Peralam under the leadership of Thiru.Vi. Kalyanasundaram.

Ramamirtham and the question of devadasi system

Ramamirtham inspired other *dasis* to leave their profession and lead an independent life. Koorainadu Tillaiammal and Chidambaram Janagaththammal were encouraged to get out of the devadasi custom. Initially, her campaign against the devadasi system happened in an unorganised manner. She visited devadasi houses and discussed about the evils of the custom secretly. She explained her experiences and asked young women to leave the life of a devadasi. She promised to help for their reformed life. She organised marriage for those girls. The furious devadasi filed cases against her, but she did not relented. With the help of T.N. Rajaraththinam Pillai, the musician and self-respecter, she protested against the initiation of Sathyamurthi, conservative Congress leader, who sent two devadasis for dance performance to England.

Usually, public criticised Ramamirtham for her public participation, but she never bothered about it.[16] The efforts of Ramamirtham were acknowledged by then Congress leaders such as Thiru.Vi. Kalyanasundaram, Varatharajulu Naidu, S. Ramanathan, E.V. Ramasami and N. Thandapani. Kalyanasundaram praised Ramamirtham as a savior of the fallen women.[17] In 1956, C.N. Annadurai, the founder of *Dravida Munnetra Kazhakam* (DMK), appreciated her efforts and specially mentioned her assistance to Gandhi during his South Indian visit.[18]

E.V. Ramasami and Kalyanasundaram were interested to establish an organisation for devadasi and abolish the institution. Ramamirtham started an association called *Nagapasaththar Sangam* (Devadasi Association) for the welfare of devadasi.[19] S.V. Lingam, a friend of Ramamirtham, assisted her in the works of association. They visited the districts of Ramanathapuram, Tiruchirappalli, Thanjavur and North Arcot in Madras Presidency. They started to recruit the members. Her initiation was supported by E.V. Ramasami, Kalyanasundaram and Varatharajulu Naidu.[20] Ramamirtham was interested to rename the *Nagapasaththar Sangam*. She felt the name was not inclusive in its nature because the dedication happened in heterogeneous way with the practice of different caste and rituals. She had a discussion with Pundit Singaravel about the name of the association and found a name as *Isai Vellalar*, which meant cultivators of music.[21]

Ramamirtham spent her money and organised the first *Isai Vellalar* Conference in Muvalur under the leadership of Singaravel. And later, she organised three conferences. The second *Isai Vellalar* Conference was held from November 15 to 16, 1925 at Mayavaram under the leadership of Perunthurai S.A. Ganeshan, Kalyanasundaram, E.V. Ramasami, and M.R. Kumarasami participated in the conference. Ramamirtham acted as a general secretary and Tillaiammal assisted her.[22] On November 6, 1925, S.A. Ganeshan paid his tribute to the people for selecting him as the leader of the Conference and also refused to accept the offer.[23] The third conference was held in Tiruvaluthur and Gandhi had been invited as a chief guest.[24]

The difficulties faced by Ramamirtham

There were a strong protest among the conservative devadasi, priest, fundamentalist, landlords, zamindars and pimps. Ramamirtham stated that we could even protest against British colonialism and Brahmanism, but not against devadasi system.[25] The agitators were trying to assault Ramamirtham. In general, Ramamirtham used to participate in the social dramas and con-demned the devadasi practice. The fundamentalist entered into the drama hall and cut her hair during the performance. The incident freed her from fear and also made her bold enough to move in public with short hair.[26] In Omampuliur, a devadasi woman gave her milk laced with poison. Fortunately, she was saved. But Ramamirtham refused to file a case against the perpetrators.[27]

Ramamirtham in her short notes on her life history has mentioned that at the age of twenty five she started to criticise her devadasi community. So, people created trouble for her. They filled a fraudulent charges and comments on her. One of the charges levied against her was that she gave one thousand rupee and fifteen thousand worth jewellries and mesmerised people. Her husband was afraid to face these encounters. Ramamirtham convinced her husband that if anything went wrong, they would again go back to singing in the street. She stated that they were expert in music taught dance and music to others and could earn lot of money.[28]

There was a murder charge filed against Ramamirtham. But, Ramamirtham proved it was a false charge and produced that the so called dead person who was allegedly said to be killed by her.[29] There was another case filed against Ramamirtham. She campaigned against the institution of devadasis and organised marriages of hundreds of girls dedicated to the immortal trade. Ramamirtham tried to help *dasi* Thangam from her diseased condition. However, her mother filed a case against Ramamirtham and six others in Mayavaram Sub-Magistrate Court that the accused used criminal force against the complaint and her two attempted to take *dasi* Thangam away with a view to rescue her from the profession.[30]

Ramamirtham in the Self-Respect Movement

The Self-Respect campaign of E.V. Ramasami gradually inspired Ramamirtham. In 1925, she left the Congress party and became actively involved in the Self-Respect Movement. She propagated the ideologies of the Self-Respect Movement and campaigned for Self-Respect marriages and women liberation. She appreciated the initiation of Muthulakshmi Reddi and had a communi-cation with her. She met Muthulakshmi in Madras. Muthulakshmi asked Ramamirtham to continue her work and assured her support.[31] Ramamirtham was invited by Muthulakshmi for the Madras Legislative Council (MLC)'s select committee meeting to witness the problem of devadasi. She advised Muthulakshmi to tackle the encounters of Sathyamurthi.[32] However, Muthulakshmi did not acknowledge or mention her association with Ramamirtham in her autobiography.[33]

She participated in various programmes of the Self-Respect Movement. In 1938, she participated in the Anti-Hindi agitation rally for creating awareness on the politics behind the imposition and construction of Hindi in non-Hindi regions such as modern Tamil Nadu, Kerala, Andhra Pradesh and Karnataka. The rally was extended to forty two days, five hundred and seventy seven miles and eighty seven public meetings. In the meantime, she was imprisoned for six months for participating in the anti-Hindi campaign in front of the school with Nilavathi and Dharmambal.

After the establishment of *(Dravidian Organisation) Kazhakam* in the Madras Presidency, Ramamirtham actively engaged herself in the public debates. In 1949, Annadurai founded the DMK, a prominent political party of South India. Ramamirtham joined the party and became its forefront campaigner.[34] During her last days, she functioned as an honorary magistrate in Mayiladuthurai Court. However, in the party, she slowly lost her significance in the movement. She was worried about her recognition in the organisation. C.N. Annadurai honoured her with the award of *Suyamariyathai Iyakka Viruthu* in 1956. She was only person to receive the award.[35] Karunanidhi, then Chief Minister of Tamil Nadu, described that her hair was like milk; along with her white dress; confident walk; speech and fire arguments.[36] He introduced a welfare government marriage scheme in her name in 1989-1991.[37] The scheme was introduced after her death in June 27, 1962.

Ramamirtham, as a writer

Ramamirtham was a prolific writer and continually wrote columns in the newspapers of the Self-Respect Movement. In her writings, she campaigned for the self-respected life of the people. In 1936, she published her semi-fictional novel called *Dasikal Mosavalai alladhu Mathipetra Minar* (*Dasis web of deceit or enlightened playboy*). The novel was written on the basis of her experience in the devadasi community.[38] Later in 1945, she started to write a fictional series in *Dravida Nadu* of *Dravidar Kazhakam*.[39] The fictional series was entitled as *Thamayanthi*.[40] Through her writings, she criticised the life of the devadasi women and explained the exploitative nature of the society.[41] Apart from fiction and novel, she extensively wrote on other social issues. Ramamirtham scripted a monograph *Islamum Indhiyarkalin Nilamaiyum* (Islam and the position of Indians) and personally published it in 1939.[42] The content analysed the principles of Islam and compared it with the values of the Self-Respect Movement.

Bangalore Nagarathnam (1878-1952)

Bangalore Nagarathnam was born to a devadasi called Puttalakshmi Ammal Vaishnavi of Heggade Devanna Kotha, a village in the Princely State of Mysore. Her mother was attached to the Sri Kanteswaram temple of Nanjangud, in modern Mysore. There was a speculation with regard to the identity of her father. Generally, Subbanna, a wealthy Brahmin from Mysore, was accepted as her father.[43] M. Subba Rao, a lawyer from Mysore, was the patron of her mother. But, in her childhood, the patron of her mother led them into poverty. The family migrated to Mysore and found a new patron Giribhatta Thimayya, a Sanskrit scholar, musician and instructor at the *Shakuntala Nataka Sabha* of Maharaja Chamarajendra Wodeyar X (1868-1894) stage plays.

Giribhatta Thimayya became the teacher of Nagarathnam. At the age of five, Nagarathnam completed her music and Sanskrit lessons from him. Bidaram Krishnappa, the leader of Mysore Palace of Yakshagana troupe, taught music to Nagarathnam.

An intelligent of Nagarathnam threatened the minds of Giribhatta Thimayya. He thought the growth of Nagarathnam would defame his existence. Threrefore, he suddenly withdrew all his support. At the age of nine, the family of Nagarathnam once again had to undergo poverty. According to *Grihalakshmi* (journal), Nagarathnam and her mother started collecting cow dung in the streets of Mysore.[44] Puttalakshmi forced to move away from Mysore. She pledged that in future, the return of her daughter to Mysore would happen only on the invitation of the kings' palace. Otherwise, she would commit suicide rather than returning to Mysore.[45] The destitute mother and daughter migrated to Kanchipuram to meet Dhanakoti sisters (Dhanakoti, Kamakshi and Palani Ammal), a famous devadasi, from Kanchipuram and a friend of Puttalakshmi. The sisters were popular in Tamil and Telugu regions. They received a warm welcome here. However, Dhanakoti could not help them and recommended to Puttalakshmi shelter under a renowned violinist in Srirangam. Financially, exhausted Puttalakshmi hesitated to migrate to Srirangam and left for Bangalore to take shelter with her brother Venkitasamappa, a violinist.

The destitute mother

In Bangalore, Puttalakshmi started working hard for her daughter's career.[46] Nagarathnam learned violin from her uncle Venkitasamappa. Her efforts were appreciated by Hyderabad Munuswamappa, a famous violinist. In the meantime, she studied Telugu and English. Later, she became proficient in many languages such as Telugu, Tamil, Kannada and English. Bangalore Kittanna, a niece of Munuswamappa, taught her dance and *abhinaya* (gesture) was taught by Madras Tiruvenkatachar. Puttalakshmi was very strict with regard to the performance of Nagarathnam. The visit of Prince Albert Victor (1889) to Bangalore encouraged the devadasi's performance and the mother and daughter witnessed the performance of devadasis.

Puttalakshmi was diagnosed with tuberculosis in 1891.[47] Puttalakshmi believed that Nagarathnam did not possess conventional beauty. Though she was short and fat, she had a flawless skin, fair complexion and possessed curly hair and great eyes.[48] The dying mother understood that her brother's intention was not good for her daughter's future. She realised that her brother would exploit her daughter, hence, she gave the responsibility of her daughter to Munuswamappa. In later days, he was loyal to the words of Puttalakshmi and rescued her.[49] Nagarathnam used to perform in the public gatherings and it established a firm place for her in field of performing art. She had a chance to perform in the house of Vina Seshanna, a legendry musician of Mysore court.

Nagarathnam and Munuswamappa travelled to Mysore as a palace artist and her performance was appreciated by the experts. The incidents fulfilled the pledge of Puttalakshmi that she made in her earlier days. Later in 1893, she was invited to perform at the Amba Vilasa Palace. This performance was witnessed by Giribhatta Thimayya and he praised her a lot.[50] She began to live in Mysore with fortune and fame.

The death of Chamarajendra Wodeyar X led the rule of Krishnarajendra, a ten years old. The widowed queen became the acting regent and she ordered to stop the dance performance at the *Muzrai* (state controlled temples) in 1895 and later in 1898 she banned the recruitment of women for dance performance. *Tafe*, the dance performance of the devadasi, was prohibited in the Princely State of Mysore. In the meantime, her *Guru* Munuswamappa passed away. Nagarathnam suffered a lot and she again migrated to Bangalore and continued her public performance. T. Narahari Rao, the Judge of Mysore Court at Bangalore, admired the performance of Nagarathnam and became her patron. Narahari Rao's wife Sethamma had a cordial relationship with Nagarathnam.

The relationship between Narahari Rao and Nagarathnam was criticised by the people of the royal court. Divan K. Seshadri Iyer opposed the open relationship and he did not question the patronage. Therefore, Narahari Rao shifted her to a new house near the hillock forest in Bangalore town. The people generously visited the house of Nagarathnam and attended her performance. Even Seshadri Iyer was also present in her performance. In later days, the hillock was known as Mount Joy or *Narahari Raya Gudda* (the hillock of Narahari Rao).[51] The shift prevented Nagarathnam from plague when it was widely spread in the Bangalore town in 1898-1899. The association with him made her happy and safe. In the course of time, a difference of opinion between the two led to separation. Narahari Rao passed away in 1902.

T. Sankaran in *Sruti* magazine had mentioned that Nagarathnam had a child, but it lived for a short period.[52] According to the devadasi tradition, the childless devadasi women could adopt the child. *Grihalakshmi* noted that Nagarathnam adopted a child and taught her traditional technique. The parents of the child tried to poison Nagarathnam with the help of the adopted daughter.[53] Later, Nagarathnam had a third daughter from Alamelumanga Thayar of Dorasani, a close friend. The relationship between Alamelumanga Thayar alias Banni Bai and Nagarathnam was cordial till her death.

Nagarathnam and her new fortune

The death of Narahari Rao led her to migrate Madras in 1903. At the age of five twenty, she decided to stay permanently in Madras city. C.S. Rajarathna Mudaliar of Madras became the patron of Nagarathnam.[54] As an extrovert, she could make friends easily. Nagarathnam who was financially sound struggled to establish her name as a singer in the new city.[55] She had a friendship with Vina Dhanam, a devadasi and grandmother of veteran Balasaraswati and Coimbatore Thayi. She was gradually able to establish herself in Madras city. She was appreciated by Ramanathapuram 'Poochi' Srinivasa Iyengar, who traced his lineage from Thiyagarajar and Vishnu Narayan Bhatkhande, a Hindustani maestro. The title *Vidyasundari*, one whose beauty is knowledge, was conferred on Nagarathnam by the queen of Bobbili.[56]

From 1905 onwards, Nagarathnam started to pay income tax and constructed a house which comprised of two floors.[57] She used to move in the city with a horse carriage which was not common in this period. She was always surrounded by her servants. During the performance, her servants used to walk in front of her with a silver pot of coffee, another with hot water and yet another with a box of betel leaves. People started to address her as BNR Ammal.[58] She conducted elaborate daily rituals and invited eminent personalities such as Kasturi Ranga Iyengar, the managing director of *The Hindu* between 1905 and 1923.[59]

Nagarathnam was eager to accept the modern changes in the field of music. In the early twentieth century, music companies introduced phonographs, blank cylinders, gramophone and discs into the British India from Europe and United States of America (USA).[60] The recording companies made efforts to record the native voices. The traditional artists such as devadasis were the first choice for the recording companies. The Gramophone and Typewriter Limited (GTTL) recorded the voice of Nagarathnam and popularised the disc as Miss Nagarathnam of Bangalore.[61] She became one of the popular recording artists in the contemporary period. The increasing *anti-nautch* agitations demanded devadasi to avoid the public dance performance and she became a vocalist.[62] Nagarathnam also stopped the dance performance from 1907-1908.[63]

The controversies over Nagarathnam

The glory of Nagarathnam created a powerful lobby. She continued to receive the patronage of the princely courts of Mysore, Travancore, Bobbili and Venkatagiri. Her talent was appreciated by the Bobbili Coronation Gazette.[64] Nagarathnam did performance throughout South India. According to *Grihalakshmi*, Nagarathnam performed in one hundred and forty six towns, especially one thousand two hundred and thirty five concerts were performed in South India and her concerts in Madras itself were eight hundred and forty nine.[65] She was the only vocalist from the devadasi tradition who performed in the All India Congress Session which was held in December, 1927 at Madras.[66] The admired Pundit Vishnu Digambur, a Hindustani musician, rewarded a gold medal to her.[67] Along with concerts, she used to perform in marriages and other festival occasions. Nagarathnam frequently attended the festival of *Ganda Penderam* at Rajahmundry, in Andhra Pradesh. Her concert raised much expectation even in Ilankai (modern Jaffna, Sri Lanka).[68]

During her travel to Tiruvarur region, she witnessed the performance of *Tyagesa Kuravanji* (kind of dance drama), which was exclusively performed by devadasis of *kondi* lineage. Nagarathnam desired to perform the drama within the temple complex. The temple authorities refused to violate the tradition. However, she sought the help of local patrons and forced temple authorities to allow her. She started to perform the dance drama with strong protection. Kutti Ammal, devadasi and the head of *kondi* family disguised as a Brahmin woman, intercepted the performance with the lawyer and brought legal stay order to stop the performance. Nagarathnam accepted the legal notice and stopped her performance.[69]

Kandukuri Veerasalingam, a social reformer who was actively engaged in the *anti-nautch* campaign, criticised the eighteenth century text of Muthupalani's *Radhika Santawanam*.[70] He condemned that several references in the book were disgraceful and inappropriate for women to hear, let alone be uttered from a woman's mouth.[71] But Nagarathnam admired the text and encountered the comments of Veerasalingam about the *Radhika Santawanam*.[72] She responded to him that did the question of propriety and embarrassment apply only in the case of women, not men? Did Veerasalingam imply that it was acceptable for Muthupalani to write about conjugal pleasures in a minute detail and without reservation because she was a courtesan? Are the 'obscenities' in *Radhika Santawanam* any worse than the obscenities in *Vaijayantivilasam*, a book that was personally reviewed and approved for publication by Veerasalingam.[73] Later, she was able to publish the work of Muthupalani in Vavilla Press, Madras. *Sasileka*, the Telugu literary magazine, commented that a prostitute had composed the book and another prostitute had edited it.[74] The book was sent to Goteti Kanakaraju, the official government translator for the censorship. He banned the book on the ground that it had obscene content and noted that both the author and editor were prostitutes.[75] The ban was lifted only after the independence in 1952.

The conventional Nagarathnam firmly believed in the devadasi tradition. During the abolition campaign, she was actively engaged for the retaining of the devadasi system in the society. She mobilised devadasi to form an organisation to counter the reformist agenda of abolition. Vina Dhanam, T. Doraikannu and Jeevarathnam were the other prominent devadasi women who encountered the *anti-nautch* activities. They formed an organisation, Jeevarathnam and Doraikannu became the official head and secretary of the organisation.[76] On November 3, 1927, a group of devadasi had sent a petition against the reformist activities.[77] They framed a memorandum titled *The Humble Memorandum of the Devadasis of the Madras Presidency.*[78] They argued that devadasi was not a prostitute, the act could damage the age old tradition and the custom was religious in nature and even the act would question the survival of devadasi women.[79] They worried that the abolition process would destroy the unique art forms of devadasi tradition and the association passed a resolution that the art of dancing and singing were the inheritance of the community. Vina Dhanam, Salem Lakshmi, Salem Thayi, Minakshi, Rajalakshmi, Lakshmirathnam and Mylapore Gowri Ammal were the supporters and issued a statement in favour of the devadasi system.[80] The pace of the organisation was slowed down in early 1928.[81] Yet, Nagarathnam was proud to refer to herself as a woman from devadasi community.[82]

Nagarathnam and Thiyagarajar, the saintly musician

Nagarathnam used to sing the canonisation of Thiyagarajar whom she considered as her first *Guru* (teacher). Her association to Thiyagarajar and his songs had led her growing devotion towards the saintly musician. William J. Jackson noted that the verses of Nagarathnam are composed when she dreamt of rare blessings of musical saint Thiyagarajar on a night in October, 1921 in the form in which she had conceived him in her daily worship.[83] In the meantime, in 1921 she received a letter from her teacher Bidaram Krishnappa regarding the ruined state of the *samadhi* (memorial) of Thiyagarajar's which was constructed in banks of River Cauveri in Tiruvaiyar (1847) where Thiyagarajar was buried. He requested her help in the renovation of the memorial.[84] She travelled to witness the condition of the memorial in the company of Nagaraja Bhagavatar, one of the organisers of the *aradhana* (musical fest in Tiruvaiyar). She was so sad to witness the pathetic condition of her *Guru's* memorial which was surrounded by thorny bushes, bamboos and snakes and it was impossible to move here even in the day time.[85]

Nagarathnam got involved in the restoration of the memorial and spent her entire money for this purpose. The work started in October 27, 1921 and the consecration was done on January 7, 1925.[86] She engaged in more public performance to earn money and sold her jewellery for the construction of the memorial. She settled the dispute which took place over the memorial land between *Chinna Katchi* and *Periya Katchi.*[87] She purchased the land. With the help of others, she was able to renovate the memorial (*See Appendix*: - 15). In between 1933 and 1935, she acquired land in and around the memorial and later in 1937 and 1938 she constructed the remaining places with her efforts.[88] In November, 1938, she completed the assignments of the temple constructions.

Nagarathnam believed it to be the shrine of the great musical legend Thiyagarajar. She got carved a marble image in the memorial and worshipped it.[89] She composed an *ashtothram* to Thiyagarajar.[90] The shrine was open to all which was not common during this period. Traditionally, the musical festival was conducted in the honour of the saintly musician Thiyagarajar which was popularly called as *aradhana*. Nagarathnam desired to participate in the musical fest. The fundamentalists restricted women to perform in *aradhana*. However, the rebellious Nagarathnam distributed handbills about her maiden performance in *aradhana* in 1927. She invited other devadasis also to participate in the fest and this became a successful event in the history.[91]

Nagarathnam firmly decided to spend the rest of her life in Tiruvaiyar to pay her homage to her *Guru*. Her songs concentrated on the musical saint. Her house was situated near Shakuntala and Kamala, the natives of Tiruvaiyar. In later days, all the three became close associates. In the meantime, she constantly sought patrons for conducting *aradhana*. In the early 1940, she toured to Mysore court to meet the then king Jayachamaraja Wodeyar and visited Nellore in modern Andhra Pradesh. There she met a protest by a group of people who were against devadasi women. But she was able to receive the patronage from C.V. Rajagopalachari and conducted *aradhana* in 1941.[92] The local administration warned the trustee not to conduct *aradhana* due to the spread of cholera in 1943. But Nagarathnam and the committee influenced the local government to permit *aradhana* celebration.[93]

In 1942, some burglars entered Nagarathnam's house, stole her jewels and attacked her. The aged Nagarathnam was frightened to stay in the house because she felt alone and no one was there who could speak in her mother tongue Kannada.[94] Then she shifted to the house of Rama Rao, a wealthy Kannada person who was in Tiruvaiyar. During her stay, she used to teach Thiyagarajar songs to Rama Rao's children. However, Nagarathnam was reluctant to go away from Tiruvaiyar. Nagarathnam devoted her entire property and wealth for the charity purpose to the trust named Vidyasundari Bangalore Nagarathnam Trust and the trustees were C.V. Rajagopalachari, T.A. Ramachandra Rao and V. Minakshisundaram Iyer. She allowed using her memorial property to Tyagabrahma Mahotsava Sabha for conducting annual functions such as *aradhana*. Moreover, she insisted the memorial should be open for the public worship.[95] In 1951, the annual fest was inaugurated by then home minister of India, C. Rajagopalachari. There he met Nagarathnam on January 27, 1951 and praised her that all musicians and *vidwans* should offer homage to this *sanniyasini* (women saint) of our times.[96]

On May 19, 1952, Nagarathnam died in Tiruvaiyar. Her body was covered with traditional red sari with *kumkum* and *vibuthi* (sacred ash) on her face and her body was seated in her usual chair. Her funeral car and image of Thiyagarajar was brought out from the memorial of her patron deity of Thiyagarajar.[97] According to her last wish, she was buried near the memorial of her patron saint. But some fundamentalists and few people in the town objected to bury a woman near the saint. With the police protection her body was buried in the place where she had wished.[98] Later, her image was sculpted and kept within the premise of Thiyagarajar memorial at Tiruvaiyar (*See Appendix*: - 16).

Thanjavur Balasaraswati (1918-1984)

Thanjavur Balasaraswati belonged to a traditional devadasi family. She had a strong matrilineal linage (*See Appendix*: - 17). Her mother and grand-mother were the great personalities and musicians of the ninteenth and twentieth century. B.M. Sundaram mentioned that Balasaraswati was considered as one of the trios in the dance tradition with Kumbakonam Banumathi and Panthanainallur Jayalakshmi.[99] Douglas M. Knight Jr, the biographer of Balasaraswati, introduced her as a globally renowned performing artist of the twentieth century.[100] Karnatakam, a columnist in *Ananda Vikatan* Tamil weekly, appreciated the dance performance of Balasaraswati at the age of ten.[101] Narayana Menon, the then secretary of the Sangeet Natak Academi, wrote a column after her death in 1984 that appreciated her contribution to the Indian dance tradition.

Balasaraswati was popularly konwn as 'Bala'. She was the second child of T. Jayammal, daughter of great devadasi Vina Dhanam and her patron Modarapu Govindarajulu, *dubash* in Madras. She was born in Madras where her ancestors migrated from Thanjavur. But she was always identified with her ancestral place Thanjavur, her initial 'T' referred to Thanjavur. The goddess Kamakshi was the family deity of the Balasaraswati's family and the temple was located in Thanjavur. Rajayi Ammal, a devadasi of Thanjavur, helped Balasaraswati's informal dedication in Thanjavur because she was minor at the time of dedication. And the dedication of minor was illegal at that time.[102] In general, the extended family lived in Ramakrishna Chetty Street in Madras city. According to the devadasi tradition, she also learnt and became an expert in Telugu, Tamil and Sanskrit language.

Balasaraswati and her family

Balasaraswati admired the performance of devadasi such as Mylapore Gowri Ammal, the contemporary of Jayammal. She mentioned that her initial inspiration for dancing came after seeing the performance of Gowri Ammal when she was young.[103] She learnt singing from her mother and dance from Gowri Ammal. Later, Jayammal selected a young *nattuvanar* Kandappa Pillai as a dance teacher of her daughter. Kandappa Pillai introduced modified traditional techniques to Balasaraswati such as the seating positions of musicians who traditionally accompanied the dancer while they danced.

Panthanainallur Minakshi Sundaram Pillai (1869-1954) witnessed the performance of the young Balasaraswati and appreciated her.[104]

The ambitious Jayammal worked hard to cultivate the talent of her daughter. She used to be seated near Balasaraswati during her practices. Balasaraswati stated that she would not have become a dancer without the efforts of Jayammal. It was her untiring efforts and push that she learned the art.[105] Further, she mentioned that her mother, Jayammal had trained her as a dancer despite strong family opposition of the *anti-nautch* campaign and also the family pressure against learning music. Jayammal restricted schooling of Balasaraswati because her teachers asked her to perform in the schools (*See Appendix*: - 18).[106] From the age of seven, she used to practice sixteen hours a day.[107] Usually, the house of Balasaraswati was a place for the amalgamation of different art forms. Balasaraswati was exposed to numerous kinds of arts. The Friday night concert at the house of Vina Dhanam was popular among the musical lovers of Madras. Douglas M Knight Jr mentioned that the every week, the performing fare was different and Vina Dhanam used to perform in the evening.[108] R. Krishnamurthy who popularly known as Kalki, the columnist in *Ananda Vikatan*, visited her house and mentioned that the house was carrying two *dhanams* (wealth) such as learning and material wealth.[109]

The art of Balasaraswati

Balasaraswati performed her *arangerram* (initiation dance) in 1925 at Amanakshi Amman temple, Kanchipuram. On September 13, 1927, Balasaraswati's first official public performance was held at the home of Doraisami Naidu, homeopathic physician.[110] However Balasaraswati's grandmother and veteran Vina Dhanam did not see her dance because since 1926 Vina Dhanam had lost her eye sight.[111] In 1932, Jayammal arranged Chinnaiya Naidu, popular dance master for the improvisation of the dance techniques of Balasaraswati.[112] In general, Balasaraswati was famous for her *padam* (expression/expressive) performance (*See Appendix*: - 19). Her repertoire of *padam* numbered nearly one hundred.[113] The dance style of Balasaraswati was known as Thanjavur style. In 1973, Balasaraswati acknowledged in the Music Academy that everything she received from her family and her *Gurus*.

Balasaraswati's maiden Music Academy performance was held at the age of fifteen in July, 1933 and later she performed on many occasions in the academy. K. Chandrasekaran, a musicologist, mentioned that Bala was not particularly beautiful, but that when she began to dance her eyes and pearl white teeth dominated and transformed her face.[114] In the same year, she was introduced to Pundit Uday Shankar, an Indian dancer. Later in December, 1934, Balasaraswati attended the All Bengal Music Conference in Calcutta where Satyajit Ray, a popular Indian filmmaker, watched the performance of Balasaraswati. Interestingly, Satyajit Ray was a teenage boy at the time of performance.[115] Rabindranath Tagore, the first Indian noble laureate, also watched the performance of Balasaraswati. She was much excited to perform in the huge platform.[116] Jayammal and Balasaraswati worked together to interpret the songs in the Carnatic style and did the Bharatanatyam.[117] Balasaraswati performed to the song *Jana Gana Mana* in 1934 at Calcutta. Later, she was invited to perform at the All India Music Conference at Banaras Hindu University by Madanmohan Malavya who was the then Vice Chancellor of the university in 1936. There she again performed for the song *Jana Gana Mana* and also performed it in Indian National Congress Exhibition in Madras in the same year. Douglas M. Knight Jr noted that these were the first and likely the last time that the song that became the Indian national anthem could be danced with *abhinaya*.[118] Again at Banaras, Rabindranath Tagore witnessed the performance of Balasaraswati and then he offered a silk shawl to Balasaraswati's drummer.[119]

The introduction of Balasaraswati in North India provided new prospects and fame to her in South India. She became famous among other performers and had opportunities of more stage performance. On January 1, 1934, Balasaraswati performed in the People's Park behind the Ripon Building, headquarters of Madras Corporation. There she met R.K. Shanmukham, the first finance minister of India, who came to watch the performance. R.K. Shanmukham admired her performance.[120] He was interested in having her as a life partner. In 1936, the family of Balasaraswati accepted the proposal of R.K. Shanmukham who was twenty six years older than her. In the meantime, in April 1936, Jayammal was able to purchase a small house in Dhanala Aravamudu Naidu Garden Street in Egmore, Madras and started living there.[121]

The grey days of Balasaraswati

On October 15, 1938, Vina Dhanam died. In the meantime, Pundit Uday Shankar invited *nattuvanar* Kandappa Pillai in 1938 to join as the faculty at the short lived Uday Shankar's Performing Arts Centre in Almora District of modern Uttarakhand state. Within a short duration, Kandappa Pillai died in February, 1941. It created a kind of rift between Balasaraswati and Uday Shankar. This incident created a great loss to Balasaraswati and her crew. She was kind enough to help and improve the life condition of Ganesha Pillai, son of Kandappa Pillai. It was reflected in her performance at the Music Academy in December, 1939. R. Krishnamurthy mentioned that he could not find any improvement in the performance of Balasaraswati.[122] The loss of Kandappa Pillai led Balasaraswati to search for a new *nattuvanar*, because the relationship between dancer and *nattuvanar* was important for the better performance. She found Kanchipuram Ellappa Pillai, cousin of Kandappa Pillai and accepted him as *nattuvanar,* but not as her *Guru*. The transition improved the musical quality of her performance.

In the course of time, the dominant behaviour of Jayammal created a rift between the relationship of the ambitious mother and daughter.[123] During the Second World War, Jayammal sold her house and moved to Chengalput, a suburban of Madras due to the Japanese bomb threat in 1942.[124] The health of Balasaraswati was also deteriorating. In 1942, Balasaraswati gave birth to a girl child, which was considered as auspicious in the matrilineal community and following that she shifted again to Madras in 1943. Lakshmi, daughter of Balasaraswati, mentioned the period of 1940s as a hard time for Bala, and that time, she was little fat and people were not asking for her performances.[125] The relationship between R.K. Shanmukham and Balasaraswati had many ups and down due to the independent nature of Balasaraswati.[126]

Balasaraswati desired to perform within the temple premises of Tiruththani, the temple of Lord Murukan. According to her statement, she dreamt about seeing Lord Murukan in 1954. She decided to travel Tiruththani with her friend C.P. Srinivasan, Jayammal and her daughter Lakshmi (*See Appendix*: - 20). But the temple priests denied her to perform in the premises, due to the Devadasis (Prevention of Dedication) Act, 1947 in the Madras Presidency. The clever Balasaraswati had sent priests to purchase the ritual objects such as coconut, camphor etc. She utilised this gap, closed the doors of the temple premise and did a short performance.[127] In the same way, Balasaraswati was interested to perform in Krishna temple at Udupi, modern Karnataka state in 1960. The temple authorities could not succeed in stopping the performance, and after her performance, they admired and presented offerings.[128]

Balasaraswati invited Kuchipudi exponent Vedantam Lakshminarayana Sastri in 1948 to improve her dance techniques. During his stay in the house of Balasaraswati, the orthodox Brahmin like him would not even touch water there. She was reluctant to continue his teaching because she could not meet his expenses [129] In the same year, Balasaraswati received an offer as a lead actor in a film which was based on the historical novel *Sivukamiyin Sabatham* (The vow of Sivakami) from R. Krishnamurthy. But she rejected the offer and wanted to continue as a stage performer only.[130]

Balasaraswati and Bharatanatyam

Balasaraswati's grace in dancing was growing stronger day by day. It reflected in the gradual increase of her programmes. She did thirteen concerts in 1943 and eleven in 1944 which included her maiden foreign trip to Ilankai in April. She was able to do three programmes in 1945. But following three years from 1946 to 1948 she did not do any public performance. In January 1945, Balasaraswati did one of the best performances of her career in the All India Dance Festival at Bombay.[131] The dance festival also carried the performances of Rukmini Devi (Bharatanatyam dancer), Achchan Maharaj (dancer), Shambhu Maharaj (dancer), Ali Akbar Khan (Hindustani musician), Vilayat Khan (Sitarist) and etc.

The growing intervention of non-devadasis' towards Bharatanatyam, questioned the existence of the devadasi dance performances. The active Bala-saraswati was fourteen years younger than Rukmini Devi who was firm to reply the counter arguments, which were imposed by revivalist especially to Rukmini Devi. Balasaraswati continually argued that there was nothing in Bharatanatyam which could be purified afresh; it was divine and was innately so.[132] The inadequacies that were felt in this art arose from the inadequacies of the dancer herself. If Bharatanatyam performances studied with devotion, dedication, patience and thoroughness, its completeness in its traditional form would have been crystal clear.[133] Balasaraswati stated in Women's World on October 25, 1953 that a dancer's basic concerns should first be to uphold the high standard of the art and then, through knowledge and practice, to pursue adaptation and innovation.[134]

To Balasaraswati dancing was natural, therefore universal expression of the human species whereby it found its unity with the cosmos and its creator.[135] Balasaraswati compared a dancer with *yogi* (saint). According to her, both *yogi* and dancer could control breath and modify their body and acquired halo of sanctity. The Yogi achieves serenity through concentration that comes from discipline. The dancer brings together her feet, hands, eyes, ears and singing into a fusion which transforms the serenity like a yogi into a torrent of beauty.[136] The dancer has to surrender herself to the art. Such surrender makes her aware of the divinity and wholeness of Bharatanatyam. And the art will continue to flourish without the aid of new techniques which aims at "purifying" it or changes in dress, ornament, make-up and the interpolation of new items which seeks to make it more "complete". She hoped for this to happen.[137] Bharatanatyam reveals the inner spiritual meaning. Bharatanatyam cuts deep into the conscious and sub-conscious levels called *Atman* or God.[138] *Abhinaya* is a gestural interpretation of songs on divinities and divine themes alone. Bharatanatyam is God oriented.[139]

She believed that the traditional order of the Bharatanatyam recital viz., *alarippu*, *jatiswaram*, *sabdam*, *varnam*, *padam*, *tillana* and *sloka* were the correct sequence in the practice of the art, which is an artistic *yoga*, for revealing the spiritual through the corporeal. [140] She wrote that if she has dedicated herself to the art, there would be no carnal distortions in her interpretations of the *padam*. Steeped in art and beauty, which are pure spiritual states, she expressed the joy which was as the basis of different moods and emotions. Such a dancer will feel no need to "purify" any item in the traditional order of Bharatanatyam.[141] She mentioned in her key note address at the Research on Dance Congress in August 1979 that many *mudras* (symbols) were common in both the *Tantra Sastra* and Bharatanatyam.[142]

Bharatanatyam is mainly practiced and performed by the fair sex. The basic reason may be that the dynamic power of the self (Sakthi) itself is always considered to be feminine and its static source of masculine.[143] It has been mainly a woman's art. But it is equally enjoyed and experienced by men as audience. By the fact of the lover being God, the union longed for is understood to be not of the physical but of the spiritual. It is the yearning of individual soul for merger in the cosmic soul. With this understanding, the dancer interprets the sensual in its spiritual settings.[144]

Rukmini Devi pointed out that the respect of dancer's was based on their choice of *shringara* elements.[145] If we approach Bharatanatyam with humility, learn it with dedication and practice it with devotion to God, *shringara* which brings out the great beauties of the dance, can be portrayed with all the purity of the spirit.[146] *Shringara* stands supreme in this range of emotions. No other emotion is capable of better reflecting the mystic union of the human with the divine. She stated this with deep personal experience of dancing to many great devotional songs, which had no element of *shringara* in them. Devotional songs were necessary.[147] Balasaraswati's Presidential address at the 33rd Annual Conference of the *Tamil Isai Sangam*, Madras. December 21, 1975, mentioned that *Chilappathikaram* and *Manimekalai* listed dance, music and the personal beauty of the dancer in that order. Yet unfortunately, today it was personal beauty, which comes first. When so much importance was attached to the looks of the dancer, it was natural that dancing was considered as carnal and *shringara* as vulgar. The truth is exactly the opposite; it was her dance and music alone that make dancer beautiful.[148]

The greatest authorities on the dance would have definitely recognized that it was the orthodoxy of traditional discipline which gave the fullest freedom to the individual creativity of the dancer.[149]

The Statesman described that it was impossible to escape the magic of her great art; the dancer disappeared, and what remained was Bharatanatyam at its most perfect, in its purest and almost divine form.[150] S. Guhan, a friend of Balasaraswati, explained his experience that in Bala's experience, the mythological characters portrayed in Bharatanatyam were not distant; they lived 'side by side' with her.[151] Lakshmi mentioned that Balasaraswati did not realise when she was transported and "became that thing".[152] Even Balasaraswati stated that she became the baby Krishna and Yasoda.[153] She created the illusion of doing *puja*, she created the illusion of the elements of the *puja*.[154] When a Balasaraswati was dancing or when she was in her room talking about her dance, she used to forget everything, such was her dedication.[155]

Balasaraswati and her international exposures

During the Eighth Tamil *Isai* (Music) Festival in Madras, Balasaraswati presented her new dance drama, *Sarabendra Boopala Kuravanji* on December 17, 1949. After seven years of gap, Balasaraswati danced in the Music Academy on January 2, 1950. In the *Ninth Tamil Isai (Music) Festival* Conference (1951), she did her dance drama in Madras. The years 1950's exposed Balasaraswati to western audiences. V. Raghavan, musicologist, was inspired by the performance of Balasaraswati and directed many westerners to her.[156] Later in May 5, 1953, R.K. Shanmukham died and Balasaraswati planned to quite her public performances. But this did not happen and she continued her dance till her death.

Balasaraswati's friends V. Raghavan, M.S. Subbulakshmi and Rajagopalan always helped in her difficult days. The Music Academy invited Balasaraswati to perform on January 2, 1950 and the following years of 1955, 1956 and 1957. In the meantime, the Music Academy and V. Raghavan established Balasaraswati School of Music and Dance in the premises of the Music Academy and V. Raghavan initiated the enrollment process and admitted her daughter Priyamvada to the dance school. The School received a liberal patronage from the Sangeet Natak Akademi.[157] Later in March 27, 1955, Balasaraswati received the President's Award from Sangeet Natak Akademi for maintaining the highest standards in music, dance and drama.[158] Kapila Vatsyayan arranged the performance of Balasaraswati at Sapru House in New Delhi on the next day itself. The Vice-President, S. Radhakrishnan watched the concert. Jayammal and Balasaraswati sang in the All India Radio, Delhi programme.[159] On November 3, 1955, she performed in the opening concert at the National Dance Festival at the Industrial Fair Theatre at New Delhi.[160] In January 1956, Martha Graham, an American dancer, toured Asia with the help of U.S. consulate. Balasaraswati observed the performance of Martha Graham and following that Balasaraswati's private dance programme was arranged for Martha Graham in Madras.[161]

In 1958, the government invited her for the tour to Russia for projecting Indian culture abroad. But before a week of trip, the government replaced another dancer for the tour and reasoned that the cancellation would save Balasaraswati from humiliation. The incident resulted in frustration and anger towards the government and understandably Balasaraswati was very upset.[162] Later, she received a request from Kapila Vatsyayan, then member of Sangeet Natak Akademi for representing the country in the festival of East-West

Encounter which was organised by the Congress for Cultural Freedom and City of Tokyo in Tokyo from April 16 to May 6, 1961. Balasaraswati was suspicious of the offer and reluctant to participate in it because of her previous experience. Even the conference Director, Nicolas Nabokov suspected that the dance performance of Bala would be a disappointment for the expecting audience and create a dent towards the image of Indian classical dance. But Kapila Vatsyayan firmly believed in the ability of Balasaraswati, she argued with others for her inclusion in the Japanese programme. Her Tokyo tour was a great success. After the programme, Nicolas Nabokov approached her and fell on his knee, kissed her hands and apologised for his second thought of replacing Balasaraswati for the concert. The Japanese newspapers declared the performance of Balasaraswati as a tremendous success and she continued her trip in Osaka and Yokohama.[163]

Balasaraswati loved the travel experience and dance in a foreign country and she felt that her performance was ideally suited to the West.[164] Later, she was invited to perform in the Asia Society in New York. The financial crisis of Balasaraswati made her to accept these offers and she left for USA in 1962. Americans received her warmly. She performed in different places such as Becket in Massachusetts, Wesleyan University, Washington D.C., University of Pennsylvania in Philadelphia, Princeton University and University of Chicago. The first lady of USA, Jacqueline Kennedy was fascinated with the performance of Balasaraswati in Washington D.C. and expressed her desire to meet Balasaraswati.[165] In 1963, she visited London and performed eight shows continually on the request of her admirers which included the Edinburg Festival in Scotland. Further, she got an offer of thirteen concerts in Europe in 1965. Balasaraswati once again toured USA in 1966.

The success of her international trips gave her enough money to purchase some land in Kilpauk, Madras and it created a new space and respect for her in India. However, she was now becoming ill. She was diagnosed with tuberculosis. But she accepted to perform at Krishna Gana Sabha in Madras (December 20, 1966).[166] Jayammal died at the age of seventy six in 1967. The late beginning of Lakshmi's career in dancing created a fear for Balasaraswati about the social stigma with regards to devadasi women. She had a dilemma about her daughter learning dance. But the international experience convinced her about her daughter's career in dance. In addition, the period between 1950s and 1960s, dancing was being accepted in the public as a cultural form and practice.[167] Balasaraswati started to teach dance from 1965. She did her daughters' formal *urangerram* in 1973.[168] Later on February 9, 1984, Balasaraswati passed away.

The honour given to Balasaraswati

The Government of India confirmed Balasaraswati with *Padma Bhushan*, third highest civilian award of India on October 14, 1957. M.S. Subbulakshmi sent a letter to inform Balasaraswati about the honour which was given by the Music Academy as *Sangitha Kalanidhi* and a request to preside over the Academy Festival in 1973.[169] In the meantime, Balasaraswati received the prestigious award of *Ratna Puraskar* (Akademi Fellow) from the Sangeet Natak Akademi in 1975 and in December she was designated as a honorary president of Tamil Isai Sangam.[170] At 1977, Balasaraswati received a *Padma Vibhushan* (Exemplary Golden Lotus) from the Government of India and honorary Doctorate in Literature and the title *Desikottama* from Visva-Bharati University in November, 1978.

The Wesleyan University was interested in producing a documentary on Balasaraswati. The documentary was titled as *Krishna ni Begane Baro* in 1960s. In the meantime, Narayana Menon approached Satyajit Ray to make a documentary on Balasaraswati. Satyajit Ray happily accepted the offer. He considered that the film would preserve the art of someone who was supreme in her field and was worth making.[171] Balasaraswati was also interested in the process of documentation. But initially the project was shelved. Satyajit Ray mentioned that the performance of Balasaraswati in 1935 at Calcutta had not appealed the sponsors.[172] In 1976, the idea was well received by then Tamil Nadu Chief Minister, M. Karunanidhi. The film was sponsored by the Government of Tamil Nadu. After ten years, Satyajit Ray received an opportunity of making film on Balasaraswati. She was fifty eight, when the film was shot. The film was released in April 19, 1977 and named as 'Bala'.

Madurai Shanmugavadivu Subbulakshmi (1916-2004)

Madurai Shanmugavadivu Subbulakshmi is a legendary Carnatic vocalist (*See Appendix*: - 21). Shanmugavadivu (1889-1962) was the mother of M.S. Subbulakshmi. Her mother was an expert in Vina playing. In general, Subramania Iyer, a lawyer in Madurai, was considered as Subbulakshmi's father but T.J.S. George speculated Madurai Pushpavanam Iyer as a father of Subbulakshmi on the basis of gossips among the musical lovers of Madurai.[173] Shanmugavadivu had a son named M.S. Shaktivel and two daughters M.S. Subbulakshmi and M.S. Vadivambal who was considered as the most beautiful woman in the family.

In general, the initials 'M' referred Madurai, an ancestral town of Subbu-lakshmi and 'S' denoted her mother Shanmugavadivu. *Sruti*, the performing arts magazine, had mentioned M.S. as Madurai Subramania Iyer Subbulakshmi.[174] But, according to the devadasi tradition, mothers' name should be used as initial. Therefore, the articulation of the magazine was incorrect and it might be a deliberate attempt at interpreting the life of Subbulakshmi. Usually, the family passionately called Subbulakshmi as *Kunjamma* or *Kunju*, which meant little one, and later her aficionados called her as 'M.S.'. G. Venkatachalam, an art critic, personally met M.S. Subbulakshmi when she was thirteen and mentioned that Subbulakshmi was not a fragile child but she was simple, matured, self-willed, strong, stubborn and silent.[175] Suyambup Pillai, a famous dance teacher, mentioned that her voice was excellent and she would become a great personality.[176]

The childhood of M.S. Subbulakshmi

Shanmugavadivu was strict with her children for their career. In general, they were not allowed to move out of their house and practiced vegetarianism. Shanmugavadivu was keen on formal western education for her son. Moreover, she encouraged him to learn *Mridangam* (kind of percussion instrument) to accompany her sisters in musical concerts. Subbulakshmi was interested in learning *tambura* and singing. On the other hand, her sister M.S. Vadivambal studied Vina. Shanmugavadivu chose Madurai Srinivasa Iyengar as a teacher for her children. Later, Seithur Sundaresa Bhattar, a violinist, and Mayavaram V.V. Krishna Iyer became teachers of Subbulakshmi. The children used to travel with their mother in different concerts in Madras Presidency and other Princely States such as Mysore, Travancore and Ramanathapuram.

The house of Shanmugavadivu was famous among the musical lovers of Madras Presidency. Eminent people such as Subbarama Bhagavathar, Ponnusamy Pillai, Karaikudi Sambasiva Iyer, Ariyakudi Ramanuja Iyengar and Dakshinamurthi Pillai (*Mridangam* specialist) frequently visited the house of Shanmugavadivu to listen to her musical concerts. At the age of nine, Subbulakshmi was asked to sing in a public gathering at Madurai. Her songs became popular and she was invited by gramophone companies such as His Master's Voice (HMV).[177] Interestingly, her first recording happened at the age of ten in the name of Madurai Subbulakshmi, but later records carried her full name as Madurai Shanmugavadivu Subbulakshmi. She started to give her public concerts at the age of thirteen and she became a vocalist.

The economic hardship compelled the family to do more concerts to lead a comfortable life. In the meantime, Shanmugavadivu sought a potential patron for her daughters' safe existence. The search ended with the offer from Rama-nathapuram royal house. However, Subbulakshmi rejected her mothers' plea to settle in Ramanathapuram palace. She was interested to be a musician for a while.[178] Subbulakshmi recalled her childhood in an interview with a Tamil writer Vaasanthi that during her childhood, men always thought to exploit her and the situations was often threatening.[179] Meanwhile, her mother found a patron Bhashyam Ayyangar, a wealthy man in Coimbatore for her younger sister Vadivambal. Unlike Subbulakshmi, Vadivambal accepted the proposal and lived a life with the selected man. But she lived a very short life and died of pneumonia at the age of twenty two.

M.S. Subbulakshmi had her debut concert at TVS Cycle Factory and following that Ramanathapuram palace invited her for solo performance. However, Shanmugavadivu was hoping for a chance to introduce her daughter in Madras to receive new prospects. In 1932, *Mahamaham* festival[180] was held in Kumbakonam, a temple town in modern Tamil Nadu. K. Subramanyam, a film director was the organiser of the *Mahamaham* festival. Shanmugavadivu approached K. Subramanyam for her daughter to perform in the grand festival. S.D. Subbulakshmi, heroine of the film *Pavalakkodi* which was directed by K. Subramanyam with whom she shared her personal life, recommended Shanmugavadivu's daughter. Subramanyam initially hesitated, but could not reject the reference of S.D. Subbulakshmi, so he permitted Subbulakshmi to perform off the prime time hours. The sixteen year old girl did an excellent performance in the festival. It encouraged others to invite M.S. Subbulakshmi to Madurai, Ramanathapuram, Mysore, Travancore and Madras. In the same year, the Music Academy of Madras conducted a talent hunt. Shanmugavadivu and M.S. Subbulakshmi participated in the competition which was held in Madras city. The performance attracted spectates such as Tiger Varadachari and Muthaiah Bhagavatar.[181]

M.S. Subbulakshmi and her association with Sadasivam

Shanmugavadivu shifted her family to Purasaivakkam in Madras city. The place was comparatively near to the house of Vina Dhanam and later, they became family friends. It improved the personalities of Subbulakshmi. *Ananda Vikatan* magazine, was interested in interviewing Subbulakshmi. Later, the interview turned her life topsyturvy. T.J.S. George mentioned that the interview unveiled M.S. Subbulakshmi to the public gaze and led to totally unexpected developments, transforming her life, her personality and career.[182] Thiyagaraja Sadasivam, a handsome advertising manager of *Ananda Vikatan*, approached Subbulakshmi for an interview for the *Dipawali* special edition of the magazine. M.S. Subbulakshmi was attracted by Sadasivam and continued to meet him. He started to organise her programmes and arranged things for her.

Thiyagaraja Sadasivam (September 4, 1902-1997) was born in Triplicane, Madras of a big family of Brahmin parents from a village near Lalgudi in Tiruchirappalli. During his childhood, the call of Gandhi made him enter into public life. He left schools and joined the revolutionary camp in independent movement in Tiruchirappalli. In 1920, C. Rajagopalachari appealed to the people to participate in the Civil Disobedience Movement in Madras Presidency. The excited Sadasivam participated in the movement and was sentenced for fifteen months imprisonment. Later in 1922, he was again jailed for a year in Tiruchirappalli Central Jail and there he shared the cell with R. Krishnamurthy alias Kalki.[183] They bonded and a close association formed between them over the period of their life. Krishnamurthy found an able salesman, propagandist and writer in Sadasivam.[184] The Congress party assigned him a task of vending *Khadhi* and later he became a manager of *Khadhi Vasthralayam* in Bangalore. When Krishnamurthy joined as an editor of *Ananda Vikatan*, Sadasivam became an advertising manager of the company.

Shanmugavadivu did not like the relationship between Sadasivam and her daughter. She decided to move back to Madurai to prevent her daughter from meeting Sadasivam.[185] In Madurai, again she started to search a patron for her daughter from a wealthy family. M.S. Subbulakshmi disliked this. She deserted her mother and moved to meet Sadasivam in Madras. Subbulakshmi found shelter in the hands of Sadasivam. Significantly, Sadasivam was already a married man with two daughters. During the visit of Subbulakshmi, the wife of Sadasivam was in her ancestral place for her second delivery.[186] After some times Sadasivam, his wife Apithakuchambal and their children and M.S. Subbulakshmi lived together in a same house. Meanwhile, Shanmugavadivu came to know about her daughter and feared her intimacy with Sadasivam. She pleaded her daughter to return from his hold. But both Subbulakshmi and Sadasivam refused to do so.[187] Shanmugavadivu abducted her daughter and Sadasivam was able to 'rescue' her from her family. Sadasivam referred to Subbulakshmi's family as 'Madurai Group' and he was cautious to keep away Subbulakshmi from her family.[188] These incidents made Shanmugavadivu frail in mind and body. In later years, Subbulakshmi became more popular and tried to establish a cordial relation with her ancestral family, but this did not happen. On August 5, 1962, her mother passed away.

M.S. Subbulakshmi and her marriage

M.S. Subbulakshmi received an offer to act in a film called *Seva Sadhanam* which was directed by K. Subramanyam in 1936. S.D. Subbulakshmi, a friend of her mother, became the source of strength for M.S. Subbulakshmi for a while. The film centred on the social issue of young woman who was forced to marry an old man. In the title card, M.S. Subbulakshmi's name was mentioned as 'Kokilagana Madurai M.S. Subbulakshmi'. Her appearance and performance attracted huge audience. The popularity of Subbulakshmi provided a confidence to Sadasivam to establish a movie company in 1938 called Chandraprabha Cinetone and he sought new stories for M.S. Subbulakshmi.

Sadasivam found *Sakunthala*, the story of Kalidasa apt for the company's fortune. He chose a brilliant team. The crew included Ellis R. Dungan as a director, Papanasam Sivan as a music composer, T.G. Rangachari as a writer and N.S. Krishnan and T.A. Mathuram as supporting actors. Ellis R. Dungan was an American who came to India and made popular movies such as *Sathi Leelathi* (1936), *Iru Sahodhararkal* (1936), *Ambikapathi* (1937) and *Kalamegam* (1940). Among the crew, he casted an amateur artist R. Parthasarathy as a protagonist of the film. T.J.S. George mentioned that Sadasivam was deliberately avoiding casting famous personality like G.N. Balasubramaniam as a protagonist of the film because he would be opposite to Subbulakshmi, the female lead.[189]

G.N. Balasubramaniam was popularly called as G.N.B. and Jawaharlal Nehru of Carnatic music.[190] In general, G.N. Balasubramaniam was considered as the prominent male in the musical and film industry who could attract much audience. However, the financial distributers refused to accept any one else other than G.N. Balasubramaniam as a lead actor in the role of king Dushyantha. T.J.S. George highlighted the growing personal relations between G.N. Balasubramaniam and M.S. Subbulakshmi.[191] Sadasivam could not tolerate the progress of the relationship which surrounded the movie set. But he could not restrict them to meet because it was his film and it could be a problem for the film too. According to the expectation, the film came out well in 1938 and received a huge success in the contemporary film industry (*See Appendix*: - 22).

After completion of the film, Sadasivam immediately wanted to marry M.S. Subbulakshmi. The discussion of marriage created a problem in the family of Sadasivam as his wife opposed this. However, the dominant Sadasivam married Subbulakshmi in July 10, 1940 at Tirunirmalai, in the outskirt of Madras city. The age difference between them was fourteen years. He also used to call her as Kunjamma. Later some time, his first wife died in her ancestral place. Subbulakshmi was submissive and being taken care. T.J.S. George referred Sadasivam as a man who completely transformed a life of women in ways no other man ever did to any women. Moreover, he stated that if M.S. made melody, Sadasivam made M.S. if music was M.S.'s career, M.S. became Sadasivam's career.[192] M.S. Subbulakshmi was babe in the woods, unable even to see the shadows around her. Sadasivam knew precisely what he wanted and precisely how to get it.[193]

Further, T.J.S. George noted that M.S. Subbulakshmi became an instrument of his strategies without realising what was meant by strategies or what their aims were in this case. Her naïve nature added to her aesthetic appeal and to the luster of her achievements.[194] T.J.S. George pointed out that M.S. Subbulakshmi became an exemplar of 'Indianness' and also he stated that she was not part of a community wide group movement for higher recognition in the social hierarchy. It was the case of an individual feeling sufficiently motivated to transform her.[195]

M.S. Subbulakshmi in the public gaze

After the marriage, Sadasivam left his job in *Ananda Vikatan*. Sadasivam for their new future. He had an idea to start a magazine with the help of versatile writer Krishnamurthy. The concept was appreciated by Rajagopalachari who was the mentor of Sadasivam. The shrewd Sadasivam wanted to use the popularity of Krishnamurthy who was popular and wrote Columns in print media as 'Kalki'. So, he named the magazine as Kalki and in later days these people were identified with the magazine as 'Kalki' Krishnamurthy and 'Kalki' Sadasivam.[196] The establishment demanded money. In the course of time, Y.V. Rao, a film director, gave a chance to Subbulakshmi in a film *Savithri* for the role of Narada. He discussed the issue with Rajagopalachari and Krishnamurthy. Then Sadasivam accepted the offer on the condition that the shooting should not be held in Madras, because he did not want to create a chance of meeting between Subbulakshmi and G.N. Balasubramaniam. The film director was ready to shift the studio to Calcutta and the film took off. M.S. Subbulakshmi received one lakh rupee as remuneration.

In between the shooting of *Savithri*, Sadasivam and Subbulakshmi met Gandhi in 1941 at Wardha, the modern district of Maharashtra. During the meeting, Gandhi asked her to sing and admired her talent. Hereafter, Gandhi used to call Subbulakshmi to perform in his gatherings. On October 2, 1947, Gandhi invited her to Delhi for his 78th birthday and requested to sing a *Hari Tuma Haro* (Thou God) of Meera *bhajans* (Songs of Meera). All India Radio requested her to record her songs and it happened on September 30, 1941. A copy of her song was sent to Gandhi who was interested in listening to her songs. After some time, the film was released in the year and the songs of Subbulakshmi made the film moderate success. Sadasivam used the money which Subbulakshmi earned from the film *Savithri* to popularise the Kalki magazine.

Sadasivam searched for a new theme for his wife which would appeal to entire India. He came to the conclusion that the story of Meera was the right choice. He felt the character of Meera, the medieval woman saint would be ideal for his singer-wife to portray in pan-Indian scenario and also the story did not require any lead actor who would pair Subbulakshmi.[197] So he convinced himself to make a film under his own banner. He carefully selected the cast crew. He chose popular and also second level actors such as V. Nagaiah, T.S. Balaiah, T.S. Durairaj and M.G. Ramachandran, who later became the chief minister of Tamil Nadu. On the technical side, he did not want to change the director, Ellis R. Dungan and chose Krishnamurthy as dialogue a writer and lyricist of the film.

The film reached pan-India level. The Tamil version was released in 1945. Subsequently, the Hindi version was premiered on April 4, 1947 which starred Subbulakshmi as a protagonist Meera (*See Appendix*: - 23). It had a major success in the South as well as North India. The critics acknowledged the film. The director responded to Randor Guy, the film collector, that M.S. did not act in the film but she herself became Meera.[198] Sarojini Naidu, the Indian poet, mentioned that the story of Meera is the story of India, the story of Indian faith and devotion and ecstasy. Subbulakshmi's performance was that she was not an interpreter of Meera, but Meera herself.[199] The film became a good launching pad for M.S. Subbulakshmi in North India. T.J.S. George stated that the North Indian political and cultural establishments would accept and honour Subbulakshmi as enthusiastically as South did.[200] The movie was able to construct a devotional aura for Subbulakshmi and she became an icon of pan-Indian culture of post-colonial India.

The high profile of M.S. Subbulakshmi

M.S. Subbulakshmi's portrayal of Meera created an opportunity to have relations with national leaders like Gandhi. On the request of Rajagopalachari, Subbulakshmi performed concerts to raise funds for Kasturba Memorial Trust. The series of concert was held in 1944 in various parts of Madras Presidency. The personality of Subbulakshmi pulled a maximum number of audiences and collected reasonable amounts. Gandhi wrote a letter to thank Subbulakshmi for her efforts. The success of the concert made her a national figure. These developments made the couple financially stabled and they were able to purchase a land in Madras in 1947 and named it as Kalki Garden. Later, the house became a vibrant place for cultural and political activities in the history of modern India.

Subbulakshmi started to perfect her Hindustani musical skills of Northern India and did more performance in North India. Following the events, Sadasivam and her well-wishers such as Rajagopalachari decided to stop Subbulakshmi from acting in feature films. Subbulakshmi continued her public concerts. Usually, she concentrated only on *bhakti* songs. Sadasivam did not like his wife to act in the film industry. So he preferred his wife to perform in more musical concert. He keenly observed the performance of Subbulakshmi and commented on it. Sadasivam was able to transform Subbulakshmi a lot, as a wife of a Brahmin. He insisted her to be fit in a caste hierarchy of the society. He removed the *shringara* element and her songs asked her to extensively concentrate on the elements of *bhakti*. It resembled what Rukmini Devi did for dance forms of devadasi. T.J.S. George critiqued Sadasivam that he 'sanitized' M.S. Subbulakshmi's music in his bid to 'Brahminize' her.[201]

Further, he stated that Krishnamurthy, Sadasivam and Subbulakshmi, with Rajagopalachari hovering as a 'presiding deity', symbolised the vanguard of a virtual cultural renaissance on the Brahmanic world of Madras.[202]

In the meantime, India got independence and Rajagopalachari, the mentor of Sadasivam, became the Governor General of Independent India. The cordial relationship between the couple and Rajagopalachari further extended the public space of Subbulakshmi. T.J.S. George noted that the political connection of Sadasivam ensured that a stream of VIPs attended the show.[203] Jawaharlal Nehru (first Prime Minister of India), Rajendra Prasad (first President of India), Radha Krishnan (first Vice-President of India), Sarojini Naidu, Edwina Mountbatten (Lady of last Governor General of British India), C.D. Deshmukh (first Indian Governor for Reserve Bank of India) and G.D. Birla (entrepreneur) attended the concert of Subbulakshmi and appreciated her performances. During the charitable performance of Subbulakshmi for Madrasi Education Association at Delhi in 1949, Jawaharlal Nehru commented, "Who am I?, mere a Prime Minister, before a Queen of Song?"[204]

M.S. Subbulakshmi and her charitable concerts

Sadasivam was selective in choosing the concerts for Subbulakshmi. The couple gave much preference to the concerts that happened for charitable trust. V. Gangadhar, the author of *M.S. Subbulakshmi: The Voice Divine* noted that nearly three hundred of Subbulakshmi concerts were organised for charity and it collected more than three crores Indian rupees for various charitable works such as schools, hospitals, cultural centres and religious institutions.[205] In 1955, Jawaharlal Nehru invited the couple to his house in Teen Murthi Bhavan at Delhi for ten days. Indira Gandhi, daughter of Jawaharlal Nehru, looked after the couple and provided a good hospitality. There Subbulakshmi participated in the fund raising concerts for Kamala Nehru Memorial Hospital. In the same year, she did a concert for Madras Music Academy Building Fund. She performed for the Prime Minister's National Relief Fund in 1976.

Subbulakshmi also performed for the benefit of Sankara Nethralaya, missionary institution for ophthalmic care in 1983. *Kundoosi*, a Tamil monthly magazine, mentioned that a performance of Subbulakshmi in December, 1947 earned ninety eight thousand Indian rupees for South Indian Educational Trust.[206] Further, she performed for Railway Women's Welfare Fund, Madras Institute of Technology, Tuberculosis Sanatorium in Sengipatti, Athirudra Mahayagam in Thalaikaveri, Mysore District Police Benevolent Fund and Adi Sankara Vimana Mandap in Allahabad, All India Manufacturers Association and Christian Medical College in Vellore.[207] In 1977, she sold her house for sixteen lakhs and moved to Kotturpuram in Madras and named their house as *Sivam-Subham*. She also gave money to different charities such as Ramakrishna Ashram in Gwalior, American College in Madurai, Mercara Hospital in Mangalore and Little Sisters of the Poor Organisation in Madras.

Subbulakshmi also gave concerts for *Vishwa Hindu Parishad* (VHP)[208] in different places in Bombay (1970), Nagpur (1972), Calcutta (1973) and Bangalore (1975). Later, she recorded the *Venkateswara Subrabhatham* in 1975 at Tirupathi and she contributed the royalty to Tirumala Tirupathi Devasthanams (TTD). In the same year, TTD conferred her with the title *Aasthana Vidwan* of Tirumala Tirupathi Devasathanam. The TTD started to broadcast the Subbulakshmi's version of Venkateshwara Suprabhatam at the temple complex of Tirupathi from 1975. She continued to urged to perform in fund raising programmes. In 1977, she toured USA to raise funds for Hindu Temples in New York and Pittsburgh.

The popularity of M.S. Subbulakshmi spread across the country. She was invited by various countries for public concerts. Her participation in the Edinburgh International Festival of Music and Drama in 1963 created a sensation. Later in 1966, she gave concerts at the United Nations and sang the English song which was specially composed by Rajagopalachari for M.S. Subbulakshmi. But her unusual English rendering did not appeal to the gatherings but the following trip to New York and Pittsburg became a successful event. Therefore, she did the India Festival in Britain, Soviet Union 1982, Festival of India in London-Concert at Royal Albert Hall, 1988 and Festival of India at Moscow on 1988.

The world renowned M.S. Subbulakshmi

Her contribution towards the art and the public activities were well-recognised nationally as well as internationally. Sarojini Naidu admired the charitable works of M.S. Subbulakshmi and addressed her as *Nightingale of India*.[209] The Board of Trustees of Ramon Magsaysay Award Foundation conferred the *Ramon Magsaysay Award for Peace* on her in 1974. The board referred to her as an idol of millions and said that this lady (M.S. Subbu-lakshmi) had remained deeply religious, unpretentious and almost childlike in her simplicity. The Board of Trustees recognised her exalting rendition of devotional song and magnanimous support of numerous public causes in India over four decades.[210] In the award function, she offered her homage to the trinity of Sadasivam, C. Rajagopalachari and Sri Chandrasekharendra Saraswathi Sankaracharya of Kanchipuram.[211]

M.S. Subbulakshmi received *Bharat Ratna*, India's highest civilian honour in 1998. The Award was given for the first time to an artist in music field. Following her death, a commemorative postage stamp was issued on

December 18, 2005 (*See Appendix*: - 24). She was honoured with the many Indian highest awards such as *Indira Gandhi Award for National Integration* (1990) *Padma Bushan* (1954) and *Padma Vibushan* (1975). And the different state governments in India honored her in multiple occasions. On July 21, 2004, the then Chief Minister of Delhi, Sheila Dikshit, conferred her *Lifetime Achievement Award*. The Government of Andhra Pradesh honoured her as *Asthana Vidushi* (1981) and *Kalidas Samman* by Government of Madhya Pradesh (1988).

M.S. Subbulakshmi's contribution was acknowledged by the most of the India's art academics. Lata Mangeshkar, popular singer, referred to Subbulakshmi as *Tapaswini* (women saint). Subbulakshmi received *Sangeet Natak Academy Award* (1956) and *Ravindra Bharathi Cultural Academy's Award* (1967). Subbulakshmi became the first woman to receive the title of *Sangeetha Kalanidhi* from the Music Academy in 1968 and in 1970 she was conferred *Isai Periaringar Virudhu* by *Tamil Isai Sangam*. Later, she was awarded *Honorary Doctorate* from *Indira Kala Sangeet Vishwa-Vidyalaya* of Madhya Pradesh in 1979. Visva-Bharati University titled her as *Desikotamma* (1981) and also be an elected Membre d'honneur by the UNESCO sponsored international Music Council in 1981. Google observed the 97th birth anniversary of M.S. Subbulakshmi with a *doodle* (*See Appendix*: - 25).

M.S. Subbulakshmi and Sadasivam

Her image satisfied the modern needs of new patriarchal society such as pious, innocent, beautiful and controllable women. Her personality could bridge the gap of the transition to the modern Indian state. M.S. Subbulakshmi had occasional critic but never an enemy. Everybody loved Subbulakshmi because she was always above controversy, politics and cliques.[212] Sadasivam was the planner, calculating one move after another, weighing pros against consequence, a thoroughly practical materialist. M.S. Subbulakshmi was an artist and nothing else. She obeyed instructions, but the art was hers and hers alone.[213] She used to wash her husband feet every day with warm water at night.[214] She mentioned her husband for his love and care and with unerring guidance and as her preceptor (*See Appendix*: - 26).[215]

Her biography also mentioned the relation between Subbulakshmi and Chandrasekharendra Saraswathi Sankaracharya of Kanchipuram.[216] Sadasivam and M.S. Subbulakshmi were fond of meeting Chandrasekarendra Saraswathi Swamigal, Paramacharya of Kanchi Kamakoti Peetham at Kanchipuram. Sadasivam believed Chandrasekarendra Saraswathi Swamigal as a spiritual leader of his life. In 1954, the couple had a chance to meet him. The Paramacharya of Kanchi Kamakoti Peetham refused to meet and bless Subbulakshmi who was attired like a Brahmin woman. 'Paramacharya' was concerned more with her non-Brahmin caste identity of Subbulakshmi and objected to her wearing *madisar*, a kind of Brahmin dress. However, Sadasivam convinced 'Paramacharya' and got the blessings with the changed attire of Subbulakshmi. Over a period, 'Paramacharya' acknowledged Subbulakshmi and mentioned her as pure as *brindavan tulasi* (a kind of medicinal plant). But while receiving the Ramon Magsaysay Award for Peace, she referred to Chandrasekharendra Saraswathi Sankaracharya of Kanchipuram as "almighty who has chosen my humble self as a tool. However, he is beyond my gratitude. Yet, in a way, I take Him to have come within my reach in the benign personality of the Sage of Kanchi, His Holiness Sri Chandrasekharendra Saraswathi Sankaracharya."[217]

M.S. Subbulakshmi was barred from media interviews too. When she gave an interview, Sadasivam sat beside her and answered all the questions. He ensured that no substantive information about their lives came out; his answers usually dwelt on the charity concerts she had given and the tributes she had received from various dignitaries.[218] Vassanthi was the only person who interviewed her and even during the interview, no one was permitted to be present.[219] During the interview with Vaasanthi, she stated that she had never been educated. She had been brought up listening to elders. Further, she replied on the question of Sadasivam that her nature was like that and no one insisted her do to what she liked and she said that naturally she never got angry with any one on any issue.[220]

Sadasivam was strict about what kind of social life Subbulakshmi should lead. She was free to go on her own only to the houses of their daughters. Social visits were not permitted unless he accompanied her. No one was expected to visit their house either without his specific approval. She was friendly only with those persons with whom he was friendly.[221] T.J.S. George mentioned that she never ceased being part of the social, business and political whirl that was Sadasivam's life. She was Sadasivam's wife, Rajagopalachari's disciple, Krishnamurthy's friend, but she was always M.S.[222]

M.S. Subbulakshmi lived her complete life as a wife and mother. M.S. Subbulakshmi did not have children but she cared for the two children of Sadasivam (Radha and Vijaya) as her own. Sadasivam's second daughter Vijaya married Rajendran, son of Krishnamurthy. She was fond of Sadasivam's daughters. The death of Radha in 1982 shattered Subbulakshmi. After this, Subbulakshmi reduced her numbers of public concert. Later, on November 21, 1997, Sadasivam died of his old age and illness. Subbulakshmi was able to continue her life after her husband's death. However she stopped her public performances. On December 11, 2004, M.S. Subbulakshmi passed away.

Conclusion

The lives of Muvalur A. Ramamirtham, Bangalore Nagarathnam, Thanjavur Balasaraswati and Madurai Shanmugavadivu Subbulakshmi represented four different devadasi lives but they had similar characteristics and experiences. The similarity starts from their birth. All the four traced their matrilineal lineage and they carried their mother's name and ancestral town as initials. Nagarathnam and Balasaraswati used their geographical location (Bangalore and Thanjavur) and Ramamirtham and Subbulakshmi used both their place and mother's name. Their mothers were strong and struggled hard to bring up their children. They were well trained and expert in many languages and arts. Their dedication to the temples did not occur in a grand manner because of the strict rules on both sides from the society and the state. Ramamirtham was not allowed to dedicate because of her lineage and Balasaraswati was secretly dedicated because of the state law. They had a tough childhood due to economic crisis especially Ramamirtham, Balasaraswati and Subbulakshmi.

Their transition witnessed the control of female sexuality over the freedom, which devadasis had enjoyed earlier on. Except Nagarathnam, all the other looked towards a man who could rescue them from the clutches of the devadasi custom. Ramamirtham married her teacher Suyambup Pillai, Balasaraswati sheltered in the hands of R.K. Shanmukham and Subbulakshmi married Sadasivam. Always their sexuality was controlled by the society. However, they gained their liberty in different forms. They were aware of the modern changes and ready to utilise the opportunities. Nagarathnam became a singer of the recording companies, Balasaraswati toured abroad and popularised the devadasi's art tradition and Subbulakshmi married a Brahmin and assimilated the Brahmanical culture.

They were seriously engaged with society. Ramamirtham actively participated in politics. Initially, she believed in Gandhi and Congress but later she campaigned for the Self-Respect Movement, *Dravidar Kazhakam* and *Dravida Munnetra Kazhakam*. She argued for the abolition of the devadasi system and moved with people to propagate the Self Respect ideas among the people. On the other hand, Nagarathnam struggled a lot but earned enough money to lead a comfortable life. She firmly believed in the devadasi practices. She wanted to continue the system. Therefore, she worked with other devadasi women and formed an organisation to retain the custom. Later, she dedicated her life in the construction and continuation of her Guru's memorial in Tiruvaiyar. Interestingly in the case of Ramamirtham and Nagarathnam, there were attempts of murder them by their close associates. However, they were strong with their ideas and practices. In the meantime, Balasaraswati and Subbulakshmi received fame due to their art forms such as dancing and singing. Balasaraswati encountered strong criticism, which was imposed by the revivalist lobbies. She was firm enough to articulate her views among the audiences. Subbulakshmi was a classic example to understand the transition of a woman in the devadasi community to Brahmin patriarchy. But she was always a great vocalist and well accepted due to this by all people. What is important is that all these four women got name and fame after they hid their devdasi identity and got amalgamated into the main stream culture.

References

1. Smith, Sidonie and Julia Watson. Eds. *De-colonizing the Subject: The Politics of Gender in Women's Autobiography*. Minneapolis: The University of Minnesota Press, 1992: p. XIV.
2. Sundaram, B.M. *Marbu Thantha Manikkankal* (The Gifts of the Tradition) (in Tamil). Chennai: Dr. V. Raghavan Centre for Performing Arts, 2003: pp. 135-136.
3. The information was collected through an in-depth interview from B. Jeevasundari, the biographer of Ramamirtham, at Chennai on March 17, 2011.
4. George, T.J.S. *MS: A Life in Music*. New Delhi: Harper Collins Publishers, 2007 (Rpt. 2010): p. 9.
5. *Ibid.*
6. *Ibid.*, p. 108.
7. Ramamirthathammal, A. Muvalur. *Dasikal Mosavalai alladhu Mathipetra Minar* (Dasis web of deceit or enlightened Playboy) (in Tamil). Erode: Unmaivilakkam Press, 1939.
8. Jeevasunadari, B. *Moovalur Ramamirtham Ammaiyar* (in Tamil). Chennai: Arivai, 2007: p. 13.
9. *Ibid.*, p. 24.
10. *Kalaimandram*. 10/04/1954.
11. Jeevasunadari, B. 2007. *Op.cit.*, p. 34.
12. *Ibid.*, p. 27.
13. *Ibid.*, p. 29.
14. *Ibid.*, p. 48.
15. The biographical notes of Ramamirtham was known as *Enathu Vazhkkai Chariththram* which meant My Life History. The work was referred in Jeevasunadari, B. 2007. *Op.cit.*, p. 51.
16. *Ibid.*, p. 52.
17. Kalyanasundaram, Thiru.Vi. *Thiru.Vi.Ka Vazhkkaik Kurippukal* (A Biographical Notes of Thiru.Vi. Kalyanasundaram) (in Tamil). Saiva Siddanta Kazhakam, 1982. p. 600.
18. Jeevasunadari, B. 2007. *Op.cit.*, p. 48.
19. Ramamirthathammal, A. Muvalur. 1939. *Op.cit.*, p. 3.
20. *Ibid.*
21. Ramamirtham. *Enathu Vazhkkai Chariththram* (My Life History) (in Tamil). In Jeevasunadari, B. *Op.cit.*, p. 55.

22. *Thanjai Jilla Isai Vellalar Mahanadu* (Isai Vellalar Conference of Thanjavur District). *Kudi Arasu*. 25/10/1925.
23. *Kudi Arasu*. 08/11/1925.
24. Jeevasunadari, B. 2007. *Op.cit.*, p. 70.
25. Ramamirthathammal, A. Muvalur. 1939. *Op.cit.*, p. 4.
26. Jeevasunadari, B. 2007. *Op.cit.*, pp. 59-60.
27. *Thuiyarkalai*, May, 1959.
28. Jeevasunadari, B. 2007. *Op.cit.*, pp. 46-47.
29. *Ibid.*, p. 33.
30. "A Social Work Prosecuted: Case Against Miss. Ramamirtha Ammal." *Revolt*. 15/09/1929.
31. Jeevasunadari, B. 2007. *Op.cit.*, p. 77.
32. *Ibid.*, p. 78.
33. *Ibid.*
34. *Revolt*. 15/09/1929.
35. Chokkalinkam. Na. Vai. "Anna Aliththa Viruthu" (The Award which was given by Anna) (in Tamil). *Yathum Ure*. April 2, 2007: p. 39.
36. *Murasoli*. 27/06/1962.
37. Chokkalinkam. Na. Vai. April 2, 2007. *Op.cit.*, p. 19.
38. Ramamirthathammal, A. Muvalur. 1939. *Op.cit.*
39. *Dravidar Kazhakam* is a social organisation which was established by E.V. Ramasami in 1944. The organisation is voiced for social justice and equality.
40. *Dravida Nadu*. 15/04/1945.
41. Anandhi, S. "Representing Devadasis: 'Dasigal Mosavalai' as a Radical Text." *Economic and Political Weekly* 26, no. 11/12. (March, 1991): pp. 743, 745-746.
42. Jeevasunadari, B. 2007. *Op.cit.*, pp. 148-165.
43. Sriram, V. *The Devadasi and the Saint: The Life and Times of Bangalore Nagarathnamma*. Chennai: EastWest Books (Madras) Pvt. Ltd, 2007: p. 1.
44. "Tyagesevasaktha, Vidyasundari, Ganakalavisharada, Life History of Srimathi Bangalore Nagarathnamma." *Grihalakshmi*, Madras. (March, 1949): pp. 11-12.
45. *Ibid.*
46. Sankaran, T. *Isai Methaikal* (The Great Musicians) (in Tamil). Madras: Tamil Isai Publications, 1962.
47. *Grihalakshmi*. March, 1949. *Op.cit.*, pp. 13-14.
48. Sriram, V. 2007. *Op.cit.*, p. 7.
49. *Grihalakshmi*. March, 1949. *Op.cit.*, pp. 13-14.
50. *Ibid.*
51. Sriram, V. 2007. *Op.cit.*, p. 11.
52. Sankaran, T. "Bangalore Nagaratnammal: A Devadasi True." *Sruti*. Issue. 4. (January-February, 1984): p. 15.
53. *Grihalakshmi*. March, 1949. *Op.cit.*, p. 52.
54. *Ibid.*, pp. 15-16.
55. Sriram, V. 2007. *Op.cit.*, p. 11.

56. Jackson, William J. *Tyagaraja and the Renewal of Tradition: Translations and Reflections*. Delhi: Motilal Banarsidass Publishers Private Limited, 1994: p. 148.
57. *Grihalakshmi*. March, 1949. *Op.cit.,* pp. 13-14.
58. *Ibid.*, pp. 52-23.
59. Sriram, V. 2007. *Op.cit.,* p. 60.
60. Kinnear, Michael S. *The Gramophone Company's First Indian Recordings, 1899-1908*. Bombay: Popular Prakashan Pvt. Ltd, 1994: p. 9.
61. *Ibid.*
62. Sriram, V. 2007. *Op.cit.,* p. 29.
63. *Ibid.*
64. Mulchandani, Sandhya. Tr. *The Appeasement of Radhika: Radhika Santawanam.* New Delhi: Penguin Books, 2011: p. xvii.
65. *Grihalakshmi*. March, 1949. *Op.cit.,* p. 15.
66. Sriram, V. 2007. *Op.cit.,* p. 125.
67. *Grihalakshmi*. March, 1949. *Op.cit.,* p. 19.
68. *Ibid.*, pp. 15-16.
69. Sriram, V. 2007. *Op.cit.,* pp. 26-27.
70. Muthupalani was a courtesan in the court of Marathas of Thanjavur. She wrote an erotic text which was named as *Radhika Santawanam*. Charles Philip Brown, an eminent English-Telugu scholar found the manuscript and printed in 1887 under the supervision of his associate Paidipati Venkatanarasu. The erotic text was edited, some portions were deleted and later it was published by Paidipati Venkatanarasu. But the scholar like Nagarathnam understood the lyrical quality and decided to publish the entire work with the prologue.
71. The arguments were rendered from the translation of Sandhya Mulchandani's *The Appeasement of Radhika: Radhika Santawanam.* (Mulchandani, Sandhya. Tr. 2011: p. xix.)
72. *Radhika Santawanam* was an erotic poem. The five hundred and eighty four verses poem was divided into four sections.
73. Mulchandani, Sandhya. Tr. 2011. *Op.cit.,* p. xix.
74. *Ibid.,* p. xx.
75. *Ibid.*, pp. xx-xxi.
76. *Tamilnadu Archives*. GO. 4079. Law Department. December 20, 1927.
77. *Ibid.*
78. *Ibid.*
79. *Ibid.*
80. Arudra. "The Transfiguration of a Traditional Dance". *Sruti*. Issue. 27/28. (December, 1986 -January, 1987): p. 19.
81. Sriram, V. 2007. *Op.cit.,* p. 124.
82. Sankaran, T. "Bangalore Nagaratnammal: A Devadasi True." *Sruti*. Issue. 4. (January-February, 1984): p. 14.
83. Jackson, William J. 1994. *Op.cit.,* p. 149.
84. *Grihalakshmi*. March, 1949. *Op.cit.,* pp. 15-16.

85. *Ibid.*
86. Jackson, William J. 1994. *Op.cit.*, p. 150.
87. *Chinna Katchi* and *Periya Katchi* were the two sections of the people who fought for the rights over the property of the memorial.
88. Sriram, V. 2007. *Op.cit.*, pp. 143-146.
89. Jackson, William J. 1994. *Op.cit.*, p. 145.
90. *Ashtothram* is a form of worship which usually offered to any particular deity with a recital of 108 names.
91. Sriram, V. 2007. *Op.cit.*, p. 95-113.
92. *Ibid.*, p. 165.
93. *Ibid.*, p. 168.
94. *Ibid.*, p. 166-167.
95. *Ibid.*, p. 177.
96. The statement was reported in The Hindu and it was quoted in Jackson, William J. 1994. *Op.cit.*, p. 149.
97. Sriram, V. 2007. *Op.cit.*, p. 184.
98. *Ibid.*, p. 185.
99. Sundaram, B.M. 2003. *Op.cit.*, p. 42, 103.
100. Knight Jr, Douglas M. *Balasaraswathi: Her Art and Life*. Chennai: Tranquebar Press, 2010.
101. *Adal Padal* (Dance and Music). 03/11/1935. *Ananda Vikatan*. p. 21.
102. Knight Jr, Douglas M. 2010. *Op.cit.*, p. 29.
103. *Ibid.*, p. 25.
104. Ramanarayanan, Gowri. "Rukmini Devi: A Quest for Beauty." Part. 1. *Sruti*, Issue. 8. (June, 1984): pp. 17-29.
105. Guhan, S. "Bala on Bharatanatyam." *Sruti*. (1991): p. 18.
106. Knight Jr, Douglas M. 2010. *Op.cit.*, p. 45.
107. *Ibid.*, p. 32.
108. *Ibid.*, p. 33.
109. Krishnamurthy, R. 20/08/1933. *Ananda Vikatan*.
110. Knight Jr, Douglas M. 2010. *Op.cit.*, p. 58.
111. *Ibid.*, p. 39.
112. *Ibid.*, p. 77.
113. Ohtani, Kimiko. "Bharata Nâ□yam', Rebirth of Dance in India." *Studia Musicologica Academiae Scientiarum Hungaricae* T. 33, fasc. 1/4. (1991): p. 306.
114. The statement was referred in Knight Jr, Douglas M. 2010. *Op.cit.*, p. 43.
115. Ray, Satyajit. "Working with Bala." *Journal of the Sangeet Natak Academi* 72-73. (April-September, 1984): p. 66.
116. Knight Jr, Douglas M. 2010. *Op.cit.*, p. 95.
117. *Ibid.*, p. 97
118. *Ibid.*, p. 96.
119. *Ibid.*, p. 99.

120. *Ibid.*, p. 111.
121. *Ibid.*, pp. 107-113.
122. Krishnamurthy, R. 15/10/1939. *Ananda Vikatan.*
123. Knight Jr, Douglas M. 2010. *Op.cit.*, p. 115.
124. *Ibid.*, p. 125.
125. The statement was quoted in the work of Douglas M. Knight Jr. (*Ibid.*, 118.)
126. Knight Jr, Douglas M. 2010. *Op.cit.*, p. 135.
127. *Ibid.*, pp. 152-153.
128. *Ibid.*, pp. 183-184.
129. *Ibid.*, pp. 138-139.
130. *Ibid.*, p. 141.
131. *Ibid.*, p. 129.
132. Pattabhi Raman, N and Anandhi Ramachandran. "T. Balasaraswati: The Whole World in Her Hands." *Journal of the Sangeet Natak Academi* 72-73. (April-September, 1984): p. 27.
133. Balasaraswati, T. "On Bharatanatyam". *Journal of the Sangeet Natak Academi* 72-73. (April-September, 1984): p. 11.
134. The statement was quoted in the work of Douglas M. Knight Jr. (Knight Jr, Douglas M. 2010. *Op.cit.*, p. 151.)
135. Balasaraswati, T. "The Art of Bharatanatyam: Reflections of Balasaraswati." *Sruti*. Issue 50. (November, 1988): p. 37.
136. Balasaraswati, T. (April-September, 1984). *Op.cit.*, p. 13.
137. *Ibid.*
138. Balasaraswati, T. (November, 1988). *Op.cit.*, p. 37.
139. *Ibid.*
140. Balasaraswati, T. April-September, 1984. *Op.cit.*, p. 8.
141. *Ibid.*, pp. 8-13.
142. The statement was quoted in the work of Douglas M. Knight Jr. (Knight Jr, Douglas M. 2010. *Op.cit.*, p. 140.)
143. Balasaraswati, T. (November, 1988). *Op.cit.*, p. 38.
144. *Ibid.*
145. The statement was quoted in the work of Douglas M. Knight Jr. (Knight Jr, Douglas M. 2010. *Op.cit.*, p. 131.)
146. Balasaraswati, T. (April-September, 1984). *Op.cit.*, pp. 10-11.
147. *Ibid.*, p. 10.
148. *Ibid.*, p. 12.
149. The emphasis is stressed by the author. (*Ibid.*, p. 13).
150. *The Statesman*. 28/03/1955.
151. Guhan, S. 1991. *Op.cit.*, p. 7.
152. The statement was quoted in the work of Douglas M. Knight Jr. (Knight Jr, Douglas M. 2010. *Op.cit.*, p. 154.)
153. *Ibid.*
154. *Ibid.*

155. Guhan, S. 1991. *Op.cit.,* p. 14.
156. Knight Jr, Douglas M. 2010. *Op.cit.,* p. 141.
157. *Ibid.,* p. 146.
158. *Ibid.,* p. 156.
159. *Ibid.,* p. 159.
160. *Ibid.,* p. 160.
161. *Ibid.,* pp. 161-162.
162. *Ibid.,* p. 178.
163. *Ibid.,* pp. 187-189.
164. *Ibid.,* p. 186.
165. *Ibid.,* pp. 190-198.
166. *Ibid.,* p. 214.
167. *Ibid.,* pp. 201-203.
168. *Ibid.,* p. 226.
169. *Ibid.,* p. 228.
170. *Ibid.,* p. 235.
171. Ray, Satyajit. (April-September, 1984). *Op.cit.,* p. 66.
172. *Ibid.*
173. George, T.J.S. 2007 (Rpt. 2010). *Op.cit.,* p. 92.
174. *Sruti*. Issue 144. (September, 1996): p. 29.
175. The statement was referred in George, T.J.S. 2007 (Rpt. 2010). *Op.cit.,* p. 73.
176. Jeevasunadari, B. 2007. *Op.cit.,* p. 34.
177. George, T.J.S. 2007 (Rpt. 2010). *Op.cit.,* p. 69.
178. *Ibid.,* p. 72.
179. M.S. Subbulakshmi's interview by Vaasanthi. *India Today* (Tamil). September, 1996.
180. *Mahamaham* was the South Indian religious festival which is equal to the famous festival of North India, *Kumbamela*. *Mahamaham* festival was held once in every twelve years in Kumbakonam in modern Tamil Nadu.
181. George, T.J.S. 2007 (Rpt. 2010). *Op.cit.,* p. 94-97.
182. *Ibid.,* p. 98.
183. Krishnamurthy, R. "*Sakunthalavin Ponvizha Andu* (The Golden Jubilee Year of Sakuntala)" (in Tamil). *Kalki*. (16/02/1946).
184. George, T.J.S. 2007 (Rpt. 2010). *Op.cit.,* p. 106.
185. *Ibid.,* p. 110.
186. *Ibid.,* p. 113.
187. *Ibid.,* p. 113.
188. *Ibid.,* p. 115.
189. *Ibid.,* p. 128.
190. *Ibid.,* p. 128.
191. *Ibid.,* pp. 129-132.
192. *Ibid.,* p. 101.
193. *Ibid.,* p. 102.

194. *Ibid.,* p. 197.
195. *Ibid.,* p. 155.
196. *Ibid.,* p. 165.
197. *Ibid.,* pp. 173-174.
198. The statement was quoted in T.J.S. George. (*Ibid.,* p. 176.)
199. *Ibid.,* p. 176.
200. *Ibid.,* p. 177.
201. *Ibid.,* p. 211.
202. *Ibid.,* p. 170.
203. *Ibid.,* p. 186.
204. The statement was quoted in T.J.S. George. (*Ibid.,* p. 186.)
205. Gangadhar, V. *M.S. Subbulakshmi: The Voice Divine.* New Delhi: Rupa and Co, 2002.
206. *Kundoosi.* January, 1948.
207. George, T.J.S. 2007 (Rpt. 2010). *Op.cit.,* pp. 195-196.
208. *Vishwa Hindu Parishad* (VHP) is a Hindu right wing organisation which propagated the *Hindutva* ideology. The organisation was formed in 1964.
209. The statement was quoted in T.J.S. George. (George, T.J.S. 2007 (Rpt. 2010). *Op.cit.,* p. 188.)
210. The content was rendered from the official webpage of *Ramon Magsaysay Award Foundation* http://www.rmaf.org.ph/newrmaf/main/awardees/awardee/profile/228 accessed on March 20, 2014.
211. *Ibid.*
212. George, T.J.S. 2007 (Rpt. 2010). *Op.cit.,* p. 216.
213. *Ibid.,* p. 217.
214. *Ibid.,* p. 251.
215. The content was rendered from the official webpage of *Ramon Magsaysay Award Foundation* http://www.rmaf.org.ph/newrmaf/main/awardees/awardee/profile/228 accessed on March 20, 2014.
216. George, T.J.S. 2007 (Rpt. 2010). *Op.cit.,* pp. 150-152.
217. The content was rendered from the official webpage of *Ramon Magsaysay Award Foundation* http://www.rmaf.org.ph/newrmaf/main/awardees/awardee/profile/228 accessed on March 20, 2014.
218. George, T.J.S. 2007 (Rpt. 2010). *Op.cit.,* p. 245.
219. *Ibid.,* p. 246.
220. M.S. Subbulakshmi's interview by Vaasanthi. (September, 2006) *India Today* (Tamil).
221. George, T.J.S. 2007 (Rpt. 2010). *Op.cit.,* p. 244.
222. *Ibid.,* p. 218.

Chapter - 7

Conclusion

Devadasi were the women who were dedicated to a specific temple or sacred object. The custom was widely spread in South Asia, especially in India and Sri Lanka. Generally, the dedication happened in a brahmanical temple. The dedicated young girls came from the different caste. The dedication ceremony resembled the rituals of the Brahmin marriages. Usually, caste played a significant role in the intra and inter relations of devadasi. There was a kind of unequal hierarchy that existed among devadasi women. The girls from the upper caste such as Brahmins were placed in a comfortable position and allowed to perform ritual services. On the other hand, the non-Brahmin girls did non-ritualistic services like cleaning temple premises. Unlike other women in the patriarchal society, the dedicated girls were educated, owned property, sexually free and had certain other privileges such as holding their flags in the medieval period and the special funeral rites of the devadasi which was not even confirmed to 'caste' men in the society.

The development of the system was not uniform in its nature. It varied according to the region and political climate of the particular historical period. The development of the system was always paralleled with the transformation of the society. The primitive Sangam society did not need the massive temple institution, the shift from the pastoral to feudal society required a kind of ideology to control the vast land. The establishment of Pallava and Pandiya in the fifth century signalled the new monarchial kingship in South India, especially in Tamilakam. The institutionalisation of the temple helped to construct their royalty and ideas over the society. The introduction of the constructed temples made a huge impact in the South Indian society. The religious institutions were a primary causative factor for the medieval pre-industrial and traditional agrarian South Indian society. The medieval temple represented as an intersection with the sacred realm that gives meaning to both kingship and the service of the devadasi.

The power structure of South India co-existed with religion, religious institution and symbols. The religious institutions such as temple played a crucial role. The firm establishment of temple order in South India strengthened the devadasi system. The temple had a huge bureaucracy at its command amongst which the temple girls, who were employed in the service of God deserve a special mention. The Brahmin-Kshatriya combination helped to preserve the patriarchal order in the society. The system had its consistent growth from the Pallava period onwards. The imperial Cholas improved the condition of devadasi system by means of donation and protection. The *bhakti* movement provided an ideological base for the existence of the system. The medieval records detailed the role of devadasi in the temple.

In medieval times, the devadasi became an integral part of the temple institution. There was no ritual and festival complete without the performance of the temple girls. All the medieval South Indian monarchs were became the patron of the institution. They were found in most of the temples of the Chola period. Pandiya paid their keen attention to the devadasi institution. During the medieval period, devadasis were honoured with several titles such as *manikkam* (ruby) and *thalaikkoli* (an expert in the dance performance) and etc. The medieval records detailed the engagement of devadasi in the family as a wife and mistress. In a feudal society, courtesans and slaves were the symbols of the wealthy men. The medieval kings and wealthy people in the society were interested in marrying devadasi as a symbol of their royalty. The Chola king Kulottungan I married devadasis, Elisaivallabhi and Theayagavalli.

The engagement of devadasi in the temple was considered as divine. The recruitment of devadasi occurred through various means such as presentation and purchase. The recruitment and appointment right of the temple servants was owned by the state, temple and village assembly. The presentation was carried into two categories. Some women were gifted as an object and the other one was a voluntary dedication. The extensive devotion, poverty, superstition and prayer were the chief factors for the volunteer dedication. Usually, the donor might be from the royal household, military generals, local chiefs, wealthy merchants and prominent devadasi. The authorisation of the temple authorities or village assembly was required to become a temple servant. The dedication occurred in the different section of the society. Kulacekara Alvar, a *bhakti* saint, married his daughter Cholakulavalli to Sriranganathar, the god of Srirangam temple.

There was a strict code of conducts drafted and maintained by the state, caste and religious institution. In the appointment of dancing girls, Rajarajan I drafted the rules for the temple services. *Koyil Ozhugu*, the Vaishnava canon, stated that devadasi would bath at dawn and adorn then they would visit the temple and stand well in sight of the deity. Temples strictly conducted the regular ritual cycles in a day, week, month, season and year. Marco Polo, the thirteenth century traveller, mentioned that the king of Malabar region performed one hundred and four prayers everyday morning and evening in honour of the deities. The functions of temple girls in the sacred realm were both ritualistic and non-ritualistic. The ritualistic works consisted of carrying lamp, maintaining perpetual lamp, bringing water for worship, fanning idol, husking paddy, cleaning rice and kitchen vessels, washing clothes, decorating surroundings waiting upon the god with fly whisk and offering sacred flowers and plant leaves. The ritualistic services consisted of dancing, performing *tirualatti* or *karpura alattai* (a mixture of turmeric, lime and camphor) and *tiruchulam* (the sacred trident).

Devadasi became the temple property as they had to serve the Brahmin and various patrons. Within the devadasi institution hierarchy existed. The devadasi of a particular temple divided according to their hierarchal gradation. The dedicated women were punch marked as a sign of life long servitude. Once the devadasi were branded with a mark, they could not enter service outside even in a royal household. Usually, devadasis of the Siva temple were branded with the trident mark and those of Vishnu temples with chunk (shell) or *chakra* (discus) marks. Siva devotees branded with the *sula* (trident), or *rishabha* (bull) mark.

Towards the end of the medieval period, the institution of devadasi was questioned. The degradation started earlier from the decline of Cholas. The political instability of the later Pandiya worsening the condition of devadasi. Devadasi did not have any agency to communicate their problems and issues. The institution of devadasi in South India, especially in Tamilakam suffered a hardship of sixty eighty years (1310-1378) due to political convulsions. The interlude of non-Hindus and non-Tamils happened in the later phase of Tamilakam. It questioned the existence of devadasihood and later it ushered in the characteristic changes in it. The political intervention of the non-Hindus led to a setback in the system.

The emergence of Vijayanagar rule brought back the old Vedic order in the Tamil country. The Nayaka rule in Tamil country brought some relief. The establishment of the Vijayanagar Empire in the fourteenth century, the Kannada and Telugu Nayakas emerged as a prominent patron of the temple institution. The emergence of the Vijayanagar rule in South India reformulated the system. Kumara Kampana, the chieftains of Vijayanagar emperor, restored the devadasi tradition and assured their protection. Vijayanagar rulers consciously promoted a high degree of Sanskritisation. They created the Vedicisation-Sanskrit 'cosmopolitan' culture for pan-Indian Vedic authentication. During this period, a new kind of ritual service was started to be practice by the devadasi women such as *kumbarthi*.

The later medieval records such as travelogues, hagiographies and other literary records give details of the devadasi's involvement in physical relation in the profane places. The moral conduct of devadasi was continuously question by the later medieval text. One can see a deterioration in their status from the Maratha rule and it reached its zenith in the colonial period. They even went to an extent labelling system of devadasi as prostitution. An epigraph of seventeenth century from Vahesvarar temple at Malayadipatti provided us with some evidence of the immoral life of the devadasi. It stated that the *devidiyal* (devadasi) named Vadvulamangal was found with a Brahmin in an amorous way. The foreign travellers such as Domingo Paes, Abraham Rogerius (1651), Francois Valentyn (1726) and Bartholomous Ziegenbalg (eighteenth century) witnessed that the devadasi tradition during their visit to South Asia especially to the Indian subcontinent. Dutch pastor Francois Valentyn (1726) was the first one who mentioned the word *devadasikal* (plural form of devadasi) in his book *Oud en Nieuw Oost-Indien* (Old and New East India). The Venetian jeweller Gasparo Balbi (1590) used the derogatory term *puttane del pagoda* (temple whore). Abraham Rogerius, a Dutch Calvinist minister, called them as 'whore' in his *De Open-Deure tot het Verborgen Heydendom* (1651). Francois Bernier mentioned that the Brahmin priests of Jagannath temple raped the young dancers after they were 'married' to the god.

The indigenous literature reflected on their condition of the later medieval period. The minor literary works such as *Virali Vitu tutu* (messenger literature), ballad and *Thanippatar tirattu* (compilation work) focused the issues of the devadasi. These later medieval literatures did not have any ambiguity between the temple women and prostitutes. They were well aware of the uniqueness of the devadasi women. The works of Arunakirinathar and Kalamekam, the later medieval poets, discussed the exploitative nature of the devadasi women. They were personally engaged with devadasi women. They had a personal relationship with devadasis. His works praised, criticised and cursed the devadasi women. Kalamekam compared the prostitute with monkey, betel leaf, coconut and palm tree. He mentioned that it was not easy to run away from them, it always moved with us until the material we had over and they have performed prank on everyone, by hugging the strong and cheating the weak.

The *Virali Vitu Tutu* (messenger) is one of the literary genres in Tamil literature that extensively discussed about the relationship of devadasi and the composer. It was popular between 1600 and 1750. The genre is structured like a conversation between *virali* who was a female messenger and the protagonist. So the literature was noted as messenger poem. The content dealt with the morality and misconduct of devadasi. Even in the *tutu* literature such as *Deivachchilaiyar virali vitu tutu*, *Muvaraiyan virali vitu tutu*, *Sethupathi virali vitu tutu*, *Nannavur Sangamechuvara Svami Vedhanayaki Amman peril virali vitu tutu* and *Kulappa Nayakkan virali vitu tutu* are the works which give much details of the devadasi institution.

The scattered and fragmentary references of the temple women, court dancers, and other public women coalesce in Thanjavur Maratha period, when these hitherto independent roles fully collapsed the identity of the devadasi. During the Maratha period, the dance of devadasi used to be called as *sadhir-attam* instead of *dasi-attam*. The Marathi word *sadar* meant durbar (court). The Maratha court described a rigorous code of conduct for devadasi and enforced it with a severe punishment. The Marathas made many rules and restrictions to control the sexuality of the devadasi. The records of the years 1820, 1846 and 1847 mentioned those rules and restrictions under the titles of *The Duties of the Dancers and Nattuvanars* and *Dress and Jewels which were restricted to the Dancers*. These rules were strictly imposed on devadasi and *nattuvanar*. It distinguished devadasi from the other women.

The colonial intervention and the nation building process changed the social relations of the Indian society. The period, eighteenth to early twentieth century witnessed a rift between traditionalism and modernity. The dominant ideologies of the colonial state and brahmanical social order discriminated and excluded the natives. The caste order was strengthened and new land relations were established. The European renaissance and industrial revolution resulted in colonial power over India. In general, the devolution of royal cosmologies to lower levels of political organisation in South India occurred in the eighteenth century. Historically, the administration of temple was state managed. The traditional kingship depended on the religious institution to retain their power structure. The colonizers understood the irrelevance of the temple patronage to sustain their imperial power over the natives. So they withdrew their support from the temple. The withdrawal of patronage created a kind of vacuum. The Brahmin priests and other temple servants started to seek their new patrons.

The introduction of the *zamindari* and *ryotwari* systems resulted in the creation of the new political lobby, who were frequently known as new elites in South Indian society. The traditional local chieftains were replaced by the new elites such as zamindars, *dubashis* etc. The temples and other religious institutions came under the power of the local elites such as little kings, zamindars, *dubashis*, wealthy Brahmins and merchants. The local landlords started to patronize it by virtue of their socio-economic power. The auspiciousness symbols of devadasi had become an important part of the ritual celebrations of non-royal elites.

The decline of temple economy led devadasi to lose temple patronage. Devadasi started to face the economic hardship and underwent difficult circumstances. Largely, it led them in engaging in concubinage and prostitution to support their basic needs. Gradually, the activities of devadasi shifted from sacred to profane sphere. The sexual activities of devadasi were highlighted rather than their earlier ritual services. Most of the devadasis became an unskilled performer. Devadasi became the de facto concubines of the new elites. The local elites funded and hosted professional performances of music and dance in the profane space. Usually, devadasis participated in most of the palace ceremonies such as coronation and festivals. But in the changed historical context, devadasis were made to dance in the private parties other than the ritualistic services which were regularly conducted in the temples and royal houses.

During the colonial period, the private dance performance was called as *nautch* or *nautch* parties. So the dance performance of devadasi was also identified with that popular term *nautch*. The dance performance of the traditional dancers was considered as an honour to the guests. The service of devadasi was demanded outside the temple and huge amount was remunerated. They travelled to different places to perform which was peculiar from the earlier custom of devadasihood. Here, the service was rendered to petty kings, zamindars and *dubashis* rather than the deities of the temple. Generally, devadasis were contracted for many days to perform in profane and the pleased masters gifted the devadasis with valuables such as money, shawls, and other gold ornaments. The *nautch* was performed on the occasions of marriage, feast, and other public occasions.

Throughout nineteenth century, the *nautch* performance was provided to English officials and elites. After the settlement, British conceived India as their second home. From 1880 onwards, Europeans in India, especially the higher officials such as Viceroys, Governors, Collectors, District Magistrates and other law enforcing echelons used to attend the *nautch* parties. The *nautch* performances were organised to honour the visit of Prince of Wales (1875) and his son Prince Albert Victor (1890) of British India. Though the British were interested in attending the *nautch* parties, missionaries and few other colonial officials regularly voiced against the *nautch* performance and participating in it. They believed *nautch* and devadasi system were symbol of degradedness.

The most of the reformers of nineteenth and early twentieth century concerned *nautch* as a social issue. Ramachandram in his monograph *The Devadasi* noted that these women of ill fame had ruined the country with their shameless trade and that the system was the creation ground for the devils. He warned people by calling them as devadasi and that would insult God under the sacred name of religion. Kalyanasundaram mentioned that he could not accept the degraded tradition of devadasi which was practiced in the name of Hindu religion. Sarma questioned the misconduct of devadasi as a prostitute. He expressed similar ideas and he stated that once devadasi were *rudrakanikai* who practiced the strict moral conduct and were well received by the devotees due to their asceticism. But the loss of their asceticism led devotees to disrespect the community. Yande stated that the holiness of the life was the prime condition and un-chastity and voluptuousness were reckoned as extreme sin, and who indulged in them were threatened with all sorts of terrible punishment in future existence.

Importantly, the reformers placed their arguments within the religious context. They tried to establish that the devadasi custom was not an integral part of the Hindu tradition. The reformers glorified womanhood. Yande explained that the dancing women were not mentioned in the Hindu text. Sarma stated that there was no truth that *vedas* and *sastras* insisted upon the dedication and on the other hand it brought bad names to the religion. Yande stated that the custom was not at all sanctioned by Hindu religion which has been based on *vedas*, and there were no records in Sanskrit and Prakrit legends which existed, regarding the idols that were supposed to require service of such dedicated prostitutes and the custom was entirely against the genius of all religious cults which have their root in Vedic teachings.

Usually, devadasi could not be compartmentalised within the inner sphere which meant spiritual because devadasis were vibrant, educated and possessed property which was not common for other women. The reformers however wanted to bring devadasi women into the private domain of a 'home', through marriage. The nationalist flagged the concept of the Indian motherhood and compared the nation with mother. They visualised the morality of a country soulfully depends on the character of the Indian women. The concepts such as purity, righteousness and discipleship played a key role in nation making.

There was a series of engagement on the issue of *nautch* performance of devadasi women. In Madras Presidency the purity and the *anti-nautch* movements found their chief advocates. The Purity Movement, the Indian National Social Conferences (1885) and Madras Hindu Reform Associations (1892) marked the significant beginning in the Indian social reform activities. It actively campaigned for the *anti-nautch* movements. It questioned the principles of the system and favoured Indian nation to compete in morals. According to them, the *nautch* was a form of impurity which destroyed the glory of the nation. They perceived devadasis were the national weakness. They condemned employing the dancing girl's for entertainment and was an open impurity wherever it was found.

In general, the social reformers believed that the engagement of the state and some individuals could stop these social problems like devadasi system. It mentioned that it was impossible to expect the custom to disappear of its own accord, for it would take a long time for education and enlightenment to reach the lowest strata of our society. The British were trying to implement various laws to ensure the moral progress in the Indian subcontinent. There were recurrent demanded to the officials to shun the *nautch* parties which were given by the wealthy Indians. The participation of Prince Albert Victor in the *nautch* performances was criticised by some of the English settlers and Indian elites. Ralph Johnson, the Bishop of Calcutta, condemned the prince participation and mentioned it as immoral. William Miller (1838-1922), the founder of Madras Christian College, expressed his disappointment with the *nautch* parties. In 1893, he organised a meeting with the help of the Indian elites to discuss the issues which was related to the *nautch*.

The colonial intervention with the devadasi system in the Indian subcontinent made a great impact. The social and economic changes affected the life of the devadasis. The 'sacredness' of the devadasi was questioned and they were forced to search their identity. The colonial officials struggled to differentiate the public women of the West and the religious women of the East. The establishment of the colonial settlement and introduction of the colonial administration initiated the new economic policies of the British which influenced the devadasi customs in a multiple way. In general, the coloniser was not able to distinguish between the devadasi and prostitutes. Most of the colonial officials compared the devadasi to prostitutes.

In the early nineteenth century, an important task of the colonial government was to document the 'native' religious practices. The coloniser made an effort to universalise the legal code in the Indian subcontinent. The colonial administration structured 'tradition' through the agency of the courts, serving to equalise structurally unequal people. The process of universalisation benefited Brahmin community in the Indian society. The process authenticated the brahmanical textual tradition and its culture as universal. Their caste customs and religious practices became the law for all. There was a little tension raised between the traditional and modern legal systems. The colonisers preferred to implement the British mode of public law and Indian mode of private law.

The patriarchal Hindu law is constructed on the sexual activity of women. Kunal Parkar noted that under the new patriarchy marriage instantiated itself in law. Marriage was absolutely indispensible for the Hindu women and it became the source for all legal status and rights. The sexual activity outside the marriage was considered as sin and designated as 'unchastity', 'incontinence' or prostitution. It was severely punished as incontinence. The Hindu community was organised around marriage. The Hindu law conditioned women's property rights upon their chastity. The devadasi institution was different in the Hindu community. And, the Hindu Law recognised the existence of dancing girls as a separate class and acknowledged their civil rights. The colonial judicial law established the rights of the temple women and it recognised the institution. The High Court observed that the dancing girls were a separate community and had no caste, or belonged to any caste, and that consequently they could adopt a girl from any caste or no caste.

In nineteenth century, the British Government enacted Contagious Disease (CD) Acts of 1864 1866 and 1869 in England to safeguard the health of the British soldiers from the venereal diseases such as syphilis and gonorrhea. The British tried to Government protect the health of soldiers through the control of the female body. According to the Act, female prostitute were instructed to undergo a regular checkups and treatment in health centres. Later, the Act was extended to all its Colonial courtiers. In 1868, the Indian Contagious Diseases Act (Act XIV of 1868) was enacted with similar provisions for the supervision, registration, and inspection of prostitute women in major Indian cities and seaports. The colonial government had to keep registers and issue the licenses to prostitutes. The examining hospitals were infamously called Lock Hospitals. The process excluded the dancing girl community from its provisions. In many cases devadasi were exempted to attend the Lock Hospital for examination and certificate due to their religious status. Ramachendrier noted that the government recognised somewhat their status by not classifying them with the common whores and prostitutes who were actually brought under the Act and compelled to attend the Lock Hospital for examination and certificate.

In the end of nineteenth century, reformers led the first phase of *anti-nautch* and anti-dedication campaign. Usually, the reformers were nationalist and believed in Brahmanical Doctrines. Their primary concern was on social purity and desired to construct a 'pure' nation. But in the early twentieth century, a section of reformers brought different arguments on the abolition of devadasi system which was centred on radicalism. The second phase got its momentum with an emergence of the Self-Respect Movement in South India. There was a significant difference between the groups of reformers regarding the reasoning for the abolition of the system in the society. The radicals understood the exploitive religious nature of the system and criticised it, because they envisaged that the degraded devadasi system could entertain the subordination, trafficking and sexual exploitation of women.

Among the reformers, Muthulakshmi Reddi was a prominent personality who tirelessly argued for devadasi abolition. Ideologically, she had a complex position. It was a mixture of two phases of the reformers. On one side, she was concerned with the puritan Hindu religion but on the other side, she argued for the abolition of the system for the empowerment of womanhood. Interestingly, the campaign of Muthulakshmi was supported by the rational arguments of the Self-Respect Movement. The effort of reformers was able to create awareness among the people. Following these development, in 1930,

Madras Legislative Council (MLC) passed a resolution to prevent the dedication of devadasi.

In general, the radicals came from the Self-Respect Movement who chiefly advocated for universal brotherhood, anti-Brahmanical and anti-ritualistic society. The Self-Respect Movement voiced for the marginalised sections of the society and questioned the hereditary monopoly of Brahmins in the caste society. The movement questioned the existing caste structure and cultural hegemony of Brahmanism. It gave priority to the self-respected life of the common people. Women liberation was one of the prominent aims of the Self-Respect Movement. It questioned the patriarchal system. It stated that in a patriarchal structure, women were treated as sexual object and property and the society treated women as a child bearing machine and equalled women with animal. The movement spoke for devadasi women and provided a space for them. It encouraged devadasi women to place their arguments in the mainstream politics. *Kudi Arasu*, the rational daily, had a column for devadasi women.

The Self-Respecters strongly believed that the abolition of the devadasi system was desirable and important. E.V. Ramasami considered the abolition of the *dasi* system and child marriages would lead to women empowerment. The rationalist considered devadasi system as a system of professional prostitution. E.V. Ramasami understood that the *pottu* ceremony that was license for the prostitution in the name of God. The Self-Respecters were able to understand the differences between prostitution and devadasihood. *Kudi Arasu* used the Tamil term *vesi* to point prostitute women and *dasi* to denote devadasi women. The newspaper actively engaged in the process of eradicating evils in Hindu temples and prostitution in the name of religion.

The Self-Respecters stressed the importance of religious reforms in the society. The Self-Respect newspapers gave its special attention to the issues of devadasi. Frequently, devadasi and other activist in the Self-Respect Movement wrote columns in the newspapers. On June 17, 1928, Masilamanip Pillai wrote a column *Devadasikalukkor Vendukol: Namathu Nokkam* which meant *An Appeal to Devadasi: Our Intension* in *Kudi Arasu*. Another column, *the Abolition of the Pottu Ceremony in the Hindu Temples in Madras Presidency* highlighted that the *pottu* that ceremony signify the acceptance of devadasi as a prostitute or concubine as their profession. The contents, *Naan Vilaimagala*? (Am I a prostitute?) on March 30, 1930 and *Swamikalum Devadiyalkalum* (Gods and Slaves of God) on December 21, 1930 stated that all the social evils in the society occurred in the name of religion alone.

Usually, devadasi and their artistic performance were inseparable. The livelihood of the devadasi was depended on their performing ability. But towards the end of 1920s, there was a new discourse around the lives of devadasi women. There was a strong protest against the devadasi system and to restrict the performance of devadasi women. The Self-Respecters did not consider the aesthetic value of the dance performance of devadasi. In more than that they visualised the exploitative and submissiveness nature of the female body through the performance. The Self-Respect Movement propagated for the restriction of the performance of devadasi women. *Kudi Arasu* mentioned that the performance of devadasi during the *puja* hours would disturb the minds of the devotees. In 1928, Youth Conference of *Isai Vellalar* at Chidambaram passed resolution that the musical system of devadasi was degraded and recommend its reform.

The entire colonial politics on the devadasi practices renamed the dance tradition of devadasi as Bharatanatyam. Revivalist claimed that the art of the devadasi was 'sanitized' and 'revived'. The so called respectable upper caste-well-read Brahmin men and women took up the task of revival of devadasi dance tradition. There was a huge debate on the renaming of devadasi's dance. It is difficult to find an exact person who first coined the word Bharatanatyam. Rukmini Devi, V. Raghavan (musicologist) and E. Krishna Iyer were the leading personalities in the process. In 1932, Madras Music Conference of the Music Academy passed resolution to renaming of *sadhir* into Bharatanatyam. The *Centenary Issue* of Krishna Iyer mentioned that it had been given a new lease of life under a new name just like a girl given in marriage.

The revivalist considered that the performance of devadasi would not satisfy the aesthetic taste of sophisticated society in which it must function. The revivalist undervalued the traditional techniques of devadasi dance. They considered the importance of the revival of the dance. Rukmini Devi was the prominent women in the process of the renaming Bharatanatyam. As Theosophist and Brahmin, she was interested to continue the age old Hindu practices especially, the dance tradition. Rukmini Devi considered that dance was an ancient culture and religion. She criticised that persons (devadasi) could do stunts which remained in the chorus because it did not have any soul in it. Further, she mentioned that art could be one of the greatest achievements of humanity. The dance transcends the physical body as a vehicle and lifts humanity into a world of higher emotion of joy and pure intellect or wisdom.

Rukmini Devi made many changes in the dance tradition, especially in music, background and presentation. She blended *sadhir attam* with the new and old forms. According to her, dance was an expression of physical body. The physical expression was both dangerous and magnificent instrument. The weakness of the physical body was its coarseness and vulgarity. She believed that the portrayal of *shringara* was "ordinary and low". She also felt that expressing *shringara* movements on the profane area would not suit her or her students. So, Rukmini Devi and other Brahmin elites thought to differentiate the so called vulgarity from sublime. She selected her repertoire carefully. Her choice was the concept of *bhakti* (devotion) and she used songs which were based on religious theme. Rukmini Devi perceived this dynamic and called as it the secularisation of the devadasi dance.

The revivalist was trying to establish the importance of the dance in the ritual tradition of Hindu religion. They continuously placed the dance and music within the religious context. They stressed the importance of the spirituality in dance performance. The revivalist voiced for spirituality. Raghavan mentioned that the temples had rare ragas and forms of composition and it serve art as well as moral and spiritual regeneration of the people. Rukmini Devi stressed the importance of the religious spirit in the dance. She noted that the dance should be influenced by religion.

Many Indologists and nationalist historians claimed that Bharatanatyam was a direct descendant of the arts of the Tamil Sangam age. The Brahmin elite claimed the dance form from the age-old Sanskrit tradition. Annie Besant stated that the dancing class women of temple was established to exonerates the ancestors from any such evil motives and were worthy of their earnest attention. Sathyamurthi mentioned that the importance of the musical revival of India, especially South India. He insisted that the music had always played a larger role in helping the achievement of freedom to other countries. The revivalist recommended that Indian National Congress should use the new spirit that emerged among South Indians in music and dance for Indian nationalism.

The Music Academy of Madras played a key role in the revival of devadasi dance. The relationship between the Music Academy and Bharatanatyam was inseparable. Usually, the members of the Music Academy were part of the cultural wing of the Indian National Congress that was projecting devadasi as performer of Bharatanatyam and identified themselves as the 'pro-art progressives'. E. Krishna Iyer, an one of the Secretaries of the Academy, played a decisive role in the renaissance of *sadhir* dance into Bharatanatyam. He who was interested to include *sadhir* programmes in the Academy. The Music Academy's attention towards dance was at its peak during the period between 1930 and 1935. The Music Academy made an effort to revive the devadasi dance tradition. The Academy started to organise the dance performances of devadasi. The various resolutions of the Academy favoured and encouraged the art of Bharatanatyam. It stated that Bharatanatyam was a great and ancient art which was unexceptionable. It appealed to the public and art associations for necessary attention and encouragement for Bharatanatyam.

The executive functionaries of the Academy continued to encourage the art of dance under its new name of Bharatanatyam. The academy provided a space for the dance performance and it allowed dancer to perform their dance. In the decade between 1930 and 1940 significant number of devadasi performed in the Academy. The Academy helped to stage dances by outstanding devadasi performers. However, after 1935 a new factor emerged in the South Indian dance tradition. A group of Brahmin women who were associated with the Theosophical Society started to learn the dance. These Brahmin dancers had infused their caste values into the dance. The Music Academy provided a platform for these 'new' dancers. The participation of the devadasi's performance in the Academy started to decrease in number.

The life stories of devadasi who were actively engaging in the discourse on devadasi at different stages, such as that of Muvalur Ramamirtham, Bangalore Nagarathnam, Thanjavur Balasaraswati and Madurai Shanmugavadivu Subbulakshmi are very interesting. All the four women were from the devadasi community and they survived during the period, when the abolition of devadasi discourse was at its peak. The life of these women directly or indirectly reflected the changes, which were with in the context of the abolition of the system in the twentieth century Indian society. These women represented the different discourse on the devadasi issue. Bangalore Nagarathnam was from Mysore who voiced for the continuation of the devadasi system. Muvalur Ramamirtham was firmly against the devadasi custom and intensively worked hard for the abolition of the system. She became a social reformer and close associate of E.V. Ramasami of the Self-Respect Movement. Balasaraswati came from the strong devadasi lineage of Vina Dhanam of colonial Madras. She questioned the Sanskritisation of devadasi dance tradition and represented the devadasi's dance to the modern world. On the other hand, M.S. Subbulakshmi, the musical legend from devadasi community, signified the transition of the autonomous nature of devadasi womanhood to a submissive woman of a modern society within the Brahmin patriarchy.

Interestingly, the entire arguments of devadasi discourse was able to prove that the devadasi institution was much influenced by its contemporary social events. Though the system was matriarchal, the patriarchal norms were continuously engaging and influencing the course of the institution. The strengthening of the patriarchy values exploited the religiosity of women. The entire historical development shifted the public women or the otherwise somewhat liberated women into the inner sphere of home in the colonial context.

Bibliography

Epigraphy

Annual Reports on Indian Epigraphy (*A.R.I.E.*). New Delhi: Archeological Survey of India.

Annual Report on South Indian Epigraphy (*A.R.S.I.E.*). New Delhi: Archeological Survey of India.

Chronological List of the Inscriptions of the Pudukkottai State Arranged According to Dynasties. 1929. Pudukkottai: State Press.

Epigraphia Indica. 1882-1977. Vols. I-XLII. New Delhi: Archeological Survey of India.

Epigraphia Indica. Ed. N.P. Chakravarti. Vol. XXII. New Delhi: Archeological Survey of India, 1933-34 (Rpt. 1984).

Inscription of the Pudukkottai State. Tr. K.R. Srinivasa Aiyar, Pudukkottai: State Press.

Inscriptions (Texts) of the Pudukkottai State. (Arranged According to Dynasties). Pudukkottai: Authority Pudukkottai Darbar, 1929.

Kanyakumari Kalvettukal. Vols. I-V. Madras: Dept. of Archaeology, Govt. of Tamil Nadu, 1972.

Modi Documentations in the T.M.S.S.M. Library. Ed. R. Vivekanandagopal. Thanjavur: Thanjavur Maharajah Serfoji's Sarasvati Mahal Library, 1999.

South Indian Inscription: Tamil and Sanskrit Inscriptions. Ed and Tr. E. Hultzsch. (Chiefly Collected in 1886-87). Vol. I. Part. 1, 2, 3, and 4 (From Stone and Copper-Plate Edicts at Mamallapuram, Kanchipuram in the North Arcot District and Other Parts of the Madras Presidency). New Delhi: Archaeological Survey of India, 1890 (Rpt. 1991).

South Indian Inscriptions: Tamil Inscriptions. Ed. E. Hultzsch. Vol. II. (Parts 1 and 2). New Delhi: Archaeological Survey of India, 1991.

South Indian Inscriptions: Tamil Inscriptions. Ed. E. Hultzsch. Vol. II. (Parts 3, 4 and 5). New Delhi: Archaeological Survey of India, 1992.

South Indian Inscriptions: Miscellaneous Inscriptions from the Tamil Country. Ed. E. Hultzsch. Vol. III. Parts i and ii. New Delhi: Archaeological Survey of India, 1929 (Rpt. 1987).

South Indian Inscriptions: Miscellaneous Inscriptions from the Tamil Country. Ed. H. Krishna Sastri. Vol. III. Parts. iii and iv. New Delhi: Archaeological Survey of India, 1920 (Rpt. 1987).

South Indian Inscriptions: Miscellaneous Inscriptions in Tamil, Telugu and Kannada. Ed. H. Krishna Sastri. Vol. IV. New Delhi: Archaeological Survey of India, 1986.

South Indian Inscriptions: Miscellaneous Inscriptions in Tamil, Telugu, Malayalam and Kannada. Ed. H. Krishna Sastri. Vol. V. New Delhi: Archaeological Survey of India, 1928 (Rpt. 1968).

South Indian Inscriptions: Collection of Tiruvarur Temple Inscriptions. 1991. New Delhi: Archaeological Survey of India.

South Indian Inscriptions: Tanjavur Temple (Tamil Inscription in the Rajarajesvara Temple (Brihadhiswara Temple) at Tanjavur. Ed. E. Hultzsch and V. Venkayya. New Delhi: Archaeological Survey of India, 1991.

South Indian Temple Inscriptions. Ed. T.N. Subramaniam. Madras: Government Oriental Manuscript Library, 1953.

Tamilnattuk Kalvettukkal (Inscriptions of Tamilnadu) (in Tamil). Ed. N. Marxigandhi. Madras: Tamil Nadu State Department of Archaeology, 1980.

Temple Inscriptions of Andhra Pradesh. Vol. I. Srikakulam District. Ed. Ramson N. Mukunda Row. Hyderabad, 1980.

Thanjai Marattiya Mannar Modi Avanath Tamizhakkamum Kurippuraiyum (Tamil Translation and notes of Modi Documents of Thanjavur Maratha King) (in Tamil). Vols. I-III. Ed. K.M. Venkatramaiah and R. Vivekanandagopal. Thanjavur: Tamil University, 1989.

The Travancore State Manual. Vols. I-III. V. Nagam Aiya. Trivandrum: The Travancore Government Press, 1906.

Travancore Archaeological Series. Ed. T.A. Gopinatha Rao. Trivandrum: Dept. of Cultural Publications, 1872-1919.

Travancore Archaeological Series. Vol. III. Part. 1. Ed. K.V. Subrahmanya Aiyar. Trivandrum: Government Press, 1921.

Travancore Archaeological Series. Vol. V. Part. 1. Ed. A.S. Ramanatha Ayyar. Trivandrum: Government Press, 1924.

Tirutturaippunti Kalvettukkal (Inscriptions of Tirutturaippunti) (in Tamil). Ed. R. Nagaswamy. Madras: Tamil Nadu State Department of rchaeology, 1978.

Topographical List of Inscriptions of Madras Presidency. Ed. V. Rangacharya. Madras: Government Press, 1919.

Varalarru Vativankal (Historical Images) (in Tamil). S. Kuppuswami. Madras: Cekar Patippakam, 1976.

Tirumala Tirupati Devasthanam Inscriptions. Vol. II. Ed. V. Vijay Raghavcharya. Madras, 1933.

Tirumala Tirupati Devasthanam Inscriptions. Vol. IV.

Inscriptions of Andhra Desa. Vol. 11. Ed. J. Ramyya Rao. Madras, 1949.

Census reports

Census of India. 1891. Vol. XIII. Madras.

Census of India, 1901, Madras. W. Francis. 1902. Vol. XV. Part 1. Madras: Government Press.

Census of India, 1901, Madras. W. Francis. 1902. Vol. XV-A. Part 2. Madras: Government Press.

Census of India, 1901, Madras. W. Francis. 1902. Vol. XV-B. Part 3. Madras: Government Press.

Census of India, 1901, Travancore. N. Subramhanya Aiyar. Vol. XXVI. Part 1. Trivandrum: Malabar Mail Press, 1903.

Government orders and legislative debates

The Madras Devadasis (Prevention of Dedication) Act. 1947. Madras Act. XXXI of 1947. The Government of Madras Law. Legislative Department. January 26, 1948.

The Proceedings of the Madras Legislative Council: Second Session of the Third Legislative Council. Vol. XXXVIII. October 31-November 5, 1927.

Proceedings of the Madras Legislative Assembly (cited as PMLA)

G.O. 4079, 1927. Law Department (Madras).

G.O. 3210, 1939. Home Department (Madras).

G.O. 23 of 1948. Law (legislative) Department (Madras).

Madras Legislative Assembly Debates. Vol. VI. 1-14 (1947).

Madras Legislative Assembly Debates. Vol. VII. 1-15 (1947).

Proceedings of the Madras Legislative Council: Second Session of the Third Legislative Council. Vol. XXXVIII. Nos. 1-5.

Proceedings of the Madras Legislative Council: Third Session of the Third Legislative Council. Vol. XLIII. (1928).

Proceedings of the Madras Legislative Council: Fourth Session of the Third Legislative Council. Vol. LI. Nos.1-10. (1930).

Travelogues

A Letter to Robert Lowe from John Bruce Norton on the Condition and Requirements of the Presidency of Madras. London: Richardson Brothers, 1854.

Bernier, Francois. *Travels in the Mogul Empire A.D. 1656-1668*. Archibald Constable. Tr. and V.A. Smith. Revised. London: Oxford University Press, 1916.

Caland, W. *Ziegenbalg's Malabarishes Heidenthum*. Amsterdam: Koninklijke Akademie van Wetenschappen, 1926.

Dubois, Abbe J.A. *A Description of the Character, Manner and Customs of the People of India*. Madras: J. Higginbotham, 1862.

——. *Hindu Customs and Ceremonies*. Oxford: Clarendon Press, 1906.

Haafner, Jacob. *Reize in eenen Palanquim; of Lotgevallen en Merkwaardige Aanteekeningen op eene Reize langs de Kusten Orixa en Chroromandel* (in Dutch). Vol. I. Amsterdam: Johannes Allart, 1808.

Major, R.H. Ed. *India in the Fifteenth Century*. London: The Hakluyt Society, 1857.

Penny, F.E. *Southern India: Lands, People and Culture*. London: A and C Black, 1914.

Penzer, N.M. *The Ocean of Story*. Vol. I. tr. C.H. Tawney. London: Chas. J. Sawyer Ltd., 1924.

——. *Poison Damsels and Other Essays in Folklore and Anthropology*. London: Chas. J. Sawyer, 1952.

Polo, Marco. *The Travels of Marco Polo*. L.F. Benedetto. Tr. and Sir E. Denison Ross and Eileen Power. Ed. New Delhi: Asian Educational Trust, 1931 (Rpt. 1994).

Rogerius, Abraham. *De Open- Deure tot het Verborgen Heydendom* (The Doors an Open to the Hidden Heathendom) (in Dutch). W. Caland. Ed. 's-Gravenhage: M. Nijhoff, 1651 (Rpt. 1915).

Taylor, William. *Oriental Historical Manuscripts*. Vols. I-II. Madras: Charles Josian Taylor, 1835.

van Linschoten, Jan Huyghen. *The Voyage of Jan Huyghen Van Linschoten to the East Indies*. Arthur Coke Burnell Tr. Vol. 1. London: The Hakluyt Society, 1885.

Valentyn, Francois. *Oud en Nieuw Oost-Indien* (Old and New East India) (in Dutch). Vol. 5. Dordrecht and Amsterdam: Joannes van Braam and Gerard Onder den Linden, 1726.

Valle, Pietro della. *The Travels of Pietro della Valle*. Gray Havers Tr. and Edward Grey Ed. Vol. II. London: The Hakluyt Society, 1892.

Autobiographies and Collected Works

Muthulakshmi Reddy, S. *My Experience as a Legislator*. Madras: Current Thought Press, 1930.

——. *An Autobiography*. Madras: M.L.J. Press, 1964.

Periyar (E.V. Ramasami). *An Autobiography of Thanthai Periyar*. Madras: Dravidar Kazhagam, 1993.

The Collected Works of Mahatma Gandhi (June-September 1927). Vol. 34. New Delhi: Ministry of Information and Broadcasting Division, 1969.

The Collected Works of Mahatma Gandhi (September 1927-January 1928). Vol. 35. New Delhi: Ministry of Information and Broadcasting Division, 1969.

The Collected Works of Mahatma Gandhi (June-October1929). Vol. 41. New Delhi: Ministry of Information and Broadcasting Division, 1970.

Thoughts of Periyar E.V.R.: Speeches and Writings of Periyar E.V. Ramasamy. V. Anaimuthu. Comp. Chennai: Periyar E.V. Ramasamy-Nagammai Education and Research Trust, 1974 (Rpt. 2009).

Thoughts of Periyar E.V.R.: Publisher's Introduction. V. Anaimuthu. Comp. Chennai: Periyar E.V. Ramasamy-Nagammai Education and Research Trust, 2009.

Newspaper and magazine

Ananda Vikatan (1926-1947). (in Tamil) Chennai: Vikatan Pirasuram.

Dravidan (in Tamil)

Dravida Nadu (The Dravidian Nation) (in Tamil)

Grihalakshmi (in Tamil)

India Today (Tamil)

Kalvettu (Inscription) (in Tamil)

Kalaimandram (in Tamil)

Kundoosi (in Tamil)

Kudi Arasu (The Republic) (in Tamil)

Nava Sakthi (in Tamil)

Murasoli (The Drum Beat) (in Tamil)

Outlook

Revolt

Sruti

Stri Dharma

Thaiyarkalai (An art of women) (in Tamil)

The Journal of the Music Academy

The Madras Mail
The Hindu
The Revolt
The Statesman
Viduthalai (The Liberation) (in Tamil)
Swadesamitran (in Tamil)
Yathum Ure (in Tamil)

Reports, monographs and pamphlets

"Abolition of Devadasi Service in Pudukotta Temples." *Stri Dharma* 14, no. 10. (1931): 457-458.

Arundale, Rukmini Devi. "Art and Culture in Indian Life." *Vallathol Memorial Lectures*. University of Kerala.

Balasaraswati, T. "On Bharatanatyam." *Journal of the Sangeet Natak Academi* 72-73. (April-September, 1984): 8-14.

——. "The Art of Bharatanatyam: Reflections of Balasaraswati." *Sruti*. Issue 50. (November, 1988): 37-40.

"Devadasi Thadai Masoda." *Grihalakshmi* 3.9 (1939): 577-579.

"Development and Preservation of Bharatanatyam: Contribution of Isai Vellalars." *Sruti* 99/100. (1992): 33-39.

"Dancing Girls in Temples." *The Indian Ladies Magazine* 4.1. (1930): 44-45.

Dedication of Girls to Gods: Plea for Prohibition by Law by Naik-Maratha Mandal. D.S. Yande, Bombay: V.P. Vengurlekar, (n.d.).

Devi, Rukmini. *The Creative Spirit*. Adyar: The Theosophical Publishing House, (n.d.).

——. *Woman as Artist*. Adyar: Theosophical Publishing House, (n.d.).

——. *Dance and Music*. Adyar: Theosophical Publishing House, (n.d.).

Inaugural Addresses of Four Presidents of the Theosophical Society. Chennai: The Theosophical Publishing House, 1946.

Krishna Iyer, E. Centenary Issue. Chennai: Music Academy, August 9, 1997.

Muthulakshmi Reddi, S. "Motion Regarding Dedication of Girls to Temples." (November 4 and 5, 1927). *PMLC*. Vol. XXXVIII.

——. *Why Should the Devadasi Institution in the Hindu Temples be Abolished?*. Madras: Central Co-operative Printing Works, Ltd, 1927.

——. *The Presidential Address of Dr. (Mrs.) S. Muthulakshmi Reddi*. Delivered at the Seventh Andhra Provincial Women's Conference held at Ellore. November 4-5, 1933.

Periyar (E.V. Ramasami). '*Chiththirapuththiran*' *Katturaikal* (Articles of Chiththirapuththiran) (in Tamil). Chennai: Dravidar Kazhaga Veliyeedu, 1959 (Rpt. 1999).

——. *Pen Yen Adimaiyanal?* (Why Women became Enslaved?) (in Tamil). Chennai: Periyar Self Respected Propaganda, 1992 (Rpt. 2004).

The Shashtiabdapurthi Celebration Committee. Sri E. Krishna Iyer's Shashtiabdapurthi Commenoration Volume. Madras: Bharathiar Sangam, 1957.

"Tyagesevasaktha, Vidyasundari, Ganakalavisharada, Life History of Srimathi Bangalore Nagarathnamma." *Grihalakshmi*. (March, 1949).

Lexicons and encyclopaedias

Abithana Chintamani: Tamil Kalaikazhanjiyam (*Abithana Chintamani*: An Encyclopedia of Tamil Language) (in Tamil). A. Singaravelu Mudaliyar and A. Sivaprakasa Mudaliyar. Comp. Chennai: Seethai Pathippakam, 1899 (Rpt. 2004).

Encyclopedia of Bharat Ratnas. R.K. Murthi. Ed. New Delhi: Pitambar Publishing Company (P) Ltd., 2005.

Encyclopedia of Religion. Denise Cush; Catherine Robinson and Michael York. Ed. London: Routledge, 2008.

Encyclopaedia of Indian Temple Architecture South India, Lower Dravidadesa 200 BC-AD 1324. K.R. Srinivasan. Ed. New Delhi: Manohar Publishers, 1991.

Dravidian Encyclopaedia. Vol. I. Thiruvananthapuram: The International School of Dravidian Linguistics, 1990.

Irupatham Norrandu Tamilp Peyaragarathi (Twentieth Century Tamil Dictionary) (in Tamil). P. Ramanathan. Comp. Chennai: Institute of South Indian Studies, 1909 (1991).

Hindu Samayach Chollakarathi (A Concise Dictionary on Hindu Religion) (in Tamil). Kokkalai Jerajan. Comp. Chennai: Maharani, 1992 (2001).

Kazhakath Tamil Agarathi (Tamil Dictionary of an Association) (in Tamil). Kazhakap Puzhavar Kuzhuvinar. Comp. Tirunelveli: The South India Saiva Siddhanta Works Publishing Society, 1964 (2000).

Koyir Kalanjiyam-Arimugam (Temple Encyclopedia An Introduction) (in Tamil). K.M. Muthusami Pillai. Ed. Thanjavur: Tamil University, 1991.

Periyar Kalanchiyam. (An Encyclopedia of Periyar). K. Veeramani. Comp. Chennai: The Periyar Self-respect Propaganda Institution, 2010.

Random House Webster's Unabridged Dictionary. New York: Random House, 1999.

Tamil Lexicon. Madras: University of Madras, 1936 1982.

The Columbia Encyclopedia. William Bridgwater and Seymour Kurtz. Ed. New York: Columbia University Press, 1963.

The Social Science Encyclopedia. Adam Kuper Ed. and Jessica Kuper. London and New York: Routledge, 1996.

Webster's Unabridged Dictionary. Random House. New York: Random House, 1999.

Dissertations

Chaganti, Anthony, "Dr. Annie Besant and Her Contributions to Society and Politics 1893-1933" PhD diss., University of Hyderabad, December, 1996.

Kambale, N.D, "Devadasis in Belgaum District: A Sociological Study" PhD diss., Shivaji University, May, 1988.

Hamsapriya, A. "Role of the Opposition in the Madras Legislature 1921-1939" PhD diss., University of Madras, Febrarury, 1981.

Hanumanthan, K.R, "Untouchablity in Tamilnadu: Ancient and Medieval Periods (Upto 1500 AD)" PhD diss., University of Madras, 1974.

Jeevanandam, S. "The Sacred Geography of Medieval Tamilakam- A Study of Saiva and Vaishnava Temples" M Phil diss., University of Hyderabad, 2009.

Jeyanthi, T. "Dr. Muthulakshmi Reddi: A Study" PhD diss., Madurai Kamaraj University, 1992.

Sathyabama, K, "Mechanize Tamil Chuvadikal Chuttum Makkal Valviyal" (Life Stories of People on the basis of Mackenzie Tamil Documents) (in Tamil)" PhD diss., Tamil University, 1998.

Pandeya, Braj Kishore. "Temple Economy under the Cholas (c. A.D. 850 - 1070)" PhD diss., Patna University, 1969.

Philip, George. "A Historical Anatomy of the Evolution of Social Revolution in Travancore" PhD diss., Mahatma Gandhi University, March, 2005.

Radhika, V.S. "Development of Sadir in the Court of Raja Serfoji-II (1798-1832) of Tanjore" PhD diss., University of Hyderabad, November, 1996.

Rajaraman, P. "The Justice Party: A Historical Study (1916-1937)" PhD diss., University of Madras, April, 1983.

Rajesh, M.N, "Socio-Religious Context of the Early Cola Temple" MPhil diss., Jawaharlal Nehru University. 1994.

Ravichandran, R, "Dravidar Kazhagam- A Political Study" PhD diss., University of Madras, 1982.

Rosana, Mathew, "Polity and Society in Travancore with special Reference to the Position of Women (1700-1900 A.D.)" PhD diss., University of Kerala, 2001.

Natarajan, Srividya. "Another Stage in the Life of the Nation: Sadir, Bharathanatyam, Feminist Theory". PhD diss, University of Hyderabad, 1997.

Shanmugam, P, "Revenue System under the Cholas (850- 1279 A.D.)" PhD diss., University of Madras, April, 1977.

Sundar Raj, M. "Studies in the History of Prostitution in Tamil Nadu (With Spccial Reference to the City of Madras, Early 19th to mid 20th Century)" PhD diss., University of Madras, 1986.

Books

Tamil books

Annamalai, P.K. and C. Arasappan. *Kalaiventhan Sarfoji* (Serfoji: the King of Art) (in Tamil). Chennai: Palaniyappa Brothers, 1964.

Arasu, V. *Sanga Noolgalin Kaalam* (The Periodisation of Sangam Literature) (in Tamil). Chennai: New Century Book House Pvt. Ltd, 2012.

Arivudai Nambi, M.S. *Thanjai Marattiya Mannar Valartha Thamizh Ilakkiyam*. (Tamil Literature Which was Grownup by Thanjavur Maratha) (in Tamil). Part. 1. Thanjavur: Tamil University, 1994.

Arivudai Nambi, M.S. *Fine Arts Under the Marathas of Thanjavur A.D. 1676-1855* (in Tamil). Puducherry: A. Kirija, 2006.

Arunachalam, M. *Tamil Ilakkiya Varalaru* (History of Tamil Literature) (in Tamil). Chennai: The Parkar, 2005.

Bakeerathan. *Kalki Ninaivukal* (The Remembrance of Kalki) (in Tamil). Chennai: Thiruvarasu Puththaka Nilayam, 1998.

Borker, Balakrishna Bagavantha. *Devadasi* (in Tamil). Chennai: Tamilnadu Writers Co-operative Association, 1966.

Civacuppiramaniyan, A. *Tamizhakattil Atimaimurai* (Monograph of Slavery in Tamilnadu) (in Tamil). Chennai: Kalachuvadu Pathippagam, 2005 (Rpt. 2010).

——. *Varalaarum Vazakkaarum* (History and its Usage) (in Tamil). Chennai: Kalachuvadu Pathippagam, 2008 (Rpt. 2010).

Devi, Nanambigai. *Thanjai Naalvar Vazhi Nattiya Isai Marabu* (The Natya Tradition through Thanjavur Four Quartet) (in Tamil). Thanjavur: Tamil University, 2005.

Eswarapillai, Tha. *Bhakthi Ilakkiyathil Samuthayap Parvai* (A Social Perspective on the Bhakti Literature) (in Tamil). Thanjavur: Tamil University, 2000.

Etiraj, A. *108, Vaishnava Divya Stala Varalaru* (The Sacred Geography of Vaishnava Temples) (in Tamil). Karaikudi: Sri Vaishnava Siddhanta Nurpatippu Kazhakam, 2006.

Jeevasunadari, B. *Moovalur Ramamirtham Ammaiyar* (in Tamil). Chennai: Arivai, 2007.

Kalyanasundaram, Thiru.Vi. *Thiru.Vi.Ka Vazhkkaik Kurippukal* (A Biographical Notes of Thiru.Vi. Kalyanasundaram) (in Tamil). Saiva Siddanta Kazhakam, 1982.

——. *Pennin Perumai allathu Vazhkkaiththunai* (The Pride of Women and the Partner) (in Tamil). Chennai: Saratha Pathippakam, 2006.

Kasinathan, Nadana and Ku. Dhamodharan. Comp. *Kalvettu* (An Inscription) (in Tamil). Chennai: Tamilnadu Governmental Archeological Department, 2009.

Kulappa Nayakkan Virali Vitu Tutu (A Tutu Literature of Kulappa Nayakkan) (in Tamil). Supradeepak Kavirayar. Karaikkudi: South India Press, (n.d.).

Kulendran, Gnanambikai. *Karaikkalammaiyar Thenninthiya Isaiyin Thaai* (*Karaikkal Ammaiyar: Mother of South Indian Music*) (in Tamil). Thanjavur: Department of Tamil Development-Culture, Government of Tamil Nadu, 1996.

Murugesan, C.S. *Varalaatril Devadasikal* (Devadasis in History) (in Tamil). Chennai: Kurinji, 2009.

Murugu, Kadhir. *Thiruvarangak Kalampakam* (in Tamil). Chennai: Saratha Pathippagam, 2008.

Muthumohan, N. *Samoogaviyal Nokkil Madham* (A Sociological Perspective on Religion) (in Tamil). Chennai: New Century Book House Pvt. Ltd, 2012.

Muvaraiyan Virali Vitu Tutu (A Tutu Literature of Muvaraiyan) (in Tamil). Mithilaippattich Chitrampala Kavirayar. Chennai: Mahamahopaththiyaya Dr. U.Ve. Saminathaiyer Library, 1982.

Nadan, Nanjil. *Naanjil Naattu Vellalar Vaazhkai* (Ethnography of Vellalars of Nanjilnadu, Kanyakumari District) (in Tamil). Chennai: Kalachuvadu Pathippagam, 2003 (Rpt. 2008).

Nagaswamy, R and M. Chandramurthi. *Tamilakak Koyir Kalaikal* (An Art forms of Tamil Temple) (in Tamil). Chennai: Archaeological Department, Government of Tamilnadu, 1973. (Rpt. 2009).

Nannavur Sangamechuvara Svami Vedhanayaki Amman Peril Virali Vitu Tutu (A Tutu Literature on Nannavur Sangamechuvara Svami Vedhanayaki Amman) (in Tamil). Bharathi Muththaiyar. Srirangam: Sri Vani Vilasa Acchakam, 1969.

Narmadha. *Thamizhagathil Thevaradiyar Marabu-Panmuga Nokku* (A Multi-Dimensional Approach towards Devadasis of Tamilnadu) (in Tamil). Chennai: Bodhi Vanam, 2006.

Natarajan, A. Tr. *Samikalin Adimaikal* (Slaves of God) (in Tamil), 1928.

Nayakkar, Venkatachala. *Hindhu Accara Abasa Dharicini* (in Tamil). Chennai: Ariviyakka Noorpathippakam.

Paramasivan, Tho. *Panpaattu Asaivukal* (A Cultural Movements) (in Tamil). Chennai: Kalachuvadu Pathippagam, 2001 (Rpt. 2010).

Perumal, A.K. *Thenkumariyin Kadhai* (History of Kanyakumari) (in Tamil). Chennai: United Writers, 2003.

Pillai, K.K. *Thamizhaga Varalaru Makkalum Panpadum* (History, People and Culture of Tamils) (in Tamil). Chennai: International Institute of Tamil Studies, 2009.

Raghavan, A. *Pennurimaiyum Mathamum* (Women's Rights and Religion) (in Tamil). Chennai: Thiravida Kazhaga Veliyeedu, 1935 (Rpt. 2001).

Raghavan, V. *Natyakkalai* (Dance Tradition of Bharatam) (in Tamil). Chennai: Kalaimagal Kariyalayam, 1974.

Raguraman, Se. *Tamizhar Natana Varalaru* (A Dance History of Tamils) (in Tamil). Chennai: Nandhini Pathippakam, 2006.

Raju, Se. *Thanjai Marattiyar Cheppedukal-50* (50 Copper Plates of Thanjavur Marathas) (in Tamil). Thanjavur: Tamil University, 1983.

Ramamirthathammal, A. Muvalur. *Dasikal Mosavalai alladhu Mathipetra Minar* (Dasis web of deceit or enlightened Playboy) (in Tamil). Erode: Unmaivilakkam Press, 1939.

Ramasamy, A. *Nayakkar Kalam: Varalaarum Ilakkiyamum* (History and Literature of Nayaka Period) (in Tamil). Chennai: Uyirmmai Pathippagam, 2009.

Rasagopalan, Sarala. *Thiru. Vi.Ka. Pennurimaich Chinthanaigal* (The Feminist Thoughts of Thiru.Vi.Ka) (in Tamil). Chennai: Olip Pathippakam, 2007.

Rasamanickam, Ma. *Thamizhakak Kalaikal* (Arts forms of Tamilakam) (in Tamil). Chennai: Pari Nilayam, 1972.

——. *Kalvettukalum Thamizh Samooga Varalaarum* (A Social History of Tamil through Inscriptions) (in Tamil). Chennai: New Century Book House, 2008.

Sankaran, T. *Isai Methaikal* (The Great Musicians) (in Tamil). Madras: Tamil Isai Publications, 1962.

Sarma, R.B. *Pottukkattum Vazhakkam Ikkalaththirkup Poruthuma?* (Is the *pottu* ceremony relevant for this Age?) (in Tamil). Madras: C. Munisawmy Mudaliar and Sons, (n.d.).

Seenivachachari, V and S. Gopalan. *Bonsle Vamsa Charithram* (History of Bonsle Family) (in Tamil). Thanjavur: Saraswathi Mahal Library, 1980.

Sethupathi Virali Vitu Tutu (A Tutu Literature of Sethupathi). Sadhavathanam Saravanap Perumal Kavirayar. Karaikkudi: Ilakkiayap Pathippakam, 1947.

Sivathamby, K. *Thamizh Ilakkiyathil Madhamum Maanudamum* (Religion and Humanity in Tamil Literature) (in Tamil). Chennai: New Century Book House Pvt. Ltd, 1994.

——. *Pandai Thamizh Samugam* (Ancient Tamil Society) (in Tamil). Chennai: New Century Book House Pvt. Ltd, 2010 (Rpt. 2011).

——. *Ilakkiyamum Karuthunilayam* (Literature and Ideology) (in Tamil). Chennai: New Century Book House Pvt. Ltd, 2011.

Soundarapandian, S and Natana. Kasinathan. *Idangai Valangaiyar Varalaru* (History of Right Hand and Left Hand) (in Tamil). Madras: Government Oriental Manuscripts Library, 1995.

——. *Kongu Mandala Varalarukal* (Histories of Kongu Region) (in Tamil). Madras: Government Oriental Manuscripts Library, 1997.

Sundaram, B.M. *Marbu Thantha Manikkankal* (The Gifts of the Tradition) (in Tamil). Chennai: Dr. V. Raghavan Centre for Performing Arts, 2003.

Subramanian, P. *Thanjai Marattiya Mannar Modi Avanath Thamizhakkamum Kurippuraiyum*. Part. III. Thanjavur: Tamil University, 1989.

Swaminathaiyer, U.V. *Ninaivu Manjari* (in Tamil). Chennai: Mahamahopadyaya Dr. U.V. Swaminathaiyer Library, 1942. (Rpt. 1991).

——. *Thiruneelakanda Nayanar Sariththiramum Iyarpagai Nayanar Sariththiramum* (A History of Nilakantar and Iyarpakai Nayanmar) (in Tamil). Madras: Madras Law Journal, 1944.

——. *Puthiyathum Palayathum* (An Old and New) (in Tamil). Chennai: Kabir Accukoodam, 1947.

Swaminathan, A. *Tamilaka Varalarum Panpadum* (History and Culture of Tamil) (in Tamil). Chennai: Deepa Pathppakam, 1992.

Thaninayagam, Xavier S. *Thamizhar Panpaadum Adhan Sirappu Iyalbugalum* (Special Features of Tamil Culture) (in Tamil). Jaffna: Thanthai Chelva Memorial Trust, 1980.

Thanapandiyan, Thu.Na. *Isaith Thamizh Varalaru* (History of Tamil Music) (in Tamil). Part. 1. Thanjavur: Tamil University, 1994.

Thomas, Annie. *Tamilaka Makaliriyal* (Feminism of Tamil Women) (in Tamil). Chennai: International Intitute of Tamil Studies, 2002.

Vaanamaamalai, Naa. *Pazhangathaigalum Pazhamozhigalaum* (An Old Stories and Proverbs) (in Tamil). Chennai: New Century Book House Pvt. Ltd, 1980 (Rpt. 2008).

Vaanadaiyar, Sundaresa. Vai. *30 Kalvettukal* (Thirty Inscriptions) (in Tamil). Chennai: Palaniappa Brothers, 1958 (Rpt. 2009).

Valarmathi, M. *Moovaloor Ramirtham Ammaiyar* (in Tamil). Chennai: Paavai Publications, 2008.

Vellaivaranan, Ka. *Panniruthirumurai Varalaru* (The History of Twelve Tirumurai) (in Tamil). Vol. I. Annamalai Nagar: Annamalai University, Rpt. 1994.

——. *Panniruthirumurai Varalaru* (The History of Twelve Tirumurai) (in Tamil). Vol. II. Annamalai Nagar: Annamalai University, 1980 (Rpt. 1997).

Venkatachary, P. *Tiruppavai* (in Tamil). Madras: Prabandh, Shri Seva Bharati, 1996.

——. *History of the Maratha Rulers of Thanjavur* (in Tamil). Thanjavur: Tamil University.

Veeramani, Ki. *Asal Manudharuma Sasthiram* (An Original *Manusruthi*) (in Tamil). Chennai: Dravidar Kazhaka Veliyeedu, 2004 (Rpt. 2011).

Venkatasamy, Mayilai Seeni. *Pazhangaala Thamizhar Vaanigam* (Trade of Ancient Tamils) (in Tamil). Chennai: New Century Book House Pvt. Ltd, 1974 (Rpt. 2011).

——. *Samanamum Thamizhum* (*Jainism and Tamil*) (in Tamil). Chennai: Naam Tamizhar Pathippakam, 2003 (Rpt. 2013).

——. *Kalappirar Atchiyil Tamilakam* (Tamilakam under Kalabhras' Rule) (in Tamil). Chennai: Naam Tamizhar Pathippakam, 2006 (Rpt. 2011).

——. *Bavuththamum Thamizhum* (*Buddhism and Tamil*) (in Tamil). Chennai: Pavai Publication, 2007.

Malayalam books

Kumari, Sugantha. *Devadasi* (in Malayalam). Kottayam: D.C. Books, 1998.

Surendran, P. *Devadasitheruvukalilude* (Within the Streets of Devadasi) (in Malayalam). Thrissur: Green Books, 2005 (Rpt. 2007).

English books

Agnihotri, Vidyadhar. *Fallen Women: A Study with Special Reference to Kanpur*. Kanpur: Maharaja Printers, 1954.

Altekar, A.S. *The Position of Women in Hindu Civilisation*. Delhi: Motilal Banarsidass, 1959 (Rpt. 1983).

Aiyangar, Srinivasa. *Tamil Studies*. New Delhi: Asian Educational Services, 1986.

Aloysius, G. *The Brahmanical Inscribed in Body*-Politic. New Delhi: Critical Quest, 2010.

Appadurai, Arjun. *Worship and Conflict under Colonial Rule*. New Delhi: Orient Longman, 1981.

Appadorai, A. *Economic Conditions in Southern India (1000-1500 A.D.)*. Vol. II and Vol. II. Madras: University of Madras, 1936 (Rpt. 1990).

Balasubramnaiam, C. *Status of Women in Tamilnadu during the Sangam Age*. Madras: Narumalarp Patippakam, 1992.

Balasubramaniam, S.R. *Early Chola Art*. Bombay: Asia Publishing House, 1966.

——. *Early Chola Temples*. Bombay: Orient Longman, 1971.

——. *Middle Chola Temples: Rajaraja I to Kulottunga I (AD 985- 1070)*. Faridabad: Thomsan Press (India) Limited, 1975.

Ballhatchet, Kenneth. *Race, Sex and Class under the Raj*. New Delhi: Vikas Publishing House Pvt Ltd, 1979.

Basham, A.L. *The Wonder That Was India*. New Delhi: Rupa & Co, 1954 (Rpt. 2002).

Bharathi, Srirama. *The Sacred Book of Four Thousand*. Chennai: Sri Sadagopan Tirunarayanaswami Divya Prabandha Pathassala, 2000.

Bhattacharya, N.N. *Indian Religious Historiography*. New Delhi: Munshiram Manoharlal Publishers, 1996.

Bhattacharyya, Kalidas. *Possibility of Different Types of Religion*. Kolkata: The Asiatic Society, 1975 (Rep. 2007).

Cranenburgh, D.E. *The Indian Penal Code Being Act XLV. of 1860 Annotated with Rulings of the High Courts in India up to July 1894*. Calcutta: Law-Publishing Press, 1894.

Chakravarti, Uma. *Shadow Lives Writings on Widowhood*. New Delhi: Kali for Women, 2001.

——. *Gendering Caste: Through A Feminist Lens*. Calcutta: Stree, 2003.

——. *Everyday Lives, Everyday Histories: Beyond the Kings and Brahmanas of 'Ancient' India*. New Delhi: Tulika Books, 2006.

Champakalakshmi, R. *Vaishnava Iconography in the Country*. New Delhi: Orient Longman Limited, 1981.

——. and S. Gopal. *Trade, Ideology and Urbanisation, South India 300 B.C. to 1300 A.D.* Delhi: Oxford University Press, 1996.

——. Kesavan Veluthat and T.R. Venugopalan. Ed. *State and Society in Pre-Modern South India*. Thrissur: Cosmo Books, 2002.

——. *Religion, Tradition and Ideology: Pre-Colonial South India*. New Delhi: Oxford University Press, 2011.

Chandra, Satish. *Historiography, Religion and State in Medieval India*. New Delhi: Har-Anand Publications Pvt. Ltd, 1996 (Rpt. 2012).

Chandrasekharan Nair, K. *Devadasi Tradition in Kerala*. Trivandrum: Kerala Historical Society, 1987.

Chatterjee, Partha. *The Nation and its Fragments: Colonial and Postcolonial Histories*. Oxford: Oxford University Press, 1993.

Chatterjee, Santhosh. *Devadasi (Temple Dancer)*. Calcutta: The Book House, 1945.

Chattopadhayaya, B.D. *The Making of Early Medieval India*. Delhi: Oxford University Press, 1997.

Chattopadhyaya, Sudhakar. *Some Early Dynasties of South India*. Delhi: Motilal Banarsidass Publication, 1974.

Chidamparanar. *Akattiyar Varalaru (Story of Agastya)*. Madras: South India Saiva Siddhanta Publishing Works, 1964.

Chintamani C. Yajnesvara. Ed. *Indian Social Reform*. Madras: Thompson and Co, 1901.

Clayton, Martin and Bennett Zon. *Music and Orientalism in the British Empire, 1780s-1940s: Portrayal of the East*. Hampshire: Ashgate Publishing Ltd, 2007.

Comaraswamy, Ananda. *Dance of Shiva*. New Delhi: Manmohar, 1982.

Craddock, Elaine. *Siva's Demon Devotee: Karaikkal Ammaiyar*. Albany: SUNY Press, 2010.

Cutler, Norman. *Songs of Experience: The Poetics of Tamil Devotion*. Bloomington: Indiana University Press, 1987.

Dalrymple, William. *White Mughals: Love and Betrayal in Eighteenth Century India*. New Delhi: Viking, 2002.

Dayalan, D. *Early Temples of Tamilnadu*. Delhi: Harman Publishing House, 1992.

de Zoete, Beryl. *Dance and Magic Drama in Ceylon*. London: Faber and Faber Limited, 1957.

Dehejia, Vidya. *Slaves of the Lord the Path of the Tamil Saints*. Delhi: Munshiram Manoharlal Publishers, 1988.

Deshmukh, Durgabai. *Chintaman and I*. Delhi: Allied Publishers, 1980.

Deva, Krishna. *Temples of North India*. New Delhi: National Book Trust, 1969 (Rpt. 2008).

Dirks, Nicholas B. *The Hollow Crown: Ethnohistory of an Indian Kingdom*. Cambridge: Cambridge University Press, 1987.

Dikshithar, Ramachandra. V.R. *Studies in Tamil Literature and History*. Madras: University of Madras, 1936.

Dorai Rangaswamy, M.A. *Religion and Philosophy of Tevaram: with Special Reference to Nambi Arurar*. Madras: University of Madras, 1958-1959.

Durai Ramaswami, M.A. and R.P. Sethu Pillai. *Selected Tamil Inscription*. Madras: Madras University Press, 1952.

Elliot, H.M. and John Dowson. *The History of India as told by its own Historians: The Muhammadan Period*. Vol. III. London: Trubner and Co, 1871.

——. *History of India as told by its own Historians*. Vol. IV. Allahabad: Kitab Malah Pvt. Ltd, 1964.

Farquhar, J.N. *Modern Religious Movements in India*. New Delhi: Munshiram Manoharlal, 1914 (Rpt. 1967).

Forbes, Geraldine. *The Cambridge History of India: Women in India*. Vol. IV. Cambridge: Cambridge University Press, 1996 (Rpt. 2004).

Frazer, James George. *The Golden Bough: A Study of Magic and Religion*. London and Basingstoke: Macmillan Press, 1922 (Rpt. 1983).

Fuller, C.J. *Servants of the Goddess: The Priests of a South Indian Temple*. Cambridge: Cambridge University Press, 1984.

Gandhi, Gopalakrishna. *Of a Certain Age: Twenty Life Sketches*. New Delhi: Viking, 2011.

Gangadhar, V. *M.S. Subbulakshmi: The Voice Divine*. New Delhi: Rupa and Co, 2002.

Geetha, V and S.V. Rajadurai. *Towards a Non-Brahmin Millennium: From Iyothee Thass to Periyar*. Calcutta: Samya, 1998.

——. *Gender*. Kolkata: Stree, 2002 (Rrt. 2006).

——. and S.V. Rajadurai. *Revolt: A Radical Weekly from Colonial Madras*. Chennai: Periyar Dravidar Kazhagam, (n.d.).

George, T.J.S. *MS: A Life in Music*. New Delhi: Harper Collins Publishers, 2007 (Rpt. 2010).

Gopalakrishnan, R. *Religion and Mysticism in the Periya Puranam*. Madras: University of Madras, 1990.

Gopalan, R and S, Krishnaswamy Aiyangar. Ed. *History of the Pallavas of Kanchi*. Madras: University of Madras, 1928.

Gurukkal, Rajan. *Social Formations of Early South India*. Delhi: Oxford University Press, 2010.

Hardy, Friedhelm. *Viraha Bhakti: - The Early History of Krsna Devotion in South India*. Delhi: Oxford University Press, 1983.

Heitzman, James. *Gifts of Power: Lordship in an Early Modern State*. Delhi: Oxford University Press, 1997.

Higgins, B. Jons. *The Music of Bharatha Natyam*. New Delhi: Oxford and IBH Publishing Co. Pvt. Ltd.

Irschick, Eugene F. *Politics and Social Conflict in South India: The Non-Brahman Movement and Tamil Separatism, 1916-1929*. California: University of California Press, 1969.

——. *Tamil Revivalism in the 1930's*. Madras: Cre-A, 1986.

——. *Dialogue and History: Constructing South India, 1794- 1895*. Delhi: Oxford University Press, 1994.

Iyengar, Srinivasa, P.T. *History of Tamils, From the Earliest Times to 600 AD*. New Delhi: Asian Educational Services, 1983.

Jackson, William J. *Tyagaraja and the Renewal of Tradition: Translations and Reflections*. Delhi: Motilal Banarsidass Publishers Private Limited, 1994.

Jamanadas, K. *Devadasis: Ancient to Modern*. Delhi: Kalpaz Publications, 2007.

Jensen, Herman. Rev. *A Classified Collection of Tamil Proverbs*. New Delhi: Asian Educational Services, 1897 (Rpt. 1986).

Jha, D.N. Ed. *Feudal Social Formation in Early India*. Delhi: Chanakya Publications, 1987.

——. *Economy and Society in Early India*. New Delhi: Munshiram Manoharlal Publishers, 1993.

Joardar, Biswanath. *Prostitution in Nineteenth and Early Twentieth Century Calcutta*. New Delhi: Inter-India Publications, 1985.

Jordan, Kay. K. *From Sacred Servants to Profane Prostitute: A History of the Changing Legal Status of the Devadasis in India, 1857-1947*. New Delhi: Manohar, 2003.

Kanakasabhai, V. *The Tamils Eighteen Hundred Years Ago*. New Delhi: Asian Educational Services, 1904 (Rpt. 1979).

Kannabiran, Kalpana and Vasanth Kannabiran. *Muvalur Ramamirthammal's Web of Deceit: Devadasi Reform in Colonial India*. New Delhi: Kali for Women, 2003.

Kailasapathy, K. *Tamil Heroic Poetry*. Oxford: Clarendon Press, 1968.

Kalarani, R. *Bharatanatyam in Tamilnadu (After A.D. 1200)*. Madurai: J.J. Publications, 2004.

Kanakasabhai, V. *The Tamils Eighteen Hundred Years Ago*. New Delhi: Asian Educational Services, 1904.

Karashima, Noboru. *South Indian History and Society: A Study from Inscription A.D. 850-1800*. Delhi: Oxford University Press, 1984.

——. Ed. *Kingship in Indian History*. New Delhi: Manohar Publishers and Distributors, 1999.

Kersenboom, Saskia C. *Nityasumangali*. Delhi: Motilal Banarsidas, 1987.

Ketkar, S.V. *History of Caste in India*. Delhi: Low Price Publications, 1909 (Rpt. 2010).

Khakar, Mohan. *Bharatha Natya Vidwan Muthukumara Pillai*. New Delhi: Sangeet Natak Academi, 1964.

Kinnear, Michael S. *The Gramophone Company's First Indian Recordings, 1899-1908*. Bombay: Popular Prakashan Pvt. Ltd, 1994.

Knight Jr, Douglas M. *Balasaraswathi: Her Art and Life*. Chennai: Tranquebar Press, 2010.

Kosambi, D.D. *The Culture and Civilisation of Ancient India*. London: Rutledge and Kegan Paul, 1965.

Krishnamurthi, S.R. *A Study on the Cultural Developments in the Chola Period*. Annamalai Nagar: Annamalai University, 1966.

Krishnamurthi Putali, N. *The Changing Conditions of Women in Andhra from the Middle of Nineteenth Century to the Middle of Twentieth Century*. Hyderabad: Navyug Publishers, 1987.

Krishnaswami, A. *The Tamil Country under Vijayanagar*. Annamalai Nagar: Annamalai University, 1964.

Krishnaswami Ayyangar, S. Ed. *Sources of the Vijayanagar History*. Madras: University of Madras, 1919.

——. *Early History of Vaishnavism in South India*. London: The Oxford University Press, 1920.

——. *South India and Her Muhammadan Invaders*. London: Oxford University Press, 1921.

——. *Some Contributions of South India to Indian Culture*. Calcutta: Bhupendralal Banerjee, 1923 (Rpt. 1942).

Kumari, Krishna M. *Studies in Medieval Andhra History and Culture*. New Delhi: Kanishka Publishers, 1994.

Kunjanpallai, Elamkulam. P.N. *Studies in Kerala History*. Trivandrum, 1970.

Lakshmi, C.S. *Face behind the Mask: Women in Tamil Literature*. New Delhi: Vikas Publishing House, 1984.

Lal, Vinay. *South Asian Cultural Studies: A Bibliography*. Delhi: Monohar Publishers, 1996.

Lerner, Gerda. *The Creation of Patriarchy*. Oxford University Press: New York, 1986.

Lewinsohn, Richard. *A History of Sexual Customs*. New York: Harper & Brothers, 1958.

Mahalingam, T.V. *South Indian Polity*. Madras: University of Madras, 1955.

——. *Kancipuram in Early South Indian History*. Bombay: Asia Publishing House, 1969.

Marglin, Frederique Apffel. *Wives of the God- King: The Rituals of the Devadasis of Puri*. Delhi: Oxford University Press, 1985.

Maureen Petterson, L.P. *South Asian Civilisation: A Bibliographic Synthesis*. Chicago: Chicago University Press, 1981.

Mayo, Katherine. *Mother India*. London: Allied Publishers, 1927 (Rpt. 1945).

Mehra, Parshotam, *A Dictionary of Modern Indian History 1707-1947*. Delhi: Oxford University Press, 1958 (Rpt. 1987).

Morgan, Sue. Ed. *The Feminist History Reader*. London: Routledge, 2006.

Mulchandani, Sandhya. Tr. *The Appeasement of Radhika: Radhika Santawanam*. New Delhi: Penguin Books, 2011.

Murthy, R.S and S, Nagarajan. Ed. *Buddhism in Tamilnadu*. Chennai: Institute of Asian Studies, 1998.

Minakshi, C. *Administration and Social Life under the Pallavas*. Madras: University of Madras, 1977.

Nagaswamy, R. *Studies in Ancient Tamil Law and Society*. Madras: The Institute of Epigraphy and Tamilnadu State Department of Archaeology, 1978.

Nair, Janaki. *Women and Law in Colonial India: A Social History*. New Delhi: Kali for Women, 1996.

Nagaswamy, R. *Art and Culture of Tamilnadu*. Delhi: Sundeep Prakashan, 1980.

Narayana Ayyar, C.V. *Origin and Early History of Saivism in South India*. Madras; University of Madras, 1974.

Narayana Rao, Velcheru; David Shulman and Sanjay Subrahmanyam. *Symbols of Substance: Court and State in Nayaka Period Tamilnadu*. Delhi: Oxford University Press, 1992.

Orr, Leslie C. *Donors, Devotees and Daughters of God: Temple Women in Medieval Tamilnadu*. Oxford: Oxford University Press, 2000.

Pande, Rekha. *Religious Movements in Medieval India*. New Delhi: Gyan Publishing House, 2005.

Pande, Susmita. *Birth of Bhakti in Indian Religions and Art*. Delhi: Books and Books Co, 1990.

Panikkar, K.N. *Culture, Ideology, Hegemony: Intellectuals and Social Consciousness in Colonial India*. Madras: Tulia, 1995.

Panjrath, Shashi and O.P. Ralhan. *Devadasi System in India*. Faridabad: Om Publications, 2000.

Paramacivanatam, A.M. *The Historical Study of the Tevaram Hymns*. Chennai: Tamilkalai Publishing House, 1982.

Parameswaran Pillai, V.R. *Temple Culture of South India*. New Delhi: Inter-India Publications, 1986.

Parabrahma Sastry, P.V. *The Kakatiyas of Warangal*. Hyderabad: Government of Andhra Pradesh, 1978.

Percival, Spear *The Nabobs*. London: Curzon Press, 1932 (Rpt. 1980).

Perumal, R. *Periyar: A Comparative Study*. Chennai: Periyar Self- Respect Propaganda Institution, 1999.

Peterson, Indira Viswanathan. *Poems to Siva: the Hymns of Tamil Saints.* Delhi: Motilal Banarsidass, 1989.

——. and Davesh Soneji. *Performing Pasts: Reinventing the Arts in Modern South India*. New Delhi: Oxford University Press, 2008.

Pillai, K.K. *The Sucindram Temple*. Madras: Kalashetra Publications, 1953.

Price, Pamela G. *Kingship and Political Practice in Colonial India*. Cambridge: Cambridge University Press, 1996.

Raghavan, M.D. *India in Ceylonese History, Society and Culture*. Bombay: Asia Publishing House, 1964.

Raghavan, V. *The Great Integrators: - The Saint Singers of South India*. Delhi: Ministry of Information and Broadcasting, 1966.

——. *Splendours of Indian Dance*. Chennai: Dr. V. Raghavan Centre for Performing Arts, 2004.

Rai, Lajpat. *Unhappy India*. Calcutta: Banna Publishing Co, 1928.

Raju, Se. *Inscriptions of the Marathas of Thanjavur*. Thanjavur: Tamil University, 1987.

Ramachandram, M. *The Devadasi*. Conjeeveram: S.K.B. Press, 1900.

Ramachendrier, C. *Collection of the Decisions of the High Courts and the Privy Council on the Law of Succession, Maintenance and C (Applicable to Dancing Girls and their issues, Prostitutes not belonging to Dancing Girls' Community, Illegitimate Sons and Bastards and Illatom Affiliation up to December 1891.)*. Madras: Scottish Press, 1892.

——. *The Law of Limitation in India*. Madras: Vest and Company, 1887.

Ramanujan, A.K. *Speaking of Siva*. Battimore: Penguin, 1973.

——. *Hymns for the Drowning: Poems for Vishnu by Nammalvar*. Princeton: Princeton University Press, 1981.

——. Velcheru Narayana Rao and David Shulman. Ed and Tr. *When God is a Customer*. Delhi: Oxford University Press, 1995.

Ramaswamy, Vijaya. *Divinity and Deviance: Women in Virasaivism*. Delhi: Oxford University Press, 1996.

——. *Walking Naked Women, Society, Spirituality in South India*. Shimla: Indian Institute of Advanced Studies, 1997.

Raychauduri, Tapan and Irfan Habib. Ed. *Cambridge Economic History of India,* Volume 1: c 1200 AD-c 1750 AD. Hyderabad: Orient Longman, 1982.

Ray, Bharathi. Ed. *Women of India: Colonial and Post-Colonial Periods*. New Delhi: Sage Publications, 2005.

Reddy, Soma. *History of Religious Institutions in Andhra Desa (1300-1600 AD)*. Madras: New Era Publications, 1984.

Roberts, Brian. *Biographical Research*. Buckingham: Open University Press, 2002.

Roy, Kumkum. *The Power of Gender and the Gender of Power Explorations in Early Indian History*. New Delhi: Oxford University Press, 2010.

Sadasivan, K. *Devadasi System in Medieval Tamilakam*. Trivandrum: CBH Publications, 1993.

Salatore, B.A. *Social and Political Life in Vijayanagar Empire*. Vol. II. Madras, 1934.

Sambamurthy, P. *South Indian Music*. Madras: The Indian Music Publishing House, 1982.

Sangari, Kumkum and Sudesh Vaid. Ed. *Women and Culture*. Bombay: SNDT Women's University, 1985.

——. and Sudesh Vaid. Ed. *Recasting Women: Essays in Colonial History*. New Delhi: Kali for Women, 1989 (Rpt. 2010).

——. *Politics of the Possible Essays on Gender, History, Narratives, Colonial English*. New Delhi: Tulika, 1999.

——. and Uma Chakravarti. Ed. *From Myths to Markets: Essays on Gender*. Shimla: Indian Institute of Advanced Study, 2001.

Sastri, K.A.N. *Foreign Notices of South India: From Megasthenenes to Mahuan*. Chennai: University of Madras, 1931 (Rpt. 2001).

——. *The Colas*. Madras: University of Madras, 1955 (Rpt. 2000).

——. *Development of Religion in South India*. Bombay: Orient Longmans, 1963.

——. *The Culture and History of the Tamils*. Calcutta: Firma K.L. Mukhopadhyay, 1964.

——. *The Pandyan Kingdom*. Madras: Swati Publications, 1972.

——. *Aspects of India's History and Culture*. The Indian Archaeological Society. Delhi: Oriental Publishers, 1990.

——. *A History of South India*. New Delhi: Oxford University Press, 2000.

Satyanarayana, K.A. *Study in the History and Culture of the Andhras*. Vol. II. *Consolidation of Feudalism*, Peoples Publishing House, 1983.

Seetha, S. *Tanjore as a Seat of Music*. Madras: University of Madras, 2001.

Sewell, Robert. *A Forgotten Empire- Vijaynagara: A Contribution to the History of India*. New Delhi: Asia Educational Services, 1901 (Rpt. 1985).

Shah, Kirit K. *History and Gender: Some Explorations*. Jaipur: Rawat Publications, 2005.

Sharma, R.S. Ed. *Indian Society: Historical Probings*. New Delhi: Peoples' Publishing House, 1974.

Sharma, Krishna. *Bhakti and the Bhakti Movement, A New Perspective: A Study in the History of Ideas*. New Delhi: Munshiram Manoharlal, 1987.

Sharma, M.J. and P. Venkateshan. *Studies in Indian Place Names*. Mysore: Geetha Book House, 1986.

Sharma, R.S. *Early Medieval Indian Society: A Study of Feudalisation*. Kolkata: Orient Blackswan Pvt Ltd, 2001 (Rpt. 2007).

Shankar, Jogan. *Devadasi Cult: A Sociological Analysis*. New Delhi: Ashish Publishing House, 1990 (Rpt. 1994).

Singer, Milton. *When a Great Tradition Modernizes: An Anthropological Approach to Indian Civilisation*. London: Praeger, 1972.

Singh, A.K. *Devadasis System in Ancient India*. Delhi: H.K. Publishers and Distributors, 1990.

Singh, K.S. *Place Names and Personal Name: An Anthropo-Historical Perspective*. Mysore: Place Name Society of India, 1986.

Singh, Nagendra Kr. *Divine Prostitution*. New Delhi: A.P.H. Publishing Corporation, 1997.

Sivathamby, K. *Drama in Ancient Tamil Society*. Madras: New Century Book House, 1981.

——. *Literary History in Tamil*. Thanjavur: Tamil University, 1986.

Shulman, David Dean. *Tamil Temple Myths: Sacrifices and Divine Marriage in South Indian Saiva Tradition*. Princeton: Princeton University Press, 1980.

Smith, Sidonie and Julia Watson. Eds. *De-colonising the Subject: The Politics of Gender in Women's Autobiography*. Minneapolis: The University of Minnesota Press, 1992.

Smith, V.A. *The Oxford History of India*. Delhi: Oxford University Press, 1958.

Soneji, Davesh. Ed. *Bharathanatyam: A Reader*. New Delhi: Oxford University Press, 2010.

——. *Unfinished Gestures: Devadasis, Memory and Modernity in South India*. Chicago: The University of Chicago Press, 2012.

Somasundaram Pillai, J.M. *The Great Temple at Tanjore*. Thanjavur: Tamil University, 1994.

Soundara Rajan. K.V. *The Art of South India: Tamilnadu and Kerala*. Delhi: Sundeep Prakashan, 1978.

Sreedharan, E. *A Textbook of the Historiography 500 BC to AD 2000*. New Delhi: Orient Longman, 2004.

Sreedhara Menon, A. *Cultural heritage of Kerala*. Kottayam: D.C. Books, 1978 (Rpt. 2008).

Srilatha, K. *The Other Half of the Coconut: Women Writing Self-Respect Moment*. New Delhi: Kali for Women, 2003.

Srinivasa Aiyangar, M. *Tamil Studies*. New Delhi: Asian Educational Services, 1986.

Srinivasa Iyengar, P.T. *History of Tamils From the Earliest Times to 600 AD*. New Delhi: Asian Educational Services, 1983.

Srinivasan, C.R. *Kanchipuram Through Ages*. Delhi: Agam Kala Parakashan, 1979.

Srinivasan, K.R. *Temples of South India*. New Delhi: National Book Trust, 1972 (Rpt. 2008).

Sriram, V. *The Devadasi and the Saint: The Life and Times of Bangalore Nagarathnamma*. Chennai: EastWest Books (Madras) Pvt. Ltd, 2007.

Stein, Burton. Ed. *South Indian Temples: An Analytical Reconsideration*. Delhi: Vikas Publishing House, 1978.

——. *All the Kings' Mana: Papers on Medieval South Indian History*. Madras: New Era Publications, 1984.

——. *Peasant State and Society in Medieval South India*. Oxford: Oxford University Press, 1985.

——. and S, Subramaniam. *Institutions and Economic Change in South Asia*. Delhi: Oxford University Press, 1985.

Stokes, Whitley. Ed. *The Anglo-Indian Codes*. Vol. I. Oxford: The Clarendon Press, 1887.

——. Ed. *The Anglo-Indian Codes*. Vol. II. Oxford: The Clarendon Press, 1888.

Subbarayalu, Y. *South India under the Cholas*. New Delhi: Oxford University Press, 2012 (Rpt. 2013).

Subramanian, K.R. *Origin of Saivism and its History in the Tamil Land*. New Delhi: Asian Educational Services, 1985.

Subramanian, Lakshmi. *From the Tanjore Court to the Madras Music Academy: A Social History of Music in South India*. New Delhi: Oxford University Press, 2006.

——. *New Mansion for Music Performance, Pedagogy and Criticism*. New Delhi: Esha Beteillie, 2008.

——. *Veena Dhanamma: The Making of a Legend*. New Delhi: Routledge, 2009.

Subrahmanian, N. *Sangam Polity*. Bombay: Asia Publishing House, 1966.

——. *History of Tamilnad*. Madurai: Koodal Publishers, 1978.

——. *The Brahmin in the Tamil Country*. Udumalpet: Ennes Publications, 1989.

——. and Theyagarajan. Ed. *Tamil Social History*. Chennai: Institute of Asian Studies, 1997.

Subramanian, P. *Social History of Tamils*. Delhi: D.K. Print World, 1999.

Subrahmanyam, Padma. *Epic Stories from Natya Sastra*. Chennai: Vanathi Pathippakam, 2004.

Sundararajan, S. *Ancient Tamil Country, Its Social and Economic Structure*. New Delhi: Navrang Booksellers and Publishers, 1991.

Sundaram, K. *Studies in Social and Economic Conditions in Medieval Andhra Desa (1000-1500 AD)*. Warangal, 1968.

Surya Narayana Murthy, J. *Devadasis and Bharatha Natyam in Tamilnadu*. Chennai: Ulaga Thamizhar Pathippakam, 2005.

Swaminathan, S. *The Early Cholas History, Art and Culture*. Delhi: Sharada Publicating House, 1998.

Tarachand, K.C. *Devadasi Custom: Rural Social Structure and Flesh Markets*. New Delhi: Reliance Publishing House, 1991.

Thakur, Pradeep. Comp and Ed. *Indian Music Masters of Our Times- I*. Ludhiana: Pradeep Thakure and Sons, 2010.

Thaninayagam, X.S. *Landscape and Poetry*. London: Asia Publishing House, 1966.

——. *History and Beyond*. New Delhi: Oxford University Press, 2000 (Rpt. 2013).

——. *The Penguin History of Early India from the Origins to A.D. 1300*. London: Penguin Books, 2003.

——. *Imagined Religious Communities?*. New Delhi: Critical Quest, 2007.

——; Jonathan Mark Kenoyer; Madhav M. Deshpande and Shereen Ratnagar. *India: Historical Beginnings and the Concept of the Aryan*. New Delhi: National Book Trust, 2006 (Rpt. 2010).

Tharu, Susie J. and K. *Lalita*. Ed. *Women Writing in India 600 B.C. to the Early Twentieth Century*. Delhi: Oxford University Press, 1993.

Thiruchandran, Selvi. *Tamil Varalarrup Padimangal Silavarril Oru Pennilai Nokku*. (*Some of the Tamil Historical Images: A Feminist Perspective*). Chennai: Kumaran Book House, 1997.

——. *Ideology, Caste, Class and Gender*. Homagama: Karunaratne and Sons Ltd, 1997 (Rpt. 2006).

——. *The Spectrum of Femininity: A Process of Deconstruction*. New Delhi: Vikas Publishing House Pvt Ltd, 1998.

——. *Women's Writings: Subjectivities and Historicism*. Colombo: Awerc Publication, 2001.

Thirumali, Inukonda. Ed. *South India: Regions, Cultures and Sages*. New Delhi: Bibliomatrix Publication, 2004.

——. *Marriage, Love and Caste: Perceptions on Telugu Women during the Colonial Period*. New Delhi: Promilla and Co., Publishers, 2005.

Thirunavukkarasu, K.D. *Chieftains of the Sangam Age*. Madras: International Institute of Tamil Studies, 1994.

Thurston, Edgar and K, Rangachari. *Castes and Tribes of Southern India*. Vol. II. Madras: Government Press, 1909.

Trevelyan, Ernest John. *Hindu Family Law: An Administered in British India*. London: W. Thacker and Company, 1908.

Van Doren B. Alice. *Lighted to Lighten: The Hope of India*. Massachusetts. The Central Committee on The United Study of Foreign Missions, 1922.

Varadachari, K.C. *Alvars of South India*. Bombay: Bharatiya Vidya Bhavan, 1966 (Rpt. 1970).

Varadachari, V. *Agamas and South Indian Vaisnavism*. Madras: Prof. M. Rangacharya Memorial Trust, 1982.

Vatsyanan, Kapila. *The Indian Classical Dance*. New Delhi: Ministry of Information and Broadcasting, 1974 (Rpt. 1997).

Venkatramaiah, K.M. *Administration and Social Life under the Maratha Rulers of Thanjavur* (in Tamil). Thanjavur: Tamil University, 1984.

Veluthat, Kesavan. *The Political Structure of Early Medieval South India*. New Delhi: Orient Longman, 1993.

——. *The 'Early Medieval' in South India*. New Delhi: Oxford University Press, 2009.

Vijaisri, Priyadarshini. *Recasting the Devadasi: Patterns of Sacred Prostitution in Colonial South India*. New Delhi: Kanishka Publishers, Distributors, 2004.

Viraraghavacharya, T.K.T. *History of Tirupati: The Thiruvengadam Temple*. Vol. II. Tirupati: Tirumala Tirupati Devasthanams, 1954.

Viswanathan, Lakshmi. *Women of Pride: The Devadasi Heritage*. New Delhi: Roli Books, 2008.

Waheed Khan, Abdul. *A Monograph on Yalesvaram Excavation*. Hyderabad, 1963.

Washbrook, D.A. *The Emergence of Provincial Politics: The Madras Presidency, 1870-1920*. New Delhi: Vikas Publishing House Pvt Ltd, 1977.

Weidman, Amanda J. *Singing the Classical Voicing the Modern: The Postcolonial Politics of Music in South India*. Calcutta: Seagull, 2006 (Rpt. 2007).

Wheeler, Talboys J. *Early Records of British India: A History of the English Settlements in India*. Calcutta: W, Newman & Co, 1878.

Williams, Monier M. *Religious Thought and Life in India: An Account of the Religious of the Indian Peoples, Based on a Life's Study of their*

Literature and on Personal Investigations in their Own Country. Part. I. London: John Murray, 1885.

Wilson, H.H. *A Glossary of the Judicial and Revenue Terms: And of the Useful Words Occurring in Official Documents Relating to the Administration of the Government of British India*. London: W.H. Allen and Co, 1855.

Yande, D.S. *Dedication of Girls to Gods: Plea for Prohibition by Law by Naik-Maratha Mandal*. Bombay: V.P. Vengurlekar, (n.d.).

Zvelebil, V. Kamil. *The Smile of Murukan, on Tamil Literature of South India*. Leiden: E.J. Brill, 1973.

Chapters in Books

Aloysius, G. "Caste in and Above History." In S.L. Sharma and T.K. Oomen. Ed. *Nation and National Identity in South Asia*. Hyderabad: Oriental Longman, 2000.

Champakalakshmi, R. "From Devotion and Dissent to Dominance The Bhakti of the Tamil Alvars and Nayanars." In David N. Lorenzen. Ed. *Religious Movements in South Asia*, New Delhi: Oxford University Press, 2005: 52.

Devi, Rukmini. "The Indian Dance." In George S. Arundale. Comp. Principles of Education. Adyar: Theosophical Publishing House, 1926.

Jeevanandam, S. "The Sacred Geography of Medieval Tamilakam-A Study of Distribution Pattern of Saiva and Vaishnava Temples." In Birendra Nath Prasad. Ed. *Monasteries, Shrines and Society: Buddhist and Brahmanical Religious Institutions in India in Their Socio-Economic Context*. New Delhi: Manak Publications, 2011: 242-252.

Mahalingam, T.V. "Inscription in Tamilnadu." In J.P. De Souza and C.M. Kulkarni. Ed. *Historiography in Indian Languages*. Delhi: Oriental Publishers, 1972.

Ogura, Yasushi. "The Changing Concept of Kingship in the Cola Period: Royal Temple Constructions." In Noboru Karashima. Ed. *Kingship in Indian History*. New Delhi: Manohar Publishers and Distributors, 1999.

Narayanan, M.G.S and Kesavan Veluthat. "Bhakti Movement in South India." In D.N. Jha. Ed. *Feudal Social Formation in Early India*. Delhi: Chanakya Publications, 1987: 348-375.

Orr, Leslie. C. "Domesticity and Difference/ Women and Men: Religious Life in Medieval Tamilnadu." In Tracy Pintchman. Ed. *Women's Lives, Women's Rituals in the Hindu Tradition*. New York: Oxford University Press, 2007: 120.

Raghavan, V. "Methods of Popular Religious Instruction in South India." In Haridas Bhattacharyya. Ed. *The Cultural Heritage of India* IV. Calcutta: R.K.M. Institute of Culture, 1956: 503-514.

Srinivasan, Amrit. "Reform or Continuity?: Temple 'Prostitution' and the Community in the Madras Presidency." In Bina Agarwal. Ed. *Structures of Patriarchy: State, Community and Household in Modernizing Asia*. New Delhi: Kali for Women, 1988. (Rpt. 1991): 175-198.

Sarkar, Sumit. "The Women's Question in Nineteenth Century Bengal." In Kumkum Sangari and Sudesh Vaid. Ed. *Women and Culture*. Bombay: SNDT Women's University, 1985: 157-172.

Spivak, Gayatri Chakravorty. "Can the Subaltern Speak?" In Cary Nelson and Larry Grossberg, Eds. *Marxism and the interpretation of Culture*. Chicago: University of Illinois Press, 1988: 271-313.

Stein, Burton. "Integration of the Agrarian System of South India." In Robert Eric Frykenberg. Ed. *Land Control and Social Structure in Indian History*. Madison: University of Wisconsin Press, 1969: 175-216.

——. "The Segmentary State: Interim Reflections." In Hermann Kulke. Ed. *The State in India 1000-1700*. Delhi: Oxford University Press, 1995: 134-161.

Tulasiraman, T. "Palaiyarai-Akalvayvu." In Nadana Kasinathan. Ed. *Arunmoli*. Madras: Tamil Nadu State Department Archaeology, 1988: 242-248.

Yadava, B.N.S. "Problem of the Interaction between Socio-Economic Classes in the Early Medieval Complex." In D.N. Jha. Ed. *Feudal Social Formation in Early India*. Delhi: Chanakya Publication, 1987: 198-219.

Articles

Acharya, Arun Kumar. "Impact of Cultural and Religious Practices of Prostitution on the Trafficking of women in India." *Trayectorias* 14, Issue. 33/34. (July, 2011-June, 2012.): 95-114.

Anandhi, S. "Representing Devadasis: 'Dasigal Mosavalai' as a Radical Text." *Economic and Political Weekly* 26, no. 11/12. (March, 1991): 739-741+743+745-746.

Anandhi S. Bharadwaj. "Women's Question in the Dravidian Movement c. 1925-1948." *Social Scientist* 19, no. 5/6. (May-Jun, 1991). 24-41.

Ali, Daud. "Reviewed work: Donors, Devotees, and Daughters of God: Temple Women in Medieval Tamilnadu by Leslie C. Orr." *The English Historical Review* 116, no. 467. (June, 2001.): 708-709.

Alyev, Leonid. "The System of Land-Rights in Southern India (900-1300 A.D.)." *Proceedings of the International Conference- Seminar of Tamil Studies*. International Association of Tamil Research. Madras. (1981): 15-24.

——. "To the Problem of Tamil Traditional Administrative System (10th centuries-13th centuries AD)." *Presented at the International Conference of Tamil Studies*. (1995).

Aravamuthan, T.G. "The Oldest Account of the Tamil Academies." *Journal of Oriental Research* 4. (1930):183-201 and 289-317.

Arudra. "The Transfiguration of a Traditional Dance." *Sruti*. Issue. 27/28. (December, 1986-January, 1987): 17-21.

Balambal, V. "Great Women of Chola Dynasty." *Journal of Tamil Studies*. (December, 1976): 71-88.

"Balasaraswati's Repotoire." *Journal of the Sangeet Natak Academi* 72-73. (April-September, 1984): 69-75.

Balasubrahmanyam, G.N. "Thirty Second Conference Presidential Address of Vidwan G.N. Blasubrahmanyam." *The Journal of the Music Academy*. (1958).

Black, M. "Women in Ritual Slavery: Devadasi, Jogini and Mathamma in Karnataka and Andhra Pradesh, Southern India." *Pakistan Journal of Women's Studies* 16, no. 1/2. (June, 2009): 179-205.

Boris, Eileen. "Politicizing Women's History, Engendering Policy History." *Journal of Policy History* 21, No. 4. (2009): 431-438.

Branfoot, Crispin. "Approaching the Temple in Nayaka-Period Madurai: The Kutal Alakar Temple." *Artibus Asiae* 60, No. 2. (2000): 197-221.

Chakravorty, Pallabi. "Bharata Natyam Mapped: Not Subjectivity but Subject Position." *Dance Chronicle* 31, No. 3. (2008): 471-475.

Champakalakshmi, R. "Urbanisation in South India: The Role of Ideology and Polity." Presidential Address of Ancient India. *Indian History Congress*, 47th Session. Srinagar. (1986): 1-58.

——. "The Study of the Settlement Patterns in the Chola Period: Some Perspectives." *Man and Environment* XVI, No. 1. Bangalore. (1989).

——. "Ideology and the State in South India." Mamimdipudi Memorial Lecture- I, *Andhra Pradesh History Congress*. Srisailam: 33rd Session. (1989).

Chandra Ghosh, Jogendra. "Devadasi in Northern and Eastern India." *Indian Culture* II. (July, 1936-April, 1937).

Chandra, Sudhir. "Whose Laws?: Notes on a Legitimising Myth of the Colonial Indian State." *Studies in History* 8, (1992): 187-211.

Chatterjee, Partha. "Colonialism, Nationalism, and Colonialised Women: The Contest in India." *American Ethnologist* 16, No. 4. (November, 1989): 622-633.

Chatterjee, Ratnabali. "The Queens' Daughters: Prostitutes as an Outcast Group in Colonial India." *CMI Report for Chr. Michelsen Institute*

Department of Social Science and Development 8. (December, 1992): 1-34.

Chettiar, Ramachandra. C.M. "Geographical Distribution of Religious Places in Tamiilnad." *Indian Geographical Journal* XVI. (I941): 42-50.

Cort, E. John. "Bhakti in the Early Jain Tradition: Understanding Devotional Religion in South Asia." *History of Religions* 42, No. 1. (August, 2002): 59-86.

Cune, Mc and B, Evelyn. "The Role of Temple in the Social and Economic Life of India." *Bulletin of the Institute of Traditional Cultures*. Part I. Madras: University of Madras. (1960): 5-19.

Cutler, Norman. "The Devotee's Experience of the Sacred Tamil Hymns." *History of Religions* 24, No. 2. (November, 1984): 91-112.

Davey, Ranganatha, T.B. "The Historical Geography of the Cauveri Delta with Special Reference to the Tanjore District." *Journal of Madras Geographical Association* 12, no. 2. (July, 1987): 83-94.

Dehejia, Rajeev H. and Vivek H. Dehejia. "Religion and Economic Activity in India: An Historical Perspective." *American Journal of Economics and Sociology* 52, no. 2. (April, 1993): 145-153.

Desai, Murli, "Challenges of Commercial Sexual Exploitation of Children in India Need for Legislative Reforms in Partnership with the Social-Work Profession." *Asia Pacific Journal of Social Work and Development* 18, Issue. 1. (June, 2008): 63-75.

Devi, Rukmini. "The Late Sri Pandanallur Meenakshisundaram Pillai." 28th *Conference Souvenir*. Madras: The Music Academy, 1954.

Domosh, Mona. "Toward a Feminist Historiography of Geography." *Transactions of the Institute of British Geographers* 16, no. 1. (1991): 95-104.

Dutta, Ranjeeta and Jamia Millia Islamia. "The Politics of Religious Identity: A Muslim Goddess in the Srivaisnava Community of South India." *Studies in History* 19, no. 2. (2003): 157-184.

Evans, Mary. "Doing gender: Gender and Women's Studies in the Twenty First Century." *Women's Studies International Forum* 34. (2011): 603-610.

Geetha, V. "Gender and Political Discourse." *Economic and Political Weekly* 26, no. 7. (February 16, 1991): 387-388.

——. and S.V. Rajadurai. "Dravidian Politics: End of an Era." *Economic and Political Weekly* 26, no. 26. (June 29, 1991): 1591-1592.

——. "Periyar, Women and an Ethic of Citizenship." *Economic and Political Weekly* 33, no. 17. (April 25-May 1, 1998): WS9-WS15.

Good, Anthony. "'Mamul' and Modernity in a South Indian Temple." *Modern Asian Studies* 35, no. 4. (October, 2001): 821-870.

Gough, Kathleen. "Modes of Production in Southern India." *Economic and Political Weekly* XV, no. 5-6-7. (February, 1980): 337-364.

Guhan, S. "Bala on Bharatanatyam". *Sruti*. (1991).

Hamumanthan, K.R. "Evolution of Caste System in Tamilnadu." *Proceeding of 5th International Conference Seminar of Tamil Studies* I, Madras: International Association of Tamil Research, (January, 1981): 6-88.

Heitzman, James. "Temple Urbanism in Medieval South India." *The Journal of Modern Asian Studies* 46, no. 4. (November, 1987): 791-826.

Iyer, Latha and Kanakalatha Mukund. "Herstory: Women in South India in the Seventeenth and Eighteenth Centuries." *Indica* 32, no. 1. (1995): 29.

Jayapragasan, S. "Aspects of Caste System in Tamilnadu during the Imperial Cola Times." *Indian History Congress*, 41st Session. Bombay: University of Bombay, 1980: 195-202.

Jha, D.N. "Temples and Merchants in South India: c. AD 900-AD 1300." *Essays in Honor of Prof. S.C. Sarkar*. New Delhi: People's Publishing House, 1976.

Shortt, John. "The Bayaderes: or, Dancing Girls of Southern India." *Council of the Anthropological Society of London* III. (1870): 182-194.

Kaali, Sundar. "Disciplining the Dasi: Cintamanai and the Politics of a New Sexual Economy." *Bioscope* 4, no. 1. (2013): 51-69.

Kandaswamy, S.N. "The Philosophical Aspects of "Paripatal". Philosophical Heritage of the Tamils." *International Institute of Tamil Research*. Madras. (1983): 117-140.

Kannabiran, Kalpana. "Judiciary, Social Reform and Debate on 'Religious Prostitution' in Colonial India." *Economic and Political Weekly* 30, no. 43. (October 28, 1995): WS59-WS69.

Karashima, Noboru and B. Sitaraman. "Revenue Terms in Chola Inscription." *Journal of Asian and African Studies* 5. (1972): 87-117.

——. and Y. Subbarayalu. "A Statistical Study of Personal Names in Tamil Inscription." Interim Report II. *Computational Analysis of Asian and African Languages* 3. (1976): 9-20.

——. and Y, Subbarayalu. "A List of Tamil Inscriptions of the Chola Dynasty." *Journal of Asian and African Studies* 11. Tokyo. (1976): 87-181.

——. and B, Sitaraman. "Nâyakas as Lease-Holders of Temple Lands." *The Journal of the Economic and Social History of the Orient* 19, No. 2. (May, 1976): 227-232.

——. and Y, Subbarayalu. "Socio and Agro-Economic Terms in the Inscriptions of the Thanjavur District." *Institute for the Study of Languages and Cultures of Asia and Africa* 1. Tokyo. (1977): 1-41.

——.; Y, Subbarayalu and P. Shanmugam. "Nagaram during the Chola and Pandyan Period: Commerce and Towns in the Tamil Country." *The Indian Historical Review* XXXV, no. 1. (January, 2008): 1-33.

——. "South Indian Temple Inscriptions: A New Approach to their Study." *Journal of South Asian Studies* XIX, no. 1. (1996): 1-12.

Kasinathan, Natana. "Pre-Historic Paintings in Tamilnadu." *The Proceedings of the Indian History Congress* 45th session. Annamalai Nagar: Annamalai University, 1985: 865-871.

Kersenboom, Saskia C. "Devadasi Murai." *Sangeet Natak*, no. 96. (April-June, 1990): 44-54.

Kosambi, D.D. "The Basis of Ancient Indian History." *Journal of the American Oriental Society* 75, no. 1. (October, I955): 226-236.

Krishna Kumari, M. "On the Significance of a Tamil Record of Kulottunga I at Bapatla." *The Proceedings of the Indian History Congress* session-45. Annamalai Nagar: Annamalai University. (1985): 918-921.

Lakshmi, C.S. "Tradition and Modernity of Tamil Women Writers." *Social Scientist* 4, no. 9. (April, 1976): 37-45.

——. "Mother, Mother-Community and Mother-Politics in Tamil Nadu." *Economic and Political Weekly* 25, no. 42/43. (October 20-27, 1990): WS72-WS83.

——. "Bodies Called Women: Some Thoughts on Gender, Ethnicity and Nation." *Economic and Political Weekly* 32, no. 46. (November 15-21, 1997): 2953-2962.

Levine, Philippa. "Venereal Disease, Prostitution, and the Politics of Empire: The Case of British India." *Journal of the History of Sexuality* 4, no. 4. (April, 1994): 579-602.

——. "Orientalist Sociology and the Creation of Colonial Sexualities." *Feminist Review*, no. 65. (Summer, 2000): 5-21.

——. "'A Multitude of Unchaste Women:' Prostitution in the British Empire." *Journal of Women's History* 15, no. 4. (Winter, 2004): 159-163.

Mahalingam, T.V. "Genesis and Nature of Feudalism under Pallavas of Kanchi." *Seminar on Socio- Economic formation in the Early Middle Ages AD 600-1200*. Allahabad. (1977)

Manjulatha, "Devdasis Inams: A Case Study of the Chittoor District." *Ithihas* XIV. (July, 1988): 116-7.

Meduri, Avanthi. "Bharatha Natyam- What Are You?." *Asian Theatre Journal* 5, no. 1. (1988): 1-22.

Mohan Ram, A. "Famines and Relief Measures under the Imperial Cholas (850-1279 A.D.)." *The Proceedings of the Indian History Congress* 45th session. Annamalai Nagar: Annamalai University (1985).

Mohanty, Chandra Talpade. "Under Western Eyes" Revisited: Feminist Solidarity through Anticapitalist Struggles." *Journal of Women in Culture and Society* 28, no. 2. (2002): 499-535.

Muthuswami Pillai, G.M. "The Glory of Chidambaram." *Saiva Siddhanta* I, no. 2. (April-June, I966): 115-120.

Nagaswamy, R. "South Indian Temple- as an Employer." *Indian Economic Social History Review* 2, no. 4. (1964): 367-372.

Nair, Janaki. "The Devadasi, Dharma and the State." *Economic and Political Weekly* 29, no. 50. (December. 10, 1994): 3157-3159+3161-3167.

——. "Beyond exceptionalism: South India and the modern historical imagination." *Indian Economic Social History Review* 43, (2006): 323-347.

——. "'Imperial Reason', National Honour and New Patriarchal Compacts in early twentieth-century India." *History Workshop Journal* 66. (Autumn, 2008): 208-226.

Narayanan, M.G.S. "Handmaids of God." in *Aspects of Aryanisation in Kerala*. Trivandrum: Kerala Historical Society, 1973.

——. "The Role of Peasants in the Early History of Tamilakam in South India." *Social Scientists* 16, no. 9. (September, 1988): 17-34.

——. and Kesavan Veluthat. "The Temple in South India." in J.S. Grewal. Ed. *Religious Movements and Institution in Medieval India*. in the series of Chattopadhyaya, D.P. Ed. *History of Science, Philosophy and Culture in Indian Civilisation*. Vol. VII. Part 2. New Delhi: Oxford University Press, 2006: 477-492.

Neild-Basu, Susan. "The Dubashes of Madras." *Modern Asian Studies* 18, no. 1. (1984): 1-31.

Ohtani, Kimiko. "Bharata Nâ□yam', Rebirth of Dance in India." *Studia Musicologica Academiae Scientiarum Hungaricae* T. 33, fasc. 1/4. (1991): 301-308.

Orchard, Treena. "In this life: The impact of Gender and Tradition on sexuality and relationships for devadasi sex Workers in Rural India." *Sexuality and Culture* 11, Issues. 1. (Winter, 2007): 3-27.

Pande, Rekha. "The Bhakti Movement: - An Interpretation." *Proceedings of Indian History Congress*. Goa. (1987): 214-221.

——. "The Bhakti Movement in Medieval Andhra. Problems and Perspectives." *Proceedings A.P. History Congress*. Guntur. (1990): 266-269.

——. "The Socio-Economic Context of Sri Vaishnavism in 11th and 12th century Andhra." *Ithihas* XVI, no.1. (1990).

——. "The Bhakti Movement and the Status of Women in 14th and 15th Century." in J.P. Mishra. Ed. *Aspects of Indian History*. New Delhi. (1991): 57-68.

——. "Transition and the Recreation of Patriarchal Ideology." *Journal of Historical Research* VIII. Assam. (1998).

——. "The Bhakti Movement- A Historiographical Critique." *Journal of Historical Research* 10. Assam: Dibrugarh University, March, 2000: 49-60.

——. and K, Sri Lakshmi. "Temple Economy, Land Grants and Women in 16th century Vijaynagara." in C.M. Agarwal. Ed. *Nari-Facets of Indian Womanhood* 1. New Delhi: Indian Publishers and Distributors, 2000.

——. "Extension of Agrarian Activity in Medieval Andhra Region. The Role of the Temples and Land Grants." in Asian Agri History. *International Journal of History and Asian Agriculture Including Environment* VIII, no.1. (January-March, 2004): 39-53.

——. "At the Service of the Lord-Temple Girls in Medieval Deccan (eleventh to seventeenth centuries)." *Deccan Studies* II, no. 2. (July-December, 2004): 25-43.

——. "Ritualised Prostitution Devadasis to Jogins. A Few Case Studies in Prostitution and Beyond, An Analysis of Sex Work in India. Rohini Sahni, V. Kalyan Shankar and Hemant Apti. Eds. New Delhi: Sage Publication, 2008: 101-117.

——. "Feudal set up of medieval Deccan and the Temple Dancing Girls." P. Chenna Reddy. Ed. Recent researches in Archeology History and Culture, Vol. II. New Delhi: Agam Kola Prakashan, 2011: 499-512.

——. "The Temple and Temple Dancing Girls of Medieval Deccan." Birendranath Prasad. Ed. *Monasteries, Shrines and Society: Buddhist and Brahmanical Religious Institutions in India in Their Socio-Economic Context*. New Delhi: Manak Publications, 2011.

Pandian, M.S.S; S. Anandhi and A.R. Venkatachalapathy. "Of Maltova Mothers and Other Stories." *Economic and Political Weekly* 26, no. 16. April 20, 1991: 1059-1064.

——. "Notes on the Transformation of 'Dravidian' Ideology: Tamilnadu, c. 1900-1940." *Social Scientist* 22, no. 5/6. (May-June, 1994): 84-104.

——. "Towards National-Popular: Notes on Self-Respecters' Tamil." *Economic and Political Weekly* 31, no. 51. (December 21, 1996): 3323-3329.

Parasher, Aloka and Usha Naik. "Temple Girls of Medieval Karnataka." *Indian Economic and Social History Review* 23, no. 1. (1986): 63-91.

Parker, Kunal M. "A Corporation of Superior Prostitutes' Anglo-Indian Legal Conceptions of Temple Dancing Girls, 1800-1914." *Modern Asian Studies* 32, no. 3. (July, 1998): 559-633.

Patil, B.R. "The Devdasis." *Indian Journal of Social Work* XXXV, no. 4. (1975): 377-389.

Pattabhi Raman, N and Anandhi Ramachandran. "T. Balasaraswati: The Whole World in Her Hands." Part. 1. *Sruti*, Issue. 4. (January-February, 1984): 17-31.

——. and Anandhi Ramachandran. "T. Balasaraswati: The Whole World in Her Hands." Part. 2. *Sruti*, Issue. 5. (March-April, 1984): 1-32.

——. "Bala: The Last Exit." *Sruti*, Issue. 5. (March-April, 1984): 33, 46.

——. and Anandhi Ramachandran. "T. Balasaraswati: The Whole World in Her Hands." *Journal of the Sangeet Natak Academi* 72-73. (April-September, 1984): 15-54.

Peterson, Indira V. "Singing of a Place: Pilgrimage as Metaphor and Motif in the Tevaram Songs of the Tamil Saivite Saints." *Journal of the American Oriental Society* 102, no. 1. (January, 1982): 69-90.

Pillai, Meenakshisundaram. "Bharatha Natyam." 28th *Conference Souvenir*. Madras: The Music Academy, 1954.

Poonacha, Veena. "Recovering Women's Histories: An Enquiry into Methodological Questions and Challenges." *Indian Journal of Gender Studies* 11. (2004): 389-404.

Prasad, Awadh Kishore. "Functions and Gradations of Devadasis." *The Proceedings of the Indian History Congress*. 45th session. Annamalai Nagar: Annamalai University, 1985: 192-199.

Punzo Waghorne, Joanne. "The Diaspora of the Gods: Hindu Temples in the New World System 1640-1800." *The Journal of Asian Studies* 58, no. 3. (August, 1999): 648-686.

Raghavan, V. "Bharatha Natya." *23rd Conference Souvenir*. Madras: The Music Academy, 1949.

——. "Bharatha Natyam-Ilakkiyam." (A Grammar for Bharatanatyam) (in Tamil). 25th *Conference Souvenir*. Madras: The Music Academy, 1951.

——. "Musical Traditions of the South." *30th Conference Souvenir*. Madras: The Music Academy, 1956.

Ramachandran, K.S. "Some Observations on the Names Occurring in the Inscriptions of Rajaraja-I in the Brihadisvara Temple at Thanjavur, Tamilnadu." *Journal of the Andhra Historical Research Society* XXXVII. (1978): 179-192.

Ramalakshmi, R. "Dissent, Protest and Movement against Patriarchy: Women's Writings in Modern India." Presidential Address. Modern Andhra Session. *A.P. History Congress Proceedings*. Hyderabad. (2001).

Ramasubramaniam, V. "'Anti-Nautch Movement'." *The Bulletin of the Institute of Traditional Culture*. Reports of Seminars: Problems facing Bharata Natyam. (1967).

Ramaswamy, Sumathi. "En/Gendering Language: The Poetics of Tamil Identity." *Comparative Studies in Society and History* 35, no. 4. (October, 1993): 683-725.

——. "Language of the People in the World of Gods: Ideologies of Tamil before the Nation." *The Journal of Asian Studies* 57, no. 1. (February, 1998): 66-92.

——. "History at Land's End: Lemuria in Tamil Spatial Fables." *The Journal of Asian Studies* 59, no. 3. (August, 2000): 575-602.

Ramanarayanan, Gowri. "Interview: Padma Subramanyam." *Sruti*, Issue. 3. (December, 1983): 36-37.

——. "Bala, My Guru." *Sruti*, Issue. 5. (March-April, 1984): 35-39.

——. "Rukmini Devi: A Quest for Beauty." Part. 1. *Sruti*, Issue. 8. (June, 1984): 17-29.

——. "Rukmini Devi: Dancer and Reformer." Part. 2. *Sruti*, Issue. 9. (July, 1984): 17-26.

——. "Rukmini Devi: Restoration and Creation." Part. 3. *Sruti*, Issue. 10. (August, 1984): 26-38.

Ramasubramaniam, V. "Anti-Nautch Movement." *The Bulletin of the Institute of Traditional Culture*. Reports of Seminars: Problems facing Bharata Natyam. Ed. T. Viswanathan. Madras, 1967.

Ray, Satyajit. "Working with Bala." *Journal of the Sangeet Natak Academi* 72-73. (April-September, 1984): 66-68.

Rege, Sharmila. "Dalit Women Talk Differently: A Critique of 'Difference' and Towards a Dalit Feminist Standpoint Position." *Economic and Political Weekly* 33, no. 44. (October 31-November 6, 1998): WS39-WS46.

Rutherford, Ian. "Theoria and Darœan: Pilgrimage and Vision in Greece and India." *The Classical Quarterly* 50, no. 1. (2000): 133-146.

Sankaran, T. "Bangalore Nagaratnammal: A Devadasi True." *Sruti*, Issue. 4. (January-February, 1984): 14-16.

-. "Bala." *Journal of the Sangeet Natak Academi* 72-73. (April-September, 1984): 4-7.

——. "Kandappa Nattuvanar." *Journal of the Sangeet Natak Academi* 72-73. (April-September, 1984): 55-60.

——. "Bala's Musicians." *Journal of the Sangeet Natak Academi* 72-73. (April-September, 1984): 61-65.

Satymurthy, S. "Greetings and Messages." *The Journal of the Music Academy* 1, no. 1. (January, 1930).

Scott, Joan Wallach. "Gender: A Useful Category of Historical Analysis." *The American Historical Review* 91, no. 5. (December, 1986): 1053-1075.

——. "Feminism's History." *Journal of Women's History* 16, no. 2. (Summer, 2004): 10-29.

Shanmugam, P. "'Tax Free' Grants During Rajaraja I'." *The Proceedings of the Indian History Congress* 45th session. Annamalai Nagar: Annamalai University, 1985.

Shanmugam, S.V. "Dravidian Studies in Indonesia." *Journal of Tamil Studies*. International Institute of Tamil Studies. (December, 1978): 1-9.

Sharma, B.N. "Varna Vyavastha and Caste System in the 7th century A.D." *Social Life in Ancient India*. Culcutta: University of Calcutta, 1975: 76-87.

Sharma, Ratna. "Devadasi: The Sacred Veil on Priestly Prostitution." *Adhyayan* VI, no. 1 and 2. (1996): 20.

Sharma, R.S. "Indian Feudalism Retouched." *Indian Historical Review* I. (1974): 320-330.

——. "How Feudal was Indian Feudalism?" *Journal of Peasant Studies* 12. (1985): 2-3 and 19-43.

Shrimali, Krishna Mohan. "Religion, Ideology and Society." *Social Scientist* 16, no. 12. (December, 1988): 14-60.

Shulman, David Dean. "The Men Who Would Be King? The Politics of Expansion in Early Seventeenth-Century Northern Tamilnadu." *Modern Asian Studies* 24, no. 2. (May, 1990): 225-248.

Singer, Milton. "The Cultural Pattern of Indian Civilisation." *Far Eastern Quarterly* XV, no. I. (November, I955): 23-36.

Sivathamby, K. "Early South Indian Society and Economy: The Tinai Concept." *Social Scientist* 3, no. 5. (December, 1974): 20-37.

Spencer, W. George. "Temple Money-Lending and Livestock Redistribution in Early Tanjore." *Economic and Social History Review* 5, no. 3. (1968): 277-293.

——. "Religious Networks and Royal Influence in Eleventh Century South India." *Journal of the Economic and Social History of the Orient* 12, no. 1. (January, 1969): 42-56.

——. "The Sacred Geography of the Tamil Shaivite Hymns." *Numen* 17, no. 3. (December, 1970): 232-244.

——. "Royal Initiative under Rajaraja I." *Indian Economic and Social History Review* 7, no. 4. (1970): 431-442.

——. "The Politics of Plunder: The Cholas in Eleventh Century Ceylon." *The Journal of Asian Studies* 35, no. 3. (1976): 405-419.

——. "When Queens Bore Gifts: Women as Temple Donors in the Chola Period." In K.V. Raman. Ed. *Srinidhih: Perspective in Indian Archaeology, Art and Culture*. Madras: New Era Publications, 1983.

Srinivas, M.N. "The Changing Position of Indian Women." *Man. New Series*, 12. no. 2 (August, 1977): 221-238.

Srinivasan, C.R. "Two Inscriptions from Tiruvanaikka." In K.V. Raman. Ed. *Srinidhih: Perspective in Indian Archaeology, Art and Culture*. Madras: New Era Publications, 1984: 157.

Srinivasan, Amrit. "Reform and Revival: The Devadasi and Her Dance." *Economic and Political Weekly* 20, no. 44. (November 2, 1985): 1869-1876.

——. "Women and Reform of Indian Tradition: Gandhian Alternative to Liberalism." *Economic and Political Weekly* 22, no. 51. (December 19, 1987): 2225-2228.

Sriram, V. "P.R. Thilagam: A Tiruvarur Kuravanji." *Sruti*. Issue. 255. (December, 2005): 25-39.

Stein, Burton. "Economic Functions of a Medieval South Indian Temple." *The Journal of Asian Studies* 19, no. 2. (1960): 163-176.

——. "The State and the Agrarian Order in Medieval South India: A Historiographical Critique." in Burton Stein. Ed. *Essays on South India*. New Delhi: Vikas Publication House, 1975: 64-91.

——. "Circulation and the Historical Geography of Tamil Country." *The Journal of Asian Studies* 37, no. 1. (November, 1977): 7-26.

——. "Temples in Tamil Country, 1300-1750 A.D." *Indian Economic Social History Review* 14, no. 11. (1977): 11-45.

——. "State Formation and Economy Reconsidered." *The Journal of Modern Asian Studies* 19, no. 3. (1985): 387-413.

Subbarayalu, Y. "Classification of Land and Assessment of Tax in Early Medieval Tamilnadu from 950 to 1300." *The Proceedings of the Indian History Congress* 38th Session. Bhubaneswar: Utkal University, 1977: 341-346.

——. "Inscriptional Sources for the History of the Colas of the early Medieval South Indian History." in N.R. Roy. Ed. *Sources of the History of India. HIS* 3. (1980): 371-379.

——. "Land Measurement in Tamilnadu from 700 to 1350." *Historia-Proceedings of the Madurai Historical Society* 1. (1981): 97-105.

——. "The Cola State." *Studies in History* 4, no. 2. (1982): 265-306.

——. "The Place of *Ur* in the Economy and Social History of the Early Tamil Nadu from A.D. 750-1350." *Sri S.R. Rao Felicitation Volume*. Delhi: Sundeep Prakashan, 1983:171-178.

——. "Sidelight on Chola Officialdom." in K.V. Raman. Ed. *Srinidhih: Perspective in Indian Archaeology, Art and Culture*. Madras: New Era Publications, 1983: 357-360.

——. "An Aspect of the Revenue System of the Cholas." *The Proceedings of the Indian History Congress* 45th session. Annamalai Nagar: Annamalai University: 172-175.

Subramaniam, V. "Tamil Romantic Poetry and Bhakti Poetry in Relation to the Temple." In M. Arunachalam. Ed. *Proceedings of the 5th International Conference-Seminar of Tamil Studies* I. Madras: International Association of Tamil Research, September, 1981: 7a-33-7a-40.

Subrahmaniyam, Sanjay. "Aspects of State Formation in South India and South East Asia. 1550-1650." *Indian Economic and Social History Review* 23, no. 4. (1986): 357-377.

——. and B. Suresh. "The Raajaraajeesvaram at Tancaavuur." *International Association of Tamil Research*. Kula Lumber. (1968): 437-450.

Swaminathan, A. "Adimaikal (Slaves) in the Cola Temple and Mathas." *Bulletin of the Institute of Traditional Cultures*. Madras: University of Madras, June, 1978: 33-38.

Talbot, Cynthia. "Temples, Donors and Gifts: Patterns of Patronage in Thirteenth-Century of South India." *Journal of Asian Studies* 50, no. 2. (1991): 308-340.

Taylor, Verta. "Feminist Methodology in Social Movements Research." *Qualitative Sociology* 21, Issue. 4. (December, 1998): 357-379.

Terada, Yoshitaka. "Temple Music Traditions in Hindu South India: Periya Malam and Its Performance Practice." *Asian Music* 39, no. 2. (Summer/ Fall, 2008): 108-151.

"The Renaming of an Old Dance: A Whodunit Tale of Mystery." *Sruti*. Issue. 27/28. (December, 1986-January, 1987): 30-31.

Tilly, Louise A. "Gender, Women's History, and Social History." *Social Science History* 13, no. 4. (Winter, 1989): 439-462.

Tirumalai, R. "Land Grants and Agrarian Reactions in Cola and Pandya Times." *Madras University Archaeological Series 6*. Madras: University of Madras, 1987.

Veluppillai, A. "Religious Traditions of the Tamils." *Lecture delivered at the Theological Faculty*. Uppsala, February 6, 1995.

Veluthat, Kesavan. "The Social Political Background of Kulasekara Alwars of Bhakti." *Proceedings of Indian History Congress* 38th Session. Bhubaneswar: Uktal University, 1977: 137-144.

——. "Royalty and Divinity: Legitimisation of Monarchical Power in South India." *Proceedings of Indian History Congress* 39th Session. (1978): 243.

——. "The Temple Base of Bhakti Movements in South India." *Proceedings of Indian History Congress* 40th Session. (1979).

——. "Religious Symbols in Political Legitimation: The Case of Early Medieval South India." *Social Scientist* 21, no.1/2. (January-February, 1983): 23-33.

Venkatachari. K.K.A. Ed. "Raja Raja-The Great." *Anantacharya Indological Research Institute Series* Series 18. Bombay: Anantacharya Indological Research Institute, 1987.

Venkatashbramanian. T.K. "Social Roots of Tamilian Religious Ideology." *Indian History Congress* 39th session, Vol. I. Aligarh: Centre of Advanced Study in History, 1978: 180-188.

Venugopal, S.V. "Facts about the Renaissance in Bharata Natya." *Sri Krishna Iyer's Shashtiabdapurthi Commemoration Volume*. Madras: Bharathiar Sangam, 1957.

Washbrook, David. "South India 1770-1840: The Colonial Transition." *Modern Asian Studies* 38, no. 3 (July, 2004): 479-516.

Yasodadevi, V. "The History of the Andhra Country (1000 A.D. to 1500)." *Journal of the Andhra Historical Research Society* XXV. (July, 1958-1960): 52-152.

——. "The History of the Andhra Country (1000 A.D. to 1500)." *Journal of the Andhra Historical Research Society* XXVI, Parts. 1-4. (July, 1960-April, 1961): 1-102.

——. "The History of the Andhra Country (1000 A.D. to 1500)." *Journal of the Andhra Historical Research Society* XXVII, Parts. 1-4. (July, 1961-April, 1962): 1-44.

Yocum, E. Glenn. "Shrines, Shamanism and Love Poetry: Elements in the Emergence of Popular Tamil Bhakti." *Journal of the American Academy of Religion* 41, no. 1. (March, 1973): 3-17.

Younger, Paul. "The Role of Landlords. Kings and Priests in the Operation of a South Indian Temple." in K.V. Raman. Ed. *Srinidhih: Perspectives in Indian Archaeology, Art and Culture*. Madras: New Era Publications, 1983: 243-255.

Zvelebil, V. Kamil. "Tamil Poetry 2000 Years Ago." *Tamil Culture* X. (1963).

Web sources

A webpage of *Ramon Magsaysay Award Foundation http://www.rmaf.org.ph/newrmaf/main/awardees/awardee/profile/228*. Accessed March 20, 2014.

Bala (1976) - Satyajit Ray Documentary on T. Balasaraswati http://www.youtube.com/watch?v=ak_a1RJ2DZc. Accessed October 22, 2013.

Dancer Dhananjayan on Bharatam and Natyam, 3rd October 2009 http://www.youtube.com/watch?v=qNBhijLh1jk. Accessed October 22, 2013.

Devadasi Marabu Vilakkam June 06 2013 *http://www.youtube.com/watch?v=F9WsVwebieo*. Accessed October 22, 2013. Hindu monk

Jamanadas, K. "Devadasis Were Degraded Buddhist Nuns". Mar 28, 2000. *http://www.ambedkar.org/buddhism/Devadasis_Were_Degraded_Buddhist_Nuns*.htm. Accessed January 30, 2012.

Remembering Smt Rukmini Devi Arundale / Founder Kalakshetra www.youtube.com/watch?v=tzVZr13OlE8. Accessed October 22, 2013.

Sex, Death and the Gods http://www.youtube.com/watch?v=zL67d0-82PA. Accessed October 22, 2013. BBC

Tamil Classical Texts such as Sangam and Post-Sangam Literature are referred from the uploaded sources of *http://www.projectmadurai.org/pmworks.html*. Accessed January 21, 2010. and

http://www.noolaham.org/wiki/index.php?title=%E0%AE%AE%E0%AF%81%E0%AE%A4%E0%AE%B1%E0%AF%8D_%E0%AE%AA%E0%AE%95%E0%AF%8D%E0%AE%95%E0%AE%AE%E0%AF%8D. Accessed January 21, 2010.

Tamil Heritage: Dancer Swarnamalya on Dance Traditions, Part 1, 3rd April 2011 (English). Accessed October 22, 2013.

Tamil Heritage: Dancer Swarnamalya on Dance Traditions, Part 2, 7th May 2011 http://www.youtube.com/watch?v=byMzczPPTAg. Accessed October 22, 2013.

Appendixes

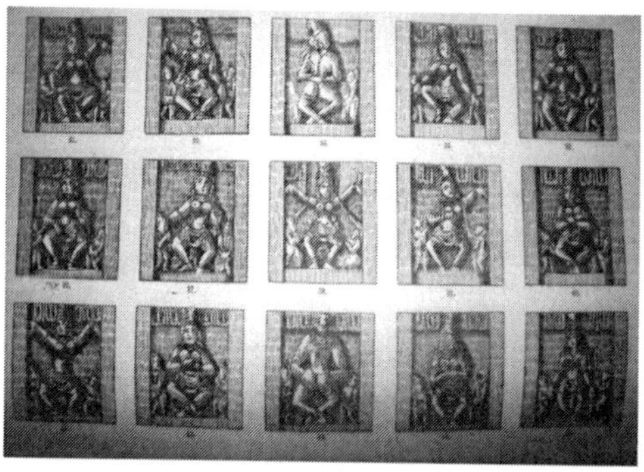

Appendix 1: Dancing images of East tower of Natarajar Temple at Chidambaram.

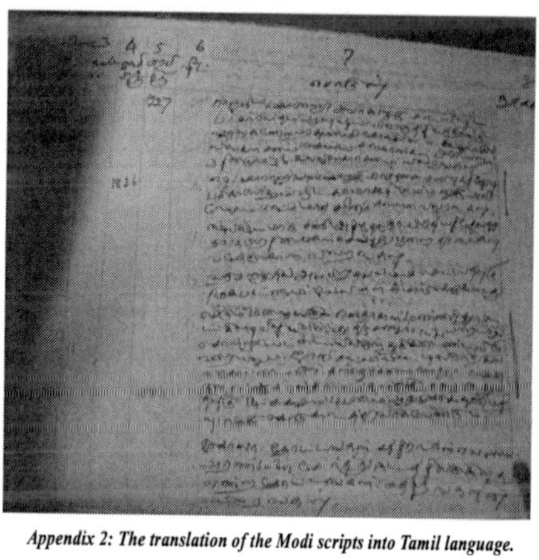

Appendix 2: The translation of the Modi scripts into Tamil language.

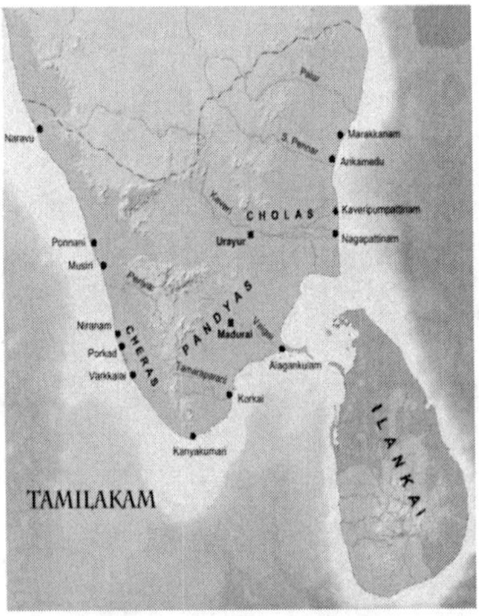

***Appendix 3:** The historical Tamilakam.*

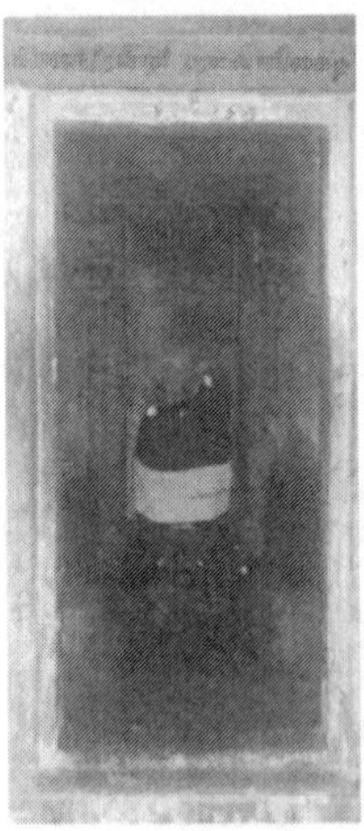

Appendix 4: Images of Paravai Nankai and Rajendran I in Thiyagarajar Temple, Tiruvarur.

Appendix 5: Shrine of Paravai Nankai and Rajendran I in Thiyagarajar Temple, Tiruvarur.

Appendix 6: Image of Manikka Nachchiyar in the North car street of Thiyagarajar Temple, Tiruvarur.

Appendix 7: Temple of Manikka Nachchiyar in the North car street of Thiyagarajar Temple, Tiruvarur.

Appendix 8: The nineteenth century C.E. portrayal of devadasi woman (Haafner, Jacob. Reize in eenen Palanquim; of Lotgevallen en Merkwaardige Aanteekeningen op eene Reize langs de Kusten Orixa en Chroromandel (in Dutch). Vol. I. Amsterdam: Johannes Allart, 1808: 219.)

Appendix 9:
Dr. Muthulakshmi Reddi.

Appendix 10: Photograph of twentieth century C.E. girls from the devadasi community (The photograph was collected by the researcher from P.R. Thilakam at Thanjavur on March 15, 2011.)

Appendix 11: 'Thanthai Periyar' E.V. Ramasami.

Appendix 12: 'Thanthai Periyar' E.V. Ramasami.

Appendix 13: Rukmini Devi at her concert.

Appendix 14: Muvalur A. Ramamirtham.

Appendix 15: The memorial of Thiyagarajar, Tiruvaiyar.

Appendix 16: The image of Bangalore Nagarathnam in Thiyagarajar memorial, Tiruvaiyar.

Appendix 17: The family of Balasaraswati.

Appendix 18: Balasaraswati.

Appendix 19: Balasaraswati during her performance.

Appendix 20: Balasaraswati with her daughter
(The image is from Pattabhi Raman, N and Anandhi Ramachandran.
"T. Balasaraswati: The Whole World in Her Hands".
Part. 1. Sruti. Issue. 4. (January-February, 1984): 19.)

Appendix 21: M.S. Subbulakshmi playing Vina.

Appendix 22: M.S. Subbulakshmi during the shooting of the movie Sakunthalai.

Appendix 23: M.S. Subbulakshmi during the shooting of the movie Meera.

Appendix 24: M.S. Subbulakshmi honored by the India Post by issuing postage stamp on her.

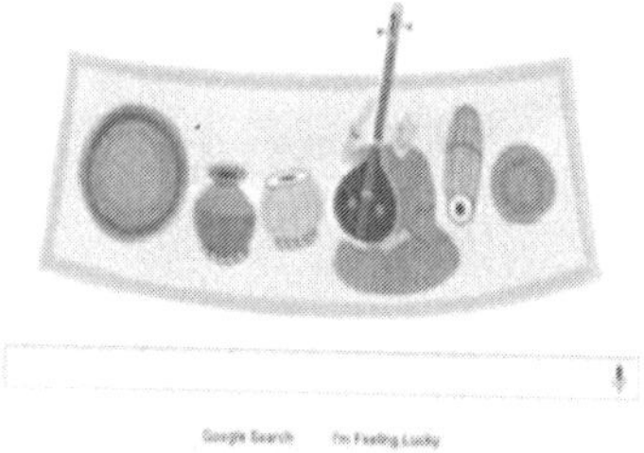

Appendix 25: Google honoured M.S. Subbulakshmi with its doodle service on her 97th birthday.

Appendix 26: M.S. Subbulakshmi with her husband T Sadasivam in 1997.

Index

A

A Corporation of Superior Prostitutes' Anglo - Indian Legal Conceptions of Temple Dancing Girls - Kunal M. Parker's , 35
A Description of the Character, Manner and Customs of the People of India - Abbe Dubois, 129
Abolition Acts/ Bills, 137
Abolition of Devadasi Act/Bill
  views on, 171-75
Abraham Rogerius
  on Devadasis, 93
Agamic Tradition, 67-68
Age of Dedication
  Issue, 134-35
Annie Besant
  on Devadasis, 183
Anti-Nautch Movements, 127, 187
  Campaigns, 153
Arunakirinathar Puranam, 95

B

Balasaraswati Thanjavur, 222
  Family, 222-23
  Dance Form, 223
  Music Performance, 223-24
  and Shanmukham, 224
  Grey days, 224-25
  and Bharatnatyam, 225-27
  International Exposure, 228-29
  Padma Bhushan, 230
Bhakti Movement, 65
  role, 67
  women in, 68
  Concept, 66-67
Bharatnatyam dance
  - Devadasis, 176-77
    Revival, 179
    origin - claims, 183
    Rennaissance, 182, 189
Bhikshunees, 19
Bhoga Culture, 65
Bill for the Suppression of Brothels & Immoral Traffic, 138
Books on Devadasis, 15-17
Brahmadayam Institution, 63
British Soldiers & Prostitution, 129

C

Caste
  role, 23
Caste System
  and Devadasis, 22
Categories of Devadasis, 28
Chastity, 162
Child Trafficking
  evidence, 129
Chinna Ummayi vs Tegarai Chetti, 133
Chola King
  crowning, 60
  Temples Construction, 62
  decline, 63
Cholas
  rise of, 55-56
Christian missionaries
  rise-impact, 119, 121
Colonial Debate, 126-28
Colonial Period, 253
  and Devadasi System, 109
  intervention, 256

Contagious Disease
(CD) Acts- 1864-69, 135, 257
Courtesan & Devadasi, 65

D

Dance/Music
- Religious Spirit, 184
Dancing Masters/Teachers
(Marathas), 112
Decline of Devadasis, 115-16, 119
Dedication Ceremony
of Devadasi, 24
Ceremony
(pottu kattithal), 25-26
Prohibition of, 174
Degradation of
Devadasi System, 98
Devadasi and Kingship, 61
Devadasi & Temple
Property, 91
Devadasi Girls Childhood
(Muthulakshmi on), 155
Devadasi System in Medieval
Tamil Nadu- Sadasivan, 34
Devadasi
Status, 14
Origin, 14
evidence, 14
Custom, 249
Duties, 81
Development, 249
Code of Conduct, 250
Moral Conduct, 252
description in books, 16-17
meaning, 15
duties, 16
rights, 17
thinkers on, 17
Medieval Period, 77, 250
Later Medieval, 251
different names, 78
priveleges, status, 78
characteristics, 78
& prostitution, 166
writings of, 168
Devadasis (Selected)
Life Stories, 209-230
Literature on, 252-53
Devadasis dance, 176-77
Revival, 179-80
Devotional Literature
(Tamils), 30
Domingo Paes
on Devadasis, 93
Donors, Devotees and
Daughters of God,
Leslie C. Orr's, 34
Dress code
Maratha Devadasis, 114
Dubashis/Zamindars
Influence/rise, 115
Duties of Devadasis, 81

E

European Impact, 120
Evolution/Origin
of Devadasis System, 18-19

F

Festival
Entertainments - Temples, 85
Performances in Temples, 111
Francois Bernier
on Devadasis, 93

G

Gandharvas, 18
Gandhi M.K.,
on Devadasis, 122-24
Gejja Puja
and puberty, 27
ceremony, 27
Ghee
importance/preservation, 188
Gifts/ donations
by Devadasis, 88
Grade hierarchy of
Devadasi Caste System, 23

H

Hindu Religious Endowments
Act-1926, 138

I

Imperial Titles/Surnames, 59
Indian Law Foundation/
  Homogenisation, 130-31
Indian/Hindu Womanhood
  Status Rethink, 121
Inheritance of Devadasis, 133
Inscriptions
  mention of Devadasis, 78-80
  on Devadasis, 14, 32

J

John Shortt
  on Prostitution vs
    Devadasis, 130

K

Kalabhra Literature
  on Devadasis, 29
Kalamekam (poet), 95
  works, 95
Karaikkal
  Ammaiyar Story, 68-69
King and Kinship
  deities, 58-59
King-God
  Concept, 60
Kings
  duties, 60-61
  Devadasi association, 61
Koyil, 58
Krishna Iyer E., 187
  role in Bharatnatyam, 187
  on Devadasi abolition, 187
Kudi Arasu (Newspaper), 17-18,
    159-60, 162
Kudis
  (South Indian Communities), 52

L

Land Gifts to Devadasis, 85
Later Medieval Period
  Devadasis, 89
Law (Hindu)
  on dancing girls, 23
Literary Sources on
  Devadasis, 20
Love
  Concept of, 164

M

Madras Music Academy, 180
Maratha Court Devadasis, 110
  Code of Conduct, 113
Masculinity Questioning
  -Self Respect Movement, 161
Medieval Rulers
  South India, 54-55
  & Temple, 58
  Identities, 58
Medieval Temples
  role, 58
  and Bhakti Cult, 58
Modi Scripts
  /Records, 32
Morality/
  Image of Women, 120
Motherhood Concept
  bringing in, 126
Mukthisvara Temple
  Kanchipuram, 62
Music Academy of
  Madras, 260-61
Musical Revival of
  India, 184
Muslim Invasions
  Impact on Devadasis, 89
Muthulakshmi Reddi
  (Reformer), 154-56
    Dilemmas/ concerns, , 156-57
  on Devadasi abolition, 171
    ...criticism, 172
Muthupalani (Devadasi), 112
Mysore Govt
  Abolition of Devadasis, 166

N

Nagarathnam Bangalore, 209, 215
  early Life, 216
  at Mysore/Madras, 217
  as Singer, 218
  Fortune/Title, 218
  Controversies, 218-19

Patronage, 218
Dance drama, 219
Campaign Against abolition, 219
And Thyagraja Memorial, 220-21
Trust/Charitable, 221
Death, 221

Naik Maratha Mandal
on Devadasis, 122, 136

Nautch
Parties -Issues, 254-55

Nautch / Dance Performances, 114
-patronage, 117-18
as Stigma, 119

Nayaka Rulers
period & kingship, 64

Nityasumangali
- Saskia Kersenboom, 34

O

Objectives of Study/Book, 37

P

Pallava Period, 54

Patriarchal Law, 256

Patriarchy
Self respect Movement on, 161

Patronage
Withdrawal/Changes, 115-16

Periyalvar, 68

Pottu Ceremony
Views on, 165-66
Abolition, 174
...ineffectiveness, 176
Writings on, 167

Princely States
opinions on Devadasis, 139
prevention of Devadasis, 139

Property Rights
Women, 163-64

Prostitutes, 135
Sangam Text on, 29
Terms Used for, 30

Proverbs on Devadasis, 31

Public Appearance – Dervadasis
(Maratha Period), 111

R

Rajarajan I (Chola)
Temple Construction, 55
& Establishment of Devadasis, 62
images of Saints, 66

Rajarajesvara Temple
Recruitment, 81

Ramanirtham Muvalur, 209-212
Novel, 210
as writer, 215
in rallies/debates, 214-15
and Self Respect Movement, 214
Protests/ difficulties, 213
Devadasi reforms, 212-13
Family/Childhood, 211
Marriage/Public Life, 212
Gandhi impact, 212
In Congress, 212

Ramasami, E.V.,
(Self Respect Movement), 140, 159

Recruitment of Devadasis, 79-80

Reddi Muthulakshmi
(Reformer), 257

Reformation of
Devadasi System, 21

Reformers Debate, 255
on Nautch Performances, 256
anti nautch campaign, 257

Reformers
impact, 121
on Devadasi Cult, 123
& womanhood, 124, 126
Twentieth Century, 154

Religion
impact, 169

Religious reforms, 169

Remuneration of Devadasis, 86

Ritualistic and
Non Ritualistic
services of Devadasis, 82-85

Ritualistic vs
Performing Roles (Devadasis), 109

Royal emblems/titles, 59-60

Rukmini Devi, 179 , 259
on Bharatnatyam, 180
Dance Performance, 180

Critique on dance methods, 181
on Nationalism, 183

S

Sadasivam Thiyagaraja, 232
Association with
M.S. Subbulakshmi, 232
and Gandhi influence, 232-33, 235
Movie company Estb, 233-34
Marriage with
M.S Subbulakshmi, 234
Magazine, 235
Political Connections, 237
Sadhir Dance
Rennaissance, 187-88
Sadhir Kacheri, 110-11
Sadhir/Sadhar Attam, 110
Sangam Text
on Devadasis, 29
Sarvadevavilasa, 116-118
Sati, 14, 163-64
Scholars Research
on Devadasi System, 34
Self Respect Movement, 140 , 258
on Patriarchy, 161
Sexual Activities
(Devadasis) Patronage, 116
Source of Information
on Devadasis, 33
South Indian Inscription
on Devadasis, 14
South Indian Society
division, 51
Basis of Stratification, 51
Subulakshmi M.S., 209, 230
Childhood, 231-32
Association with Sadasivam,
232, 239-241
Bharat Ratna, 238
Film Offers/Marriage, 233
in Savithri Film, 235
Meera - Portrayal of , 236
Charitable concerts, 237
World fame, 238
Superstitious Attitude
of Devadasis, 170

T

Tamilakam Temples, 57
Tax Remission/ exemption, 88
Temple , 54
functioning, 54
Devadasis role, 54
expansion/endowments, 56
role, 20, 57
Temple Women Rights
establishment, 131-32
Thanjavur
Maratha Kings Patronage, 110
Theogony, 18
Theosophical Society
on Devadasis, 183
Thiru.V. Kalyanasundaram
on Devadasis, 122-14
on Womanhood, 125
Travancore State Manual, 17
Travellers Accounts
on Devadasis, 92-93

V

Varna System, 52
vs Caste System, 52
Vedic Brahiminical Structure, 53
Vengamuthu vs Pandaveswara
Gurukul (1883), 132
Vibachari (Prostitute), 162
Vijayanagar Empire
& Devadasi Restoration, 90
establishment , 63
period, 64
Village/Land Grants
to Devadasis, 87
Virali Vitu Tutu, 95-97, 252

W

Women Status, 14
evidence, 14
Women's Conferences
criticism, 172
Women's Education, 160
Women's History, 13
Goals, 13

Women's Liberation, 158
World Ambassadors
on Devadasis, 33
World Travellers Records
on Devadasis, 33
Writings of Devadasis, 168

Z

Zamindari
Introduction of
- impact, 253
Ziegenbalg Bartholomous
Travelogue, 94